The Churches and the Indian Schools, 1888–1912

The
CHURCHES
and the
INDIAN
SCHOOLS
1888–1912

Francis Paul Prucha

University of Nebraska Press
Lincoln and London

Library of Congress Cataloging in Publication Data
Prucha, Francis Paul.
  The churches and the Indian schools, 1888–1912.

  Bibliography: p. 259
  Includes index.
  1. Indians of North America—Education. 2. Indians of North
America—Missions. 3. Church schools—United States.
4. Church and state—United States. I. Title.
E97.5.P78   377'.6'   79–12220
ISBN 0–8032–3657–3

Contents

Illustrations

Preface

THIS book is about tension and conflict between Protestants and Catholics over Indian mission schools at the end of the nineteenth century and the beginning of the twentieth. It grows out of an earlier study of the Protestant humanitarian reform organizations that dominated American Indian policy in the late nineteenth century. The goal of those reformers was to Americanize the Indians, to destroy tribalism with its communal base, and to substitute the individualism which marked white society. Since the Americanism that they sought to impose upon the Indians was conceived in terms of the evangelical Protestant heritage of America from which the reformers came, the Catholic missionaries did not fit well into the proposed patterns.

The conflict between the two religious groups was perhaps inevitable and unavoidable, for the fundamental expectations of each of the antagonists clashed sharply with those of the other. There was no disagreement about the absolute necessity of religious (specifically Christian) influence upon the civilization of the Indians as they were prepared for assimilation into the white man's society. The conflict arose, rather, over differing Protestant and Catholic views about the place of each other within American society.

Protestants, of course, had long been the dominant force. The United States was, after all, a Protestant nation. In origin and development it had been formed in an evangelical pattern, a "chosen people" with a new covenant, witnessing before the world the radical effects of the Reformation upon political society. When Protestants saw threats to their traditional preeminence and to their dream of a Christian nation, they often reacted strongly, as they did in the 1830s and 1840s with a great nativist thrust against the increasing Catholic immigration from Ireland and Germany. But there was, more fundamentally, a lack of understanding, an inability to concede that the social and religious fabric of the nation could or should change. Latent anti-Catholicism surfaced only occasionally, but even good men who prided themselves on their impartiality and lack of bias often ignored the Catholics and, when they did advert to them, harbored feelings that Catholics were not quite to be trusted in American society.

Catholics, for their part, were aware of their position of inferiority. They professed strong adherence to the nation and sometimes outdid themselves in patriotic fervor. But they were sensitive to what they considered slights, to receiving less attention than deserved in public affairs and being denied full participation in government programs. And they fought mightily to make their own way, thus still further stimulating Protestant antagonism.

The system of Catholic mission schools on the Indian reservations, established to spread the Catholic faith among the Indians and to preserve the faith of those converted by earlier missionaries, became a major obstacle to a universal public school system maintained by the federal government for the Indians. The Protestants, finding that the Protestant outlook and ideals that permeated the government schools fulfilled their own goals, abandoned many of their mission schools. The Catholics, who looked upon the government schools as institutions that would pervert the faith—and sometimes the morals as well—of the Catholic Indian children, fought valiantly to maintain the Catholic schools. When they sought federal aid for these enterprises, the Catholics unloosed a wave of anti-Catholicism, which bolstered the agitation against the Catholic schools carried on by more fair-minded Protestants who worried about the principle of separation of church and state.

Protestant groups had long been accustomed to arousing public opinion in favor of measures they promoted, through dissemination of publications, through correspondence with church leaders and laymen across the country, and through the press (both religious and secular). They knew how to bombard the President and other officials of government with protests and memorials, and they were adept at bringing pressure to bear on key members of Congress. Catholics, as they increased in numbers and became a political force at the polls, adopted the same techniques with considerable success. Such political activity by Catholics, however, was condemned by anti-Catholics as "un-American" and as ecclesiastical meddling in affairs of state, although it differed little from their own efforts.

As Catholics entered into national political affairs, Indian affairs became a primary arena, for the federal government was responsible for relations between the whites and the Indians, and Indian education and civilization was a national issue. Catholic engagement in Indian education brought the Catholics into national politics in a direct and visible way. The conflict that developed was not an edifying story. It created bitterness between individuals and groups who professed charity toward their neighbors, and it hardened into irrational positions, views and opinions that were frequently built on suspicion and misinformation. Men of otherwise broad outlook were caught in a narrow sectarianism that was at odds with their humane professions.

This study begins in 1888, when it first became clear that the Catholic Indian school system was the principal beneficiary of federal funds for mission schools and when the drive began in earnest for a public school system for the Indians. It ends in 1912, when the last great Protestant-Catholic flare-up over Indian schools occurred, this time over the issue of religious garb in government schools. The quarter-century between those two dates witnessed the end of the direct federal appropriations for mission schools and the fights waged by the Catholics for the right of Catholic Indian children to attend Catholic schools, for the restoration of rations to Indian children who attended mission schools, for the use of Indian trust and treaty funds (at the request of the Indians) to support Catholic Indian schools, for Catholic religious instruction in the government schools, and for the right of nuns to wear their religious habits when teaching in schools taken over by the federal government.

The battles—and the conflicts at the time were described by the participants in military terms—were directed by the Bureau of Catholic Indian Missions on one side and by the Indian Rights Association (allied with the mission boards of the chief Protestant denominations) on the other. They involved the President, the Secretary of the Interior, and the Commissioner of Indian Affairs, were fought out bitterly in the halls of Congress, and touched the federal courts, including the Supreme Court of the United States. The success of the Catholics in these struggles after 1900 indicated their growing weight in the political life of the nation and their acceptance as part of American society. It indicated the decline in influence of the Protestant-dominated Indian reform groups in directing the Indian policy of the United States. It showed, too, that the virulent anti-Catholicism of the 1890s had spent itself as far as Indian affairs were concerned and that fair-minded persons were willing to concede the reasonable requests of the Catholics without fear that the Pope was about to take over America.

The Indians were only obliquely a part of the story. The Catholic missionaries were dedicated men and women; they were convinced that the salvation of the souls of the Indians whom they served depended upon their efforts and were determined that Indian parents should have the right to choose the schools to which they sent their children. The Indian Rights Association, on the other side, prided itself on its long history of work in defense of Indian rights and for Indian welfare, and the Protestant missionaries with whom the Association worked had the concern of their Indians at heart. But one cannot escape the conclusion that in the battles described here the Indians were on the outside, the ones in whose name the religious groups fought but with little direct part in the events. In some cases, it seems fair to say, they were but pawns in the hands of the managers of the campaigns.

The sources for the study are numerous and full. I have relied chiefly on three groups of material: the voluminous records of the Bureau of Catholic Indian Missions, which have recently been deposited in the Marquette University Library and many of which have not been used for serious historical research before; the magnificent collection of Indian Rights Association Papers in the Historical Society of Pennsylvania and now available for convenient use on microfilm; and the records of the federal government preserved in the National Archives. These three collections give excellent coverage of the part played by the two religious antagonists and by the federal government, from which each side tried to gain official support. There are, in addition, the papers of persons who were participants in the controversy, printed government documents from all three branches of the federal government, and newspaper and periodical accounts. Secondary literature has been of relatively minor help, for the subjects treated here have been little studied by historians.

I owe gratitude to many archivists and librarians for making materials available, particularly in the Marquette University Library, the National Archives, the Library of Congress, the State Historical Society of Wisconsin, the Milwaukee Public Library, and the Historical Society of Pennsylvania. I appreciate, too, the gracious assistance given me in using the archives of the Sisters of the Blessed Sacrament and the archives of the Archdiocese of Baltimore. Research on the project was materially aided by a grant from the DeRance Foundation through Marquette University.

FRANCIS PAUL PRUCHA, S.J.

Marquette University

The Churches and the Indian Schools, 1888–1912

Beginnings of the Controversy

THE Protestant-Catholic controversy in Indian affairs came to the fore first in the decades after the Civil War, when the government, almost despairing of finding a solution to the Indian wars on the frontiers and the corruption in the Indian Office, adopted the "peace policy" of President Grant's administration.[1] This policy had two structural elements. First, Congress authorized a civilian group, called the Board of Indian Commissioners, to advise the Bureau of Indian Affairs and to serve as a watchdog over funds appropriated for Indian administration. Second, in a move to end political appointments in the Indian service, the Indian agencies were turned over to church missionary groups, who nominated the agents and other personnel. In both of these new departures the Catholics were slighted.

The Board of Indian Commissioners was composed of prominent Protestant laymen. While it was not intended that the members should be formal representatives of their church bodies or nominated by them, the connection of the Board with the Protestant churches was close. There was no Catholic on the Board, and there was no indication that one was seriously considered—despite the long interest of the Catholic Church in Indian affairs.[2] It was just taken for granted that such a religiously oriented public body would be Protestant.

The Board of Indian Commissioners each year had a meeting in Washington with representatives of missionary societies engaged in Indian work, and the Board considered itself a sort of liaison between the missionaries and the Indian Office. Except at the very start, there were no Catholic representatives at these meetings. Whether there was overt pressure against Catholic attendance or whether the Catholics voluntarily stayed away is difficult to determine. But the annual meetings reinforced the idea that Christian cooperation with the government in Indian affairs was strictly a Protestant matter.[3]

In the distribution of Indian agencies among the denominations the

Catholics fared little better. President Grant offered the guideline that an agency should be assigned to the missionary group that was already working among the Indians there, but this did not provide for determining between competing groups on a given reservation. Vincent Colyer, secretary of the Board of Indian Commissioners, to whom fell the task of signing up the churches for the program, seems to have had only limited information about the actual state of missionary endeavors. By their own calculation—on the basis of missions established and priority in mission work—the Catholics expected to get thirty-eight agencies in the distribution. They received only seven. The Methodists, who had relatively little mission work to their credit, were assigned fourteen. The Orthodox Friends received ten, the Presbyterians nine, and so on down the line through Episcopalians, Hicksite Friends, Reformed Dutch, Baptists, Congregationalists, Lutherans, and Unitarians.[4]

The Catholics objected, but no corrective measures were taken, and the program gradually deteriorated as the Catholics and Protestants fought over mission fields and as the Protestants fought among themselves. The Catholics, already irritated about what they considered discrimination in the assignment of the agencies, complained sharply about being excluded entirely from reservations under the control of some other denomination. Making a point of religious freedom for the Indians to choose whatever Christian church they wanted, the Catholics finally won their point in 1881, when the government decided that reservations would be open to missionary activity by all groups.[5]

Catholics did not sit idly by as the Protestants seemed to reap the benefits of government policy. In order to gain the strength that comes from unity of action, the Catholics established in 1874 a central agency in Washington to coordinate and direct Catholic Indian mission work and through which all Catholic missions would deal with the federal government. At first there was simply a commissioner, appointed to look after Catholic interests, but in 1879 a formal Bureau of Catholic Indian Missions was established, which was officially recognized as an institution of the Church by the Third Plenary Council of Baltimore in 1884. Its work was carried on by a director and a small staff, under the direction of a committee of prelates. The Bureau became an important force in directing the mission activities of the Catholics, a rallying point for Catholic positions, and an aggressive lobby in Washington for Catholic interests.[6]

The establishment of the Catholic Bureau signaled—indeed helped to stimulate—a new surge in Catholic activity. As Catholic population steadily increased in the United States, a vigorous and growing Church stepped up its mission work. Much of it, of course, was the work of religious orders and congregations of men and women, which, like the Catholic Church in the United States in general, were heavily staffed by foreign immigrants. Significant, too, was the continuing benefaction of Katharine Drexel, daughter of the wealthy Philadelphia financier Francis Drexel. She and her two sisters used large sums of their inheritance to build schools for Catholic Indian missions and to help staff them. And in 1891 Katharine founded a new congregation of nuns— the Sisters of the Blessed Sacrament—to work exclusively among Indians and Negroes. This work of the Drexels was coordinated and directed by the officers of the Bureau of Catholic Indian Missions and the members of the hierarchy who had missions within their dioceses.[7]

The federal government, lacking a comprehensive school system for the Indians, relied heavily upon schools conducted by the various missionary societies and in the 1870s began the practice of making contracts with these mission schools by which the government agreed to pay an annual amount for each student enrolled. The contracts were especially attractive to the Catholics, since the government funds, together with the gifts of Katharine Drexel and the teaching staffs of priests and nuns, provided the necessary support for the schools, and it was easy to expand under such circumstances. The director of the Catholic Bureau saw this expansion as a necessary means to outmaneuver Protestant educational efforts. He urged building more Catholic schools on the reservations. "If we do this," he said in soliciting Drexel funds, "we do an immense deal of good, get the Indians into our hands and thus make them Catholics; if we neglect it any longer, the Government and the Protestants will build ahead of us schools in all the agencies and crowd us completely out and the Indians are lost."[8]

How successful the Catholics were can be seen in a report circulated by the president of the Catholic Bureau, Bishop Martin Marty, in May 1889. He summarized the Catholic advance:

> The rapid growth of the Bureau almost surpasses belief. When the Bureau was first organized, in 1874, the Catholic Missions and Sisters had two boarding and five day schools, supported by the United States government at an expense of $8,000; there were, June 30, 1883, eighteen boarding schools, receiving a government allotment of $54,000. Our contracts with the Government during

the year just closing aggregate $394,533, and we estimate that during the year about to commence the amount will be $431,933. Since the Council of Baltimore was held, five years ago, the Bureau has acquired property to the value of one million dollars. These results have not been accomplished without labor. We have fought every inch of the way. We must not let this work flag.[9]

The result of the aggressive Catholic action, coupled with declining Protestant interest, was a dominance of Catholics in Indian missions and receipt by their schools of the overwhelming proportion of contract funds.[10] In addition, an increasing number of Catholics appeared on the rolls of Indian service personnel during the Democratic administration of Grover Cleveland. Squeezed out, as they viewed it, under Grant's peace policy, the Catholics had come back in force.

This resurgence was not lost upon the Protestant formulators of American Indian policy, who themselves had organized a number of associations to promote their own particular Christian vision of the Indian's future in America. The Boston Indian Citizenship Committee and the Women's National Indian Association, both founded in 1879, were established to protest wrongs done to the Indians and continued to work for Indian rights and welfare. They were soon joined by the Indian Rights Association, established in 1882, the work largely of the scion of a wealthy Philadelphia family, Herbert Welsh, who directed the activities of the Association from its headquarters in Philadelphia. This organization, with an agent in Washington, numerous reports and publications, and branches throughout the country, became the focal point for Indian reform. Representatives of all the groups, together with a revitalized Board of Indian Commissioners, met each year beginning in 1883 at a resort hotel at Lake Mohonk, New York, as guests of Albert K. Smiley, a Quaker member of the Board of Indian Commissioners. These so-called Lake Mohonk Conferences of Friends of the Indian became the great forum for discussion of Indian affairs. Their purpose, as the host of the conferences noted, was "to unite the best minds interested in Indian affairs, so that all should act together and be in harmony, and so that the prominent persons connected with Indian affairs should act as one body and create a public sentiment in favor of the Indians." The goal was the complete Americanization of the Indians and their absorption into the body politic as individuals no different from other citizens. The Indian reform organizations and the Lake Mohonk Conferences were exclusively Protestant affairs, and their view of Americanization did not have room for foreign elements;

it was from them that there came renewed stirring of suspicion and antagonism toward Catholic success.[11]

The Protestant leaders were alert to complaints and rumors, and they made a good deal of isolated examples. But even a few cases gave them an opportunity to express their fears and to contemplate action against the trends they saw or suspected. Thus in October 1887 Charles C. Painter, the agent of the Indian Rights Association in Washington, wrote to Herbert Welsh to inform him that he had heard from the Reverend Edwin Eells, an Indian agent in Washington Territory, that the Commissioner of Indian Affairs intended to replace him with a Catholic from West Virginia. "These are Protestant Indians under missionary care of the Congregationalists & Presbyterians," Painter wrote. "Edwin Eells the Agent has been there since 1871, and is acknowledged to be one of the best of Agents." "It comes up from all points of the compass," Painter continued, "that this process is going on, a decanting of Protestant influence from the control and education of the Indian and an injection of Catholic. It is not accident, but evident design. I think it evident that other influence than that of our friends is beginning to be felt in the allotment of lands. There never has been a time when we so much need to be on the alert as now."[12]

Welsh immediately took up the cry. He sent a copy of Painter's remarks to a number of influential friends—to spread the alarm and to seek advice. To General Samuel A. Armstrong, head of Hampton Institute, he wrote: "I believe this is a very serious question." And he noted, "It was admitted to me by Agent [James] McLaughlin [at Standing Rock Agency], with whom I spoke frankly on the subject last summer, that the Romanist influence in the management of Indian affairs was too great. What can we do to improve matters?"[13] Welsh also wrote to the Reverend William Hayes Ward, editor of the Protestant weekly the *Independent*, and to Dr. James E. Rhoads, president of Bryn Mawr College, a Quaker much interested in Indian affairs. To Rhoads, Welsh repeated the remarks of McLaughlin to the effect that "this policy has been carried beyond the line of fair play." Meanwhile Painter sent Eells's letter on to Welsh for his information, with the suggestion: "It w^d perhaps be best not to use it publickly . . . unless the time comes when we must make an open fight to prevent a surrender of all Indian work to the Catholic Church."[14]

In large part it was a struggle about schools on the reservations, for missionary influence over the Indians came from their boarding schools. Welsh, an Episcopalian, was deeply interested in the schools of that denomination and did much to support his church's mission work among the Sioux. In writing to Anna L. Dawes, daughter of Senator Henry L. Dawes, about the Episcopal mission at Standing Rock and the need for a church school there, his prejudices were clear. "One of the Roman Catholic priests at this Agency is very hostile to our work," he wrote, "—in fact, I suppose that all of them may be so considered, —and does everything that he can to discourage the Indians connected with it. The object of the Roman Catholics is to get the children into their school and so to interfere with the influence of their parents over them." He repeated his concern that "very significant favoritism is being shown the Roman Catholic church by the Indian Bureau." Anna's reply was significant, for it indicated the close connection that politics had with the question. She wrote: "I have told Father about Mr. Eells. He thinks that cannot be reached by *politicians*, but thinks the denominational agencies are the ones to complain. They can object on the score of partiality to one sect, but there seems to be no other way to reach the evil—except indeed a new President!" [15]

The anti-Catholic sentiment of the Indian Rights Association and its friends did not abate, and accounts of "the Romanizing process" and the "aggression of the Roman Catholic church upon the patronage of the government and the mission work of the various Protestant bodies among the Indians" continued to be circulated.[16] Finally, in the summer of 1888, Welsh sent a formal complaint to Secretary of the Interior William P. Vilas. He used as his entry point an article published in the official organ of the Presbyterians, the *Church at Home and Abroad*. The article, based upon the report of the Superintendent of Indian Schools and upon the experiences of the Presbyterian Board of Home Missions, asserted that the government had given a much larger number of contracts for Indian schools to the Catholic Church than to any Protestant group and that the Presbyterians had been compelled as a result to abandon schools they had undertaken at the request of the Indian Office. The article itself was very anti-Catholic in its tone. It spoke of "Roman aggressiveness, viz., its growing power with the government at Washington, in every department, and in nearly all the state and city governments. It is a power so insidious and relentless that it becomes all true lovers of this land to be instantly on the alert in order to defeat its purposes. . . . The Romish Church is un-American. It is controlled by a power outside of our commonwealth. Its priests and people are subject to the mandates of the pope. In case of a conflict of authority, he must be obeyed at all hazards." [17] Welsh added to this his own views. "My own acquaintance with Indian affairs during the past four years," he said, "has led me to the conclusion that the work of Protestant Churches among the Indians, representing large expenditure of money and labor was being put in jeopardy, or actually robbed of fruition by the appointment of many Roman Catholic teachers and employees at agencies or schools where heretofore the appointees were Protestants." Since, Welsh noted, a great many persons both in and outside the Indian Rights Association were concerned about the matter, he inquired of Vilas whether the government had any policy for dealing with the matter in the future.[18]

Vilas rebuffed Welsh with a vague reply, which must have been less than satisfactory. It was, Vilas said, his "earnest desire and purpose to feel or manifest no partiality to any sect in making appointments, employments, or arrangements for the education of the Indians." Instead, he would welcome all cooperation from anyone who was willing and able to contribute toward civilizing the Indians. "The relative share which any sect may secure in this work," he concluded, "must, therefore, depend upon the zeal and labor they bring to it."[19] And the Commissioner of Indian Affairs, John H. Oberly, took pains to refute the charge that the Indian Bureau had discriminated in favor of Catholics. No organization with adequate facilities that had asked for contracts had ever been refused, he said; the Catholics received more contracts simply because they had expended larger sums of money in the erection of school buildings and could accommodate more pupils under contract. In fiscal year 1887 the Catholics had spent $115,000 for Indian school buildings and furnishings, Oberly reported, and altogether had laid out about $1,000,000.[20]

At this point the Friends of the Indian at Lake Mohonk turned to Indian education in earnest. Although rejoicing in the victory they had attained in legislating land allotments for the Indian in the Dawes Act of 1887, they realized that more was needed. They wrote into their platform for 1888: "Neither the land in severalty, nor law administered by competent courts, will suffice for the protection of the Indian. More fundamental than either is his education."[21] The meeting of that year began with a long paper on education prepared by the Reverend Lyman Abbott, noted Congregational minister, reformer, and editor of the *Christian Union* (later the *Outlook*).[22] He condemned the existing "no-system" of Indian education, with bits and pieces of government and religious schools put together without order, and he recommended in its stead a universal, compulsory school system for Indians run entirely by the federal government. He was opposed absolutely to any government funds for church mission schools, the "*quasi* partnership" between the government and the churches, which was "as perplexing in its results as it is anomalous in its nature." It was, he said, "simply an incidental evil of this anomalous condition of affairs" that in 1886 out of fifty religious schools supported in part by the government and in part by religious societies, thirty-eight with 2,068 pupils were under Catholic control and only twelve with 500 pupils under Protestant. The missionary groups, he contended, would do better to leave secular education to the government and spend their own energies and moneys on strictly religious training for the Indians.[23] The paper was a forthright and challenging one, for Abbott was never one to speak hesitantly, and much of the time in the three days of the conference was devoted to discussing it.

Some accepted Abbott's position fully and called for an absolute end to any church-state union in Indian education, speaking of the contract schools as "un-American." The conference members were well aware of the critical question of public aid for Catholic parochial schools in the states, as the Catholics, because of the secular or Protestant character of the public schools, established their own schools and then sought public funds to support them. The memory was still fresh of violent agitation in Boston in 1887 and 1888. The Reverend Addison P. Foster, a Congregational minister from that city, told the conference: "The only protection from the rivalry of denominations, and the only defense against a *quasi* union of Church and State, is to have no aid to denominational schools afforded by Government. This principle is as sound in Dakota as it is in Boston."[24]

Others, however, were not ready to accept Abbott's recommendations. There were two main obstacles. First, it was insisted that secular education alone was insufficient to work the transformation in the Indians that the reformers all wanted.[25] Second, everyone admitted that there was no likelihood that the government could at once step into the void that would be created if the religious schools were closed. No matter how firmly one condemned the use of government funds by religious societies, practical concern for the Indians dictated that the change would have to be made gradually, and some of the Protestant denominations foresaw disastrous effects upon their own establishments.[26]

In the end the conference of 1888 compromised. It accepted the principle that Indian education should become totally the responsibility of the government, while urging the liberty of the Christian churches to continue their religious training of Indians and to supplement the work of the government by schools supported entirely by the missionary societies. But it proposed that aid be continued to contract schools until the government was prepared to assume the entire work of secular education.[27]

Before the next Lake Mohonk Conference met, fundamental changes had taken place, which deeply affected the mission school issue.

Commissioner Morgan and Father Stephan

THE national election of 1888 ousted Cleveland and the Democrats from office and returned the Republicans under Benjamin Harrison. The change of political parties was of great significance in the contract school question, for the Protestant reformers could expect support from the Republican Party, to which most of them belonged. Harrison did not disappoint them. To the post of Commissioner of Indian Affairs he appointed Thomas Jefferson Morgan, a Civil War general, Baptist minister, and public educator. For Superintendent of Indian Schools he picked the Reverend Daniel Dorchester, a Methodist clergyman.[1]

Morgan was a man of singular qualities as Commissioner of Indian Affairs, for despite his variety of experience he was primarily a professional educator. He fitted well into the strong Americanizing currents of the day and appeared as a most welcome leader in Indian educational reform. Born in Franklin, Indiana, on August 17, 1839, he graduated from Franklin College in 1861, although he left school during his senior year to enlist in the Union Army. As a Civil War officer, he served in a regiment led by Benjamin Harrison and later won a name for himself as a commander of black troops. When the war ended, Morgan entered Rochester Theological Seminary and in 1869 was ordained a Baptist minister. He held a number of ministerial posts, but soon he moved into secular education, serving as principal of state normal schools in Nebraska, New York, and Rhode Island. That a Baptist clergyman could move so easily between denominational and public institutions is an indication of the dominant place held by Protestants and their general acceptance in the growing public school system of the states. Morgan's continual insistence upon the need for Christian education not only reflected his own personal commitment to religion but was a part of the spirit of the age.[2]

After his old Civil War commander, Benjamin Harrison, was elected to the presidency, Morgan hoped to be appointed United States Commissioner of Education, and when he failed to obtain that position, he eagerly accepted the post of Commissioner of Indian Affairs.[3] He came to the Indian Office with firm opinions on the value of education as an essential means for the promotion of American citizenship and on the necessity of a public school system. In his *Studies in Pedagogy* he extolled the virtues of the "free schools of America," which would create a universal Americanism. The goal of the teachers, he wrote, should be to bring about a common life among the various peoples who made up the nation. "Nothing, perhaps, is so distinctly a product of the soil," he declared, "as is the American school system. In these schools all speak a common language; race distinctions give way to national characteristics."[4] In his new office Morgan would soon add the American Indian to this vision.

After assuming office at the beginning of July 1889, Morgan went right to work on a comprehensive scheme for a national Indian school system. In October he appeared at Lake Mohonk to present his ideas to the assembled philanthropists. He told them: "When President Harrison tendered me the Indian Bureau, he said, I wish you to administer it in such a way as will satisfy the Christian philanthropic sentiment of the country. That was the only charge that I received from him. I come here, where the Christian philanthropic sentiment of the country focusses itself, to ask you what will satisfy you."[5] Morgan proposed just the sort of system that Abbott had so urgently advocated the year before, but he walked softly on the issue of contract schools. He straightforwardly announced his opposition to them in principle, yet he insisted that he would not abruptly close the ones in existence. In the lengthy discussion of his report, the questions of church and state that had engaged the conference in 1888 were worked over again in a modest way. The conference voted its strong confidence in Morgan and his program and gave its full support. Men who often represented quite different views at the conferences rallied behind the Commissioner. Lyman Abbott said he thought the conference was ready to stand behind Morgan and give him hearty support in the endeavor to provide universal education for the Indians, and his remarks were greeted by warm applause. General Armstrong urged strong backing, and Herbert Welsh spoke in Morgan's favor. The Board of Indian Commissioners in a special business meeting voted formally to aid the Commissioner in carrying out his plans for educating the Indians and for their progress to full American citizenship.⁶ The more moderate tone of the debate indicated how comfortable the Lake Mohonk reformers felt with Morgan at the helm and their assurance that their particular interests, after four years of difficulties, would now be well looked after.

If indeed they did relax for a moment, they were soon jolted out of their complacency. The Catholics began an aggressive and virulent attack upon Morgan and Dorchester. In this they were led by the Reverend Joseph A. Stephan, who had been appointed director of the Bureau of Catholic Indian Missions in 1884. Born in Baden, Germany, in 1822, he had been educated in technical schools in preparation for a military career. When his vision returned after an attack of blindness, however, he determined to become a priest. In 1847 he came to the United States and completed theological studies at Cincinnati. Throughout the Civil War he served as an army chaplain, and after the war, when Grant's peace policy went into operation, he was Indian agent at the Standing Rock Agency in Dakota. An ardent zeal for the conversion of the Indians marked his apostolic work, and his appointment to head the Catholic Bureau gave that organization a new and aggressive energy. Stephan was a man of striking appearance, with erect carriage and a long white beard that gave him a patriarchal look. He was also, unfortunately, a man of immoderate views and irascible temper.⁷

The Catholics were understandably edgy about having two Protestant ministers in such key spots in the Indian service. Charges of bigotry against Morgan and Dorchester soon filled the air, as Stephan and the Catholic press, aided by Democratic papers, fought to prevent the confirmation of the two men by the Senate. Despite the continued public assertions by the Indian Office appointees that they had no anti-Catholic bias of any kind, their records were far from clean in Catholic eyes. Dorchester was the more vulnerable, for he had been active in the Boston public school controversy in 1888 and in that year had published a book called *Romanism versus the Public School System*, in which he violently attacked the Catholic school system. "Its crying defect," he declared, "is that its teaching is not only un-American but anti-American, and will remove every one of its pupils, in their ideals, far from a proper mental condition for American citizenship, and enhance the already too difficult task of making them good citizens of a republic."⁸

With such a man in charge of Indian schools, it is no wonder that the Catholics feared for the future of their Indian educational work, but for some reason Dorchester was nearly forgotten, and the main attack

HERBERT WELSH. One of the founders of the Indian Rights Association, Welsh served as executive secretary and then as president from 1882 to 1927. (Photograph from the Historical Society of Pennsylvania)

THOMAS J. MORGAN. Morgan was the designer and energetic promoter of a government Indian school system during his term as Commissioner of Indian Affairs, 1889–93. He was a leading opponent of the contract schools. (Portrait from James M. King, *Facing the Twentieth Century*)

was leveled against Morgan. Perhaps this was because he was Dorchester's superior and more influential in formulating Indian policy, perhaps because he seemed more vulnerable on grounds other than his religious bias. To be sure, however, Morgan was on record with anti-Catholic statements that matched Dorchester's for sweeping denunciation of the Catholic position on the schools. In a discussion at the National Educational Association meeting in 1888 devoted to the criticism that the public schools failed to cultivate morality and religion, Morgan from the floor lashed out at the Catholics, whom he accused of trying to destroy the public school system and substitute their own. "I have traced this matter to the source," he said. "I have studied it, and it simply means that it is a challenge to our civilization, it is a challenge to our Christianity, it is a challenge to our political life, it is a challenge to everything that we Americans cherish today." He denied that the public schools were godless simply because they were not Catholic and urged his listeners not to yield to Catholic criticisms. "If you yield, if you accept the criticism as just," he concluded, "you yield everything that we prize in the civilization of the nineteenth century, represented by Martin Luther, and represented in its outflowering by American ideas; you recognize that all that is a sham and a pretense, that it is to be thrown aside, and that we are all to go back to mediaevalism, with all that condition implies." [9] A man of such mentality was not likely to be enthusiastic about government-supported Catholic Indian schools, no matter how much he protested his impartiality.

Morgan, appointed during a recess of the Senate, had served as Commissioner of Indian Affairs for more than five months before his name was formally sent to the Senate for confirmation on December 4, 1889. In that time he had formulated his policies and won the support of the influential groups represented by the Board of Indian Commissioners and the Lake Mohonk Conference. But that time also allowed his opponents to organize a campaign against him.

The specific charge made by the Catholics was that Morgan and Dorchester were dismissing Catholics from the Indian service because of their religion. The officials replied that the persons dismissed were guilty of incompetence, insubordination, or intemperance and that religion had nothing to do with the cases. But more fundamentally, the Catholics worried about losing the contract schools and the improved status the church had acquired in Indian affairs. The Protestants, on the other hand, worried about interference of Catholics in political affairs as only the beginning of a "Romanist" advance. Both sides, while preaching fairness and impartiality, took whatever measures they thought prudent and effective to gain their ends—the Catholics to prevent Morgan and Dorchester from remaining in office, the Protestants to assure their confirmation at all costs.[10]

Public opposition to Morgan at first seemed to be of a political nature. Certain senators who did not get the appointments for their constituents that they wanted openly opposed Morgan's confirmation, and Democrats were not above some harassment of the new administration. But by mid-October Herbert Welsh began to see Catholic influence and felt it necessary to bolster Morgan's cause. He wrote to Talcott Williams of the *Philadelphia Press*, "I fear also that the Roman Catholics are hostile to him, because he found it necessary to dismiss a number of them, not because of their religion, but on account of their inefficiency. If a chance occurs for you to say a good word for Morgan in the Press, I trust you will avail yourself of it. It will both help a good man in a trying position, and strengthen the best elements in the Republican party." Welsh kept up a sizable correspondence on the matter—to Charles E. Briggs of the *Press*, for example, urging favorable notice of Morgan; to General Armstrong, telling him that he feared the Roman Catholics would oppose Morgan because "he will undoubtedly thwart their scheme to gain control of the Indian service"; and to Morgan himself to get exact figures on money given to Catholics for contract schools compared with that given to other denominations. "It is unpleasant to engage in warfare with any body of persons under the name of a Church," he told Morgan, "but if such a body tries to force the Government, by the power of its Church membership, to do that which is clearly unjust, the contest cannot be avoided. I do not hesitate to engage in such a contest if I am absolutely sure that I am right, and if I have all the data necessary to show that I am right."[11]

Morgan himself, in the meantime, had tried to soften Catholic attacks upon him by an appeal to James Cardinal Gibbons, Archbishop of Baltimore and the leading American prelate. He wrote a polite letter, assuring Gibbons of his desire to have "the sympathy and cooperation of all good people" in his work of preparing the Indian children for American citizenship. The Cardinal replied with a stiff note, in which he invited Morgan to confer with him prior to a meeting of bishops called to discuss their grievances against the new administration. Morgan was unable to arrange the conference with Gibbons, but he sent him a private and informal letter, in which he took a conciliatory stance:

I have been both surprised and pained at the character of many of the articles in Catholic newspapers reflecting upon my personal character, and my official actions. Almost all of the criticisms which have fallen under my eye are wholly without foundation, and some of them, I am sorry to add, are false and slanderous.

Of course I cannot make any public reply to such criticisms, and I go to the verge of personal humiliation in alluding to them even in this communication to you. I do so only from my sincere desire to remove, so far as it is in my power, any obstacle that may prevent a harmonious cooperation between myself as the representative of the Government, and yourself as the representative of the Catholic Church in the work of promoting the education and civilization of the American Indians.[12]

Welsh, too, tried to prevent an open conflict with the Catholics over Morgan's policies, and he turned to Catholic leaders to see if they might help to avoid an open rupture. He wrote to Cardinal Gibbons saying that if unfair action had been taken against Catholics, the Indian Rights Association would fight to correct the injustice. Then he turned to the prominent Catholic layman Charles J. Bonaparte, of Baltimore (a grand-nephew of Napoleon and a Republican), to ask for help. "I may be mistaken in fearing that the Roman Catholic Church will oppose Gen. Morgan's confirmation," Welsh wrote, "but what I already know seems sufficient to warrant my making this appeal to you for counsel as to the best means for averting such a result."[13] Bonaparte arranged a meeting in his office between Welsh and Archbishop John Ireland, of St. Paul, and Archbishop Patrick W. Riordan, of San Francisco, who had come to Baltimore to discuss the issue with Cardinal Gibbons. The prelates clearly voiced their objections, charging that Morgan intended to abandon the contract school system and that both Morgan and Dorchester were obnoxious to them because of alleged enmity toward the Catholic Church and because they had been sweeping Catholics out of positions in the Indian service. Welsh wrote a detailed account of his visit in a letter to Morgan and sent copies of the letter to his supporters in the fight for Morgan's confirmation.[14]

On November 20 Archbishop Ireland, accompanied by Secretary of the Treasury William Windom and Secretary of State James G. Blaine, called on President Harrison. They talked for an hour, and the question of the Indian schools was fully discussed. Written statements drawn up by the Bureau of Catholic Indian Missions were left with the President, and Ireland thought that a favorable impression had been made on Harrison even though no conclusions had been reached. But as to Morgan, the Archbishop reported, "I have no confidence in him. He is a bigot and a liar."[15]

The Catholics did not relent. Charges of anti-Catholic bias on the part of Morgan were widely circulated in the Catholic press. The *Catholic Columbian* (Columbus, Ohio) was especially active, printing and distributing ten thousand petition forms to be signed and sent to the Senate protesting against the confirmation.[16] Nor was anti-Catholicism the only charge leveled at Morgan, for his enemies dredged out a court-martial from his Civil War career. Although Morgan had not been dismissed from the army and was subsequently promoted, the court-martial was not forgotten by his political and religious opponents. The *National Democrat* (Washington) for December 7, 1889, for example, had a long article opposing confirmation on the basis of the court-martial, and Stephan and his friends never quite let the issue die.

In mid-December Father Stephan sent to the Senate Committee on Indian Affairs a long statement entitled "In the Matter of the Confirmation of Thomas J. Morgan as Commissioner of Indian Affairs," in which he summarized his attack on Morgan under three heads with extensive argumentation attached: (1) that Morgan was not a truthful man; (2) that he conducted the Indian Office in the sectarian manner, in prejudice to the Catholic Church; and (3) that his military record rendered him, if not unfit for public office, at least less worthy than others. When a copy reached Morgan, the Commissioner reported that he was "both humiliated and outraged at being obliged to reply to such charges, and to waste time on this which ought to be spent in the very greatly needed and much neglected work of the office." But reply he did, with a massive rejoinder to Senator Henry L. Dawes, chairman of the Senate committee, in which he justified his policy in regard to Indian schools and answered one by one the charges made against him. He reiterated his position that he was against contract schools in principle but that he had maintained those in existence without any discrimination against Catholics.[17]

Father Stephan was indefatigable and did not let up his attack. "I am indeed so overloaded with official business and constant worrying to defeat the confirmation of Morgan & Dorchester by the U.S. Senate," he wrote in December to Katharine Drexel, "that I hardly am aware whether I took a meal or not. I have to see Senators & members of congress constantly to explain questions, and as the newspapers are full of our fight and attacks are made direct on our Bureau and the Cath.

church, it keeps me not only exceedingly busy, but also sleepless at night." As the vote on confirmation neared, he redoubled his efforts, seeing every senator and gaining the support of influential members of the Senate. He worked secretly, he said, in the hope that his opponents would "fall into a lull and stupor and neglect to work untill they are at once, unaware, confronted in the Senate session by too heavy guns for them." [18]

As the Catholic Bureau and the Catholic press stepped up their attack, Welsh countered with increasing efforts of his own on Morgan's behalf. From the middle of November 1889 to the beginning of February 1890 he devoted much of his time and effort to the cause. He kept in close touch with Morgan and enlisted support from many friends. "I wrote long since," he noted at the end of December, "to all our Branch Associations, to all our members, and to the Bishops of the Methodist and Episcopal Church asking their assistance in this matter, and I know that in response to my appeal a great many letters have been written to Senators asking them to vote for Morgan's confirmation." [19] He persuaded the *New York Tribune* to publish a long letter in support of Morgan, which appeared on November 25, and the next month he submitted to the *Times* another long letter that dealt largely with the court-martial issue, which was printed on December 25. Welsh circulated copies of these two letters widely, and he continually alerted his correspondents to the future dangers he saw of Catholic interference in political affairs. [20] But finally he began to tire. "I begin to feel some of the strain and annoyance of this controversy," he wrote to General Armstrong at the beginning of 1890, "though I was never more convinced of being in the right than I have been throughout it. The Romanists have not raised themselves in my estimation by what I have seen of their bearing and methods in this matter." [21]

Welsh in the end was victorious, for the Senate on February 12, 1890, confirmed Morgan and on the following day, Dorchester. [22] Morgan's friends were jubilant at the favorable outcome. "It is gratifying," one of them wrote to Senator Dawes, "to see a chosen victim escape the toils of intolerance." Morgan himself spoke of it as "a great and far reaching victory," and he repeatedly argued that the Senate confirmation meant a complete quashing of all the charges made against him. Welsh, however, reverted at once to the role of peacemaker. In writing to Morgan to congratulate him on his confirmation, he remarked: "There is one point very strongly impressed upon my mind, and in regard to it Bishop Hare fully agrees. The importance, as an act of wise policy, of your doing whatever is in your power, consistent with your duty, to show the liberal spirit toward the Roman Catholics in dealing with Indian matters in order that their feeling of hostility may be allayed, and further hostile criticism upon you on this score obviated." [23]

The Lake Mohonk Conference in October 1890 devoted much of its time to debating the advisability of continuing the contract schools. Opponents, including the Reverend James M. King, secretary of the National League for the Protection of American Institutions, who read a paper on "The Churches—Their Relation to the General Government in the Education of the Indian Races," argued vehemently that any government appropriation for church schools was unconstitutional. Supporters, on the other hand, pointed to the good work being done by the contract schools and insisted that the system of government schools could not at once provide for all Indian children if the mission schools were closed down. In the end the conference unanimously adopted a resolution approving Morgan's proposal for a common school education for all Indian children at government expense, but until that could be done, it advised that the work of the contract schools be continued and fostered. [24]

During 1891 the bitter recriminations came to a head as Morgan fought a violent verbal battle with the Bureau of Catholic Indian Missions. It was clear to the Catholics that neither Morgan nor his philanthropic supporters had changed their ultimate position about the contract schools, and a campaign of abuse against Morgan got under way. Morgan's public reaction was circumspect and gentlemanly, but the attack in no way influenced him to weaken his original principles. At the January conference of the Board of Indian Commissioners with the representatives of the missionary boards, Morgan asserted that he had never "uttered a word either in public or private about suddenly destroying that system [contract schools]." He pointed out that instead the money granted to the contract schools had increased since he took office— $530,000 the year before he entered office, $562,000 during his first year, and $570,000 for the current year. He left no doubt, however, about where he stood in principle. "But I do not believe in the system," he declared. "It is utterly untenable." He did not intend to disturb good schools in existence, but he was adamant against extending the system by approving new schools. "I believe the churches would spend their money more wisely," he told the missionaries, "if they spent it in missionary work rather than in the secular education of Indians." [25]

The issue was soon joined between Morgan and the Bureau of Catholic Indian Missions. The Commissioner, in fact, had early identified his foe. In January 1891 he noted stirrings of opposition to him in Congress, which he attributed partly to partisan purposes, partly to a "little bit of spite" against him by a dismissed clerk. "The gist of the whole matter, however," he wrote to Harrison's private secretary, "is the desire of the Roman Catholic Bureau to get rid of me, because of my attitude on the question of Indian education."[26]

In the *Congressional Record* for February 14, 1891, entered as part of the remarks of Congressman Joseph E. Washington, Democrat from Tennessee, was a letter of Stephan to Morgan of September 3, 1890, about reduction of contracts, to which was appended the following paragraph: "The Catholic bureau accuses Commissioner Morgan not only of withholding from the Indians what Congress had enacted that they should have, but also of displaying marked religious bigotry and of treating certain religious denominations with gross unfairness."[27]

In a strong letter to the Bureau, Morgan took exception to the statement, absolutely denying bigotry or gross unfairness. He pointed to numerous examples of his good will toward Catholic incumbents in the Indian service and claimed that the Senate had vindicated him of all accusations made prior to his confirmation. He charged the Bureau with failing to fight in the open but resorting instead to "a policy of personal assault, malice and untruthfulness" to advance their position and break down his personal character and thus injure the success of his administration.[28]

Stephan replied in kind. He countered Morgan's complaint about malicious entries in the *Congressional Record* with a reference to a speech in the same debate by "the unsavory McCord" and to page after page of "American League protests—American Alliance remonstrances —Committee of One Hundred resolutions, and the vile libels and calumnies of a Bailey, all, all, it is said, either written, made up or inspired by you, Sir, while holding a Government office, when you should have been engaged in more profitable business." He insinuated that a man of Morgan's past history had no business speaking of untruthfulness and brought up again the matter of the court-martial, in which, he noted, no Catholics had been involved. After watching Morgan in office for nearly two years, he concluded, he could see no reason to change the opinions of Morgan that had led him to oppose his confirmation in the first place.[29] With this blast off his chest, Stephan left for Europe for his health. The work of the Bureau devolved upon the Reverend

P. A. Chapelle, rector of St. Matthew's Church in Washington and vice-president of the Bureau, and upon Charles S. Lusk, secretary of the organization.

Before he had read Stephan's angry letter, Morgan proceeded on a conciliatory course. He held a meeting in his office on June 10 with Chapelle and Lusk. Most of the discussion dealt with problems of the Catholic Indian school at Santa Fe, but Morgan took the occasion to raise the question of attacks made upon him, and he received assurances from Chapelle that they would cease. Morgan was hopeful that the controversy had been quieted. He sent a copy of the stenographic report of the meeting to President Harrison's secretary with the comment: "It is a great satisfaction to me that these people are seeing the error of their ways." [30]

His optimism was unfounded, and the fires soon flared up again. In the *New York Sun* for June 28 appeared an article attacking Morgan, which he was convinced emanated from the Catholic Bureau and which broke his forbearance since it seemed to fly directly in the face of the promises he had received from Chapelle less than three weeks before. Morgan acted almost at once. On July 2 he severed all official relations with the Bureau of Catholic Indian Missions; he did not cancel the contracts for the Catholic Indian schools, but in the future he intended to deal directly with each school, bypassing the central Washington office, which had heretofore handled all the official business of the various missions.[31] Morgan sent a copy of the letter he had written to the Catholic Bureau to Cardinal Gibbons, reasserting his friendship for Catholics while complaining bitterly about the treatment he had received from those connected with the Bureau. "The assaults which have been made upon my personal character," he said, "charging me with being a perjurer, a liar, a bigot, a pagan, a dishonored soldier, a persecutor, a brute, a corruptor of morals, a destroyer of the faith, &c. &c., attacks which have not spared my wife nor the sacredness of my home, could hardly have been pleasing under any circumstances." But what really irritated him was that these attacks came forth "under the sanction of a great Bureau, styling itself Christian." [32]

Morgan, of course, gained much support for his action from the opponents of the Catholic schools. Herbert Welsh praised Morgan for his action. "I fail to see," he wrote, "how you could continue to have any relations with the [Catholic Bureau] so long as the present Director maintained his position. His letter to you, of which you sent me a copy, was so grossly insulting that it was certainly impossible for you to have further dealings with him." The attacks of the Bureau had been "as unfair as they were persistent." The Reverend H. L. Morehouse, of the American Baptist Home Mission Society, wrote to the President to express his hope that the decision would be unalterable, and James M. King, of the National League for the Protection of American Institutions, told Harrison that he hoped the administration would stand behind Morgan's decision.[33]

The Catholic Bureau, on the other hand, was greatly disturbed by Morgan's action. Cardinal Gibbons wrote directly to Morgan, saying that the cutting off of relations with the Bureau was "a very grave step, and one that I fear will be fraught with much embarrassment to all concerned in the great and necessary work of educating our Indian wards." He urged the Commissioner to reconsider the matter and revoke his action, and he promised to use his influence to prevent attacks upon Morgan "of a malevolent or personal character." The Bureau held emergency meetings of its board of directors and used every means it could to get the Commissioner to reverse his decision.[34] But Morgan would not budge, and he moved ahead with his policy of ignoring the Bureau in his official actions. Lusk wrote to Stephan, who was still recuperating in Germany: "Things look rather dark for us at present, but I have an abiding faith that we will pull through all right, and that Morgan will find that he has made a great blunder in attempting to 'knock us out.'"[35]

The sharp Catholic reaction to his decision of July 2 clearly disturbed Morgan, who began to wonder if he had acted too quickly in an important matter without the prior approval of President Harrison. He sent a series of letters to Harrison's private secretary, E. W. Halford, and to the President himself, describing in detail the positive reaction to his measure and repeating the justification for it. He wrote to Halford on July 20: "One man writes me that my letter to the Bureau will be 'historical,' another that it will be a 'turning point in the history of the country'; another . . . that I 'deserve the thanks of the nation,' and so on and so on. Of course, they [the Catholics] will not yield the point without a struggle, and what form that struggle with take, I am not as yet advised. I see no reason as yet to think that I have made a mistake, although I sincerely wish that the controversy might have been honorably avoided." To the President he reported that the step had been taken with full consultation and approval of the Secretary of the Interior and that it had been necessary for his self-respect and the dignity of his office. "The truth is," he wrote, "that this crisis and change had to come sooner or later, the Catholic Bureau could not forever run the Indian Office, and *any* man whom you would have been willing to place in charge of these great interests, would have rebelled against such a form of slavery, to say nothing of the particular attacks on me. You will not fail to notice that this is not a blow at the Catholics, but at an insolent, dictatorial Bureau, whose usefulness, if it ever had any, it has outgrown." He hastened to add that the political effects of the action, if any, would be favorable to the President and the Republican Party.[36]

Morgan's views on the relationship between Catholic schools and the government school system that was his dream came into sharp focus in a conflict between the Catholic contract school at Santa Fe and the newly established government schools at Santa Fe and Albuquerque. In his attempts to carry out the rules for schools he had drawn up, Morgan called attention to what he considered to be weaknesses in St. Catherine's School for the Pueblos at Santa Fe. He asked about non-English-speaking employees, questioned the facilities for industrial training, and noted reports that the dining room was not heated—legitimate enough concerns for a man whose goal was to upgrade all Indian schools.[37]

John Baptist Salpointe, Archbishop of Santa Fe, sent his reply to Morgan by way of Father Stephan at the Catholic Bureau. He brushed off the questions and criticism lightly, while stressing all the points of information that were in his favor. The main import of the letter, however, was a complaint that the establishment of a government school for the Pueblos at Santa Fe was an attempt to destroy the Catholic school, that the government agents intended to fill up the government school at the expense of the mission schools, thus destroying the results of the missionaries' long years of hard work. Furthermore, Salpointe asserted, the Indians wanted Catholic rather than government schools. He suggested that Morgan leave the education of the Pueblos to the Catholics and set up government schools for Indians who had no schools at all. Although the bishop explicitly denied any direct opposition to the government school, he was very critical of the federal school officials and charged that they tried to get students for their school by intimidation. He wrote:

> Harassed and frightened by the menaces of these men, speaking in the name of the Government, the Indians come to us and ask, if really they will be punished for not sending their children to schools which they consider as opposed to their religious convictions. Of course, our answer is that the Government has neither the right nor the intention to interfere with their religion, and that they

must pay no attention to the threats of subalterns, whose position depends upon the success they may have in the proselytizing work committed to their care. Is that opposing the Government institutions? Not directly indeed, but on account of the religious principles therein taught, which principles are in opposition to the religion the Indians have professed for over two centuries and which they earnestly wish to be the religion of their children.

He predicted that the Santa Fe government school would be a failure. "It may be that the intentions of Mr. Morgan are right," he concluded, "but, taking things as they are, his action in regard to our schools looks, in the opinion of all fair-minded people, as a religious persecution." [38]

Morgan's reply to Salpointe indicated the conflict between his position and that of the missionaries. He was appalled that the bishop could construe the establishment of "national schools" among the Pueblos as an attempt to destroy the Catholic faith of the Indians and that thereby he was bent on religious persecution. "I certainly would have supposed that you understood," he said, "that the public school system of the country is designed, primarily, for the preparation of children for the duties of citizenship, and it is no part of the work of the public school system to propagate any particular creed." He asserted that the former training of the Indians had utterly failed to fit them for the demands of modern life, and that unless measures were quickly taken to give the Indian children improved industrial training, they would continue "in a semi-lethargic condition, making little progress in civilization and more and more threatened with disaster from the stronger civilization that is surging about them." [39]

After suggesting to Salpointe that if he wanted strictly Catholic schools he should solicit funds for them from Catholics, not from the federal government, he laid down a set of propositions upon which he based his case:

> First. The Government of the United States has entered upon the work of establishing and maintaining a system of Government schools for the education of the Indians, and these schools are being pushed with energy and the Government is committed to their defence.
>
> Second. That the Government not only has the right to do this but is under strong obligations to do it.
>
> Third. That the Government will protect these institutions against any unwarranted interference with their work and it cannot be expected that the Government will quietly allow the enemies of

these national institutions to interfere with their work without inter-
posing an objection and, if necessary, a protecting arm.

Fourth. It is not to be expected that the Government will pay
out of the National Treasury for the establishing and maintaining of
institutions of any kind in the Indian country, when it is boldly
avowed by those having these institutions in charge that they have
the exclusive right to that work, and that they look with disfavor
upon the work of the Government in national schools. . . .[40]

Morgan wanted assurance that St. Catherine's would provide satisfactory industrial training, that only English-speaking persons would be
employed, and that opposition to the government schools would cease.
The bishop made a weak response. He denied any hostility to the government schools but continued to protest against the use by agents of
those schools of "threats, intimidation and coercion for the purpose
of filling these schools at the expense of ours." When the Commissioner learned that a priest in Santa Fe was stirring up the Indians to
resort to the courts to get their children out of the government school in
Albuquerque by writ of habeas corpus, he threatened to withdraw all
support from the contract school.[41]

Morgan's supporters continued their attack on the contract schools
with a new emphasis on the separation of church and state, which reflected to some extent no doubt the growth in anti-Catholic prejudice
exhibited in the nation. The discussion moved from criticism of the
disproportionate amount of money going to Catholics to condemnation
of Catholic schools per se. In 1892 James King was back at Lake
Mohonk to renew his attack. Referring to an "unscrupulous" attack
made by Father Stephan on the government schools because of their
Protestant character, he made his final point: "In this Columbian year
it becomes us to remember that our civilization is not Latin, because
God did not permit North America to be settled and controlled by that
civilization. The Huguenot, the Hollander, and the Puritan created our
civilization. Let us not put a premium by national grants on a rejected
civilization in the education of a race who were here when Columbus
came." King concluded that "much Roman Catholic teaching among
the Indians does not prepare them for intelligent and loyal citizenship." [42]

The Protestants could not escape the logic of their position. If separation of church and state was demanded in the case of the Catholic
schools, it would have to be applied also to their own. So the Protestant
missionary societies withdrew from the contract school system, ending

the long years of partnership between their societies and the government in Indian educational and missionary work, and promoted instead government schools for the Indians.[43]

The presidential election of 1892 made much of the contract school issue, for Stephan and the Catholic Bureau did all they could to tie Morgan and his alleged anti-Catholicism to Harrison's coattails.[44] Of special note was a remark in Stephan's 1892 report to the president of the Bureau, in which the priest referred to "the bigoted Commissioner, and the not much less bigoted President," a statement widely repeated in the religious and secular press.[45] The Catholic newspapers urged Catholics to throw out the Harrison administration, continuing the bitter attacks on Morgan that had begun at the very start of his government career. The editor of the *Catholic Columbian* had written to Stephan at the time of the fight against Morgan's confirmation: "If Morgan and Dorchester are confirmed the conviction is eternal as truth itself, in the minds of Catholics that the outrage will be resented by the hundreds of thousands of Catholic voters throughout the country. The ballot box will right the wrong."[46] The same paper had kept its readers alert to Morgan's transgressions, writing in 1891: "Indian Commissioner Morgan advertises himself as a full-blooded religious bigot by his treatment of the bureau of Catholic Indian missions. Morgan is an arrogant, dictatorial, domineering fanatic, who is utterly unfit, by training and temperament, for the position which he occupies. But there is evidently a close bond of sympathy between him and the president."[47] Such charges were met by the Protestant and "patriotic" press with equally bitter tirades against usurpations by the Catholic power, which they saw threatening the very foundations of the nation.

The Catholic press was jubilant over Cleveland's victory in November. The *Catholic Herald* of New York declared: "The Republican Party, led by bigots, invaded the sanctuary of the home, usurped parental rights, and robbed the Catholic Indians of their only treasure, their faith; but the people, true to the best traditions of America, hurled it from power. Cleveland's victory was, in truth, the defeat of bigotry."[48]

The End of The Contract Schools

IF the election of 1892 was indeed a victory for the Catholics, in which the people of the United States had "beaten bigotry black and blue," it was a hollow victory for the proponents of direct government support of the mission schools.[1] The removal of Morgan and Dorchester could not stem the tide of support for public schools or quiet the winds of opposition to the contract schools that had begun before Morgan had taken office and of which he was more the servant than the master. But the Catholic leaders hoped that a sympathetic Commissioner would protect their interests. At the beginning of 1893, Archbishop Ryan and Cardinal Gibbons began a campaign to persuade the new President to appoint such a man to succeed Morgan. Ryan reported that the Protestant clergy were hard at work and had sent a delegation to Cleveland to have a Commissioner similar to Morgan appointed, and Gibbons quickly wrote to the President-elect in an attempt to forestall such action. "I have no desire to ask for the appointment of a Catholic for that office," he told Cleveland, "as such a selection might embarrass you, and might be construed as an act of undue partiality to the Catholic Church. Moreover no matter how fair and equitably might be his acts, they could be viewed with suspicion and distrust by unfriendly critics." What he and Ryan and the western bishops wanted was the reappointment of John H. Oberly, who had held the office during the latter part of Cleveland's first term. But the prelates were unsuccessful. Cleveland appointed Daniel M. Browning, a circuit judge from Illinois, who had hoped to get the position of Commissioner of the General Land Office. Browning, described by one group of supporters as "a lawyer of ability with many years experience on the bench, a trained judicial mind, a scholar, a gentleman, and with all a live acting working democrat," followed closely in Morgan's footsteps.[2]

The old contract school system was, in fact, doomed. Pressures from the Indian Rights Association and others in the anti-Catholic lobby convinced Congress to cut the appropriations for the Catholic Indian schools until by the end of the century the funds were stopped altogether.

Although the controversy between the Protestants and the Catholics over the Indian schools was based on the sincere differences of opinion of reasonable men about religious beliefs and the principles of American society, it could not help but be colored by the outbreak of strong anti-Catholic bigotry that occurred in the 1890s. A reaction to the growing numbers of Catholics arriving with the "new immigration" and the threat they seemed to offer to the traditional Protestant hegemony, the anti-Catholicism took form in the numerous "patriotic" societies that sprang up across the nation, although principally in the Middle West, and was propagated by an outpouring of periodicals and other publications. The "movement" focused finally in the American Protective Association (usually referred to as the APA), which, at least in the public mind if not in actual fact, became the embodiment of the anti-Catholic forces. The APA was founded in 1887 and reached its peak in 1895, after which it declined as a formal organization, even though a strong residue of exaggerated opinions remained.[3]

The great charge of the anti-Catholics was that Catholicism was alien to American principles and ideals, that Catholics owed blind allegiance to a foreign power, the Pope, and that the hierarchy was an ecclesiastical-political power set on undermining the American nation. The extreme and often foolish attacks on the APA and similar groups riled the Catholics, who looked to political activity to protect their just interests, thus aggravating the fears of their opponents that the Catholic Church was a dangerous political force within the nation. Of special importance to the Catholics in maintaining the faith were the parochial schools which were prescribed by the Third Plenary Council of Baltimore in 1884, and which grew in significance at exactly the time that the public school system of the states was burgeoning.[4] The public school controversy between Catholics and Protestants was an immediate prelude to the controversy on the national level over Catholic schools for Indian children. The APA, in fact, latched on to the Catholic Indian school issue as one of its chief exhibits. And the Catholics, in turn, by their charge that the APA was behind all opposition to its programs and projects, strengthened beyond due measure the public visibility of that organization.

The APA was aided in its attack upon the Catholics in the matter of the Indian schools by Thomas J. Morgan. He had resigned at the end of Harrison's term and accepted the position of corresponding secretary of the Baptist Home Mission Society and editor of the *Home Mission Monthly*. From this position he continued his agitation for Indian education and other reforms, and for several years he gave himself over to a torrent of attacks upon the Catholic Church. The APA eagerly welcomed Morgan to its roster of speakers and writers, and the ex-Commissioner responded with more alacrity than was becoming for one who so recently had been proclaiming his lack of bias. On Sunday, April 16, 1893, at the Music Hall in Boston, he delivered an address, "Roman Catholics and Indian Education," which was a violent attack upon the Catholics. "The Roman Catholics have assumed an attitude on the Indian question," he told his audience, "that is un-American, unpatriotic, and a menace to our liberties. I challenge the course they have pursued, as that of a corrupt ecclesiastico-political machine masquerading as a church, a course that has been without precedent, and is without justification. Its spirit has been that of the Inquisition, its methods those of the disreputable politician, and its agencies, intrigue, secrecy, conspiracy, falsehood and slander." [5]

He continued to speak in a similar vein around the country. In October 1894 he spoke at Minneapolis for an hour and a half on "Rome in Politics," recounting his experiences in Washington with the Catholic Bureau and charging the Catholics with conspiracy to defeat Harrison. He concluded by saying that no man could be a good Catholic and at the same time a good American citizen. The following year he gave the main address at a meeting in San Francisco sponsored by the APA, in which he noted that President Cleveland had endorsed his administration of Indian policy by appointing a successor who followed the same line. "The Roman Catholic Hierarchy," he proclaimed, "is now confronted with the certainty that the contract school system shall absolutely cease." [6] The American Citizen Company distributed his anti-Catholic messages in their pamphlets, and Morgan contributed a substantial chapter to a volume published in St. Louis in 1895 with the suggestive title *Errors of the Roman Catholic Church and Its Insidious Influence in the United States and Other Countries*. He kept the Baptist faithful alert by his editorials in the *Home Mission Monthly*, proclaiming in November 1893, for example, that the Roman Catholic Church was opposed to freedom of any kind and was "alien in its spirit, unrepublican in its organization, a corrupter of politics, and an enemy to American institutions." As the APA movement subsided after 1895, Morgan too seems to have moderated his views or at least quieted his utterances. He kept his position with the Baptist Home Mission Society, however, until his death on July 13, 1902.

The APA agitation surfaced in Congress in 1894. In debate in the House on June 7 over the Indian appropriation bill, strong anti-Catholic argument against continuing the contract schools came from Congressman William S. Linton, Republican of Michigan, who thus began a debate over continuation of support for the Catholic mission schools that lasted through the decade. He wanted to end at once the funds for sectarian schools and he demanded the replacement of those schools by public ones. He read into the record statistics on the contract schools, pointing to the large percentage of the money going to Catholics, and he produced the documents from the Methodists, Presbyterians, Episcopalians, and Congregationalists by which they withdrew from the contract school system. His clear antagonism to the Catholic schools was seen in his charge that the Catholics were "foisting upon the people of this country schools that do not belong to the civilization of to-day." [7]

Nor could he abide the fact that the Catholic missionaries belonged to immigrant groups. He wanted to prevent subsidizing "the schools of Mother De Chantal, Gerard Terhorst, Pius Boehm, Balthasar Feusi, S.J., Sister Kunigunda, Rev. Aloysius M. Folchi, and others whose euphonious names have not been heretofore called to the attention of American people." The sentiment of the American people, he said, was aroused by the "unholy and unconstitutional union of church and state." He protested, of course, his lack of bias and his high regard for persons of all sects and denominations, but he ended by lecturing the Catholics. If they would stop using their church as a "political machine" and acknowledge the government under which they live as the highest civil authority, "then, and not until then, will these anti-Catholic societies in this country, with their millions of members, to which they are adding thousands monthly, cease to exist." [8]

Linton did not go unchallenged. One of his Congressional colleagues from Michigan, Democrat Thomas A. E. Weadock, bluntly accused him of being the mouthpiece of the American Protective Association, which he condemned as an "oath-bound secret political society" with "un-American, illegal, traitorous, lamentable operations," offering for the record a long array of APA oaths and other anti-Catholic documents. Linton denied that his speech had been prepared for him by any secret organization, but when asked outright by Weadock whether he was a member of the APA, he replied, "I do not propose to be catechised at this time." [9] Whatever the outcome of the debate, the vicious anti-Catholicism behind the movement to curtail the contract schools could no longer be ignored.

The debate over the sectarian schools continued in the House, and on June 14 an amendment was introduced that would have prohibited the payment of any money to sectarian schools. But a point of order was raised against the amendment on the ground that it changed existing law, and the point was sustained by the chair.[10] In the end Congress directed the Secretary of the Interior "to inquire into and investigate the propriety of discontinuing contract schools and whether, in his judgment, the same can be done without detriment to the education of Indian children" and to report back to Congress the results of his investigation and his recommendations.[11]

Secretary of the Interior Hoke Smith made note of the problem in his annual report of November 21, 1894. Although he agreed fully with those who opposed the use of public money for sectarian schools, he thought the question should be "considered practically." The schools had been encouraged by the government and had grown up under that encouragement, and Smith did not think that the intense feeling of opposition to sectarian education should induce the government to disregard the existing situation. The contract schools were still needed. It would not be good, he thought, to "abandon instantly a policy so long recognized." His recommendation was to decrease the appropriations for the contract schools by at least 20 percent a year, so that in a few years they would cease to be made. In that time the government could prepare to get along without them, and the schools, if they chose, could gather money to continue without government aid.[12]

The recommendations of Smith were accepted by President Cleveland in his message to Congress of December 3, 1894. The President favored the reduction in the number of contract schools so that "in a comparatively short time" they might be replaced altogether by government schools, and he hoped that the transition would be gradual and without too much expense to the government or undue disregard of the investments made by those who ran the contract schools. Commissioner of Indian Affairs Browning noted in his report for the year that a reduction of over 20 percent had been made in money laid out for contract schools. "Contracts have been declined or reduced," he said, "wherever it could be done without depriving children of school privileges."[13]

This was the position also of the Indian Rights Association, which reaffirmed its stand in 1893 against continuation of the contract schools. While admitting that support of the mission schools by the government had been necessary at one time and that the schools had done good work, the Association now contended that "the contract system was an emergency measure, and not one necessarily expedient as a permanent policy. . . . It is manifestly contrary to the American idea to aid religious bodies in the propagation of their faith, and the dangers and entanglements growing out of such a policy are evident, and prove in practice serious." The report commended the Protestant bodies for withdrawing from the contract system and urged the Indian Bureau to "develop and perfect a first-class system of Government schools," following the "bold, firm step" taken in that direction by Commissioner Morgan.[14]

With the withdrawal of Protestants from the system of contract schools, the contest was between the government schools and the Catholic mission schools, and the continuation and growth of the latter threatened to weaken the development of the former. This worried Herbert Welsh a good deal, and he lamented to his friends that the government's educational work for the Indians was being undermined and that, with the Protestants gone, the education of the Indians was left in the hands of Roman Catholics. He urged Protestants to throw strong support to the government schools, and he even attempted to enlist Cardinal Gibbons in his crusade when he thought the Cardinal might be turning toward his own position.[15]

Welsh's big campaign came in the spring of 1894, when opposition arose against William N. Hailmann, who had been appointed to succeed Dorchester as Superintendent of Indian Schools, and when demands were made to eliminate Hailmann's position altogether. Welsh was convinced that these moves originated with the Bureau of Catholic Indian Missions and that the attack on Hailmann was at bottom an attack upon the government Indian school system itself. He spoke of a coming "struggle between Roman control of our Indian schools and the American Public School idea," and he wrote to many of the friends—Protestant religious leaders and laymen alike—to whom he had appealed earlier in the confirmation struggle.[16]

Welsh wrote to Hailmann in November 1894 that pressure should be brought to bear on Congress to gradually withdraw appropriations for support of denominational schools. He insisted, however, on gradual withdrawal. He strongly opposed, he said, "a sudden and violent extinction of it [the contract school system], as such a course would, in my judgment, be exceedingly unjust to those who in good faith and at the call of the Government have entered into this work." [17]

The continuation of opposition to the contract schools was a serious blow to the Catholic Bureau, for it defeated hopes that the departure of Morgan and the Harrison administration would bring a new day for the Catholic Indian schools. In a report to his superiors at the end of 1894, Father Stephan expressed his dismay over the new men in public office. No preceding administration, he asserted, had ever been "so actively and persistently bitter in antagonism to Catholicism and persecution of Catholics, as the present one," and he saw the President, his cabinet, and all the leaders of the party acting as a unit. Morgan's "malign influence survived his retirement," Stephan wrote. The priest saw in Hoke Smith, whom he described as being "a prominent Sunday-school teacher" and "closely identified with elements of organized prejudice and enmity against Catholicism," a new and determined enemy, who was intent upon driving the Catholics out of Indian work. So pessimistic was he over the future prospect of the schools that he recommended to the bishops the sale of the Catholic Indian schools to the government and the use of the money to promote missionary work and thus "to save the cause of Catholic Christianity from annihilation" —a proposal that never was seriously considered. [18]

Smith and Browning moved ahead with their reduction plan, and Congress accepted the principle of the 20 percent annual cut. In the Indian Appropriation Act for fiscal year 1896, under the section headed "Support of Schools," appeared this statement:

> *Provided*, That the Secretary of the Interior shall make contracts, but only with present contract schools, for the education of Indian pupils during the fiscal year ending June thirtieth, eighteen hundred and ninety-six, to an extent not exceeding eighty per centum of the amount so used in the fiscal year eighteen hundred and ninety-five, and the Government shall, as early as practicable, make provision for the education of Indian children in Government schools. [19]

The action infuriated Stephan, for he saw the carrying out of what he considered Secretary Smith's nefarious anti-Catholicism. The priest was irked, to begin with, because he had been kept waiting in the anteroom to Smith's office, while representatives of the Indian Rights Association were ushered in immediately. The Secretary was determined,

Stephan charged, to implement Morgan's plan in regard to Indian schools. "In carrying out this policy," he wrote, "Secretary Smith has out-Morgan'd Morgan, and has injured our Catholic Indian schools far more than Morgan did, or ever attempted to do." He saw the influence of Smith behind the opposition of Congress to the contract schools and behind it all the shadow of the APA.[20]

Father Stephan himself carried on an aggressive campaign in Congress on behalf of continued support for the contract schools. He argued that the government had invited the missionaries to set up schools in the first place, that the federal schools could not adequately provide for all the Indian pupils, and that the sectarian argument was not a valid one, for it was a question simply of educating the children, not of preaching religion, but if sectarianism was a sound charge, then it should apply also to the Protestant-run Indian schools, Hampton and Lincoln Institutes. "In the name of justice and in the spirit of fair play," he wrote to Congressman James S. Sherman, chairman of the House Committee on Indian Affairs, "I therefore protest against the proposed annihilation of the contract schools, which are eminently satisfactory to the Indians and economical to the Government."[21]

Stephan worked in many ways to secure legislative support. Congressman Sherman was from the start a firm supporter of the Catholic position, and when he was unable to swing the House, the Catholics depended upon friends in the Senate to insert a provision for the schools into the bills, with the hope that the House would concur, or, if not, that the conference committee would favor the measure. Stephan's assistant, Father E. H. Fitzgerald, went out to South Dakota to support Senator Richard F. Pettigrew when he was seeking reelection. Pettigrew, chairman of the Senate Indian Committee, Stephan said, "in return for this help will stand by us." Against his opponents Stephan carried on an active battle, by writing to bishops and other influential Catholics asking their aid for or against various senators, depending upon their stand on the contract school issue. The results were satisfying, and he argued against any public agitation on the part of Archbishop Ryan or Cardinal Gibbons in 1896. "With the chairman of the Senate and House [Committees on Indian Affairs] and several other Senators and Congressmen, all of whom we have secured, there is no reason for undue alarm," he wrote, "and the less we show our hands outside—hidden to the eyes and knowledge of the "A. Perjurers Ass.' —the less friction, and surer our success."[22]

Stephan was not mistaken, for Congress in its support of schools provided for the continuation of the contract schools in fiscal year 1897. It had been, however, a long and determined struggle on both sides. In the debate on the Indian appropriation bill on February 24, 1896, Congressman Linton had renewed his attack. The bill included a provision to allow 60 percent of the 1895 sum for contract schools—a following of the 20 percent annual reduction recommended by the Secretary of the Interior. Linton introduced an amendment to cut off funds to sectarian schools altogether. After considerable debate, in which Linton was supported by Congressman Eugene J. Hainer, of Nebraska, and others, Congressman Sherman proposed to eliminate Linton's motion by a point of order, which was overruled by the chair. In the vote, Linton's absolute prohibition was approved by the House. Francis E. Leupp, the Washington agent of the Indian Rights Association, reported that Linton's measure "was carried by a large majority, chiefly composed of members who have a considerable element of the 'A.P.A.' in their home constituencies." [23]

When the bill reached the Senate, there was immediate objection to the House's action, and Senator Thomas A. Carter, Republican of Montana, introduced an amendment to continue the contract funds at the 60 percent rate. He thought it unfair to cut off instantly the support of schools started at the instigation of the government, and he doubted the ability of the government to provide at once for the children who would lose their schools. He proposed, moreover, that when the funds were finally ended for the contract schools they be ended also for Hampton and Lincoln, as nongovernment schools. [24]

On April 21, when the bill was considered again, Senator Francis M. Cockrell, Democrat of Missouri, offered as a substitute for Carter's amendment a new one, which provided for a 50 percent grant of funds and which declared opposition to grants for sectarian schools as the settled policy of the government. The amendment was agreed to on April 22, but the House would not concur, and the item went to a conference committee. After considerable delay because of disagreement within the conference committee (the bill was sent to conference six times), on June 9 an acceptable version was agreed upon, which read as follows:

> And it is hereby declared to be the settled policy of the Government to hereafter make no appropriation whatever for education in any sectarian school: *Provided*, That the Secretary of the Interior may make contracts with contract schools, apportioning as near as

may be the amount so contracted for among schools of various denominations for the education of Indian pupils during fiscal year 1897, but shall only make such contracts at places where nonsectarian schools can not be provided for such Indian children and to an amount not exceeding 50 per cent of the amount so used for the fiscal year 1895.[25]

Despite the limitations, Father Stephan seemed pleased. He informed the superintendents of the contract schools that the schools were safe for another year, and he hoped, if the government did indeed cut off all funds in the future, that the bishops would be able to provide alternative support.[26]

So the struggle went on year by year, Catholic hopes rising and falling as their interests were opposed or supported in Congress. The House usually showed the strongest opposition, and when no headway could be made there, attention was concentrated on the Senate. In the appropriations for Indian schools for fiscal year 1898, there was violent debate again, for Senator Henry Cabot Lodge argued that the statement of policy not to appropriate money for sectarian schools agreed to the previous year had ended the question, and he fought the inclusion in the new bill of contract money at any percentage. Senator Joseph R. Hawley, of Connecticut, and Senator Pettigrew retorted that the government was not yet equipped to handle all the Indian pupils, and the whole question was threshed out once again on February 20, 1897. Pettigrew's remarks caused a special stir, for he lashed out against the Indian Rights Association for its opposition to the contract schools:

. . . because those Indians happened to believe the doctrines of the Catholic Church, they would drive them from the schools, turn them loose on the prairies, and make no provision for them whatever. Oh, Mr. President, I am tired of the contemptible hypocrisy of the Indian Rights Association. I am sorry that it finds representation on this floor. Whilst it may contain many philanthropic and excellent people, its affairs are controlled and directed by persons who have no respect not only for the interests of the Indians but in many cases for truth itself.[27]

These remarks so rankled Herbert Welsh that he published a special rebuttal, in which he asserted that the Indian Rights Association's attitude toward the Indian work of all religious bodies had been "friendly and fair." He reaffirmed the Association's position that the granting of money to religious groups for the education of Indian children should be "gradually, not violently or harshly, abandoned, so that the Government might in time be freed from sectarian entanglements." In private, Welsh characterized Pettigrew as "a very unscrupulous and unreliable man." [28]

On February 22 the Senate approved a 40 percent figure by a heavy majority. At that point Senator Jacob H. Gallinger, of New Hampshire, insisted on adding the phrase from the 1896 act "And it is hereby declared to be the settled policy of the Government to hereafter make no appropriation whatever for education in any sectarian schools," which the Senate agreed to without debate. Gallinger then attempted to add an amendment to stop all appropriations for sectarian schools absolutely on June 30, 1898, but the proposal was voted out of order. The bill went again to conference, since the House refused to concur in the amendment; the committee held to the Senate version, which the House finally agreed to on March 3. [29]

The success led Stephan to conclude that opposition to the contract schools was lessening—not only in Congress but throughout the country. As illustration, he pointed to the defeat of Congressman Linton and Congressman Hainer, both of whom had been leading spirits in the fight against the Catholic schools. Stephan took some credit for their defeat, for he had spent ten days in Linton's district and a week in Hainer's, rallying Catholics and "well meaning Protestants" against them. [30] The priest had in fact been an active campaigner in the election of 1896, switching his support from the Democrats, whom he had rallied behind four years earlier in order to unseat Harrison, to McKinley, from whom he hoped to gain support for the Catholic schools that had not been forthcoming from the Cleveland administration. [31]

But the change of administrations in 1897, as the Republican McKinley succeeded the Democrat Cleveland, in fact, had little significance for the Catholic fight for the contract schools. The new President's choice for Commissioner of Indian Affairs was watched with care by the Catholic Bureau, for Browning had been hostile to the Catholic schools, and a more sympathetic officer in his place would be a good omen. Stephan, with his usual exaggerated fears, reported that "great efforts are made to get an A.P.A., or at least a sympathizer with them, into the office of Commissioner to wipe out the Catholic schools and drive us from the field of Indian education." He hoped, he said, that the McKinley administration would be "a clean, strong, harmonious and successful one," and he did not want a poor choice of Commissioner to spoil it in the minds of Catholic voters. His own

JOSEPH A. STEPHAN. As director of the Bureau of Catholic Indian Missions from 1884 to 1901, Father Stephan was the chief promoter of the interests of the Catholic Indian mission schools. (Photograph from the Marquette University Library)

MOTHER KATHARINE DREXEL. Mother Katharine, founder of the Sisters of the Blessed Sacrament, used her sizable inheritance to support the Catholic Indian mission schools. (Photograph from the Sisters of the Blessed Sacrament)

choice, which he pushed upon McKinley, was a former Indian agent and inspector, William J. Pollock.[32] The new President, however, nominated William A. Jones, of Wisconsin, and Stephan sought information on him in order to plot his strategy, by writing to the Archbishop of Milwaukee to find out about Jones's "antecedents, his character, his church affiliations, his business, and his attitude towards the Church, particularly in the matter of Indian education." He was reassured to learn that the new Commissioner was "an honest, just and reliable man," who was "liberal and unprejudiced in religious affairs" and likely to treat the Catholic Church in a fair and impartial way.[33]

Despite some grounds for optimism, the Catholic Bureau could see the handwriting on the wall for its schools, and it began to plan for the future in case the appropriations were entirely withdrawn. On September 24, 1897, it drew up a "Memorandum Relative to Catholic Indian Schools," which proposed these alternatives:

FIRST—That an effort be made to secure from Congress, at its next session, another appropriation for contract schools, thereby insuring the continuance of practically all of them until June 30, 1899; after which it is thought to be possible to continue them in the following way:

The two schools among the Osages will be provided for out of the tribal funds of the Indians; five of the schools at what are known as "ration agencies" can be maintained from the rations and clothing furnished by the Government to the pupils in attendance; it is fairly probable that the three schools among the Sioux and the one among the Menominees will be supported out of the tribal funds of those Indians, as is done in the case of the Osage schools, while the remaining 21 schools can be carried on as day schools, a priest and two or three Sisters for each being supported out of the Annual Collection for Indian and Negro Missions.

SECOND—To make no further effort to secure an appropriation by Congress; but instead, to rent the school buildings to the Government, under an arrangement whereby the present teaching force would be retained as Government employes.

By this plan the owners would receive a revenue from their property and the teachers a good income, while the schools would remain practically Catholic institutions. This system has been tried at several of our schools, and has so far worked to the satisfaction of the Government officials and of our people. There is good reason to believe that the Indian Department would be entirely willing to agree to an extension of this system.[34]

The Catholic leaders, for the time being, sought to persuade Congress to continue the appropriations. The decline in funding, however, continued. For fiscal year 1899 the House, in the face of the Catholic agitation, voted only 20 percent of the 1895 figure. Stephan had gone to Europe again for his health, but the fight was carried on vigorously by Charles Lusk, who sent a lengthy memorandum to the Congressmen on the Indian Committee. Then he turned his attention to the Senate, hoping for 40 percent of the old amount. In this he was aided by Archbishop Ryan, who appeared before the Senate Committee on Indian Affairs to deliver a fervent plea for the religious education of Indian children and to urge a continuation of appropriations for the contract schools.[35] The Senate compromised at 30 percent, and the conference committee supported that amount.[36]

Although the legislation allowed $142,362 worth of contracts for the year, the continued reduction of the funds pointed clearly to the end of federal aid. "If this dire calamity takes place," Stephan wrote to the Bureau's board of bishops, "it means the closing of the schools, and the return of the pupils to their homes, with the certainty that in the near future they will be placed in Government schools, where, subject as they will be to Protestant influences and instructions, they will lose their faith, probably never to regain it."[37] The response was a formal resolution at the annual meeting of the country's archbishops that Cardinal Gibbons prepare a statement of Catholic grievances for presentation to Congress. Gibbons soon sent a formal petition in the names of the Catholic archbishops to members of both houses of Congress, in which he set forth in bold language the necessity of religious education for the Indian children and the impossibility of supplying it in secularized government schools. He traced once more the history of the Catholic Indian schools and the preference that Catholic Indians had for them. In the end he urged Congress "to reopen the question of the contract school system, and to go over again, with deliberation and care, the whole subject of Indian education, so that, in some way to be determined by the Congress, both the Government school system and the contract school system may be considered upon their merits."[38]

Gibbons sent a copy of the petition to the American bishops, with a sharp criticism of the attack on the contract schools, which was due primarily, he said

to the efforts of the organization known as the American Protective Association, aided and abetted by the various Protestant sects, which, because of their jealousy of our success in the work of Indian education and their belief that if our schools were out of the way they could gain control of the entire governmental school system, desired to break down the contract school system. By raising the cry of "sectarianism," and by their boldness and pertinacity, these enemies of the Church were able to intimidate both political parties to such an extent as to frighten Congress into the adoption of the unwise and unjust policy now in force in regard to contract schools.[39]

One of the primary pieces of evidence of official antagonism to the Catholic Church adduced by the Cardinal was the stance taken by Richard Henry Pratt, head of the government Indian boarding school at Carlisle, Pennsylvania. He, in fact, appended to his letter to the bishops a copy of the correspondence that Father Stephan had had with the Secretary of War about Pratt's anti-Catholic statements. Stephan had pointed to the *Red Man*, a periodical put out at Carlisle with public funds, in which utterances of an extreme nature had been published. The priest had tried to get the federal superiors of Pratt to condemn his blatant anti-Catholicism, so unfitting for a man in official position, to stop any further demonstrations, and if Pratt did not cease, to remove him from office. When the protests were ignored, the Catholics concluded that Pratt's statements were supported by the administration.[40] And Pratt kept up his tirades against the missionaries. At an Indian teachers' institute in Los Angeles in July 1899, he alleged that the mission schools instructed the children in a "spirit alien to the Nation," and that the Catholic Church was the "greatest hindrance to the Indian, in getting into the broad life of the Nation." The Los Angeles statement caused considerable stir in the Indian office, for the Catholics seized upon it as more ammunition for their battle against Pratt. Commissioner Jones wrote privately to warn him. "The officers of the Catholic Bureau," he said, "have been here at the Office and I judge from what they dropped, that they expect to make a determined fight against you, and I think this is the beginning." At the end of the year, Jones passed on to Pratt a request from the Secretary of the Interior, "as a personal favor not to come out in the school paper as attacking the Catholic Church."[41]

Cardinal Gibbons saw the Protestant success as a result of the Catholics' failure to oppose the attack courageously and vigorously. Thinking that the hostility was but temporary and would soon disappear, the Catholics had been too quiet and had allowed matters to drift.

Gibbons urged now that Catholics let members of Congress know of the grave injustices done and use the polls to see that "fair-minded men" were elected.[42]

Cardinal Gibbons's petition to Congress and his letter to the bishops were too late to save the issue. The appropriations act for fiscal year 1900 reduced the sums available for contract schools to 15 percent of the 1895 base, and it included the decisive phrase "this being the final appropriation for sectarian schools."[43] So ended the long partnership between the United States government and the Catholic Indian mission schools based on support of the schools by direct appropriations by Congress. It had been profitable for the Catholic schools; Father Stephan totaled up the funds received from the federal government through fiscal year 1899, including estimates of the value of rations and clothing given to the pupils, as $4,493,276.[44]

The Catholic Crisis, 1900

THE ending of Congressional aid for the mission schools was a tremendous blow to the Bureau of Catholic Indian Missions. But the work it had built up over the past decades was too important to give up without a struggle, and the Bureau had no intention of abandoning its schools. Father Stephan sent a circular to the superintendents of the contract schools informing them that the new Indian appropriation bill had passed both houses of Congress without any provision for the education of Indian children in contract schools and that as a result all government aid would cease on June 30, 1900. He directed them, however, to keep their schools open with no diminution of pupils. The bishops, he said, would seek to raise enough money to keep the operations going. When Commissioner Jones wrote to inquire what schools the Bureau intended to discontinue, now that it would receive no more federal funds, so that he could take the necessary steps to provide for the displaced children, Stephan fired back a terse note informing Jones that he did not intend to discontinue any schools and that the same enrollment would be maintained during the coming year.[1]

It was a bold, almost defiant, stand, which was an earnest of the Catholics' determination not to forsake the Indian children of Catholic faith. There were twenty-five boarding schools on Indian reservations that had been receiving contract support. The average attendance at these schools in 1900 was 2,078, the cost to the Bureau about $150,000 annually. In addition the Catholic missions ran another fifteen boarding and thirteen day schools for Indians.[2] Where was the money to come from? The Catholic Bureau undertook with great energy and purpose a two-pronged campaign. It continued its pressure upon the federal government for assistance, in one form or another, to the Catholic Indian schools. At the same time, it began a serious effort to collect the necessary funds from Catholic sources.

From the moment that it was clear that Congress did not intend to

continue the appropriations it had made for so many years to the contract schools, the Bureau of Catholic Indian Missions looked for ways
to reverse or offset the legislative action. Father Stephan, indeed, could
not bring himself to believe that Congress would stand by its prohibition on the use of funds for mission schools, and he sought the aid of
Bishop Ignatius F. Horstmann, of Cleveland, to push Senator Mark
Hanna toward favorable consideration of the Catholic goals and to call
on President McKinley for the same purpose. And it appeared at first
that Horstmann's intervention had effect, for Charles Lusk noted a few
days later that his letter to Hanna had "done a world of good." Hanna
now thoroughly appreciated, Lusk said, the "necessity of keeping the
Catholics in good humor with the Administration, and that, unless
something is done this Winter for our schools, there is a great danger
of the concentration of the Catholic vote against the Republican
Party." [3]

The Catholics attempted to introduce into Congress a measure that
would explicitly continue expenditures for contract schools. In the
middle of January 1900, Stephan handed to Congressman John J. Fitzgerald, of New York, the draft of an amentment which he hoped could
be inserted in the Indian appropriation bill for 1901:

> Provided, That the Secretary of the Interior may make con-
> tracts with present contract schools for the education of Indian
> pupils during the fiscal year ending June 30, 1901, but shall only
> make such contracts at places where the Government has not pro-
> vided school facilities for all the children of school age residing
> thereat, and to an extent not exceeding the number of children in
> attendance at said contract schools at the close of the fiscal year
> ending June 30, 1900. [4]

Fitzgerald introduced the amendment on February 2 and spoke at
length then and on the following day in support of the contract schools.
A point of order against the amendment raised by Congressman John
S. Little, of Arkansas, was sustained by the chair, and when Fitzgerald
offered a second amendment to authorize the use of Indian trust and
treaty funds for the contract schools, it met the same fate. [5] The ma-
neuvering, Lusk thought, had not shown the full force of Catholic support, for "we have more friends in the present House than we have had
at any time since the crusade against the Catholic schools began." But
he was not discouraged. "Our batteries will now be brought to bear
upon the Senate," he told the directors of the contract schools, "where,

as you know, we have always been stronger than in the House."[6] At first his optimism seemed justified. Stephan advised against sending out an appeal for private funds while the possibility of Congressional aid held out "so alluring a prospect for our schools." But these high hopes were dashed to the ground. Although Senator James K. Jones, of Arkansas, offered an amendment, it was rejected, on the basis, Stephan charged, that it would not be "good politics."[7]

Father Stephan was bitter about the outcome. There was no escaping the fact, he told Archbishop Ryan, that "the Administration and the Republican majority in Congress are our enemies; that it is a fact which all Catholics should know, and against which all Catholics should earnestly protest."[8] To Bishop Henry Elder, of Cincinnati, he laid bare his soul:

A fixed determination was apparent to crush out our schools on the part of the present administration and the dominant party in Congress. Arguments and facts were of no avail; the work of destruction must go on. No word of criticism was uttered against the schools. Every one admitted the good work they were doing. But it was a repetition of the scene before Pontius Pilate. The Jews could show no evil in Jesus, but they must have his life, and so the cry went forth, Crucify! Crucify! And today our Indian schools are being subjected to the same kind of persecution. This action of Congress was rank injustice, it is true, both to the Indians and the Church, but that made no difference. Our educational work among the Indians, in a great measure started and carried on upon the invitation of the Government, must receive no further recognition. Political expediency demanded it, and the righteousness of our cause and the welfare of the Indians, the wards of the nation, could not avert the disaster that has befallen us.[9]

Congress had proved unfavorably disposed. Anti-Catholic sentiment was strongly expressed in the House and Senate. "No one opened his mouth to stop the calumniation," Stephan lamented. "If the Catholics had attacked the Protestants, what a howl they would have raised against us."[10]

What especially galled Stephan and his friends was the undiminished support that Congress gave to Hampton Institute for the Indian students enrolled there. The head of the school was a Congregational minister, the school had a resident chaplain, it at one time had had a missionary department and prepared students to become missionaries, and the whole life of the school was permeated with a religious atmosphere.

Yet contracts with it were provided year after year without fail. "Congress has been guilty of the rankest discrimination in renewing the appropriation for the Hampton School," Stephan charged, "while denying an appropriation for our schools upon the plea that they are sectarian. But this inconsistency and discrimination do not seem to trouble our lawmakers. They can see sectarianism whenever a Catholic institution is involved, but are able to completely overlook it in the case of a Protestant institution." [11]

Stephan wanted some kind of organized support for Catholic causes —especially Catholic Indian mission and school work—and he urged the federation of various Catholic societies throughout the nation, "with the object of resisting aggressions against the Church and affording protection to her interests." [12] What he had in mind, largely, was political pressure to gain what the Catholics wanted. "Catholics have been too long divided," he said; "they should get together. The time has come when they must let it be known that they will not submit quietly to unjust treatment." Someone was needed to keep the fires stirred up. "Now is our time, and we dare not let this coming election pass without making ourselves felt," he confided to Mother Katharine at the end of July, "because our Senators and Representatives give us justice only when they fear our votes, and if our laymen confront those officials with demands of justice towards our Indian schools and missions we will get their support. Some Senators who voted against us were taken to task and spoken to by some influential men lately, whom I had aroused, and they promised to change their attitude and satisfy us." [13]

One senses that Stephan would have reveled in the campaign, but his health once again gave out, and his doctor advised him to give up his work. He sailed for Europe at the beginning of August in the hope that the complete change of scene and absolute rest would restore his shattered health and enable him to once more take up the work of protecting and advancing the work of the Indian schools. [14] Although he returned to work the following year, his days were numbered, and he died on September 13, 1901.

The torch fell to the Reverend William H. Ketcham, who indefatigably carried on Stephan's work in defending and promoting the Catholic missions until his death in 1921. [15] Ketcham was born in Sumner, Iowa, June 1, 1868, but he lived his early life in Texas. While attending grade school and high school he became interested in Catholicism, and in 1885, after a year at St. Charles College, a Jesuit school at Grand

Coteau, Louisiana, he was baptized a Catholic. After graduating from St. Charles in 1888, he began study for the priesthood under the sponsorship of the Bishop of Galveston, in whose diocese he intended to work as a priest. He spent a year at Mount Saint Mary's Seminary in Norwood, Ohio, but then, after his father moved to Oklahoma City, continued his theological studies at Sacred Heart Monastery in Indian Territory. There he became interested in Indian work and came in touch for the first time with contract schools. On March 13, 1892, after release from the Diocese of Galveston, he was ordained at Guthrie by Bishop Theophile Meerschaert, Vicar Apostolic of Indian Territory. He was the first priest ordained for that jurisdiction. For eight years Ketcham labored as a missionary priest among the Indians, first at Muskogee and later at Antlers (in the Choctaw Nation). He built mission churches, established schools, and became thoroughly committed to spreading and developing the faith among his Indian charges.

Ketcham came to the attention of the Bureau of Catholic Indian Missions because of his work in Indian Territory. He and Stephan met for the first time at the Chicago Exposition in 1893, and Stephan sought then to get him as an assistant, without success. When Stephan's ill health in 1900 made it imperative to find an assistant who could succeed him as director of the Bureau, eyes turned to Ketcham. At the beginning of August 1900, just as Stephan was about to leave for Europe, Archbishop Ryan invited Ketcham to come to the East, and he presented Ketcham to the prelates of the Indian Bureau at their early October meeting. Cardinal Gibbons and Archbishop Michael A. Corrigan, of New York, agreed, and Ketcham was informed that he was to aid Stephan and, when the older priest could no longer work, succeed him. He was instructed to visit Indian schools before coming east at the end of November to assume charge of the office.[16]

It was a crucial time, but Father Ketcham did not seem to be fazed by the problems. Even as assistant director of the Bureau, he immediately began aggressively to seek aid for the Catholic Indian schools from the federal government, and he turned his attention first of all to the President. Late in December he had a brief interview with McKinley and then a few days later another conference.[17] He left with the President a memorandum containing four points on which he wanted him to take action. It was, to all intents and purposes, the blueprint for reform in federal relations with the Catholic Indians that would occupy Ketcham for more than a decade. He asked:

1. Permission to use the Indians' own money (that is, Indian trust and treaty funds) for education of their children in schools of their choice
2. Abrogation of the "Browning Ruling," which denied to Indian parents the right to designate which school their children should attend
3. Modification of Rule 202 of the *Rules for the Indian School Service*, which declared that once enrolled in a government school, Indian pupils would be considered members of that school until separated from it by authority of the Commissioner of Indian Affairs
4. Permission for priests to give religious instruction to Catholic pupils in government Indian schools.[18]

The most important of the points, beyond doubt, was the first, the use of the Indians' tribal funds—due them for cession of lands or under other treaty stipulations—to replace the direct appropriations for support of the Catholic contract schools, for the continuation of the schools was the first priority of Ketcham and the Catholic Bureau. Ketcham said that the Indians wanted the Catholic schools continued and that, in fact, large and expensive school plants would have to be erected to replace them, thus raising the cost of educating the Indians. The Menominee Indians, he noted, had actually signed a formal petition expressing their desire to use their funds for the Catholic mission school on their reservation. He insisted that the policy of the government to make no appropriations for education in sectarian schools was no "insuperable barrier" to granting his request, for that prohibition applied only to the use of *public* funds. "It in no wise related to the use of money belonging to the Indians," he said. "There can be no question that it is clearly within the discretion of the Executive to expend these tribal funds for the benefit of the Indians concerned."

The President sent the memorandum to the Secretary of the Interior, who in turn passed it down to Commissioner Jones for an answer. While he waited for Jones's reply, Ketcham's spirits were high. He was ready, if a favorable reply came from the President, to revise the text of the appeal for private funds, omitting any reference in it to the tribal funds.[19]

Jones's answer to Ketcham's memorandum was a devastating rejection of the Catholic request and the arguments on which it was based. The Commissioner cited the laws of the 1890s by which the appropriations for contract schools had been gradually eliminated, ending with a quotation of the 1897 statement that it was "the settled policy of the government to hereafter make no appropriation whatever for education in any sectarian school." He denied Ketcham's contention that the statement applied only to public funds and did not touch the money belonging to the Indians. This was not a "fair construction of the wishes of Congress." Jones believed that Congress's intention was not simply to prohibit the use of public funds but to announce "the well settled and fixed policy that the Government in its management of Indian Affairs should not in any way enter into partnership with any sectarian organization for school purposes." Even the contracts for the Osage Catholic schools, which had drawn upon Osage tribal funds since 1898, Jones now believed were in violation of the law and the settled policy of the government. As for the Menominees, he quoted from directives from the Department of the Interior in 1893 and 1898 denying the use of Menominee funds for that purpose.[20]

Jones enunciated here in brief the position used by the opponents of the Catholic schools. There is no doubt that the Commissioner was firmly and sincerely convinced of his reading of the documents, but there was also a touch of anti-Catholic animus in his mind. In a private confidential letter to the Secretary of the Interior less than five months earlier, Jones had reviewed in great detail his problems with the Catholic Indian mission schools. He laid out all the information, he said, so that the Secretary could realize "the persistent tendency of the Catholic Sisters on some of the reservations to resist sending pupils to the regular Government schools. Opposed as they are to the public school system of the country, they extend the same hostilities to Indian schools maintained by the Government upon strictly non-sectarian principles." His treatment of the Catholics, he insisted, had been more liberal than that accorded any other denomination, yet the Catholics were not satisfied but were "constantly grasping for more."[21]

It was precisely the nature of the nonsectarian government schools that worried Ketcham. He was convinced that to send a Catholic Indian child to a government school with its nonsectarian services and atmosphere was to endanger if not destroy his Catholic faith. "It would be just as reasonable to expect a man to live in an Arkansas swamp and breathe for years a poisoned atmosphere without contracting malaria," he wrote in his annual report in 1902, "as to expect a Catholic child in a Government school to escape perversion. In the one case, the man's life may be prolonged by the aid of medicine; in the other, religious instruction may prevent open apostasy, but it will seldom succeed in producing a good Catholic." To Cardinal Gibbons, Ketcham lamented the "impending peril to so many souls" if the mission schools had to be closed or suspended, for he considered the school in almost every case absolutely essential to the mission, and he urged heroic efforts to keep the schools open. "Your Eminence," he concluded, "it is very hard to convince one's self that our Indian Missions are really to be abandoned —that Protestants will shortly reap a harvest in the fields long tilled by devoted Catholic Missionaries—." [22]

Ketcham wrote to the Catholic archbishops in October 1901 in an attempt to secure their firm support for the mission schools. He asserted that the government schools were "often bitterly anti-Catholic, and at best totally indifferent in religious matters," and he charged them with a "moral tone such that no Catholic could in conscience patronize them." He inserted a strong plea:

> Even if our schools must eventually be crushed by the insidious policy of the Indian Department—and here let me remark that this Department seems always to commit the same mistakes, it matters not which party is in power, for along with Morgan and Dorchester we have the unpleasant memory of Hoke Smith and Browning— let us not be guilty of aiding that Department in its work of crushing Catholic schools, by withdrawing our Church support from them; let us, on the contrary, support them to the last, until they are destroyed, if destroyed they must be, by this blind policy; so that on the Day of Judgment our skirts, at least, may be found clear of the Red Man's blood. [23]

So, while the legislative efforts were in progress, their outcome problematical, the Catholic Bureau developed and carried on an active program of solicitation for nongovernment support to replace the federal funds. As soon as Father Stephan saw the need clearly, he took the matter to the bishops. There was already an annual Lenten collection in Catholic churches for Indian and Negro missions, but the results were meager and by no means enough to pick up the bills previously paid from the government contracts. "The mere reading of the Notice, with a few perfunctory remarks, in the various churches on the Sunday preceding and the Sunday on which the collection is taken up," Stephan said, "arouses little or no interest among our people." He wanted the bishops to detail Indian missionaries to solicit funds—men who "from actual experience and knowledge, know the wants of our Red brethren and what they suffer, and thereby are best fitted to give an intelligent idea of the worth of this work of the Church and its claim to recognition and help." And he urged the archbishops at their annual meeting to give attention to the matter.[24]

There was some response. A few bishops and priests from the West collected money in the East for the Indian schools. The Bureau of Catholic Indian Missions sent out to Catholics an appeal, which Archbishop Ryan supported with a strong letter of approval "in favor of the thousands of poor Indian children in immediate danger of being lost to the Church and to Christian civilization." A special allotment was obtained from the collection for Indian and Negro missions, and, in addition, there were generous personal donations from Cardinal Gibbons and Archbishop Ryan, and, of course, a large contribution from Mother Katharine. But this was a stopgap approach. "The all important and unsolved problem confronting the Bureau," Father Ketcham said in his first report, "is: *By what means can $140,000 be raised annually for the support of the Catholic Indian schools?*" The future of the schools, he noted, depended upon finding some permanent source of revenue.[25]

Ketcham's answer to the problem was the establishment in the fall of 1901 of the Society for the Preservation of the Faith among Indian Children. One friendly critic declared that the organization was one that "must necessarily fall under the weight of its own name," and it was usually called simply the Preservation Society.[26] The object was to enroll Catholics in the Society, each to pay an annual membership fee of twenty-five cents and to pray for the success of the Society. The hope was to obtain four hundred thousand members, whose annual fees would bring in one hundred thousand dollars for the mission schools. Ketcham made it "the chief feature of the year's work" in 1902. He sought the formal approval of the bishops for introducing the Society into their dioceses, prevailed upon hundreds of priests to promote the cause in their parishes, and solicited aid from the Catholic press. Membership forms were printed up, and the usual paraphernalia of such an enterprise were developed.[27]

For Father Ketcham it was a matter of tremendous apostolic urgency. In the letter he wrote to Cardinal Gibbons seeking the prelate's support for the Preservation Society, one can see the intensity with which the director of the Catholic Bureau viewed the necessity of maintaining the Catholic Indian schools. He wrote:

> The thought of the responsibilities of my position; more than this, the interest with which almost ten years of missionary work

among Indians has inspired me; more still, the zeal for the salvation of souls, especially of the poor, helpless and abandoned, which every priest and every Catholic feels, fill me with grief and apprehension at the prospect which presents itself of the suspension of our schools, knowing as I do that in ninety-nine cases out of every hundred this means the loss of Catholic faith, and in all probability the loss of eternal salvation. Is it possible that we have labored so long and so diligently among Indians only to bring upon them and their children a greater damnation? I fear it might have been better for them never to have known the truth, than after having been incorporated in the Church to be perverted and corrupted. And the pity of it is, the poor Indian is helpless—no slave is more fettered. The only way to "save our children," said one of them to me, "is for us to kill them before they are carried away from us to lose their faith and their innocence in the schools of the Government." No czar is so absolute and tyrannical as most Indian Agents are.[28]

In the spring of 1902 the Catholic Bureau inaugurated the *Indian Sentinel*, an annual magazine devoted to the work of the Preservation Society. In a salutatory editorial in the first issue, Ketcham declared that there was no more vital question confronting the Catholic Church in the United States than that of the Catholic Indians. "The life or death of the Catholic Indian schools is the issue of the hour," he said, "and view it as we may in all its vast responsibilities, the time and opportunity for action are now upon us, and delay in any event is most hazardous." In an "Appeal in Behalf of Catholic Indian Mission Schools," the *Sentinel* presented the history of the contract school question and urged generous contributions to keep the schools running. "For a number of years to come, boarding schools among the Indians will be an absolute necessity," it said. "Were these schools discontinued, all the children would be forced into the 'non-sectarian' Government schools, where, in the course of a few years, they would lose every vestige of the Catholic faith. Moreover, our schools must be so equipped and conducted as to compete successfully with the schools of the Government." For the future, the Bureau intended to devote its energies to raising funds for the schools and the missions.[29]

In this search for funds Ketcham enlisted the aid of an energetic and remarkable priest of the Harrisburg, Pennsylvania, diocese. He was the Reverend Henry George Ganss, who since 1890 had been pastor of St. Patrick's Church at Carlisle, Pennsylvania, where his proximity to the Carlisle Indian Industrial School of Richard H. Pratt brought him into contact with Indian problems and stirred his interest in Indian education. Ganss, born on February 22, 1855, in Darmstadt, Germany, came with his parents to Lancaster, Pennsylvania, when he was six weeks old. He was educated at St. Vincent College, Latrobe, Pennsylvania, from which he graduated in 1876 with the degree of doctor of music. Two years later he was ordained to the priesthood. Although he spent most of the next thirty years as a parish priest in small central Pennsylvania parishes, he earned a national reputation for his musical and scholarly efforts. He composed a number of masses, including a requiem, and his hymn "Long live the Pope" was translated into twenty-five languages. In a musical competition to commemorate the heroism of American sailors in the disastrous Samoan hurricane of 1889, he won first prize among 145 entries for his naval hymn "The Banner of the Sea." In addition he wrote widely on religious subjects, including a *History of St. Patrick's Church, Carlisle, Pa.* and the article on Martin Luther in the *Catholic Encyclopedia*. His library of five thousand volumes included more than eight hundred titles on Luther. Ganss was also a builder, constructing new churches in the little towns he served.[30]

Ganss had been introduced to the work of the Preservation Society by Father Stephan through the good offices of Mother Katharine shortly before the old priest's death, and he became interested in the cause. For two years, beginning in January 1902, he devoted his tremendous energies to the task of raising money for the Indian schools. He was appointed financial agent of the Catholic Bureau and sent out by Ketcham to solicit donations from the wealthier Catholics of the country and to establish the Society for the Preservation of the Faith among Indian Children in the various parishes he visited. He worked chiefly in Philadelphia and New York, drumming up members for the Preservation Society with an energy and zeal that at times outran the ability of Ketcham to supply the forms and funds that such aggressive promotion demanded.[31] But then, because of ill health, Ganss gave up the appeal work and returned to Carlisle, although he did not give up his Indian interests.

All these efforts to raise money got off to a slow start. Ketcham reported that from the establishment of the Preservation Society on October 1, 1902, to the end of 1902, he had collected $30,192.86, of which about $12,000 came from the general appeals of the Bureau, $9,500 from Bishop Horstmann in Cleveland, and $8,000 from Father Ganss's efforts in the Archdiocese of Philadelphia.[32]

In the next year, 1903, the Bureau received $2,634.10 from its annual appeal, $3,862.76 from the Association of the Holy Childhood, and $25,937.55 from the Preservation Society. In view of the large Catholic population in the United States, Ketcham concluded that the returns were "very meagre." The rest of the money to make up the $140,000 came in part from the Indian and Negro collection, but again chiefly from Mother Katharine, who regularly contributed more than $100,000 a year to replace the missing federal funds.[33] Year by year the reports were far from encouraging. Despite repeated statements of support from Cardinal Gibbons and other prelates, appeals of the American Federation of Catholic Societies to its members, and formal papal approbation from Pope Pius X in 1904 and again in 1908, the amounts collected by the Preservation Society declined. The differences were made up by the steady donations of Mother Katharine. "The tremendous burden that the thirteen million Catholics of the United States impose constantly upon Mother Katharine Drexel," Ketcham exclaimed in 1906, "cannot be other than a subject of amazement to any thinking person."[34]

One staunch ally of the Catholic Bureau and of the Preservation Society was a group organized by Catholics in New York City in 1904 —the Marquette League. The origin of the League can be traced to the work of Father Ganss in New York. He aroused interest among a number of clergy and laity, who determined to do something to aid the Indian schools. It was suggested at first that a club might be organized in the city which would undertake to support one Indian school, and that then the plan might be spread to other cities. But instead, the League was formed with more general goals, though it hoped to establish centers throughout the country. Ketcham urged the leaders to concentrate on gathering support for the Indian schools. The mission work proper, he thought, could be cared for by the annual Indian and Negro collection; it was the schools where the need lay. Moreover, Ketcham candidly reported another difficulty with the annual Lenten collection in the churches. "We have learned by experience," he said, "that the connecting together in the eyes of the people of the Indian and Negro work has been a great detriment to the cause of the Indian, as many people who would give to the Indian work refuse to do so because they fear that some of it will be spent upon the Negroes. This is a disposition which is to be lamented and reprobated, of course, but the fact that it exists is beyond question." Furthermore, there was a decided difference between mission work among the two races. The efforts among the blacks was almost entirely among a non-Catholic people, while those among the Indians were aimed at "saving of Catholic people to the Faith." [35]

The organizers in New York followed Ketcham's suggestions, and in May 1904 Ketcham was sent notice of the establishment of the League. A printed circular (the work of Father Ganss) listed the officers and outlined the purposes of the new organization. [36] To quiet fears that the new League might confuse the public and direct attention away from the Preservation Society, the League was constituted as an auxiliary of the latter organization, but it clearly intended to operate on a different level. It appealed to "the well-to-do Catholics for a more generous support than that provided by an annual membership fee of twenty-five cents" and urged sizable contributions to support one child for a year (seventy dollars), to erect a mission chapel (one thousand dollars), to support a missionary for a year (five hundred dollars), or to support a catechist for a month (ten dollars). It set its annual membership fee at two dollars and hoped to find fifty thousand members. The League had the blessing of Pope Pius and the endorsement of numerous archbishops and bishops. Its mission, it said, was to crystallize growing sentiment for the Indians into "energetic and effective action, and procure the salvation of the souls of a race to which we owe the debt of Catholic charity and national reparation." The time was now, the circular asserted. "Ten years hence will be too late. Within that period the Indian's destiny for good or evil will be decided. Delay means loss of opportunity and disaster for souls." [37]

The Marquette League collected between one thousand and three thousand dollars a year, not very significant amounts in the total costs of the Catholic Indian schools. [38] But it had considerable influence beyond its financial aid, for the prominent men who directed it turned out to be an effective lobbying force when the Catholic Bureau reopened a drive to obtain money for its schools through the federal government.

While the Catholic missionaries worried about collecting enough money from the faithful to support the Indian schools and while new attempts in Congress to gain additional contract funds met with the old opposition to sectarian schools, there were some rays of light. The death of Father Stephan in 1901 removed from the scene a man, who, although of undoubted zeal and dedication, was not a diplomat and whose intolerant outbursts hindered the Catholic cause. Father Ketcham, though no more willing to compromise than his predecessor, won the respect of those he dealt with. The advent of Theodore Roosevelt to the Presidency with the death of McKinley on September 14, 1901, moreover, heartened the Catholic leaders, for they saw in the new President a man of fair dealing. Roosevelt reacted favorably when Ketcham and a group of priests in Washington proposed to him that he appoint a Catholic to the Board of Indian Commissioners to replace the Episcopal bishop Henry B. Whipple. Ketcham proposed Archbishop John J. Keane, of Dubuque, as a man who lived in the West and was interested in Indian schools and who knew how to get along with non-Catholics. The nod went instead to Archbishop Patrick J. Ryan, of Philadelphia, one of the prelates who directed the work of the Bureau of Catholic Indian Missions and who had the support of Cardinal Gibbons and of Herbert Welsh of the Indian Rights Association.[39] Along with Ryan, Roosevelt appointed the Baltimore lawyer Charles J. Bonaparte. Bonaparte, a staunch Catholic layman, was a Harvard graduate and a personal friend of Roosevelt's. He became the most influential of the lay supporters of the Catholic Bureau in its campaign to preserve the Catholic Indian schools.[40] Roosevelt's action in the appointments was deeply appreciated. "His courage and sense of justice in appointing two Catholics on the Board of Indian Commissioners," Ketcham wrote in his 1903 report, "will ever be remembered with gratitude by his Catholic fellow-countrymen. That action of our President marked the turning point for the better in the tide of Catholic Indian affairs."[41]

An apostle of a Protestant-Catholic rapprochement was Father Ganss, who had an ecumenical and irenic spirit that was far in advance of his time (and which sometimes set him at odds with the Catholic mission leaders). Early in 1902 Ganss undertook to make friends with the Indian Rights Association. He wrote to Herbert Welsh to obtain copies of the proceedings of the Lake Mohonk Conference and used the request as an opening. "Personally, I may add," he told Welsh, "that by the death of Monsig. Stephan,—the policy of the Catholic Indian missions and schools will undergo some radical changes. I have no doubt, the workings of the Indian Rights Association could be brought into harmony with the new policy of the Catholic Church, and the fusion would be a factor of incalculable weight and influence." And he arranged for a personal interview with the Indian Rights Association head. Welsh responded quickly and favorably, noting that there were many points where united efforts between the Catholics and the Association were possible. Welsh thought Ganss was "a very liberal and sympathetic type of man," and he entered into friendly correspondence with him and with Archbishop Ryan. After a chat with Ganss in March 1902, Welsh wrote: "I am deeply impressed with the belief that there is a broad common ground on which our own Catholic friends and ourselves can meet and work without compromise which would invade the essential principles of either party. . . . Father Ganss has shown so broad and humane a sympathy, so just an appreciation of what was good, and what was not good, outside of religious limits, that I feel quite sure this is not too bright a view to take of the situation." [42]

Ryan, Bonaparte, and Ganss all appeared at the Lake Mohonk Conference in October and addressed the meeting in conciliatory terms. Father Ganss was the most effusive. "Our future prospects are encouraging," he said; "in fact most hopeful. Catholic charity never exhausts itself in its help to the poor and oppressed; and the more the status of our Indians is known to them the more liberal is the response. But a still more hopeful condition prevails in the fact that under the broad, enlightened, and charitable policy of His Eminence Cardinal Gibbons and Archbishop Ryan, who control the destinies of our Indian work, the most amicable and helpful relations exist between the church and Government schools; between ecclesiastical and State authorities. And why should they not?" The Catholic delegates were warmly received, and in closing the conference the Quaker host, Albert K. Smiley, noted that it had been "a source of extreme satisfaction this year that we have had a strong delegation from the Roman Catholic Church." Ganss later wrote to Smiley about the conference that "such an elevating and spiritualizing atmosphere as that which pervades the deliberations of the Conference, cannot fail to soften sectarian asperities and bring us nearer to that Christian unity which was the uppermost thought of our Redeemer." [43]

Ganss was sincere in his desire for cooperation with the Indian Rights Association and attempted to get members for it. "It is my desire to work in the fullest and heartiest accord with your or rather *our* Society," he wrote to the secretary of the Association, "and it will always afford me great pleasure to do so." [44] He appeared, in fact, to be more favorably inclined, at times, to the Indian Rights Association than to the Bureau of Catholic Indian Missions, which irritated him with its tone of criticism toward those who did not agree with it. He complained to Archbishop Ryan about Father Ketcham's lack of tact in criticizing the Commissioner of Indian Affairs in his annual report.

The report was one more in a list of blunders committed by the Bureau, he thought, and he suggested that the Bureau ought to be abolished altogether, since it had lost the confidence of the government.[45]

The rapprochement between Catholics and Protestants that was the ideal of Father Ganss, unfortunately, was short-lived. The Catholic aggressiveness in seeking to protect and expand its interests in Indian education and the Protestant opposition that countered it renewed an antagonism between the two groups that could not be easily erased.

The Browning Ruling

MUCH of the tension that the Catholic missionaries experienced came from the fact that the government Indian schools and the mission schools were in competition for students. As the government schools expanded in the 1890s under the drive of the humanitarian reformers for a full-blown public school system for the Indians to match the public school system of the states, the mission schools felt the pull of recruitment of children for the new federal schools. The Catholic missionaries were worried. If the children could be sucked away from them into the government schools, their work would be seriously impeded and their schools might ultimately be forced to close down. And what of the faith of the Catholic pupils? Could it withstand the "godlessness" of the government schools or, what was often considered worse, their strong Protestant atmosphere? There ensued a sort of tug of war between the missionaries and the Bureau of Catholic Indian Missions on one side and the Indian agents and government school superintendents on the other. Each side accused the other of stealing pupils from its schools.

The government officials argued that the Indians were wards of the United States and that the government as a consequence had the right and obligation to provide for the education of the Indian children. They insisted that they should be the ones to determine where the children would attend school and that the children should be assigned in a way that would most effectively maintain the government schools and provide the best industrial education for the students and thus fit them best for rapid entry into the white man's world. Commissioner Morgan had been much concerned about the matter and strove earnestly to provide students for the government schools, even at the cost of taking students already enrolled in mission schools. The Catholic missionaries looked upon the matter in quite a different light. They argued that the Indian parents had a right to determine where their children would be educated, to choose, that is, the school in which their children would be enrolled.

This issue of parental right to select a school that would preserve and enrich the Catholic faith of the children had loomed large in the controversy of the early 1890s.

The government was adamant in its position. Although the Commissioners of Indian Affairs considered the individual circumstances as case after case of enrollment problems came before the Indian Office, they backed the agents and denied the claims of the Catholic Indian parents (as expressed through the Catholic school authorities). Thus in 1891, Morgan wrote to the Indian agent at the Green Bay Agency in Wisconsin, "If the government school is full it would then be proper to give the parents their choice of schools, but if the government school be not yet filled, such choice ought not to be allowed." Similarly, Morgan's successor, Daniel M. Browning, advised the Indian agent at the Rosebud Agency in South Dakota that "where a [government] day-school is established, children should not be taken from its territory and sent to contract or non-reservation schools until the day school is filled to its capacity, or is so nearly so that it will not interfere with its efficient operation." [1]

The classic statement of the government's position, however, came in September 1896, when Commissioner Browning, in a reply to a question from the acting Indian agent at the Pine Ridge Agency, restated his policy—a statement that became known as the "Browning Ruling." Captain W. H. Clapp, an infantry officer serving as acting agent, wrote that there was controversy on the reservation between the government day schools and the school at Holy Rosary Mission. He had ruled that the mission school could not enroll students in excess of their contract unless such students were unable to attend a day school. This decision, he wrote to Browning, "provokes opposition from certain parents who prefer to have their children at the Mission, and from the people of the Mission, who desire to retain all their former pupils, and take in others with little, or any regard to the interests of the day-schools." He remarked: "The question hinges upon the right of the parents to decide where their children shall attend school." Browning answered the letter forthrightly: "It is your duty first to build up and maintain the Government Day Schools . . . , and the Indian parents have no right to designate which school their children shall attend." [2]

The Catholic leaders immediately opposed this ruling. In October 1897 Archbishop Ireland, of St. Paul, and Bishop O'Gorman, of Sioux Falls, called on Commissioner William A. Jones (Browning's successor) to see if he intended to continue the rule, and the prelates understood him to say that it would not be enforced. But Jones took no action to abrogate it and in fact declared that he had been misunderstood; he regarded the rule as entirely proper and would maintain it. There was even an attempt to insert into the Indian appropriation bill on January 26, 1898, a provision strengthening the Commissioner's hand, which read as follows:

> And the Commissioner of Indian Affairs may transfer advanced pupils from any boarding or day schools on or off any reservation to advanced schools on or off such reservation in the same or other States, without the consent of their parents or guardians, whenever, in his judgment, the interest of such pupils will be subserved by such transfer.

Stephan fought successfully to have this stricken from the bill by having one of his friends in the House of Representatives make a point of order that the provision changed existing law and was not germane to the bill, and the point was sustained by the chair. If the measure had been passed, Stephan charged, it would have enabled the Indian Office "to deplete our contract schools completely." [3]

The Catholic missionaries complained bitterly about the enforcement of the ruling, which cut down attendance at their schools. "The carrying out of this ruling," Stephan asserted in 1899, "is unwarranted invasion of the natural and legal rights of the Indians, and means in a short time the virtual destruction of our Indian mission and school work. Without pupils we cannot have schools, and without schools we can make little headway in the Christianization of the Indian." He urged the archbishops to adopt some course of action to secure a revocation of the Browning Ruling. [4] Stephan enlisted the aid, too, of Bishop Horstmann, to whom he appealed as a personal friend of President McKinley and of Senator Mark Hanna. He urged the bishop to come to Washington and present to the President the wishes of the Catholics regarding the Indian schools, and he prepared for the bishop's use a long memorandum on the Catholic position on the Browning Ruling and other topics. Horstmann decided against a direct contact with McKinley but instead saw Hanna, to whom he forcefully presented the Catholic views, dwelling at length on "the iniquity of the Browning ruling," which he insisted the President could remove simply by giving private instructions to the Commissioner of Indian Affairs to suspend its execution. The Senator promised to convey the message to the President—but no revocation of the ruling was forthcoming. [5]

The problem was left to Father Ketcham. Early in 1901, when he submitted his requests to the President, he included abrogation of the Browning Ruling. It was, he said, "a denial of the inherent, natural right of the Indian parents," and for those Indians who had received allotments of land in severalty and had become citizens, it was, in addition, an interference with their legal rights. Ketcham asserted that the Catholic Indians, as well as many non-Catholic ones, preferred to send their children to Catholic mission schools, where they could get religious training as well as a sound secular education. If they were free to choose, they would select the mission schools; but the ruling denied the freedom of choice of the Indian parents and forced them to send their children to schools that were "obnoxious to them." The priest maintained that the average Indian parents were as competent as the average white parents to decide on the school they wanted. "This Ruling," he concluded, "is un-American and offensive to every Catholic in the land. If carried out to the letter, it would in time deplete every Catholic Indian school of its pupils." [6]

Since Ketcham's memorandum was referred by the President to the Secretary of the Interior, who in turn called upon Commissioner Jones for a careful reply or refutation, it was Jones who answered Ketcham. In regard to the Browning Ruling he took issue with every one of Ketcham's contentions. [7] "Under the law," he began, "Indian parents and children are known as wards of the Government. It is the duty of the Commissioner of Indian Affairs to look closely after their welfare, and endeavor to do all that can legitimately be done for their education and civilization." He noted the money the government was spending for schools, which were "modern in construction, sanitary in arrangement, providing the best literary and industrial training," schools which were generally better equipped than private ones. Filling the schools was a duty of the government, he admitted, but even more important were the interests of the children, which were "vastly more important than those of parents or other persons."

Jones stood firmly behind the Browning Ruling. It was based, he said, on years of experience in Indian education and had been the policy of his predecessors. To allow the missionaries to fill their schools without reference to the responsibility of the agents for the education of the children would "certainly not be in harmony with efficient and effective service." Without the ruling, the agents would be powerless to maintain discipline and to compel attendance at schools, and the

WILLIAM A. JONES. Serving as Commissioner of Indian Affairs from 1897 to 1904, Jones was a key figure in the controversy between Catholics and Protestants over support of Indian mission schools. (Photograph from the State Historical Society of Wisconsin)

WILLIAM H. KETCHAM. Father Ketcham, who succeeded Father Stephan as director of the Bureau of Catholic Indian Missions in 1901, was
an effective promoter of the interests of the Catholic Indians and the
Catholic mission schools. (Photograph from the Marquette University
Library)

parents might use religious preferences as a cloak to get a dissatisfied child out of a government school, to the child's detriment.

The Commissioner disagreed flatly with Ketcham that all Catholic Indians preferred the mission schools, that the average Indian was as capable as the average white man in choosing schools, and that the ruling was un-American. He himself, he declared, had never invoked the ruling arbitrarily but had always considered all the facts pro and con in each case and had decided according to the best interests of the child. "I do not believe that the best interests of the Indian children will be subserved by any change in the rule," he concluded, "but on the other hand its abrogation would frequently create clashes of authority between the government and the mission people consequently resulting in no good but much harm to the Indian children."

Father Ketcham and his friends did not rest with this rebuff. They appealed directly to President McKinley, and they insisted that the President had assured them that the Browning Ruling would be revoked and that he had in fact directed Secretary of the Interior Ethan Allen Hitchcock to do so. But no formal revocation occurred, and Ketcham and other Catholic leaders continued their campaign of urging the Secretary of the Interior and the Commissioner of Indian Affairs to accede to the President's wishes.[8]

At the end of August 1901, Jones retreated a bit from his adamant stand and became willing to "tentatively abrogate" the rule, with a clear proviso, however: if after a trial the abrogation was found to be detrimental to the Indian children, the ruling would be reestablished and adhered to.[9] Yet he continued to hold firm to his opinion. He informed the Secretary of the Interior that he believed the Browning Ruling was "the only interpretation of the law which will enable the Commissioner of Indian Affairs to properly apply the amounts appropriated by Congress for Indian educational purposes." He insisted that he had always considered only what was best for the child, and that he was "very careful to see that no injustice was done to the natural rights of an Indian parent competent to understand what was desired."[10]

In October, a month after the assassination of McKinley and the accession to office of Theodore Roosevelt, Secretary Hitchcock took a cautious step in the direction of satisfying the Catholics. He temporarily suspended the ruling for a reasonable period, "with the distinct understanding that if such suspension be to the disadvantage of Indian children or detrimental to their best interests, that this authority shall then be revoked and the said so-called ruling reestablished." He directed Commissioner Jones to require the agents to report fully upon the effects of the suspension.[11] But Hitchcock did not wait for the temporary suspension to be tested. On October 30 he orally informed Jones that the ruling was abrogated, and Jones immediately notified the Catholic Bureau in a terse note. The Commissioner, however, was clearly unhappy with the turn of events and reminded the Secretary again that he believed that "the Commissioner of Indian Affairs has the unquestioned right under the law and under good policy to designate which school an Indian child shall attend upon a reservation, and that the 'Browning Ruling' was a correct statement of that policy." [12]

It took another two and a half months for the abrogation to be promulgated officially. In Education Circular No. 62, dated January 17, 1902, Jones notified the agents and school superintendents of the abrogation and directed them to send to him full reports concerning any children affected by the new policy.[13] Jones could not quite let the matter rest with that. On November 1, 1902, he sent another circular to the agents and superintendents to make sure that they watched carefully the transfer of students to mission schools. The effect of the abrogation, he told them, was "to grant latitude to Indian parents in the selection of the school to which their children shall be sent, but not to permit whimsical or capricious persons to defeat the education of their children by frequent and unwarranted changes." He directed the government officials to make sure that the consent of the parents was given freely and voluntarily. Before any transfer could be approved, the parents were to appear in person before the agent or superintendent and make a voluntary statement of their wishes, which was to be recorded and filed with the records of the agency. Each case was to be reported to the Indian Office, and the agents were to visit and inspect the mission schools and report on their condition and the care and education of the pupils. Jones continued to fear that "ignorant Indian parents" could be unduly influenced and persuaded by the Catholic missionaries to send their children to the mission schools.[14]

Father Ketcham complained that it had taken eight months from the time that President McKinley had directed the revocation of the Browning Ruling to the formal abrogation in January 1902, but he was pleased with the outcome of his agitation. He reported: "Statements appeared in the daily papers to the effect that many protests against the revocation of the Browning Ruling had been filed with the Secretary of the Interior by the different Protestant sects of the United States. Nevertheless the recognition of the rights of Indian parents was hailed with delight by Catholics. Mission priests and teachers were inspired with renewed hope and courage. They are easily satisfied; they only ask for justice; and it is a creditable commentary on their work that the Indians patronize their schools without being forced to do so by such regulations as the Browning Ruling." [15]

Bishop William Hare in South Dakota, on the other hand, saw trouble arising from the abrogation and wrote to Commissioner Jones to point out that St. Francis School at Rosebud was inducing students to transfer to it from other schools. "Marauding of the kind which I have described," he told Jones, "if permitted by the Government, will, I am sure, lead in the future to contests which will be most humiliating to all honorable persons, which will spoil the Indians and their children by giving them the impression that attendance at school is not a privilege to the pupils, but a favor to the school, and make the relations between the officers of the different schools almost intolerable." The Commissioner replied that it was not possible "to rectify the evils complained of" since the Secretary of the Interior had abrogated the Browning Ruling. [16]

There is no doubt that both sides considered it a religious controversy. The Catholics thought of it as a matter of freedom of conscience and believed that the Browning Ruling had been aimed specifically at them and their Indian schools. The Protestants saw in the abrogation of the ruling the sinister specter again of Roman Catholic influence and power. Commissioner Jones drew up a dossier of copies of the essential correspondence related to the ruling, which he sent to Merrill E. Gates, secretary of the Board of Indian Commissioners and a sort of listening post or unofficial agent for Protestant interests in the capital. Gates was to transmit the material to Lyman Abbott, editor of the *Outlook* and an ardent champion of government Indian schools and of the Protestant understanding of the principle of separation of church and state. In sending the collection of documents to Abbott, Gates commented on the affair. Jones had supported the ruling. "But the Roman Catholic Church," Gates charged, "through its prelates and its Bureau here in Washington have been strenuously opposed to the Ruling. Commissioner Jones has been overruled by the Secretary of the Interior, who has first suspended, and then under further pressure from the same people, has abrogated the Browning Ruling." Gates saw insidious political bargaining in the background. "The point which the Commissioner wishes to have understood, although he does not wish to have it needlessly bruited about," Gates told Abbott, "is that there appear to have been campaign promises made by some persons high in authority in party councils, in the campaign of 1900, that in case of the reelection of President M'Kinley, this Browning ruling would be suspended or abrogated." [17]

The revocation of the Browning Ruling was the first victory in Ketcham's campaign. It indicated that Catholic interests were receiving a favorable hearing in high administration circles.

The Rations Question

The federal government for a long time supported the Indian mission schools in an indirect way by supplying the children with rations. Some of the rations rested upon treaty obligations or similar agreements with tribes, whereby rations and other supplies were promised for a set period of time or until the Indians were capable of self-support. The agreement made by the Manypenny Commission on September 26, 1876, with the Sioux and Northern Cheyenne and Arapaho Indians, for example, provided that in consideration for the cession of territory the United States would furnish, among other things, a subsistence ration for each individual "until the Indians are able to support themselves." [1] Other rations were gratuities provided by the federal government to Indians who were in desperate need, although there was no formal agreement calling for such distribution. The children in government schools received the rations to which they would have been entitled had they been at home with their parents, and the same arrangements had been customary also in the mission schools. Father Stephan in the 1890s estimated the value of rations received by children in the Catholic mission schools at twenty-five thousand dollars a year.

The provision of rations to the children in mission schools was formalized in 1900. On July 28 of that year the Acting Commissioner of Indian Affairs, in response to an inquiry from the Shoshone Indian agent, laid down a set of principles and procedures. Schools on the reservations "conducted by religious, philanthropic or other approved societies" were to receive such rations and clothing as the Indian children in their schools would have received living at home. "In other words," the directive read, "so far as the matter of rations and clothing is concerned, the mission schools will be presumed to stand *in loco parentis*." The ration table of each reservation was to be followed and detailed regulations were provided for requisitioning the food and clothing from the agent. These provisions were given universal application and were appended to the *Rules for the Indian School System* for 1900.[2]

Commissioner Jones soon had second thoughts about these regulations. On August 27, 1901, he rescinded them and announced:

> Schools on the various reservations which are conducted by religious, philanthropic, or other societies, will, in the future, receive no supplies whatever from the Government for the Indian children therein whether the children would be entitled to such supplies or not if living as reservation Indians with their parents. Neither will the rations etc. be issued to the parents of such children as attend these schools or any other schools.[3]

It is impossible to determine why Jones suddenly and without warning reversed the position of the Indian Office at this particular time. That he was opposed to rations in general, as impeding the movement toward self-support among the Indians, is clear, and he no doubt had honest scruples about any support to sectarian schools after Congress had absolutely cut off appropriations for contract schools after 1900.[4]

The first uproar against Jones's new policy came, not from the Catholics, but from William H. Hare, the Episcopal missionary bishop among the Sioux. In a letter to the Secretary of the Interior on November 15, 1901, Hare remonstrated against the order. The Episcopal Church, at the instigation and with the encouragement of the government, had established four boarding schools for the Sioux, and for twenty-five or thirty years the children there had received "at least as much rations and annuities as they would have received if running wild in the camp." Jones's order, issued without warning and after the arrangements for the year had been made, was a penalty inflicted on the children merely because they attended a mission school. Hare denied that Congress's ending appropriations for education in sectarian schools had any applicability here. Nor did he think Jones could justify his action on the fact that the Episcopal Church had resolved not to take subsidies from the United States Treasury for its Indian schools. "Subsidy is defined by the dictionaries as a *direct pecuniary* grant," Hare wrote. "The issue of rations and annuities to an authorized proxy, such as a Boarding School principal is, is not a subsidy."[5]

Jones refuted Hare's contentions in a long and detailed justification of his action sent to the Secretary of the Interior.[6] The gist of his argument was that the distribution of the rations to the children in sectarian schools was against the wishes of Congress and that as an agent of the government he was bound to follow the Congressional directive. He saw in the Congressional action reducing and finally abolishing altogether aid for sectarian Indian schools, not isolated acts, but the formulation of a broad policy of gradually substituting regular government schools for contract schools. "A definite policy," he wrote, "thus appears to be fixed upon the Government's scheme of Indian education." He rejected flatly Hare's view that the Congressional prohibition referred only to cash subsidies or direct pecuniary grants and not to rations or other supplies. "In my judgment," Jones declared, "this seems a refinement not in accordance with a fair construction of the wishes of Congress in this matter. It is not believed that it was the intention of Congress to prohibit *only* the use of public or trust funds, but to announce a well settled and fixed policy that the Government in its management of Indian affairs should not in any way enter into partnership with any sectarian organization for school purposes, should hold aloof, should furnish no aid, should permit these schools to work out their own destiny unaided by the Government."

Jones noted that the Episcopal Church had taken formal action in 1892 to oppose "subsidies" from the government and that it had reemphasized this stand in 1894. And he dug out a letter from his files in which the general secretary of the church's Domestic and Foreign Missionary Society had protested in 1895 against an Indian Office report (which turned out to be erroneous) that government money had gone to an Episcopal mission.[7] Despite Hare's argument to the contrary, the Commissioner absolutely equated the rations and clothing with money grants. He reported that in 1901 all the mission schools among the Sioux had together received more than sixteen thousand dollars' worth of rations. "Rations mean dollars and cents," he declared; "dollars and cents mean rations. The Episcopal Church, through its Board of Missions, does not desire any *pecuniary subsidy* from the United States Treasury; this Office fails to see any distinction between $16,000.00 and $16,000.00 *worth of rations*." Hare's statement that rations and clothing were not a subsidy, he rejected as "a distinction too fine to be perceptible."

In Jones's view, Indian children in mission schools, not being under government control were, "for all practical purposes, off the reservation." If an Indian parent placed his children in a mission school in order to give them denominational religious training, Jones held that the government was relieved of "any further expenditure of public or trust funds for the purpose of their support and education." He went so far as to declare that the distribution of rations under the order of July 28, 1900, had been illegal.

After the Commissioner's rejection, Hare carried his case to the Secretary of the Interior, who upheld Jones. Then he appealed to the President, who sought a decision from the Attorney General, Philander C. Knox.[8] Knox drew up a decision, dated February 10, 1902, in which he supported Jones. Noting that the acts of Congress might be interpreted to refer to direct appropriations to sectarian schools, he nevertheless declared that "the issuance of rations to them for the benefit of Indian children in their care would certainly offend the spirit of the acts of Congress . . . for in saving the necessary expense of maintenance, it would have the beneficial effect of a direct appropriation." [9]

Bishop Hare accepted the decision, but he noted the deleterious effect it had on his mission schools. Two of them he was forced to give up altogether—St. Paul's at the Yankton Agency, and St. John's on the Cheyenne River Reservation—and he concentrated all his available funds on his two remaining boarding schools. He reported that he ultimately was forced to sell St. Paul's for half its value and St. John's for one-tenth its. "The only comfort," he remarked, "lay in the fact that the highest executive officers of the Government seemed to have been driven to a seemingly pitiless act by a high and imperative sense of public duty, that public duty being not to use funds in the hands of the Government for denominational schools." [10]

The official policy statements of Commissioner, Secretary of the Interior, and Attorney General came in response to Bishop Hare's complaint, but the Catholics almost immediately took up the issue, for their schools, like those of the Episcopalians, were seriously affected by Jones's order. Unlike Bishop Hare, who quietly acquiesced, the Catholic authorities made a concerted effort to get the rations restored, for they considered the "ration issue" as part of the broader question of the rights of Catholic Indians in the education of their children in Catholic mission schools. "With the exception of the persistent enforcement of the obnoxious Browning Ruling," Ketcham wrote, "no action of the Government in regard to mission schools, not even the abolition by Congress of the 'contract system,' has called forth such universal and fierce denunciation as the withdrawal of the rations." [11] Enlisting the aid of the prominent Catholic lawyers and of sympathetic members of both houses of Congress, the Bureau of Catholic Indian Missions kept up the agitation.[12]

It is not known how much Father Ketcham was aware of Bishop

Hare's case, but he had plenty of evidence on his own about the hardships caused by the sudden and unexpected cutting off of rations, and at the end of January 1902, despairing of succor from the Commissioner of Indian Affairs or the Secretary of the Interior, he sent a long letter of argument and appeal to President Roosevelt. He spoke of the "great chagrin and surprise" with which those in charge of the mission schools learned of the Commissioner's order, for the system of distributing rations to the children had always worked well. His main argument was that the rations were due as partial payment to the Indians for cessions of land, that the food and clothing merely represented the money that would otherwise be paid to the Indians in settlement of debts. In no way, therefore, were the rations an appropriation by the government for sectarian schools and they did not fall under the ban of Congress, upon which Jones rested his case. Ketcham asked that the "decided injustice to the Indian children" attending mission schools, both Catholic and Protestant, be revoked and the old order of things restored.[13]

The two Catholic members of the Board of Indian Commissioners, Ryan and Bonaparte, took up the issue, treating it within the context of ongoing Protestant hostility to Catholic mission schools. Bonaparte became the leading spokesman for the Catholic cause, a position he continued to hold in relation to all questions relating to the church-state controversy. In a letter to Archbishop Ryan on October 1, 1902, he set forth in outline the argument he would continue to develop.

He maintained, first, that furnishing rations to children at mission schools was not, in any proper sense of the term, an appropriation of money by Congress for the benefit of these schools. Second, he argued, as had Father Ketcham, that the rations were authorized in consideration of cessions of land. Their refusal, then, constituted "a breach of the agreement or treaty by imposing a condition on its performance by the Government not justified by its terms." He characterized the Commissioner's action as punishing Indians who sent their children to mission schools by withholding from them something which the government otherwise would pay them; he could find no justification for such action in any legislation. Ketcham had supplied Bonaparte with a printed copy of Knox's February 10 opinion, and Bonaparte disagreed sharply with it. He regretted, he told Ryan, that the matter had been submitted to the Attorney General without "any adequate discussion, by brief or printed argument, of the legal merits of this construction, at least on the part of those injuriously affected by it." The lawyer saw little hope in getting redress from the executive, for how could one expect the President to overrule two members of his cabinet, one of whom was his legal adviser. He thought, instead, that the best course would be to apply to Congress to authorize the distribution of rations. If the President could be persuaded to recommend such legislation, fine, or perhaps some action could be stirred up at the forthcoming meeting of the Board of Indian Commissioners at Lake Mohonk. He lamented to Ryan, "I suspect that the action of the [Indian] Department has met with the secret, if not avowed, approval of persons so hostile to religious, and especially Catholic, schools, whether for Indians or other people, that they cannot fairly weigh considerations of justice, humanity or public policy affecting the welfare of such schools." [14]

Bonaparte approved Ryan's suggestion that a copy of his letter be sent to the President, although he felt that Knox's adverse opinion precluded any Presidential action other than a recommendation to Congress. He thus got himself more deeply involved than he had perhaps intended, for Roosevelt later took to heart the complaint that the injured parties had not been given a hearing before the Attorney General's opinion had been rendered and directed the Attorney General to request from Bonaparte and Ryan a full brief on the question. [15]

Before Bonaparte set to work on such a brief, he and Ryan fought out the issue in the meetings of the Board of Indian Commissioners. At the Board's meeting at Lake Mohonk in October 1902, Ryan presented a paper by Hare and statements of his own about the cutting off of rations. A committee of three was appointed to consider the question and to decide what action, if any, the Board should take. Merrill E. Gates, secretary of the Board, originally appointed to the committee, begged off because he had already expressed himself as not favoring application to the government for a continuation of rations to schools run by the American Missionary Association (of which he was formerly president). In the end, by vote of the Board, Darwin R. James, president of the Board of Indian Commissioners, was named chairman of the committee; Bonaparte and Eliphalet Whittlesey were the other two members. [16] Bonaparte had left Mohonk before the discussion on rations had been completed and before the committee had been appointed, and he later told Ryan that he inferred from the tenor of the debate that any action taken "would almost certainly not be satisfactory to us, or calculated to assist in securing favorable Congressional action." [17]

The procedure of the committee surprised and irritated Bonaparte, for the committee of three never met, and he was simply given a report prepared by James. He refused to sign the report, which referred to previous statements of the Board and of the Lake Mohonk Conference opposing issuance of rations to Indians capable of self-support, to the action of Congress in the Indian appropriation bill of 1897 stating the policy of making no more appropriations for education in sectarian schools, and to Attorney General Knox's opinion upholding the action of Indian Commissioner Jones.[18]

Bonaparte took issue with all three points. The earlier resolutions about rations and self-support had nothing to do with the issuance of rations to children, "who are not expected or desired to support themselves." The question was one of impartiality. "If rations are arbitrarily granted to one set of Indians, and arbitrarily refused to another," he said, "such action on the part of the Government must seem unjust and oppressive as well to those who think rations should be as to those who think they should not be given to all alike." The real question, Bonaparte insisted, was whether the Indians should be permitted to send their children to religious schools without suffering for it. The provision in the Indian Appropriation Act of 1897 Bonaparte found irrelevant. The question was not one of appropriating funds for any class of schools but whether the children in mission schools "should be treated as *quasi* outlaws, entitled neither to their just claims nor to what all others of their class are given by way of bounty." As for Knox's decision, it established nothing but the legality of Jones's action and did not affect either the equity of his course nor the propriety of Congressional reversal. And he candidly asserted that Knox's opinion was "by no means satisfactory even on the question of law."[19]

Bonaparte was afraid that the majority report of the committee might be used to forestall any Congressional action in favor of rations, and he hoped to confer with Archbishop Ryan before the Board of Indian Commissioners' next meeting in January. "I think it very improbable," he wrote to Ryan, "that we can induce our colleagues to take any action which would be of benefit to our schools; in fact I have a suspicion that one or two of them may have had something to do with inspiring the original order of the Indian Commissioner." He felt that the best that he and Ryan might be able to do was to prevent the Board from intervening in the matter at all.[20]

The Washington meeting of the Board of Indian Commissioners in January 1903 was a heated affair, quite an unusual occurrence, for never before had there been such a strong difference of opinion. Never before had there been Catholic members on the Board, resolutely determined to uphold the interests of the Catholic mission schools and upsetting the Protestant hegemony which had existed since the very founding of the Board in 1869. At the meeting on January 21, Darwin James presented the report of the committee of three, and Bonaparte submitted his minority report. The two reports were referred back to the committee. But Bonaparte was not willing to go along with the other members of the committee by accepting their report or any modification of it. When the matter was considered the next day, he moved that the committee be permitted to resubmit to the Board the two reports as the individual opinions of those who signed them and that the discussion be postponed for another day. The next morning Bonaparte offered a resolution, which after more discussion and suggested amendments was referred to Bonaparte and Philip Garrett for further consideration.[21]

That afternoon Bonaparte's resolution (amended by Garrett) was considered by the Board. It was a statement of Bonaparte's views, modified somewhat to reflect the majority report of the committee. In very guarded language it affirmed the Catholic position:

> *Resolved:* That the Board of Indian Commissioners reaffirms its views as heretofore expressed respecting the impolicy of issuing rations to adult Indians capable of self-support; it has no purpose and no wish to criticise the policy of refusing all appropriations of public funds for the support of denominational institutions; and it recognizes the fact that the opinion of the Attorney General has sustained as lawful the order of the Commissioner of Indian Affairs issued on August 27th, 1901, but the Board regrets that the order appears to work a hardship to the children who if they were not at a certain class of school would continue to receive rations from the Government by reason of the fact that their parents have not yet attained self-support, and who are therefore entitled to rations under their treaties or by the established practices of the Department, and the Board ventures to express the hope that Congress may be able to devise a plan whereby the rations provided in said treaties or granted by the said practice, may be granted to such children notwithstanding their attendance at private or nongovernmental schools.

Commissioner Andrew S. Draper's motion to delay a vote on the resolution because it sounded like criticism of the Commissioner of Indian Affairs was lost, and the Board voted four to three to approve the resolution. James, Gates, and Draper, traditional evangelical Protestant

PATRICK J. RYAN. Archbishop of Philadelphia, Ryan was prominent in the cause of Indian education as one of the directors of the Bureau of Catholic Indian Missions and as a member of the Board of Indian Commissioners. (Photograph from the Library of Congress)

CHARLES J. BONAPARTE. A prominent Baltimore lawyer and Catholic layman, Bonaparte was the chief legal adviser of the Bureau of Catholic Indian Missions in its fight for the Catholic Indian schools. He was a close friend of Theodore Roosevelt and served as Secretary of the Navy (1905–1906) and Attorney General (1906–1909). (Photograph from the Library of Congress)

stalwarts, voted against the resolution. Ryan and Bonaparte were joined by Episcopal bishop William D. Walker and Philip C. Garrett in support of it.[22] Bonaparte reported to Ketcham that the resolution had passed "after a long controversy and by a very close vote." He feared that it would not, for the moment, be of much practical utility to the schools affected, but he added, "I regard it as a matter of some importance as indicating a change in the policy and sentiments of the Board."[23]

There was less success with Congress. An attempt in the Senate to add a remedial clause to the Indian appropriation bill was stricken out on a point of order—as Ketcham charged, "through the bigotry of Senator Lodge."[24] So Ketcham turned again to his lay friends to influence President Roosevelt, whom he suspected at that point to be less sympathetic to the Catholic schools than McKinley had been. "Now, as we are not unfriendly to President Roosevelt," he wrote to Eugene Philbin, "as we recognize the fact that if the rations are not restored in some way or other during his term of office it will militate against him very seriously among the Catholic voters of the U.S. in case he should be the next Republican nominee for President, we think that not only for our sakes, but for his, this matter should be speedily and satisfactorily adjusted." He added that "we suffer exceedingly from the present unjust, unconstitutional and uncalled-for policy of persecution." Philbin, a New York attorney and a personal friend of Roosevelt, spoke with the President, but he did not push the matter aggressively, fearing to interfere with the course undertaken by Bonaparte.[25]

Bonaparte's complaint to Archbishop Ryan in 1902 that the Attorney General's opinion in support of Jones's order had been too hasty and without hearing from the advocates of the mission schools reached President Roosevelt when Ryan forwarded him a copy of the letter.[26] The President did not act on it then, but he was stirred into action in the summer of 1903 by personal conversations with Catholic representatives. One of these was Philbin, who took great interest in the cause of the Catholic mission schools and who became an adviser to the Catholic Bureau and a regular correspondent with Bonaparte on the rations issue. Philbin in early July had a brief interview with Roosevelt in which he presented the Catholic arguments, and Bonaparte himself brought up the matter when he visited the President at Oyster Bay on July 15.[27]

On July 25 Roosevelt wrote to the Attorney General, calling attention to Bonaparte's remarks that the matter of Jones's order had been submitted to the Department of Justice without full information. "I think I was in error in failing to secure for the Catholic and Episcopalian people the chance to present their brief in full," the President wrote. "I therefore ask the Department of Justice to request from Mr. Bonaparte or from Archbishop Ryan, both of them members of the Indian Board, a full brief on the question. I should then like the Department of Justice to give me its decision on the brief." The Attorney General's office wrote to both Ryan and Bonaparte on July 29, 1903, requesting a brief, and Ryan asked the lawyer to present one document for both of them, which Bonaparte agreed to do.[28]

Bonaparte began work on the brief almost at once. He had at hand not only his own report to the Board of Indian Commissioners, on which he drew heavily, but a sixteen-page printed brief, dated February 4, 1903, prepared by Congressman Edward Morrell of Pennsylvania, and other material sent to him by Archbishop Ryan, and he hoped to be able to submit it quickly. By August 13, in fact, he had a draft completed, which he expected to change in phraseology, perhaps, but not in substance. He sent copies of it to Ryan, Ketcham, and Philbin.[29]

Ketcham objected to Bonaparte's contention that the parents of children in mission schools also were deprived of rations. "I do not know of any case," he wrote, "where parents have lost *their* rations for the reason that they sent their children to other than a Gov't school. The Indian Dept strictly denies that this has ever been done. . . . At Pine Ridge, S. Dak., some children were deprived of their rations while *at home in vacation* but the matter being brought to the Commissioner's attention he at once ordered that the rations be restored to them while they were home." Bonaparte acceded to this comment, albeit reluctantly. He told Archbishop Ryan that he would insert a paragraph indicating the disclaimer but also pointing out that Jones's order of August 27 was equivocal and broad enough to warrant the interpretation he had given it. "My own belief," he added, "is that the ambiguity is intentional and that, if it should be found that our schools prosper, notwithstanding the loss of the children's rations, those of the parents will be likewise cut off; or would be if the Secretary had a free hand."[30]

Philbin, too, continued to exhibit fears of anti-Catholic prejudice in connection with the ration question. "I have been informed," he wrote to Bonaparte, "that there is a very strong feeling of bigotry against the Church in relation to the Indian Missions, and that it would require considerable moral stamina on the part of the government officials to give the Church that to which it is entitled." As a result, he hoped that the brief could show that the granting of rations was "obligatory, as a matter of law." And he wanted the President as little involved as possible, for he reported that there was a strong feeling among Protestants that the President had been too friendly to Catholics. Bonaparte agreed about the Protestant views, but he saw no way to satisfy Philbin in regard to the obligatory nature of the ration distribution. He pointed out that many of the rations were, by law, gratuities, and therefore at the discretion of the Indian Office—and those that were due under treaties he thought were only *morally* due, not strictly legally. Moreover, he understood the problem that the Attorney General would have in going back on his original opinion, and he would be happy, he said, with any little change for the better.[31]

But when should the brief be submitted? After some initial haste and then indecision (occasioned by various readings of the temper of the government officials), it was decided to wait for the proper "psychological moment."[32]

Before any action was taken, a new interruption occurred. Bonaparte was appointed a special investigator of abuses in the Indian Territory and in that position was a special assistant to the Attorney General. He felt that he ought not submit the brief while in that special capacity lest it be thought to represent an official government view, and the President authorized him to withhold it until his report on the investigation had been submitted to the Secretary of the Interior. And finishing his report on the Indian Territory was dragged out for considerable time. At one point he promised Father Ketcham that he would have the brief ready to submit on January 5, but more delays ensued. A month passed —during which a disastrous fire in Baltimore destroyed a large amount of Bonaparte's property—and he kept promising the imminent completion of the Indian Territory report. Finally on February 20 he sent in the report to Secretary Hitchcock and then began a final revision of the brief on the rations question, "omitting some references in it, which seemed to me, in the view of the present information, impolitic." He wrote first to Roosevelt, however, to get his approval to submit the brief at that time, noting the Catholic pressures that were building up. "Father Ketcham," he reported to the President, "has been keeping some Catholic Societies quiet (very much against the inclination of sundry fussy individuals of Irish descent and strongly Democratic proclivities among their members) by telling them the brief would be submitted very shortly; and I was finally obliged, about a week ago, to

back him up by a similar announcement." At long last, after getting
a go-ahead signal from Roosevelt and turning in a supplementary report
on the Indian Territory, Bonaparte, on February 27, 1904, submitted
the brief on rations to the Attorney General.[33]

Bonaparte's brief, entitled "In the matter of Withdrawal of rations
from Indian Children attending Schools conducted by religious, philanthropic or other Societies on the several Reservations: Brief submitted
by Order conveyed July 29th, 1903," for the most part repeated the
well-worn arguments of the Catholics and included verbatim much that
was in Bonaparte's minority report to the Board of Indian Commissioners. In one respect he added a new element—a strained interpretation of what the revocation of the Browning Ruling had meant for Indian policy. "I submit," he said, "that the withdrawal of rations gives
effect *per indirectum* to the very purposes avowed in the 'Browning
Ruling'; it coerces Indian parents in the choice of schools for their
children." It was a policy, that is, consistent with the Browning Ruling.
With the abrogation of the ruling on January 17, 1902, it became "a
grievously oppressive anomaly." The discrimination against religious
schools in Jones's order, he found, was based entirely on the religious
or at least the private nature of the schools affected, not on any characteristics that made them bad schools. Such legislation in a state or territory of the United States, he insisted, would be considered "abhorrent
to the spirit of the Constitution and the principles of our American
polity." He concluded: "I claim that a grave error has been committed;
I believe that as soon as may be this should be corrected." [34]

Bonaparte and his friends hoped, of course, that the Attorney General would be impressed with the arguments thus formally presented
and would issue a new opinion in favor of rations for children in the
mission schools. "If this victory can be won," Ketcham declared, "the
condition of our Indian schools will be very much improved, in fact
far beyond what we ever dared to hope for." But the brief would be
useful, too, in cementing the favorable posture that President Roosevelt
showed to the Catholics, and in strengthening the growing signs of
good will on the part of the Secretary of the Interior and the Commissioner of Indian Affairs, which the Catholic leaders began to detect in
the fall of 1903.[35]

Catholic interest in the rations question (as well as other aspects of
the Indian schools) was reflected in the conventions of the American
Federation of Catholic Societies, a recently founded national organiza-

tion representing Catholic groups across the nation. The Federation's plan to propose a resolution in support of rations for Indians at mission schools was intended to impress the President (and the country) with the importance of the matter to the Church. Bonaparte was worried about the proposed action, lest it be immoderately worded and offensive to the President. As he expressed his concern to Archbishop Ryan, it would be "*very* inexpedient to have such a resolution couched in denunciatory language; and, while a reference to the subject would be thoroughly appropriate, it seems to me eminently desirable that it should be so framed as to give no needless offense, and to recognize the unquestionable desire of the President to deal fairly with *all* agencies working for the benefit of the Indians without regard to religious faith." He urged the Archbishop to impress upon the managers of the coming convention of the Federation in Atlantic City "the importance of avoiding a lurid description of the iniquities and oppressions whereof we complain." [36]

His fears were not unfounded, for in the Federation's meeting in Chicago in the previous year the assembly had been treated to a long address on Indian affairs delivered by Father Henry Ganss. Ganss spoke of how the Catholics had responded enthusiastically to President Grant's peace policy and had built schools for the Indians in the West, which had thrived until attacked by those who envied them and urged Congress to cut off appropriations for the contract schools. "And, be it said to the eternal shame of the American Congress and Senate," the priest declared, "and we must hang our heads in mortification when we do say it, in a moment of weakness, vacillation and alarm, panic-stricken and terrorized, yielding to the pressure, they revoked the appropriation given to our Catholic schools." Ganss made a strong overture, however, toward President Roosevelt, which drew repeated applause from his audience. "We have reason to expect much from our present Chief Executive of the Nation, President Roosevelt," he said, ". . . and I contend that we have received more, as far as the Catholic Indian work is concerned from our present Chief Executive than we have from any President since the days of General Grant." If Roosevelt had not done more, Ganss asserted, it was because Catholics had not presented their claims to him "in the proper light and under proper influence and under proper auspices." [37]

Ganss gave another long and flowery address at the Federation's convention in Atlantic City in 1903, in which he covered much the same ground. He spoke approvingly of the revocation of the Browning Ruling and praised the new rules governing religious instruction and services in the government Indian schools. But he could not rest with that. "The ruling depriving children who attend contract schools of their rations," he proclaimed, "is such a flagrant violation of the very gist of almost every Indian treaty, is so glaringly unjust, not to say brutally inhuman, that we may rest assured that the high sense of duty and justice, which has thus far signalized the career of President Roosevelt, as well as the conciliatory policy of the Commissioner of Indian Affairs, will have it relegated to the national chamber of horrors to rest by the side of its twin brother, the Browning monstrosity."[38]

But Bonaparte need not have worried about the formal resolution of the convention on the rations issue. The resolution on Indian schools declared in part: "We most heartily endorse this part of the resolution of the Board of Indian Commissioners: 'That Congress may be able to devise a plan whereby the rations to Indian children provided in treaties, or granted by practice, may be granted to such children notwithstanding their attendance at private or non-government schools.' We pledge our co-operation in this measure, as well as in all wise and beneficent legislation calculated to ameliorate the conditions and safeguard the rights of our Indian wards." A copy of the resolution was sent by the secretary of the Federation to every Congressman and Senator.[39]

Bonaparte's brief was delayed in being submitted, and no opinion was forthcoming on it from the Attorney General when he finally received it. Something needed to be done, Ketcham declared, lest the Catholics be "headed off all around." "If the rations are long withheld," he wrote in November 1903, "they will come too late. The delay means money to us every day—it is a case of administrative robbery." Ketcham and Archbishop Ryan, however, disagreed on the proper approach in Congress. Ryan wanted to continue attempts to amend the Indian appropriation bill. Ketcham disliked this tactic, for it was subject to obstruction by the technicality of a point of order, and he preferred to have a separate bill introduced to restore the rations.[40] In fact, Congressman Henry S. Boutell, of Illinois, had introduced a bill in November 1903 to prohibit discrimination against the mission schools, but when Congressional action to answer the Catholic demands came in the Indian appropriation bills, Boutell's measure was allowed to die in the Committee on Indian Affairs, to which it had been referred.[41]

Although Congressman John H. Stephens, of Texas, the chief spokesman for anti-Catholic interests in the House, managed to kill a proposed amendment by a point of order that it constituted new legislation, the Committee on Indian Affairs, Ketcham reported, "got together and so manipulated the English language that they have now an item restoring the rations against which the point of order, they assure me, cannot possibly lie. This in all probability means the correction of the rations question by Congress." And he exulted: "Fortune seems to smile on us." [42] The item read: "That no part of the moneys herein appropriated for fulfilling treaty stipulations shall be available or expended unless expended without regard to the attendance of any beneficiary at any school other than a Government school." [43]

When the Senate passed the measure on March 24, Ketcham's enthusiasm knew no bounds. He printed up and distributed a one-page congratulatory flyer, which he sent out to the Catholic press. "RATIONS RESTORED!" the sheet proclaimed. The item in the bill, Ketcham announced, made it "impossible for the Indian Department, in the distribution of rations to Indians who receive such rations from the Government, to discriminate against Indian children attending Mission Schools." And he listed by name the men in Congress to whom the Catholics were especially obligated. "There was no opposition whatever to the measure in the Senate," Ketcham noted, "and in the House the only man who placed himself on record against it was Mr. Stephens of Texas. The restoration of the rations is due chiefly to Senator Aldrich and Representative Sherman." Bonaparte, the cautious lawyer, expressed the hope that Ketcham had not been a little "previous" in his congratulations, since the bill was still in conference. But Ketcham insisted that they were "out of the woods." There were in fact no slips, and Roosevelt signed the bill on April 21, 1904, with the item intact. [44]

In the following year the rations issue was overshadowed by the fight over the use of trust funds for mission schools, and the rations item was omitted from the Indian bill for 1906. [45] The measure was restored, however, in the appropriations for 1907 and in clear wording that eliminated the confusion of the earlier enactment. It now read:

> Mission Schools on an Indian reservation may, under rules and regulations prescribed by the Commissioner of Indian Affairs, receive for such Indian children duly enrolled therein, the rations of food and clothing to which said children would be entitled under treaty stipulations if such children were living with their parents. [46]

The effect of the victory was small. Under the appropriation bill for 1907, five mission schools received rations. Two years later the number was reduced to two, since rations were withdrawn from the schools that had received contracts payable out of tribal funds. By 1909, only one ration school remained.[47] Rations did not provide the support the Catholic Indian schools needed, and they were used chiefly to enable the schools to carry a larger number of pupils than would otherwise have been possible.[48]

The Protestants followed the action from a distance. The mission school item, the Washington agent of the Indian Rights Association noted in 1906, had been "inserted at the request of Catholics," although it was what Bishop Hare had contended for for some time. Hare, for his part, thought it was locking the barn after the horse was stolen, since his schools that would have benefited were now closed. But because he considered the principle "intrinsically right," he saw no grounds for opposing the policy, even though the Catholics would get the benefit from it.[49]

The rations issue showed the success of the Catholic leaders in finding strong political friends who could be counted on to look favorably upon the interests of the Catholic Indian schools. After some initial misgivings about Theodore Roosevelt, Ketcham became an ardent supporter of the Republican President and publicly and officially pointed out to his fellow Catholics the excellent qualities of the man. In his report of April 8, 1904, Ketcham praised him as a man who found time to give personal attention to questions affecting the Indians. "President Roosevelt, in his official as well as private acts," he wrote, "has risen above unchristian racial and partisan prejudices, and has manifested a determination to mete out equal justice to all men." When Roosevelt held firm in his support of the Catholic mission schools, in the face of strong anti-Catholic opposition, he won further praise from the Catholic Bureau, which rejoiced, of course, in his reelection in 1904. "He was threatened with defeat at the polls," Ketcham wrote, "and there were among his friends some who feared that he had endangered his prospects for the Presidency. But when the *American people* spoke, they did so with no uncertain sound. They put the seal of approval upon his fairminded, just and liberal policy. They gave him a victory unique in the annals of Presidential elections. . . . All honor to Theodore Roosevelt!"[50]

Roosevelt's concern to treat the Catholics fairly in their Indian interests was reflected in the actions and attitudes of Commissioner

Jones, and Ketcham was quick to observe it. "Although a Protestant of the most pronounced type," the priest wrote of Jones in April 1904, "he has learned from actual observation the great power for good which the Catholic Church wields among the Indians, and is disposed to foster her Indian interests together with those of all other religious bodies, and in doing so has manifested a spirit of strict impartiality." And when Jones retired from office at the end of 1904, Ketcham was among those extolling his good qualities. He noted that while Jones's "natural bias was not favorable to the Catholic Church," his views had gradually altered as he dealt over the years with the Catholic Bureau. "During the close of his official life," Ketcham remarked, "Commissioner Jones did everything in his power to encourage our work. We take this occasion to express our appreciation of his character as a man, his assiduous work as an official, and his courtesy and generosity as a friend." [51]

While courting the executive officials, Ketcham learned, too, the value of staunch friends in the House and Senate to fight for support of the mission schools, and he was assiduous in promoting the reelection of those who were most influential and important for the Catholic cause. Foremost among these was Senator Nelson W. Aldrich, of Rhode Island, and when Aldrich ran for reelection in 1904, Ketcham was busy pushing his case with Catholic leaders in Rhode Island. To Bishop Matthew Harkins, of Providence, he wrote in March, extolling the work of Aldrich in the restoration of the rations. He noted the opposition in the House and the inability of the Democrats to control Congressman Stephens, although Catholics had long been ardent supporters of the Democratic Party. He noted, too, the strong opposition in the Senate of Senators Lodge and Gallinger. "But, fortunately," he added, "Senator Aldrich was equal to the emergency, and I believe he is the only man in the Senate who could have succeeded in silencing all opposition. Aldrich appealed to the President, and the President prevailed upon Mr. Lodge to make no opposition to the measure; Aldrich appealed to [Orville H.] Platt of Connecticut, and Platt prevailed upon Gallinger to keep quiet, and consequently through Mr. Aldrich's faithful advocacy the measure passed the Senate unanimously, without any carping or discussion whatever." Ketcham expected Aldrich, too, to be of continuing help in the fight to get the use of tribal funds for the Catholic mission schools, for he believed that he was "more influential with the President than any other man." After quoting Senator Platt to the effect that it was a mistake for Republicans to seriously champion

Catholic interests, since Catholics were so closely attached to the Democratic party, Ketcham continued:

> Senator Aldrich does not seem to share these views of Mr. Platt, but what I am very solicitous about is this: Regardless of party politics, I would like to see our Catholic people ready to show their appreciation of favors, especially great favors, such as we have received from Senator Aldrich. Even should there be little danger of Senator Aldrich's defeat, I would like to have him feel very perceptibly that the Catholics of Rhode Island recognize and reciprocate his kind offices in behalf of Catholic interests. I believe this should be done in the case of any of our public men, regardless of party, who have the candor and the courage to do as he has done. I desire more than I can say to have Senator Aldrich's confidence in Catholics confirmed, and Senator Platt convinced that he has been mistaken in his opinion that Catholics are too blindly attached to party and party leaders to recognize substantial work done in their behalf by Republicans. I would not like to see Catholics too fickle in the matter of politics, but I do believe that they have clung too persistently and unanimously to the losing side, which has also within itself strong elements of bigotry.[52]

As election time drew near, Ketcham addressed a confidential letter to each of the priests in Rhode Island, urging support of Aldrich. He said in part:

> For my work it is imperative that the Senator should be returned to the Senate and this for two reasons:
> 1st. That the policy he has caused to be inaugurated may be safeguarded and perpetuated.
> 2nd. That more favorable legislation may be secured. The Executive has given us every thing that he can. We need legislation by which tribal funds, that can be used for the support of schools, will be set apart for tribes who do not have such funds.
> I know the situation well and I have canvassed among the senators and representatives extensively, and I can state with certainty that Senator Aldrich is the *only power* that can accomplish what we need and want, and that he alone, out of all of his colleagues be they Democrats or Republicans, has been willing to support and further our claims, and, in fact, has taken them up and brought them to a successful issue.[53]

Whatever may have been the effect of Catholic switching from the Democrats to the Republicans in the election of 1904 and whatever part

Catholics played in the reelection of Aldrich, Ketcham expected some return from the Republicans. "Our Republican friends are under great obligations to us, and they realize it," he wrote to Cardinal Gibbons shortly after the election, "and there is one good feature about the Republican Party, viz: that it has the disposition and the courage to stand by its friends. I am perfectly sure that they feel that they must do something for us." [54]

The Contracts of 1904

Rations, even if applied to all the Catholic Indian schools, could not relieve the critical situation. And the failure of Catholics across the nation to rally to the appeals for funds to keep the schools open in lieu of government support brought a new surge of activity on the part of the Catholic Bureau at the beginning of 1904. It tried then to persuade President Roosevelt to approve the use of tribal funds for new contracts with the schools—a matter that had lain more or less dormant since Jones's adverse recommendations of 1901.

The Catholic Bureau submitted a memorandum to Roosevelt in which it set forth its appeal for the use of tribal funds, pointing out the difference between these funds and the direct appropriations of Congress and urging that the Indians be allowed to determine how their own funds should be used. The memorandum was sent to the President "in the firm belief that he will recognize its equity, both as permitting the Indian parents to exercise the right freely conceded to all others in the country of educating their children in such proper schools as may be approved by their own judgment and conscience, and also as relieving wholly or in part his fellow citizens of the Catholic faith from a very severe tax on their resources involved in the unaided support of these numerous schools." [1]

At an interview with Father Ketcham on January 4, 1904, Roosevelt asked for specific information and plans for the possible use of tribal funds, and Ketcham readily replied the next day with a letter and an attached memorandum. The priest, "assuming that the Attorney-General will advise the President that, as a matter of law, the Executive may properly use what are known as 'tribal funds' . . . for the education of Indian children in schools carried on by the various religious denominations located on Indian reservations," suggested eight schools as a beginning—two among the Osages in Oklahoma (already so supported), two among the Chippewas in Minnesota, one among the Menominees in Wisconsin, and three Sioux schools in South Dakota. The tribes concerned had tribal funds that could be drawn upon, and Ketcham asked that the funds be applied to the schools beginning on January 1, 1904. He listed four schools among the Sioux conducted by Protestant churches that he thought could also apply for use of the funds.[2]

Ketcham was a bit touchy about how the Indians' request for or approval of the use of these funds should be handled. He believed, he told Roosevelt, that no special action was necessary. The fact that the Indian children were now attending the schools should be considered sufficient evidence of the willingness of the parents to have the funds used for that purpose. Thus the friction and delay that might result from requiring the Indians to sign formal petitions might be obviated. He pointed to the case of the Osages, where the funds were being used without appeal to the individual Indians concerned, and hoped that that case would furnish a model for the others. Ketcham offered a considerable argument, too, to show that these mission schools would not materially affect the number of children in attendance at the government Indian schools.[3]

Roosevelt was favorably inclined toward the Catholic appeal, and he called a meeting of cabinet officers for Friday, January 22, to consider the appropriateness of honoring the request in light of the Congressional declaration of policy against the use of funds for sectarian schools. Ketcham wrote to Mother Katharine on the 21st: "Tomorrow the question of the 'tribal funds' will be settled finally. I know only one thing, and that is that the Attorney General has given a favorable opinion. We will probably have opposition. The only question is, will the President be firm enough in his promise to us."[4]

The Friday meeting was attended by Attorney General Knox and his assistant, Charles W. Russell, Secretary of the Interior Hitchcock, Secretary of Agriculture James Wilson, Postmaster General Henry C. Payne, and Secretary of Commerce and Labor George B. Cortelyou. The meeting considered a long memorandum submitted by the Attorney General's office and explained by Russell, which favored the legality of the use of Indian funds on the ground that they were not appropriations in the sense of the Congressional prohibition. The paper asserted that "at least Indian trust funds are now, so far as they were formerly, within the discretion of the Secretary to apply to sectarian schools. The mere declaration by Congress of what it intended not to do would not repeal the laws under which that discretion had existed." In regard to treaty funds appropriated annually by Congress, the memorandum suggested that they could "probably be used to support sectarian schools" since they were "probably not the moneys contemplated by the declaration of policy, not being, practically speaking, moneys of the United States but moneys owing and paid to the Indians." But a final decision on the treaty funds question was postponed.[5]

On the basis of this favorable opinion, Roosevelt gave approval for issuing contracts, but he considered it essential that there be requests from the Indians concerned for such application of their funds. For the Menominees and Osages, petitions were already on hand. There was one signed by more than two hundred Menominees, dated April 19, 1897, praying for use of tribal funds to keep their mission school open. "This school is an excellent one," the petition read, "and we love it and are proud and happy that so many of our children have received a good education in that institution." The signers were disturbed by news that no more funds would be available for contract schools and said: "What is to be done? Shall we close our school, where our children have been educated for so many years as good citizens and Christians? No. If the Government has declared to make no more appropriations for that school, then we, the Menominees, will rather spend our own tribal funds for the support of this school."[6] From the Osages there was a petition from the chiefs and headmen, dated June 1902, asking for the continuation of St. Louis and St. John schools, with a $125 per capita payment to be taken from Osage funds.[7] On the basis of these petitions, contracts for the Menominee school and the Osage schools were issued as of January 1, 1904, to run for the remaining six months of fiscal year 1904.[8]

For Indians at the other agencies, however, it was necessary to obtain petitions, and the Catholic Bureau proceeded to draw them up and have them signed by interested and willing Indians. The petitions from the three Sioux reservations—Rosebud, Pine Ridge, and Crow Creek—were sent to the Commissioner of Indian Affairs by the Catholic Bureau on August 3, 1904, with a formal request for contracts.[9] They were almost identical in wording. They noted the ending of the contract system by Congress and the "great sacrifice of labor and money" on the part of the fathers and sisters in maintaining the schools without government aid. The petitions read in part:

> The work of these good Fathers and Sisters has been of the greatest benefit to us and to our children, and we most earnestly desire to have them continue among us. We do not feel, however,

that they should devote their lives to the work of educating, civiliz-ing, and Christianizing our children and receive no recompense from us when it is in our power to give it. We are amply able to give such aid from our trust funds in the United States Treasury and the money annually appropriated by Congress, in pursuance of treaty stipulations, for our civilization and the education of our children. A portion of this money should, in all justice, be devoted to paying these Fathers and Sisters for the splendid work they are doing for our children, and it is our earnest desire that this should be done.

The petitions bore the signatures (mostly *X*'s) of a large number of Indians, with certification by the interpreters that the documents had been explained and that they were fully understood by the signers.[10] A similar petition, dated June 15, 1904, from the Tongue River Agency, praying use of tribal funds for St. Labre School for the North-ern Cheyennes, was sent to Commissioner Jones on August 15, with a formal request for a contract.[11] The Quapaw national council on Sep-tember 3, 1904, adopted a resolution that the President use the thou-sand-dollar appropriation due each year from the treaty of November 15, 1824, for St. Mary's School, and Ketcham used that as the basis for his request for a contract.[12]

Contracts, dated July 1, 1904, to cover fiscal year 1905, were then issued to the Bureau of Catholic Indian Missions as follows:

School	Tribe	No. of pupils	Rate per capita	Total amount
St. Joseph	Menominee	170	$108	$18,360
St. Louis	Osage	75	125	9,375
St. John	Osage	65	125	8,125
Immaculate Conception	Sioux (Crow Creek)	65	108	7,020
Holy Rosary	Sioux (Pine Ridge)	200	108	21,600
St. Francis	Sioux (Rosebud)	250	108	27,000
St. Labre	Northern Cheyenne	60	108	6,480
St. Mary	Quapaw	10	50	500
			Total	$98,460 [13]

In addition to these Catholic contracts, one was issued to the Lu-theran Board of Indian Missions for Zoar Boarding School on the Menominee reservation, for forty pupils at a per capita rate of $108.[14]

The Bureau of Catholic Indian Missions had attained its objective.

Through the sympathetic action of President Roosevelt, the executive branch of the federal government had agreed to supply support which the legislative branch had effectively stopped in 1900. The success was too good to be true; the contracts were barely in hand when a new and violent storm of opposition to support of the Catholic mission schools arose.

The work of the Catholic Bureau in arranging for contracts paid out of the Indians' trust and treaty funds could hardly be kept secret. News of the activities filtered in to the Indian Rights Association, which immediately began vigorous agitation against the practice and initiated what became a full-blown campaign against the contract schools that rivaled in intensity and bitterness the fight in the 1890s. While protesting a complete lack of a "sectarian point of view," the Indian Rights Association stirred up its old friends and allies. The new campaign was managed by Matthew K. Sniffen, who had served as assistant to Herbert Welsh in directing the work of the Indian Rights Association since 1884 and who formally became executive secretary in 1909. Because Welsh was absent for long periods, spending much time in Europe for his health, Sniffen ran the office during the whole controversy over the use of tribal funds for mission schools. In this he was ably seconded by Samuel M. Brosius, who had assumed the duties of Washington agent of the Association in 1898, as successor to Francis E. Leupp. The two men, one in Philadelphia and the other in Washington, were in constant contact by correspondence and occasional visits, and generally they saw eye to eye in their opposition to any advances made by the Catholics.[15]

The first cry, however, came from Protestant missionaries in the Sioux country. In the September–October 1904 issue of the *Word Carrier*, a newspaper published by the Reverend A. L. Riggs at the Santee Normal School in Nebraska, the editor reported: "A new scheme has been inaugurated by our Roman Catholic brethren with the aid of the Commissioner of Indian Affairs for getting church schools supported from Indian tribal money." He pointed to the petitions collected and the contracts made, and he argued that it was "farcical" to assume that a majority of the adult Indians on the reservations had ever signed petitions for "giving these school contracts to the Romanists."[16]

At the same time the alarm was raised by Bishop William H. Hare, who began by making a discreet inquiry of the Commissioner of Indian Affairs. The Commissioner's reply substantiated the bishop's fears, for he was informed that contracts had indeed been made with the Bureau of Catholic Indian Missions for schools in South Dakota, on the Osage

MATTHEW K. SNIFFEN. Long-time assistant to Herbert Welsh in directing the work of the Indian Rights Association and his successor as executive secretary, Sniffen was a leader in the drive against the Catholic contract schools. (Photograph from the Historical Society of Pennsylvania)

SAMUEL M. BROSIUS. Brosius was Washington agent of the Indian Rights Association from 1898 to 1933 and a key figure in the association's controversy with the Catholic Indian schools. (Photograph from the Historical Society of Pennsylvania)

Reservation in Oklahoma, and among the Menominees in Wisconsin, all of whom had requested that the schools be maintained out of the interest from their trust funds.[17] When the Commissioner later indicated that Hare, too, could request such contracts and that it was not necessary to get the consent of the whole tribe in order to get the funds, Hare declared: "My eyes began to be opened, not to say, to stare." He remembered how he had been forced to close two of his boarding schools when the federal government had decided that it was against the acts of Congress prohibiting payments to sectarian schools even to allow rations to the students, and now here were the same officials conniving to supply funds to Catholic mission schools.[18] He carried his concern to the Indian Rights Association with the assertion that the contracts with the Catholics were a "gross breach of trust," and he inquired about the possibility of carrying a suit from some of the disaffected Sioux Indians against the Commissioner of Indian Affairs or the Secretary of the Interior.[19]

Sniffen went right to work. He explained the matter to Brosius and urged him to speak to the Commissioner of Indian Affairs about it at once. The Washington agent needed little urging. "This is quite an interesting question," he replied to Sniffen, "and will not down without some effort I am beginning to see, as the Catholics are such workers."[20] At Sniffen's suggestion he began by obtaining from the Commissioner of Indian Affairs copies of the Sioux petitions on which the contracts were based, hoping that the names on the lists would furnish clues to Bishop Hare about the Indians involved on the Catholic side, while Sniffen began to confer with the Law Committee of the Indian Rights Association (of which N. Dubois Miller was chairman) about the legal side of the question. With the contracts in hand, Sniffen expected that they would be "in a position to go ahead vigorously."[21]

The vigor was soon evident, for the Indian Rights Association leaders tried every avenue open to them as they began "to make a stir" over the issue. Sniffen wrote confidential letters to the editors of the *Springfield Republican* and to the *Independent* (upon whom he knew he could rely for a sympathetic hearing), alerting them to the problem. He alluded to a recent conversation he had had with Charles J. Bonaparte in which Bonaparte had clearly intimated that the President had taken his action in favor of the contracts in order to win Catholic political support. "I have no doubt," he quoted Bonaparte as saying, "that this brought the President a great deal of support from the Catholics. Father Ketcham (head of the Catholic Indian Bureau) promptly became an ardent supporter of Roosevelt, and the Catholic papers, notwithstanding their intense opposition to the Government's Philippine policy, also came out strongly for Roosevelt." Sniffen noted that the contracts had been entered into about July and thought it would be interesting to see when such Catholic journals as the Boston *Pilot*, the New York *Freeman's Journal*, and the *Irish World* changed their political allegiance.[22] It seemed necessary, too, to deal directly with the President, and Brosius was urged to seek a meeting with him—perhaps through an intermediary such as Mrs. John Markoe of Philadelphia, a friend of Roosevelt's who had been helpful to the Indian Rights Association in previous Indian issues.[23]

Meanwhile the Association began to seek statements from Protestant Indians protesting the use of trust funds for the Catholic schools. Sniffen wrote to Bishop Hare to secure such appeals from the Sioux Indians, with the request that the Indian Rights Association protest on their behalf. Such Indian documents, Sniffen wrote, would relieve the Indian Rights Association of the charge of unwarranted interference and put it in a stronger position to press its case.[24] Such protests were not long in coming. A letter from Reuben Quick Bear and other Indians to the president of the Indian Rights Association, dated December 5, 1904, was just what the officers wanted:

> We, members of the Sioux tribe of Indians having rights and residing on the Rosebud Reservation, appeal to you to aid us in trying to prevent the paying out of our tribal trust funds, or interest of the same, by the Government for the support of Roman Catholic mission schools. For three months we have been trying to arouse the friends of Indians in our behalf to oppose the unjust contracts made with the "Catholic Bureau of Indian Missions." We write and appeal to you on behalf of the great majority of the people of this tribe.[25]

Quick Bear was the special darling of the Protestant protesters, for he was one of the Indians through whom the Indian Rights Association ultimately directed its legal fight against the Catholic contracts. Soon after he wrote to the Indian Rights Association, other Sioux protested directly to the Commissioner of Indian Affairs, being careful to have their competence and their signatures attested. Still other groups of Indians sent their protests to Congress when the movement against the contracts moved from the executive to the legislative branch of the federal government.[26] Sniffen used the Indians' appeals as the grounds for a direct protest to the Secretary of the Interior. "On behalf of a large majority of the members of the Rosebud and Pine Ridge bands of Sioux Indians . . . and at their request," the letter read, "we earnestly protest against the proposed diversion and expenditure of any of their trust funds, or interest thereon, under and in control of the United States for the support of any other than Government schools." They objected to the payment of any undivided trust funds of the Indians to representatives of the Catholic Church for the support of schools "conducted according to the peculiar form and faith of that church organization and wholly within its control." Sniffen asserted that there had not been even "a pretended petition" from the majority of the tribe whose funds were used and that the contracts went against "the well-settled policy of the Government proclaimed by statute law enacted March 1, 1899, that no further aid should be given Indian sectarian schools." [27] The Protestant Indian cause was backed up by Protestant missionaries at Rosebud. The Reverend Aaron B. Clark, of the Episcopal Church, and the Reverend James F. Cross, a Congregationalist, wrote to the Indian Rights Association early in December asking for the immediate cancellation of the Catholic contracts. [28] Although the action of the Indians gave the Indian Rights Association a cover for its anti-Catholic crusade, no one was fooled into thinking that the Indians acted independently.

From the first Sniffen and his advisers toyed with the idea that the Catholic contracts should be challenged in the courts. This had been the initial response of Bishop Hare, and the bishop for some time continued to be of that mind. [29] One problem with that approach was the cost involved, and Sniffen sought to face that problem by an appeal to the old allies in the anti-Catholic struggle of the 1890s—the secretaries of the Protestant missionary societies in New York. Accordingly, on December 3, he addressed letters to the following men: the Reverend H. L. Morehouse, corresponding secretary of the American Baptist Home Mission Society; the Reverend Charles L. Thompson, secretary of the Board of Home Missions of the Presbyterian Church in the United States of America; the Reverend A. B. Leonard, of the Missionary Society of the Methodist Episcopal Church; the Reverend A. L. Lloyd, general secretary of the Domestic and Foreign Missionary Society of the Protestant Episcopal Church in the United States of America; the Reverend F. P. Woodbury, of the American Missionary Association (Congregational); and Joseph J. Janney, of the Society of Friends.

To them Sniffen sent a statement about the contracts made with the Catholic Bureau. Because they had been made in "a surreptitious and illegal manner," he urged the church boards to protest at once to the President of the United States and to the Secretary of the Interior. Then he spoke of possible legal action in case the appeals to the President accomplished nothing. Several lawyers of high standing had been consulted, he said, and they thought that legal action would be successful, even though it might have to be taken all the way to the Supreme Court. "If such a suit were deemed advisable it could be undertaken by our Association," Sniffen wrote, "without being open to the charge of sectarianism—and on behalf of individual Indians." The cost of such a suit he estimated at five hundred to a thousand dollars, and he asked for a statement from the secretaries on the willingness of their boards to assume a proportionate share of the expense.[30]

Sniffen was somewhat disappointed in the response. Only the Baptists came through with a prompt and forceful protest to the President. On December 12 their board addressed a three-page letter to Roosevelt, in which it protested the contracts as a violation of the principle of separation of church and state; the board requested that the order for any such payment be revoked and the contracts declared null and void. The Episcopalians and the Congregationalists referred the matter to their boards in a noncommittal way; the Presbyterians replied with a bland statement that they had long regarded any plan of contract schools as "un-American and adverse to the best interests of the Indian."[31] At the end of the month Sniffen reported to Hare, "It seems strange that we have heard nothing from the Methodists." But he said that Herbert Welsh had strongly advised that the Indian Rights Association continue to push the matter as vigorously as possible. The Methodist board, however, did finally write a remonstrance to the President against the use of trust funds for mission schools.[32]

In the matter of money for a legal suit, even the Baptists were not enthusiastic. Morehouse wondered if the appropriation of missionary funds for such a purpose would be proper and thought the money might be raised instead by appeal to individuals; at any rate, the board preferred to wait to see if its protest to the President had any success before committing itself to legal action. The Quakers, in their response, flatly refused to get involved, especially in a legal suit against the government. "We have always thought it unwise to assume an attitude of hostility or antagonism to the Government," Janney wrote to Sniffen; an attack by a law suit he thought would greatly imperil their influence.[33]

Sniffen sought support also from an array of Protestant bishops. He sent them a copy of Bishop Hare's letter of November 7, supplied information about the size of the contracts and the number of pupils involved, and urged the bishops to write to the President.[34] Most of the bishops replied favorably and some wrote to Roosevelt, but others were too busy. John Scarborough, Bishop of New Jersey, said that he did not think that private letters would do much good. "The Roman Catholic clergy & Bishops," he told Sniffen, "are shrewd politicians— & we are not. In the late election, I am credibly informed, the Roman Catholics as a body turned from the Democrats to the Republicans—& they will claim their pay from the party they helped, as a matter of course. They all pull together." [35]

The protests to the President by the mission boards and by the bishops all received the same response from Roosevelt. He politely asked his correspondents to write directly to the new Commissioner of Indian Affairs, Francis E. Leupp. "The situation has been a difficult one," Roosevelt wrote. "I think Mr. Leupp has the right idea for its permanent solution in his desire that all these funds held for the tribes should be allotted to individuals. Then there could be no question, as there sometimes is now, of either doing injustice to the Indians of a given faith who want schools of that faith, by refusing them schools; or to the Indians of another faith who have not joined in the request, by granting it." [36]

Having been thus rebuffed by the President, whom it believed to have sold out to the Catholics in return for support in the election, the Indian Rights Association sought to attain its ends by other means than influencing the executive by a protest campaign. At first it continued to explore the possibilities of instituting a legal injunction against the government's paying out trust fund moneys to the Catholic mission schools. Brosius was firm in his advocacy. He believed that the suit ought to be instituted "simply for the purpose of publicity—with the possible result of a decision in our favor." And he told Sniffen that the missionary boards who hesitated to get involved in a suit against the government by direct contributions for that purpose could keep their names out of the case by giving something to the Indian Rights Association for its general support, "which to us will amount to the same thing as a direct contribution for the *suit*." [37]

Sniffen, for his part, continued to confer with Dubois Miller of the Law Committee and proceeded somewhat cautiously. "As you know," he wrote Brosius, "most everything in which we have had to take legal action in late years, has always resulted in a decision by the court in favor of the government, and under these circumstances we have to be very cautious about seeking legal redress through the ordinary channels." But he, too, saw advantages from a suit, if the missionary boards could be persuaded to share the expenses. "Even though the action of the President were supported finally [in the courts]," he wrote, "it would tie the money up for the time being and probably cause the Romanists to work for a segregation of these trust funds—an end which we desire to see accomplished. In this way the objection to the support of such schools would be removed, since the expense would fall directly on the individuals who are most anxious to have them aided." [38] He drew some encouragement, too, from the fact that Commissioner Leupp seemed to be favorably inclined toward the idea of a suit, which would decide the prickly question of the legality of the contracts.

But it did not take long for the two men to give up the idea of a suit for the time being. Brosius decided that the hesitancy of the boards about financial aid and the probability of losing the suit, once instituted, made it inadvisable to commence an action. He wanted instead to push the plan of securing publicity by having resolutions introduced in both houses of Congress calling upon the executive branch for full information regarding the contracts and to continue agitation for segregating the tribal funds. Meanwhile the campaign of protest to the President should be renewed and stepped up. He wanted all the churches to imitate the Baptist protest, and he himself intended to write to some missionary on each reservation to secure a protest signed by the Indians for forwarding to the President. Even Bishop Hare, by the end of the year, had changed his mind about legal action. "At first I was inclined to think that an injunction suit would be the best mode of meeting the matter," he confided to Sniffen; "but that would be expensive and uncertain of results, and I am inclined now to think that publicity and agitation are the best recourse." [39]

Sniffen agreed and began in earnest to stir up the other denominations to follow the lead of the Baptists. He wrote again to the Episcopalians, the Presbyterians, and the Congregationalists, urging attention to the Baptist resolution, for he felt it was necessary that the various groups put themselves on record "in order that the President may have no doubt as to how the contracts with the Catholic Bureau are regarded." [40] Then, egged on by Brosius, Sniffen made a special trip to New York to speak personally with the secretaries of the missionary boards—to sound them out once more on their willingness to contribute funds for a suit if it became necessary and to prepare them to support a fight to segregate the trust funds if the campaign moved in that direction. He came back from "a pretty interesting time" with the secretaries, encouraged once more that funds might be forthcoming.[41]

But soon, while not giving up their campaign with the President and while keeping the idea of a suit in the back of their minds, the Indian Rights Association leaders turned to Congress.

The Fight in Congress

ADOPTING an old ploy for getting executive activities before the public, the Indian Rights Association engineered resolutions in the House of Representatives and in the Senate calling upon the Secretary of the Interior to furnish information about the granting of contracts to the mission schools. While Sniffen sorted through names of Congressmen who might be persuaded to offer a resolution, Brosius drew up an appropriate measure. He asked Congressman John H. Stephens to introduce it in the House, which Stephens did on December 13, 1904.[1]

The resolution, passed on January 10, 1905, asked the Secretary to report whether or not any principal or interest of Indian trust funds or any other moneys of Indian tribes had been spent to support "any Indian contract schools other than Government schools" and to indicate purposes, amounts of money, and authority for such expenditures for the period since January 1, 1903. And it wanted to know "whether or not the consent of the Indians interested" had been secured. The Secretary's reply, forwarding a report prepared by Commissioner Francis E. Leupp, dated January 17, 1905, supplied the Protestant crusaders with excellent ammunition. Leupp provided a table of contracts awarded for fiscal year 1904 (the two Osage schools) and for fiscal year 1905 (one Lutheran and eight Catholic schools). As to authority for the grants, Leupp was extremely vague: the contracts, he said, were made by his predecessor and forwarded to the Interior Department "without any statement relative to the authority under which such recommendation was made," and that they had been approved by the Department. He reported that petitions from a number of Indians at the reservations where contracts were requested were on file in his office, and he listed the trust funds that had been drawn upon.[2]

The resolution requesting information was but a prelude to a vigorous attempt to persuade Congress to prohibit explicitly the expenditure of the tribal funds for the Catholic schools. Father Ketcham saw it coming. "The President stands firm in the position which he has taken," he wrote to Bonaparte on January 21, 1905, "and has informed these people that the only recourse they have is Congress or the courts. I do not think they will try the courts, and while they very probably, through Stephens of Texas and others, will begin an agitation this session, I think it is too late for them to get any measure through. We hope by next Congress to have testimony from the reservations which will supply our friends with 'powder' for a successful fight." [3]

The strategy of the Indian Rights Association was to seek an amendment to the Indian appropriation bill for fiscal year 1906 which would prohibit the use of the funds. Stephens introduced such an amendment in the Committee on Indian Affairs, and Sniffen began an all-out campaign to gain support for the measure. The Executive Committee of the Indian Rights Association at its meeting on January 4 directed him to write the missionary boards to add their voices and to urge Leupp, too, to come to their support. [4] Sniffen was all ready. On that very day he sent a battery of letters to the missionary board secretaries (omitting this time the Quakers, who had been so unresponsive to his former appeal), urging letters to Congressman Sherman, chairman of the House Committee on Indian Affairs, to Stephens, and to other Congressmen. "If this clause is inserted in the Indian bill," the letters read, "we will have accomplished what we are aiming for, namely, a rule of law that Indian trust funds shall not be used for the purpose indicated; for when the law becomes applicable, the present contracts cannot be continued or new ones made." The following day the Indian Rights Association's Executive Committee sent a formal request to Sherman for the incorporation of Stephens's clause and a similar letter to Leupp. Sniffen also wrote to Lyman Abbott, editor of the *Outlook*, suggesting that he call attention to the matter in his journal. [5] He tried to leave no stone unturned. Finding that Congressman Charles Curtis of Kansas, a member of the Indian Committee, was "lukewarm on the subject" and had "shown evidence in the past of being more or less subject to Catholic influence," Sniffen wrote again to the missionary board secretaries on January 6; he asked them to request officers of their churches in Kansas to apply pressure on Curtis to vote right on the issue. And Darwin R. James, president of the Board of Indian Commissioners, was sent a copy of the letter to the missionary boards. [6]

Then Sniffen approached the Reverend James M. King, the well-known anti-Catholic publicist, who as general secretary of the League for the Protection of American Institutions had played a significant role in the 1890s crusade against the contract schools and whose book, *Facing the Twentieth Century: Our Country, Its Power and Peril* (published in 1899), was a massive compilation of anti-Catholic sentiment. What he wanted especially from King was a list of persons to whom he could send a form letter that he had drawn up. "The main thing now," he wrote "is to reach people living in the states represented in the make-up of the House Committee on Indian Affairs, namely: Arkansas, Colorado, Indiana, Iowa, Illinois, Kansas, Minnesota, Nebraska, New York, New Mexico, North Dakota, Missouri, Oregon, South Dakota, Texas, and Wisconsin." [7] King, unfortunately, disappointed him. While he had headed the League, he said, he had had at his disposal "a large list of names of influential citizens throughout the several states upon which I could depend to communicate with members of Congress concerning any legislation which we desired to effect," but since he had left that office he no longer had access to the list. Nevertheless, he supported the drive, for he considered the use of the funds for sectarian Indian education "not only unwise but illegal." He suggested that Sniffen write to Josiah Strong, head of the American Institute for Social Service. This Sniffen did. He asked Strong for a list of the names of five hundred to a thousand people who would be apt to respond to his suggestion, but Strong was no more help than King. He told Sniffen that his Institute was "composed of all parties and sex including Roman Catholics," and his membership list was not especially geared to the interests of the Indian Rights Association. [8]

As part of the fight, the Indian Rights Association prepared a pamphlet concerning the history of the contracts made with the Catholics, which it intended to distribute widely. After some modifications to make it "seem much less anti-Catholic," the circular was published on January 12 under the title *Indian Trust Funds for Sectarian Schools*. It began with a citation of the act of Congress of June 7, 1897, which set the policy of making no further appropriations for education in any sectarian school, and then asserted that this policy had been violated by the new contracts. By giving in to Catholic pressures and using the undivided tribal funds without the consent of the Indians interested, the government was guilty of a "gross breach of faith." The pamphlet printed the protest of the Rosebud Indians and the letter from the missionaries, Clark and Cross. The position of the Indian Rights Association was that the tribal funds were "quasi public funds" and therefore fell under the Congressional prohibition. The statement ended with an appeal to the readers to urge their Congressmen and Senators to enact legislation to prohibit further expenditures of the trust funds for the support of sectarian schools. Sniffen was sure that the pamphlet would "stir things up somewhat," and he sent copies out with his correspondence and asked churchmen to distribute copies to their people.[9]

The publication of the pamphlet snapped the bond of friendship between the Indian Rights Association and its greatest supporter among the Catholics, Father Henry Ganss. When Ganss received a copy of the publication in late January, he blasted Sniffen in an angry three-page letter. He complained that as a member of the Association he should have received a copy from the Philadelphia headquarters; instead a copy had only by chance come to him secondhand. But his chief point against Sniffen was that, "as a matter of courtesy and fair play," the Catholic side of the question should have been given a hearing before the Protestant argument was spread broadcast over the country. "The surreptitious manner of publishing the circular, and the precipitate haste in circulating it," he told Sniffen, "shows a lack of prudence, not to say a deep animus, on the part of the sponsors of the publication." He spoke in support of the Catholic missionaries among the Sioux: "Why should not the missionaries at Rosebud and Cheyenne River, whose honesty and truthfulness is impugned, who are accused directly and by implication of having misled the Indians and hoodwinked the Government, why should they not have had a chance to explain, as much as Revs. Clark and Cross had to exploit, their side of the question?" He concluded that he could not consider the publication in any other light than "an outbreak of jealous, intolerant bigotry." Sniffen replied in a moderate letter to Ganss, pointing out that the pamphlet "carefully avoids any attack on your Church, but simply stands for the principle involved." But he was more candid with Brosius, to whom he sent a copy of Ganss's letter for his amusement. "It is hard to see what would have been accomplished by giving the Catholics a chance to state their side of the case," he wrote. "The matter had been put through, and the way in which it was carried out was enough to condemn it."[10]

The Protestant missionaries at Rosebud, Pine Ridge, and Crow Creek reservations sent to Congress petitions from the Indians there, and Brosius declared that the Reverend H. Burt, of Crow Creek, reported that not more than one-tenth of the Indians favored the present use of their funds.[11]

All the letters and protests addressed to Congressman Sherman did no good. The Congressman answered his correspondents brusquely:

"So far as the appropriation is concerned, it has never attempted to change the declared policy of Congress of some years ago. So far as the Indians' disposition of their own funds is concerned, it seems to me that we ought not to say that they cannot expend their own money for the education of their own children in schools of their selection." [12] This answer not only disappointed the protesters but in a sense infuriated them, for Sherman bypassed an essential argument, namely, that in the present situation of undivided trust funds, all the tribal members had an interest in all the funds. To use any of the money at the request of only a part of the tribe—and the Indian Rights Association insisted it was only a small part—violated the rights of all the rest, who did not want the funds used that way. Morehouse thus wrote of Sherman's reply, "If the money were given by the Indians for these schools after each man had received his quota, that would be a different thing. Or, if the money were so applied by a general council instead of having it worked up through individual solicitation, there would be some show of reason in his position." The pamphlet *Indian Trust Funds for Sectarian Schools* put it this way: "There is no objection to any Indian *making choice* of having his share of funds used in the manner indicated, but a share of undivided tribal funds cannot well be segregated from the others, until the final segregation of tribal funds is directed by Congress into individual holdings, a statute very much desired by friends of the Indian." [13]

Of special note was a series of editorials in the *Outlook*, in which the editor, Lyman Abbott, strongly endorsed the anti-trust-fund crusade. Early in January 1905, Sniffen had sent Abbott information on the controversy and remarked, "If you see your way clear to treat this matter in THE OUTLOOK, we shall be much indebted." Later in the month the journal published his material. In the issue of January 21, in an editorial called "A Mischievous Appropriation," Abbott called attention to $102,780 in contracts (including one for a Lutheran school), and strongly objected to them as being against Congress's declarations and against the principle of separation of church and state. He urged his readers to write in protest to Congressman Sherman. Abbott, unfortunately, misunderstood the precise issue at stake, which was not a direct appropriation for mission schools, and he was set straight by Sniffen, who informed him that it was a question of the President applying trust funds without reference to Congress. But a week later Abbott renewed his attack, opposing the use of tribal funds that was based on petitions from the Indians. "This does not seem to us to make the policy involved in this appropriation any more defensible. . . . The tribal funds of the Indians are public funds. The executive order appropriates these public funds for sectarian purposes." He commended the proposal to divide up the trust funds among individual Indians, but for the present he insisted that the funds belonged "to the tribe as a tribe." [14]

The reply sent to protesters by Sherman, in which he noted the difference between Congressional disapproval in 1897 of direct appropriations of public funds and the use by the executive of the Indians' own funds at their request, drew a new attack from Abbott in an editorial of February 4, called "Unfair Indian Fighting." A week later, the *Outlook* continued its campaign. It repeated the details of the case and declared that it had not said that the contracts were illegal, only that they were "unjust to the Indians, unwise for the Government, and injurious to the churches." Such use of funds was inevitably pernicious, the paper said, for "jealousies, heartburnings, deceptions, wire-pulling, and sectarian conflicts and animosities follow in its train." The "immediate practical thing" to do was to have Congress divide the trust funds in severalty, so that each Indian could use his share of the funds as he saw fit without any intervention of the government. [15]

The *Outlook* articles, coming as they did in a widely read and respected journal, worried Father Ketcham and his friends, who sought ways to counteract them in the press. Ketcham drew up a draft of a reply to the "vicious article" of January 21, which he sent to editors of Catholic papers. He hoped thereby to dissipate the confusion in the Catholic public mind about the matter, and he urged the editors to "make thin air" out of the "mischievous appropriation." [16]

The strongest blow against the *Outlook*, however, came from Congressman Sherman in his argument on the floor of the House of Representatives on March 2, 1905, against legislation to prohibit the use of the trust funds. He took Abbott severely to task for irresponsible journalism. "I have never known so much misinformation to be disseminated through the country by the press, both daily, weekly, and monthly," he said, "as has been disseminated upon this subject." He then called special attention to the *Outlook*, "which opened the discussion of this question." Abbott had sent him, he said, an advance copy of his January 21 editorial about proposed appropriations for contract schools. Sherman went on:

I took the trouble to write Doctor Abbott quite fully, explaining exactly what the law was, and that there had been no such estimate, that it was not proposed to appropriate one cent of Government funds, that the Congress had declared some years ago that we would not further appropriate from Government funds for sectarian purposes, and that so far as I knew there was no thought on the part of anybody to backstep from that position; and I further explained exactly where the money came from—this $102,000—and where it had been expended; and with that letter before Doctor Abbott, the Outlook published the article which they had sent to me, without changing it by the crossing of a "t" or the dotting of an "i." And that sort of thing has gone on through the press. The local press up in my part of the State have disseminated misinformation broadcast on this subject.[17]

Sherman's outburst, to be sure, did not lose him any friends among the Catholics, and his remarks in the House won a prominent spot in the Catholic arguments.[18]

Sherman did not need to worry about the subtleties of the arguments to gain his point against the Stephens resolution. The Indian appropriation bill was reported out of his committee without the restricting clause, and when Stephens attempted on January 21, 1905, to add the amendment from the floor of the House, it was ruled out on a point of order by Sherman that it was introducing new legislation. The House passed the bill, therefore, without the prohibition.[19]

Responses from the executive branch had not been much more helpful. Secretary of the Interior Ethan Allen Hitchcock replied by sending to those who wrote to him a copy of a memorandum drawn up by Francis E. Leupp shortly before he became Commissioner of Indian Affairs. Bypassing the question of a legislative prohibition on the use of trust funds, such as that sought by Stephens, Leupp instead presented two general positions. First, he said that the President would welcome an injunction suit such as Bishop Hare had proposed, for it would define judicially the status of the Indians' rights in the matter. Leupp would, he wrote, "consider the irrevocable settlement of the question of the limitations of the Government's authority as trustee of the Indian funds in the United States treasury as in the highest degree desirable." Moreover, such a decision would go a long way to teach the Indian "the great moral lesson of discipline which every citizen of every color has to learn one day—that the very foundation of our social order rests on law, and that we must all accept the law as expounded for us by the courts." Second, he wanted legislation for the individualizing of the funds of the tribes, keeping them under government control but opening a separate account for each Indian. "I wish to treat the tribal funds just as the tribal lands have been, or are presently to be treated. The allotment of lands in severalty has done more for the Indian, in spite of all the incidental defects of the system and of all the mistakes and abuses which in isolated cases have occurred under it, than any other single measure. It has snapped one of two demoralizing bonds of tribal communism, and as soon as the trust funds are individualized the second will be broken also." In thus setting forth his policy, which he intended to follow as Commissioner, Leupp wanted his readers to "get a view of the rounded whole instead of seeing only a single phase." But he did note that one particular object to be gained by the individualization of the trust funds was a solution to the problem of using the trust funds for denominational schools.[20]

Making no headway with the administration and stymied in the House for the time being, the Indian Rights Association shifted its campaign to the Senate, where it found a faithful servant in Senator Thomas R. Bard, a lame-duck Senator from California and member of the Indian Affairs Committee, who had been defeated for reelection after serving a partial term in the Senate. Bard submitted to the Senate Committee on Indian Affairs an amendment to the Indian appropriation bill that read as follows: "That no portion of the funds appropriated by this act nor the principal nor interest of any Indian trust or tribal funds held by the United States for the benefit of any Indian tribe shall be available nor be expended for the support of any sectarian or denominational school."[21]

The first stage was to arrange for hearings before a subcommittee of the Committee on Indian Affairs, at which the matter of the contracts could be fully aired. The planning began about January 25, when Brosius started to collect names of persons who could testify at the hearing. Sniffen himself wrote to the missionary boards, asking their availability to come to Washington to make a protest before the committee. When a hearing was scheduled for January 31, he drew up a form letter, which he sent to interested groups to urge representation at the hearing and to ask for letters of protest against the use of tribal funds.[22]

Two sessions of the hearing on the Indian appropriation bill were devoted to the question of the use of tribal funds for sectarian schools. The first of these, on January 31, was devoted largely to the Protestant attack on the use of the funds. Senator William M. Stewart chaired the meeting, with Senators Porter J. McCumber, Moses E. Clapp, Fred T.

Dubois, Henry M. Teller, and Bard on hand. Present also were Brosius, Commissioner Leupp, and a staunch ally of the Indian Rights Association, Dr. Wilbur F. Crafts of the International Reform Bureau. At that session Senator Bard entered into the record statements of protest from the Presbyterian Board of Home Missions, the Boston Indian Citizenship Committee, the Baptist Home Mission Society, and the Board of Indian Commissioners. Leupp began the actual discussion with a statement about what had been done in the matter of using trust funds for the contract schools. "There is no law authorizing it," he said. "But there is no law, either, that we know of, against it." The practice had been carried on under the authority of the President, and Leupp freely acknowledged the questions that arose from the practice of thus using tribal funds. "Opinion may differ," he admitted, "not only as to the expediency of doing this, but as to the right to do by indirection of any sort what the law forbids by direct methods, and the question may always come up as to whether Indian trust funds are public funds until they pass into the Indians' hands, or whether they belong actually to the Indian from the start." These questions, he noted, had been turned over to the Attorney General for an opinion. "Meanwhile," he added, "Congress, of course, will have a perfect right to go ahead and legislate that no trust funds shall be used for these purposes, if that is desired." [23]

The big events of the hearing on January 31 were the statements made by Brosius and by Senator Bard. They brought forth in dramatic fashion the charge of Catholic political influence behind the contracts that was so deeply imbedded in the Protestant position. Brosius spoke first, reading a four-page statement alleging the illegality of the contracts, which had been made by arbitrary executive authority. He argued that the Indians protested such use of the funds and that the Indians who benefited from the contracts received more than a proportionate share of the funds. Then he drove home his point about an "ecclesiastical lobby" by dragging in the antics of a certain E. L. Scharf, who ran a small news agency in Washington and who seemed to take it upon himself to act as protector of Catholic interests and bitter critic of anti-Catholics. Brosius asserted that Scharf, "representing the Catholics," had proposed to deliver the necessary Catholic votes to carry twenty close Congressional districts, if an appropriation of two hundred thousand dollars for Catholic mission schools was continued. The material for the charges had been supplied to Brosius by Bard, and the Senator amplified the Scharf story at the hearing.[24]

It was a petty performance, for the alleged action of Scharf had occurred in the Congressional election of 1902, more than two years prior to the hearing, and no notice of it had been brought before the public until the hearing on January 31, 1905. There was no corroborating evidence for Bard's assertions, and no indication, if Scharf had indeed done as charged, that he was in any way an official spokesman for the Catholic Church.

Bard's charges, however, furnished the sort of sensational copy that the press loved. Once the charges had been publicly aired at the hearing, Brosius immediately gave out the news to the papers. Much of the press carried the story. The Scharf revelations caused enough stir to excite the Catholics, and Cardinal Gibbons issued a statement disclaiming any official connection between Scharf and the Church.[25] The Scharf episode hurt. Ketcham complained to Archbishop Ryan about Scharf and others who had "persistently meddled in Catholic Indian affairs and matters pertaining to the Bureau, greatly to my embarrassment and annoyance." What bothered Ketcham most was that the Scharf affair was seized upon by "the bigots of the country, and especially those who have been using the Republican Party to serve their ends," who were alarmed by the way many Catholics had voted for the Republicans in the last election. The Scharf "sensation" was a way of alarming Republicans and "inspiring fear and creating confusion among Catholics." The Catholic press, in fact, had diverted its attention from the real issue at stake and gave too much attention to refuting Scharf and his methods.[26]

Some papers, of course, carried stories in defense of the Catholics; the *Washington Post*, for example, printed a statement prepared by Father Ketcham. The Indian Rights Association leaders, however, were not impressed with the articles favorable to the Catholics. "The NORTH AMERICAN reporter was a 'mick,' as I got him to admit in an indirect way," Sniffen wrote to Brosius after that journal published an article, "but his article was harmless."[27]

The Catholics got a chance to reply to the Protestant protests of January 31 when the Senate subcommittee on February 3 allowed them to have their day, without the presence of their adversaries. Ketcham presented his position before the committee and answered polite questions posed by the committee members and by Commissioner Leupp, who was again on hand. He spoke firmly but without rancor, trying to make clear how the Catholics felt about the matter and why they were justified in seeking assistance for their mission schools. He first read into the record the prepared statement that had appeared in the *Post* the day before. "The question at issue is simply this," he said: "Shall an Indian parent have the right to use his own money in the education of his own children in the school of his choice?" The Catholics contended that the tribal money—both that held in trust and that appropriated annually by virtue of treaty stipulations—could be drawn upon by the Secretary of the Interior for the benefit of the Indians. Furthermore, where Indians expressed a desire to use these funds to educate their children in mission schools, the government should pay for that education out of the tribal funds. If the funds could be properly used for that purpose once individualized, Ketcham argued, a portion of the common fund could be used while the funds were yet undivided. In fact, he noted, the government had long admitted the legality of such use of tribal funds in its uninterrupted support of the two Catholic schools on the Osage Reservation. "It seems strange," Ketcham remarked, "that during all these years the opponents of the Indian contract school system have taken neither offense nor alarm at what they now please to term 'a breach of trust by the Government.'" As for the more recent contracts, he noted that after Roosevelt had become President, the Catholic Bureau had consulted Charles J. Bonaparte, for whose legal ability and integrity they had high regard, and that the lawyer had thought that the use of the funds was legal. Roosevelt agreed that the Catholic proposal was a fair one and he would do whatever was lawful. The President had referred the matter to the Attorney General and acted upon his advice.[28]

Ketcham reviewed the history of the contract school system, recalling how the Catholics had entered into the work of Indian education at the instigation of the government and had poured in their own funds. When Congress killed direct appropriations to contract schools, the Catholics—unlike the Protestants, who closed their schools—continued their work on their own resources. And he made a fervent plea to the Senators:

> I appeal to you in the name of 12,000,000 of your Catholic fellow-countrymen, in the name of the Catholic Indians of this country, in the name of fair-minded people of all religions or of no religion at all. We feel that your seal of disapprobation should not be placed upon our work, but that rather any encouragement that could possibly be given us should be afforded. The church has nothing to gain from a material point of view from this work among the Indians. Every year she is sinking treasure and spending lives in this

work from the highest motives of religion and philanthropy. She is endeavoring to extend the benefits of civilization to a people who must perish from the earth, who can only leave a trace behind them, and who can never be of any material benefit to the church.[29]

Ketcham told of his previous cooperation with Brosius when the Indian Rights Association had asked for help and how Catholics had supported Bishop Hare in his efforts to secure rations for the children in mission schools. "Now," he concluded, "when a measure comes before the country that affects the Catholic missions, as this measure does, we feel surprised and, of course, more or less hurt, that these people have formed themselves into an opposition." Ketcham made a point, too, to dissociate the Bureau of Catholic Indian Missions from Scharf, who, he asserted, was "in no sense of the word an agent of the Catholic Church or the Bureau of Catholic Indian Missions." Scharf was no more than a private tutor, with some students at the Catholic University.[30]

When members of the committee asked about the ability of the government schools to handle all the Indian pupils, Ketcham cited the number of pupils, the capacity of the government schools, and the residue of pupils left over, many of whom were being cared for in the Catholic mission schools.[31]

At the end of the hearing, Leupp questioned Ketcham about his position on individualization of the trust funds.

> Mr. LEUPP. . . . Now, if the subcommittee will allow me to ask Father Ketcham a question, I should like to bring out one point. Would you, Father Ketcham, or would your church object to legislation which would individualize these Indian funds—open an account with each individual Indian instead of keeping these sums in a lump, and then allow each individual Indian to say how his money shall be spent for the education of his children?
> Fr. KETCHAM. I have no objection to that, Mr. Commissioner.
> Mr. LEUPP. That would be a very fair solution.
> The Chairman. Would that satisfy Bishop Hare?
> Mr. LEUPP. Entirely. . . .
> Mr. LEUPP. This plan of individualizing the funds, Senator, will give every Indian a chance to say what he wishes done with his money and no question could arise thereafter as to the Government's handling of this money.[32]

In the midst of all the brickbats flying in the direction of the President as well as of Congress, Roosevelt issued a strong statement of his position in a letter to the Secretary of the Interior dated February 3, 1905. Roosevelt noted the Attorney General's report that the legislative prohibition on the use of public moneys for sectarian schools did not extend to moneys belonging to the Indians themselves. "There was, in my judgment," he said, "no question that, inasmuch as the legal authority existed to grant the request of the Indians, they were entitled as a matter of moral right to have the moneys coming to them used for the education of their children at the schools of their choice." He, however, laid down two prescriptions to be followed: first, that care be taken to see that "any petition by the Indians is genuine" and, second, that "the money appropriated for any given school represents only the pro rata proportion to which the Indians making the petition are entitled." If these conditions were fulfilled, he thought it "just and right" that the requests of the Indians should be honored, and he expected to continue the practice until Congress or the courts should decide otherwise. He did put in a strong word, in addition, for a bill introduced in the House by Congressman John F. Lacey, of Iowa, which provided for permission to allot the Indian tribal funds in severalty, exactly as had been done with land. Such legislation would obviate the questions now so actively agitated about the payment for mission schools out of the funds.[33] The statement led Ketcham to rejoice that "so far as the President is concerned, we came out all right."[34]

The Protestants saw in the letter one more indication that the President had given in to the Catholics. Lyman Abbott in another editorial in the *Outlook* took strong issue with Roosevelt's decision to approve the use of the Indian trust funds, calling it a violation of "a vital and fundamental principle of the unwritten constitution of the American commonwealth." He argued that the funds were public funds and held in trust by the federal government, which as guardian had the sole authority to dispose of them. He called attention again to the Scharf affair—"an agreement testified to and not denied"—and he declared that the President had unintentionally given his support to that section of the Catholic Church that was seeking to destroy the public school system of the nation. He urged him to admit his mistake and reconsider his decision. Abbott sent an advance proof of the article to Roosevelt, as a courtesy and to make a personal plea for a change in policy. Roosevelt replied immediately with a strong rebuke. In regard to the Bard-Brosius disclosures, he wrote: "There has been no testimony to this effect of a kind to merit denial, and as far as I know the statement is a lie pure and simple. I shall be astonished if the *Outlook* repeats such a slander, absolutely without basis of any kind." And he took issue with Abbott's accounting of the prorated funds. At the end he challenged the editor's analogy between the Indian school question and the question of nonsectarian public schools. "The public moneys on the Indian reservation can not be used for denominational schools," he said, "but the funds held to be divided among the Indians individually are properly to be used as the individuals prefer. Any other course seems to me radically unjust." Unfazed by the President's declarations, Abbott printed the editorial as written.[35]

The Indian Rights Association, of course, did not rest with its testimony before the Senate subcommittee. It began a new campaign to bring pressure upon Senators to vote in favor of the Bard amendment. Brosius himself proposed to make an appeal to every Senator, but to secure the "interest from the *outside* that is so *important*," he relied on Sniffen. "Is it possible for you," he asked, "to get a list of influential persons ready—all the religious papers, etc., so that we can send out literature to them, asking that they immediately appeal to the Senators, on the contract school question." Sniffen at once drew up a form letter, dated February 4, which he sent (together with pertinent statements and newspaper articles) to a long list of persons, with the admonition to vary the form of their letters and to write at once.[36]

A great many avenues were used to bring influence to bear on the Senate. Material was supplied to friendly newspapers, and articles they published were circulated. This was especially the case with the *New York Evening Post*, which on February 6, 7, and 15 had strong articles against the use of trust funds. After the first of these appeared, Sniffen thanked the editor, Oswald Garrison Villard, "for so fully ventilating this perversion of the Indian trust funds for the support of sectarian schools."[37] Meanwhile the Executive Committee of the Indian Rights Association, not unmindful that the President's action in approving contracts was still of concern to them, drew up a long statement addressed to Roosevelt. After being sent to Brosius for checking, the letter was dispatched on February 10, 1905. On February 14, copies of the letter were sent to the *Evening Post* and to a number of other newspapers.[38]

On the same day Senator Bard introduced a resolution in the Senate, calling upon the Secretary of the Interior to furnish information on the education of Indians in sectarian schools. "We hope to get additional facts," Brosius wrote. "All has not yet been disclosed. When all is disclosed there may [be] a sensation." The resolution, passed by the

Senate on February 15, elicited a tremendous file of documents from the Commissioner of Indian Affairs.[39] Brosius also prepared a resolution for Stephens to introduce in the House asking for information on the use of rations for subsistence in sectarian schools.[40] On February 16, Brosius addressed a letter to all the Senators to urge support of Bard's amendment. "This question," he said, "should not be regarded as an issue between Protestant and Catholic, but should be viewed and decided upon the broader principle of entire separation of Church and State." Large numbers of copies of the hearing before the Senate subcommittee were ordered, to be sent out under Senator Bard's frank.[41]

Protests to Congress flowed in. On February 21, 1905, Senator Bard presented a miscellaneous batch—from Reuben Quick Bear and other Rosebud Sioux and from Indians at Crow Creek and Pine Ridge, as well as from the Boston district secretary of the American Missionary Association and other laymen.[42] Lodges of the Junior Order of United American Mechanics, a strongly anti-Catholic organization that was considered by some to be a successor to the APA, sent printed appeals to the Senate.[43] There were, of course, some Catholic memorials too, but these were nothing in the face of the Protestant onslaught. The president of the Marquette League and the president of the American Federation of Catholic Societies each sent urgent telegrams to fourteen selected Senators for defeat of the amendment. And a clergyman from Iowa wrote to Roosevelt asking him to veto any amendment such as that proposed by Bard.[44]

Both the Protestants and the Catholics were apprehensive about the outcome. Brosius and Sniffen corresponded regularly throughout February, watching and measuring the effect of their agitation, but they relaxed a bit when the Senate Committee on Indian Affairs reported the Indian appropriation bill with the Bard amendment in it. "It is to be expected," Sniffen reported, "that the Romanists will fight this clause, but I believe it will be adopted by the Senate. . . . At any rate, we shall keep up the fight to the last ditch." [45]

The Senate committee agreed to the Bard amendment by a vote of seven to three. Stewart, the chairman, voted against it, arguing that it would be a reflection on the President, but Leupp testified that the President would not see the amendment in that light. This turned Father Ketcham deeply pessimistic. He wrote to Bonaparte on February 18: "All pledges to the contrary, the 'Bard amendment' was placed on the bill today. I do not know what may be done in the Senate. A point of order should lie against the item, yet I do not know on whom to *rely* to make it. Mr. Brosius has kept Congress flooded with newspaper protests. The Indian Rights Ass'n have been reenforced, so I am told, by the W.C.T.U. and kindred societies. Every one seems to be afraid to openly take our side, in fact I find it next to impossible to see any one. I think that Mr. Brosius played his winning card when he put Bard forward and introduced Mr. Scharf to the public. I have not given up entirely, but candidly I see little to inspire hope." Bonaparte, too, was dejected and thought the situation "critical and unpromising." He feared the "decided hostility" of Leupp and that the Scharf incident had done more harm than had appeared at first.[46] Ketcham shared Bonaparte's hesitancy about Leupp. "Mr. Leupp has done everything in his power to thwart us and assist Bard, his pretences of friendship to the contrary," he wrote to Bonaparte. "I still have faith in the President but not in Mr. Leupp. . . . It now begins to look as if we were 'up against' bad faith."[47]

Since the Senate committee reported the Indian appropriation bill with the Bard amendment intact, supporters of the Catholic cause tried to remove the clause by a point of order—a tactic that had proved successful in the House—but to no avail. They did, however, succeed in modifying it a bit by an amendment to the amendment, offered by Senator McCumber, which made Bard's addition less drastic. McCumber added this proviso:

> *Provided, however,* That the individual owner or beneficiary of any interest in such fund who may desire to educate his ward, child, or children in any school other than a Government school may, by written order signed by him, direct that any portion of the interest accruing to him, or which would be allotted to him on such fund, be paid to the school in which such ward, child, or children may be educated.[48]

The Senate approved the appropriation bill with the amended Bard amendment. Then, because the House had rejected the amendment when proposed by Stephens and passed the bill without it, the matter fell to a conference committee. To the surprise of both sides, the conference committee rejected the amendment, and since the Senate acquiesced in that decision (even Bard made no further move to restore it), the Protestants lost at the crucial final moment.[49]

The Catholics, of course, were jubilant. "I was much gratified," Bonaparte wrote to Ketcham, "to hear that the obnoxious Bard amendment had been defeated, and that Congress adjourned without gratifying our friend Brosius and his allies in any way." The Marquette League congratulated Ketcham for having "won a great battle in Congress," and Ketcham himself rejoiced in the "complete victory over Mr. Bard." But he by no means considered the victory a final one. "We will have another fight on hand next Congress," he said.[50]

Brosius and Sniffen, to all appearances, took the defeat calmly, but Sniffen, as usual, saw Catholic machinations in the background. "I suspect the Romanists did some fine work with the Senate Conferees," he wrote, "to nullify what had been accomplished." Congressman Stephens was the only one who held out; he refused to sign the conference report without the amendment.[51]

The Catholics were right in suspecting that the Protestants intended to renew the fight in the next Congress. The 1905 battle was only part of the total campaign, and Sniffen was satisfied that they had developed "a powerful public sentiment," which could be marshaled again when the new Congress met.[52] The Indian Rights Association consoled itself with the thought that the President's letter of February 3 had set definite guidelines for a continuation of the contracts, and it looked especially at the determination of an exact pro rata share of the trust funds for the mission schools. The problem would be "in keeping the President to his word" in the matter.[53]

Both sides geared up for the next fight by publishing extensive material from the House and Senate debates, which each spread widely to the public in order to keep the fires burning. The major effort of the Indian Rights Association was the printing of choice excerpts from the *Congressional Record*. A sixteen-page pamphlet was printed up in large numbers by the Government Printing Office for the Association. Sniffen and Brosius, in fact, had been active in supplying material for Congressman Stephens to read into the *Record*. And Brosius gathered together some letters that Leupp had written to Senator Bard, in reply to the Senator's request for data on the contract schools.[54]

The booklet contained debate from the Senate of February 28 on the amendment to the Bard amendment offered by Senator McCumber. The chief extracts were from the speech of Senator John T. Morgan, of Alabama, who was the chief speaker against the McCumber amendment. He argued that it was wrong to allow the parent of the Indian child to determine ahead of time where the interest on the trust funds should go, that instead this was the right of the guardian, namely, the United States government. He objected, moreover, to doing indirectly what Congress had prohibited directly. "I would rather vote, in cases where Indian children are being educated by the Catholic Church," he said, "to apply to the extent of the necessities of the Indians, the money directly out of the Treasury than to authorize the ward of the United States, who is supposed to be incapable of attending to his own business, to give an order to a priest to go to the Treasury and get the money under a continuing order, and let the school or the church have the benefit of the appropriation in that form continuously as long as that annuity remains payable by the Government of the United States. . . . [The churches] will absorb every dollar the Indians have if we start this system." The second part of the pamphlet contained extracts from Congressman Stephens's speech in the House on March 3, when the conference committee report on the Indian appropriation bill was considered. And it printed letters of Brosius to Stephens of February 15 and 27 about the evil of the contracts, letters of Commissioner Leupp to Bard of February 16 and 20, with details of the contracts awarded, and the letter of Episcopal missionary Aaron B. Clark to Stephens of March 1, in which Clark declared: "Congressmen should understand very clearly that these contracts with sectarian schools work greatly to the prejudice of other school work. By this scheme the Government becomes, nolens volens, a close partner with the body to whom contracts are issued, quite contrary to the spirit of our American institutions." [55]

It was a neat package of propaganda for the Indian Rights Association, mailed at government expense under Congressman Stephens's franking privilege, a saving in postage that more than covered the cost of the printing. The arrangement, however, precluded any identification of the Indian Rights Association on the pamphlets or the envelopes, a fact that disturbed the publicity-conscious Sniffen. Five thousand copies were ordered, and Sniffen sent copies of the reprint to newspaper and journal editors, with the request that they notify their readers that copies were available at the Indian Rights Association office. [56]

In May, an additional five thousand copies of the Morgan-Stephens pamphlet were ordered and the same number of a new extract from the *Congressional Record* of January 21, which were mailed out together in franked envelopes. "The Romanists show signs of new activity," Sniffen noted, "and we want to be also on the alert." [57]

The chief user of the extracts from the *Congressional Record* and indeed the principal instigator of the extra printing and the additional extracts was a strange figure, a lawyer from New York City named

DeWitt C. Morrell. He wrote first to Sniffen about the trust fund fight in February 1905. Sniffen supplied him with printed material for distribution, and the two developed an extensive and friendly correspondence that continued throughout the controversy over the mission schools. Morrell's motivation, first and foremost, was a violent anti-Catholicism, and his intemperate flaying at the Catholic hierarchy, the Jesuits, and public officials who seemed to favor them, marked him as a bigot of the first water. Soon after he surfaced and began to take an active interest in the Indian Rights Association's work, Brosius cautioned Sniffen to investigate the man and his standing in the community before they paid much attention to him. Sniffen's reply was candid: "Although he is a Quaker, he is a most ardent A.P.A.," he wrote, "which accounts for his strong anti-Roman Catholic tendencies. In this respect he is an extremist, and believes that the Catholic Church is trying to secure temporal power in the affairs of this country—a danger which he thinks cannot be too strenuously resisted at every point. He is inclined to be too egotistical concerning the influence he personally commands, but he is a tireless worker and can't be daunted by temporary defeat." [58]

Aside from the Catholic Church, Morrell's two great dislikes were President Roosevelt and Congressman Sherman. Of the former he wrote, "I know of no act in the history of our Executive that compares for meanness and disgrace with this act of Roosevelt's of paying the trust funds of Protestant Indians to Roman sectarian schools without the consent or knowledge of the Protestant Indians. . . . There can be no terms of censure of Roosevelt too severe." Sherman's support of the Catholic position on the contract schools maddened Morrell, who made it his chief aim in life to defeat the Congressman's reelection. He attempted to saturate Sherman's district with hostile literature, and he used up hundreds upon hundreds of the Indian Rights Association publications in the campaign to inform the voters that Sherman was under the influence of Roman Catholic interests. [59]

Morrell also tried to draw James M. King into the fight. He attempted to use King's *Facing the Twentieth Century* as "a sort of fertilizer of the ground," but the publisher of the book refused to cooperate by making the book available. He then approached King directly for an article that he could print and distribute in his fight against Sherman— "so as to keep the pot boiling, and maybe Sherman will wish he had never been born"—but King was too busy with other things. "It is probable the Jr. O.U.A.M. will get into the fight," Morrell wrote to Brosius. "Be assured the old APA's are in it." [60]

The willingness of Sniffen and Brosius to accept the support of men like Morrell, who joined the fight out of anti-Catholic animus, and to give them full encouragement in their activities makes it impossible to accept at face value their repeated disclaimers of any anti-Catholic or sectarian motivation. In fact, when Morrell spoke of the resurgence of anti-Catholic organizations, Sniffen told him, "I am very glad to learn the possibility of a re-birth of the Patriotic Society to which you refer, and I trust it will soon be an accomplished fact. Our experience shows that we need the strongest kind of organizations to combat the subtle influence of the hierarchy." Sniffen also carried on a long correspondence with Charles R. Saunders of Boston, who sent contributions to the Indian Rights Association specifically to support the anti-Catholic drive, who distributed the Association's literature, and who agitated with Congress in support of the anti-trust-fund drive. But Sniffen was unwilling to go as far as Morrell in his criticism of the Catholics. When Morrell referred to the work of Roman Catholic schools as "notoriously defective," Sniffen told him that the Catholic mission schools he had visited in the West were well taught in English. "Of course," he added, "the Roman dogmas are strongly hammered into the pupils." [61]

To counter the propaganda of the Indian Rights Association and its allies, the Bureau of Catholic Indian Missions prepared a collection of materials to present its side of the question. Lacking the funds itself to bring out the documents in pamphlet form, it relied upon the Marquette League to do so. The pamphlet, *Indian Tribal Funds: The Case for the Catholic Indians Stated, with the Record Made in Congress of the Debate by the Senate on the Issue of the Mission Schools*, appeared in the spring of 1905. Its language was strong, in spots intemperate, and it was given to name-calling. "The Brosius-Bard episode," it began, "opened at once the flood-gates of anti-Catholic bigotry and the members of Congress were deluged with petitions and letters against the use of the tribal funds for the support of Catholic schools. Prominent in this work was the Women's Christian Temperance Association. Many screeds, emanating from this source, were neither Christian nor temperate. Charity also prompts the inference that a number of violent diatribes from ministers of various denominations were written through a misapprehension of the facts of the case." It then pictured the Catholic groups coming to the rescue: "In defense of the rights of the Indians the Marquette League, the American Federation of Catholic Societies, and other associations, and the Rev. W. H. Ketcham, Director of the Bureau of Catholic Indian Missions, put themselves in communication with the members of Congress and so fortified them with the truth that the action of President Roosevelt was upheld and the rights of the Catholic Indians to the use of their own tribal funds was maintained when the next attack was made." [62]

The pamphlet was filled with pertinent extracts from the proceedings of the Senate of February 23, 1905 (debate on the Bard and McCumber amendments) and from the proceedings of the House of Representatives of March 2 (on the conference report), with emphasis on Sherman's attack on Lyman Abbott and the *Outlook*. In a final section headed "Calumnies against the Catholic Missionaries" it refuted the charges made by the Indian Rights Association that the petitions on which the contracts had been made were not genuine and that the Indians had been forced or bribed to sign. It printed the petitions and letters from Catholic missionaries and from agents attesting to the integrity of the petitions. It concluded with a statement of a Sioux Indian that his name had been put on a counterpetition against his will, probably by an Episcopal catechist.

The pamphlet was aimed more at informing Catholics and strengthening them in their resolve to withstand the attacks of the Protestants than at convincing those who did not support the contract school system. Ketcham thought that the pamphlet was "gotten out in a very satisfactory manner," and he was convinced that its circulation would do a great deal of good. He lamented, however, that "very few even of our most enlightened people" took the trouble to read such publications once the press stopped agitating a matter. He thought that in the fall, when the tribal funds issue would once again become news, the League's pamphlet would be much in demand. "The Indian Rights Association has already applied to me for a number of copies, with which I supplied them," he wrote. "I received information only today that these people are busy laying deep plans for the defeat of the 'tribal funds' next Congress." [63]

Petitions and Contracts

IF any Catholics thought they had won a complete victory over their foes in the defeat of Stephens's and Bard's measures in the House and the Senate, they were soon disillusioned. Instead of an easy, automatic renewal of the 1904 contracts for the eight mission schools, they faced what seemed like an interminable delay on the part of the executive branch and then active opposition on the reservations when at last the petitions on which to base new contracts were gathered.

On June 6, 1905, Charles S. Lusk, secretary of the Bureau of Catholic Indian Missions, made a formal request of the Commissioner of Indian Affairs for a renewal of the contracts that had been made the year before, "upon the same terms and conditions." He asked for contracts for the twelve months beginning July 1, 1905, for the schools among the Osages, Menominees, Sioux, Northern Cheyennes, and Quapaws, payable from the trust and treaty funds of the tribes among which the schools were located. And he supplied exact figures for numbers of pupils and per capita payment asked at each school. The Indian Office acted with extreme caution, uncertain just what authority it had and what funds it could draw on. The casual way in which Commissioner Jones had acted once he got approval from Roosevelt was now to be replaced by the careful niceties and bureaucratic finesse for which Leupp was famous. When the Indian Office got Lusk's letter, it at once forwarded the request to the Secretary of the Interior and asked for an authoritative decision about the availability of funds. It informed the Catholic bureau that the granting of contracts would be held up until a definite determination had been rendered on the availability of funds for such contracts.[1]

Leupp, however, took two steps during the summer that touched the matter substantially. First, he decided that the President's directive that the petitions be "genuine" meant that new petitions were necessary for new contracts and that he and his agents would determine the form of the petitions and how they were to be signed and attested. In the middle of June, Lusk wrote to Father Digmann at St. Francis Mission that the Catholic Bureau would not be sending out petition forms, for the Indian Office had taken the matter into its own hands. Second, Leupp drew up a method for determining the pro rata shares to be allowed to Indians who petitioned for the use of the tribal funds for the mission schools. He isolated the funds in the Treasury which appeared to be the sort intended. His procedure was first of all to deduct from the funds the educational costs of the government schools for the specified tribes, then to divide up the remainder of the money due by the number of Indians involved. This left very little to be applied on a pro rata basis for the mission schools under contract.[2]

There was no answer to the Catholic Bureau's request for new contracts. The Commissioner would not move without direction from the Secretary of the Interior. The Secretary of the Interior depended on word from the President. The President awaited legal advice from the Attorney General. Throughout the summer the Catholic Bureau corresponded with its friends in high places (Eugene Philbin, Senator Aldrich, Bonaparte, Archbishop Ryan, and Cardinal Gibbons), trying to bring sufficient pressure to bear on the President to break the logjam. At the request of Philbin, Roosevelt in the middle of August instructed the Department of the Interior to submit the matter to the Attorney General, but no opinion was forthcoming.[3]

Ketcham was seriously worried, not only over the financial situation of the schools if the contracts were not renewed, but over the political implications. He had proclaimed to everyone that the President would continue the contracts, and if, now that the election was past, they were forgotten, he would not know what to do; and he spoke of the "baneful effect, politically speaking, upon the Catholic public." "As a Republican myself," he wrote to a supporter, "and naturally wishing to see a greater number of our people in the ranks of the Grand Old Party, I have no hesitancy in lamenting . . . the damage that will be done to our efforts along these lines. Our people have always been shy of the Republican Party because they have believed it to be antagonistic to the Catholic Church. It has been hard work to make them believe otherwise, but now, after a great number of them have torn themselves away from old political traditions, if they find that they have been trapped and duped, there will be no hope whatever of healing the wounds that have thus been opened afresh."[4]

More weeks passed without any action. Through the good graces of

Senator Aldrich, Roosevelt then agreed to call a meeting of Aldrich, Attorney General William Moody, and Bonaparte (who on July 1, 1905, had been appointed Secretary of the Navy). Ketcham was asked to prepare a statement for the meeting, and he felt "quite a bit encouraged." By December 1 he had a rough draft ready, which Lusk took in person to Bonaparte for the settlement of certain dubious points.[5]

The completed memorandum, signed by Gibbons, Ryan, Archbishop Farley, and Ketcham, was submitted to President Roosevelt on December 8, 1905. It was a clear and forceful statement of the Catholic Bureau's concern about the delay in approving the contracts for the year. After outlining the history of the contracts of the previous year and the request for new contracts, the prelates entered their complaint: Although the Commissioner of Indian Affairs had asked for authorization early in June, it was not until about August 10 that the Secretary of the Interior had transmitted the matter to the Attorney General, who still had not rendered an opinion. The contracts, if given, would have been operative from July 1 and the school year began on September 1, yet the schools did not know what to expect in the way of contracts. The schools were kept open, and the delay in granting the contracts had burdened the Catholic Bureau with large and unforeseen expenses, which it could not bear without great detriment to its other schools. Now, with winter set in, it would be difficult if not impossible to comply with the detailed requirements of Leupp that all the Indians appear in person before the agents to sign the new petitions. "The question now is, what shall be done to bring this chaotic state to an end, and to insure fair, just treatment to all concerned?" the prelates said. Their recommendation was a continuation of the previous year's status without any new petitions.[6]

On December 20 and 21 Bonaparte had two conferences with Roosevelt and the Attorney General about the contract schools; at the first Senator Aldrich was present, at the second, Commissioner Leupp. In addition, he met individually with the Attorney General and with Leupp. Bonaparte reported to Ketcham in detail. "The situation, as developed by these conferences," he wrote, "was substantially as follows":

It was agreed that the ratio adopted by Mr. Leupp for calculating the portion of the trust funds available for the support of contract schools would result in their getting substantially nothing, and that this basis of calculation must be abandoned. It was also agreed that, for the present year, the schools which were started in good faith and under the expectation that they would receive contracts, ought to be treated on the same basis as last year. With regard to next year, however, it will only be possible to secure contracts in cases where the funds in the hands of the Secretary of the Interior are trust funds in the stricter sense, and not such as require annual appropriations by Congress, unless, in the meantime, some Congressional action can be secured doing away with the prohibition of or declaration against appropriations for sectarian purposes. The Attorney General is very unwilling to give an opinion in the case, as there is a decided difference on the subject among his subordinates. If, however, the President should insist upon an opinion from him, I feel quite confident that it would be adverse to the interests of the schools. Under these circumstances, I think you will agree with me that the President has treated the schools as equitably, and even liberally, as the situation permits. I had a very frank talk with Mr. Leupp about the situation, and I think that if you and Archbishop Ryan would call to see him, and discuss matters from an amicable standpoint, a *modus vivendi* could possibly be reached which would be of considerable service in the further intercourse of the [Catholic] Bureau and the Indian Office.[7]

Bonaparte was caught in a ticklish situation. He was strongly behind the Catholic Bureau's position and indeed had been an important architect of its legal arguments. Yet as Secretary of the Navy he faced delicate questions which were the business of other cabinet members, namely, the Secretary of the Interior and the Attorney General. He took part only at the express request of the President and could speak out only on that condition.

Out of the conferences came a forthright letter from Roosevelt to Leupp, charging him to move ahead on the contracts. The President repeated quite fully his original instructions to the Secretary of the Interior of February 3. He then gave specific directions for the two types of funds. One was the trust fund, "which requires no appropriation by the Congress, and which clearly is to be administered as the Indians request." He told Leupp to use that fund as the Indians directed—"each Indian in a tribe is to be credited with his pro rata share of the funds, which you will apply for him to the Government school where that is the school used, or to the Church school where that is the school used, instead of segregating any portion of the fund for the support of the Government school and pro-rating the balance." The other fund consisted of moneys appropriated by Congress according to treaty stipulations. Roosevelt was uncertain whether or not the prohibition of Congress against the use of funds for sectarian schools applied to this category. But since some of the contract schools were being run on the belief that Roosevelt's letter of February 3 authorized the use of the treaty funds and because it would be a great hardship to cut them off arbitrarily, Roosevelt directed that the treaty funds be used in exactly the same way that the trust funds were—but only for the current year, with no additional contracts based on the treaty funds until some authorization had been given by Congress or determination made by the courts.[8]

Shortly after the President wrote to Leupp, he heard from the Attorney General. Moody, in a letter of January 4, 1906, furnished information on the question of the use of the trust and the treaty funds. He divided the funds into three classes: (1) money held in trust by the government for certain tribes, (2) money appropriated by Congress in pursuance of treaty obligations to provide for the education and civilization of the Indians, and (3) money appropriated voluntarily by Congress for the support of Indian schools. For the first, Moody relied on the opinion of his predecessor of 1904 that the Secretary of the Interior might use such funds for sectarian schools. In regard to the second, Moody hesitated, in spite of the fact that Assistant Attorney General Charles W. Russell had prepared an affirmative opinion. He hesitated to adopt the reasoning of Russell and therefore submitted the question, without disclosing his doubts, to Assistant Attorneys General Charles H. Robb and James C. McReynolds and to Solicitor General Henry M. Hoyt. All three disagreed with the Russell opinion, and Moody said his own view leaned strongly in their direction. Understanding, however, that "in view of certain temporary arrangements you have made, the question for my opinion is held in abeyance . . . ," Moody told Roosevelt, "I have not found it necessary to arrive at a final conclusion."[9] Roosevelt had made sure that he—and the contract schools relying on treaty funds—would be off the legal hook for the time being. Soon an injunction suit by the Indian Rights Association would start the legal determination of the question in the federal courts.

It seems clear that Ketcham did not see Roosevelt's letter of December 23 to Leupp. He got instead a relatively brief note from the Commissioner, dated January 2, 1906, in which Leupp relayed the substance of the President's directive. Leupp reported also that petitions had been prepared for the trust fund schools and that similar ones would be made ready to send to the treaty funds schools. He suggested that Ketcham notify the Catholic schools and the Indians affected.[10] Ketcham immediately panicked. He apparently did not know that Leupp had been told to change his system of determining pro rata shares (putting Catholic school Indians on a par with government school Indians). And he had an abiding fear that new petitions—especially on account of Protestant agitation—might seriously cut the number of those who would sign. He fired off letters of lament to his staunchest supporters, Senator Aldrich and Charles Bonaparte.

To Aldrich he made clear his dislike of having to seek new petitions. Ketcham wanted the contracts made on the basis of the previous expression of Indian intent. "The Commissioner, however, takes a different view of the matter," he told Aldrich, "and in consequence the whole thing has to be gone over again very greatly to my disappointment, and, I fear, to the detriment of the schools concerned." The Menominees were rent by internal dissension over financial matters, and he feared that it would not be possible to obtain favorable action from them. As for the Sioux, the opponents of the Catholics on their reservations had been at work and it was possible that many of the Indians who had been favorable to the Catholics might be induced to withhold their signatures from the petitions sent to them by the Commissioner. The Commissioner's view on how the pro rata shares would be determined he thought would be disastrous for all the schools except for the two among the Osages. Ketcham sent a copy of this letter to Bonaparte, who replied with a consoling message: "My understanding of the President's instructions," he said, "is that the schools paid for out of the trust funds in a stricter sense should remain just as they were last year, and that schools paid for out of treaty funds should also remain as they were last year for the present year only. The regulations prescribed by Mr. Leupp were regarded as unsatisfactory because for practical purposes, they defeated this intention." [11]

Leupp, in fact, had drawn up petitions embodying the specifications of the previous contracts in regard to the number of pupils and the per capita payments. On January 11, 1906, he sent to the agents at Pine Ridge, Rosebud, and Crow Creek, and to the superintendent of the Tongue River Training School a packet of documents which embodied the procedures he had decided upon and to which he held adamantly despite Ketcham's laments: a copy of the directive of the President of February 3, 1905, a blank petition for the Indians to sign, a certificate to be signed by the interpreter, and a certificate to be signed by the agent. With these was a pointed letter of instruction. The agent was to place the petition in the agency office and immediately notify the mission school authorities that this had been done. Then he was to notify the Indians under his care that the petition was ready to be signed by all who wanted to do so, and an opportunity was to be given them to sign. "This advertisement must be made with the utmost publicity," Leupp directed, "and you must see that all the Indians interested are given ample notice and full time for consideration, to which end you might briefly call attention to the principal parts of the petition, and even furnish copies of it to representative Indians." When an Indian appeared before the agent to sign, the agent (through the interpreter, if necessary) was to explain the terms of the petition and see to it that the proposed petitioner understood what he was doing before he would be allowed to sign. Leupp insisted that the Indian be told that education for his children did not depend upon the petition, for the government would provide it in any case in government schools, and that signing would mean that his share of the trust funds or treaty funds would be taken for the purpose of supporting the mission schools. But the agent was told: "You will studiously refrain from giving the Indians advice on the subject; simply give the facts, explained in detail." No change in the language or terms of the petition or the attesting certificates would be permitted. Leupp's purpose was plain. "You must be extremely careful not to give anyone ground for complaint that a surprise of any sort was sprung upon him," he told the agents. "Everything in connection with the petition must be done candidly and in the open, without favor or prejudice." There was some flexibility, of course, all carefully set forth by Leupp. Certain days were to be fixed for signing the petition, but Indians who did not come on those days must still be permitted to sign. And in the case of bad weather, when old, infirm, or sick Indians could not come in personally, a deputy with an interpreter was to be sent to their homes, and separate certificates by the deputy and the interpreter attesting to the integrity of the signing were required.[12]

One can easily see why Ketcham preferred the free and easy and somewhat vague procedures of 1904 to this administrative masterpiece. Leupp was going to be sure that the petitions were genuine even if it meant bureaucratic overkill; and he was going to know exactly how many pro rata shares were to be directed to the Catholic schools among the Sioux and Cheyennes.

In regard to the St. Mary's school among the Quapaws, the procedures were somewhat different, following the traditional patterns there.

Those Indians, accustomed to express their wishes through a tribal council, were to follow that method again. Leupp sent directions to the superintendent of the Seneca Training School in Indian Territory to lay the Catholic Bureau's request before the council, to make sure that every member had an opportunity to express his views fully and freely, and to get a properly attested act or resolution from the council.[13]

As Leupp moved ahead, sure that he was right, the Catholics continued to long for the old ways. On January 18 Ketcham sent to Aldrich, who was preparing another meeting with the President, a detailed memorandum, which he called "a plain, unvarnished statement of our views of the question and of the crisis in which we find ourselves." "These contracts," he sighed, "could be executed in a day and the whole question settled, which is so harrowing to us." It was the signing of new petitions that Ketcham feared. Missionaries informed him, he told Aldrich, that the new regulations were "inflicting the greatest blow to their work that it has ever sustained, as the Indians are indignant over the sacrifices required of them, and begin to look upon the missionaries and schools as mercenaries." Ketcham saw only one way to settle the difficulty—the President should have the orders for the new petitions countermanded and the contracts immediately drawn up and executed. "This cannot be done too soon," he concluded, "as our schools cannot hold out much longer, and as the evil effects that are being wrought by the present canvass among the Indians is in some places threatening to undo in a few days a work that has been built up by the toil and sacrifice of many years."[14]

President Roosevelt was irritated by Ketcham's complaints to Aldrich, which he considered unwarranted criticism of what the administration intended to do. He sent Aldrich a statement prepared by Leupp that he thought answered Ketcham "convincingly and finally." Then, after a conversation with the Senator on the matter, he prepared for him a summary of his own position:

> (1) I will not stand for any fraud, direct or indirect. The Commissioner of Indian Affairs is to be satisfied that the petitions from the Indians are bona fide and not faked.
> (2) The Commissioner of Indian Affairs has not the slightest intention and never has had the slightest intention of construing this to mean that he will cast obstacles in the way or be unreasonable about the signatures. His action in the Osage Tribe conclusively proves this. He has given orders that every facility shall be afforded to enable the opinion of the Indians to be expressed,

and that no technicality of any kind will be permitted to block this attempt.

(3) The purport of the order is that as regards the tribes affected, including those covered by it up to the end of the present fiscal year and the smaller number covered thereafter, each child that goes to a church school is to have for its share of the school fund the same amount as the child that goes to a Government school; that is, that, according to the number of pupils, the church schools and the Government schools will severally be treated on exactly the same basis, the same pro rata going to the maintenance of each.

When Roosevelt sent a copy of the statement to Leupp, the Commissioner replied that it seemed to him "to cover the ground." But he, like the President, felt hurt by Father Ketcham's agitation. "If the Bureau of Catholic Indian Missions," he told Roosevelt, "would do me the compliment of believing in my fairness and charity as heartily as it expects me to believe in its own, I think there would be no question between us."[15]

However fair the intentions of Roosevelt and Leupp, Ketcham's distress about opposition to the petitions on the reservations was not unfounded, for the Protestant missionaries (particularly at Rosebud and Pine Ridge) intended to do everything possible to obstruct the signing. As early as May 10, 1905, Sniffen had written to Brosius, trying to get prepared if new petitions were to be required. If the government decided on new petitions, he said, it would be good to have the Indians informed on the matter, for if they realized that their own money was being given up, they would probably be less enthusiastic.[16] And this was precisely the tactic used on the reservations. An active campaign was undertaken to discredit the Catholic missionaries, painting them as greedy men who were trying to obtain the Indians' funds for their own purposes. The Indians were to be frightened into believing that they would sustain great loss of their funds if they signed the petitions. "It is an iniquitous piece of business," the Episcopal missionary at Rosebud, Aaron B. Clark, wrote to Bishop Hare, "and I am doing what I can to make the people all understand the matter fully." He did not think that many Indians would wish or dare to sign the petition since they now understood that it would lead "to the carrying out of a scheme of robbery against all their neighbors." And counterpetitions were circulated, a practice approved by the Indian Office if carried on under conditions similar to those required for the original petitions.[17]

The attack, in Catholic eyes, was unfair and unconscionable. A contemporary history of the Rosebud mission school, St. Francis, gave the Catholic missionaries' views about the new petition.

> Several months before this petition was laid before the Indians, Protestant Catechists, Deacons and Helpers had gone all over the reservation warning the Indians, Catholics included. "When a petition is laid before you," they said, "do not sign it; otherwise you will lose all your money and will have to starve." When the President ordered all Rosebud Indians to contribute—inasmuch as they possessed their funds in common—their anger was aroused. The Catholic missionaries were publicly called thieves and robbers, who were trying to burst a bank and help themselves to the deposits of other people. "If you can not run your school without our money, close it and give it up," one said at a meeting. A picture was drawn representing a priest stretching out his hands after a bag of money (trust and treaty funds) and behind him Indian children crying for bread. Doggerel verses were circulated ridiculing Catholic priests as trappers, scheming for the money of the Indians. The Episcopalian minister himself did not blush to give an instruction on Confession in the presence of the Catholic missionary, insisting especially on the duty of restitution of ill-gotten goods, and telling the Indians to ask for the money the priests had received the previous year out of their funds.[18]

Father Florentine Digmann, Jesuit superior of the St. Francis Mission, was right in the midst of the controversy. He could hardly be expected to view the whole business objectively, for his commitment to the mission school was absolute, and the Protestant opposition had long irritated him. The journal entries for February 1906 in his unpublished "History of St. Francis Mission" give a blow-by-blow account of the battle over the petitions on the Rosebud Reservation. As the agent moved from village to village with the petition to be signed, he was accompanied by Father Digmann and by the Reverend Mr. Clark and his helpers. The Protestants attempted to frighten the Indians so they would not sign, asserting that signing would deprive them of substantial sums. Digmann would reply to the charges, quoting Leupp as to the nature of the funds to be used. Clark asserted that the signers of the petition had been "fixed," that Father Digmann was "pushing the people to sign, by some means or other," and he promised to get tangible evidence of the coercion. "There were 64 signers yesterday," Clark reported on February 13, "but there will be hundreds of protestors in a list to be sent the Commissioner shortly. There is a strong and general feeling that this business is altogether wrong and that a contract should not be allowed." Bitterness and tension filled the air, but numbers of Indians signed at each stop.[19]

The agents tried to restrain open hostility and to maintain fair play on both sides. When Ketcham complained to Leupp about agitation on the part of a Rosebud Indian, George Fire Thunder, to prevent the signing of the petition, the Commissioner referred the complaint to the agent, who reported that Fire Thunder had gotten into a heated argument with one of the Catholic missionaries in which the Indian had used inflammatory language. But, he continued, "This is the only case of unseemly disturbance that has occurred. Fire Thunder is one of those old time returned students who hardly ever labors for a living, hangs around and finds fault with the Indian Office and management of affairs generally, and, as I am reliably informed, devotes most of his time to writing letters to the Indian Rights Association." The agent reported that the parties favoring the petition and those opposed to it had indulged in a great deal of unnecessary talk and argument. "Much was said on both sides that could have been left unsaid to the credit of both factions," he noted. At the time he wrote, the days seemed to be "wholly occupied in hustling for signatures to the respective petitions."[20]

The outcome at Pine Ridge and Rosebud was beyond Ketcham's expectations; his pessimism proved unfounded, for the Catholic Indians signed the petitions in larger numbers than in the previous year. The vindication delighted Ketcham. He reported:

> It will be remembered that last year our missionaries were accused of all manner of fraud, of bribery, misrepresentation, etc., in the matter of inducing Indians to sign the petitions then presented to them. This year the Commissioner himself supervised the signing of the petitions through his agents, and by rigorous regulations rendered even the suspicion of fraud and misrepresentation impossible. His action in this regard has vindicated our missionaries and placed their calumniators in a very unenviable light.[21]

The contracts for Pine Ridge, Rosebud, Crow Creek, and Tongue River were drawn up by the Indian Office and sent to the Secretary of the Interior in May with a recommendation for approval. When Roosevelt heard of the injunction suit entered against the Rosebud contract, he directed that all the other contracts pending be approved without delay. The Rosebud contract also was approved, on June 26, 1906, but payments under it were withheld pending the outcome of the suit.[22]

The final outcome of the 1906 canvass, reported by the Commissioner of Indian Affairs in his annual report was as follows:[23]

Osages: The business committee or council of the Osage Nation, by a unanimous vote on January 12, 1906, approved the request of the Bureau of Catholic Indian Missions, and contracts were made out for 65 students for St. John's school and 75 for St. Louis's school, at $125 per capita, a total of $17,000. Because the average attendance, however, fell below the figures in the contracts, only $11,995.25 was actually paid.

Menominees: The petition, signed by 100 members of the Menominee Tribe representing 269 shares out of 1,370 on the rolls, was returned on March 28, 1906. Because there was no government school on the reservation, the full request—170 pupils at $108—was granted, but because of low student attendance, the sum was cut to $13,922.20 from the $18,360 of the contract sum.

Quapaws: On March 16, 1906, the Quapaw council approved the request for the contract, which called for 10 students at $50 per capita (from funds appropriated under a treaty provision of May 13, 1833).

Cheyennes: The Tongue River Cheyennes did not sign the petition for the use of the funds in numbers large enough to support the original Catholic Bureau request for $7,020. The Catholic Bureau then modified its request and got a contract for 39 students at $108—a total of $4,212. (This meant a loss of 11 pupils at Tongue River, but the Bureau decided to reduce the number of pupils rather than the per capita payment.)[24]

Sioux:

Holy Rosary Mission, Pine Ridge: A petition dated March 16, 1906, was signed by 224 members of the tribe, representing 801 shares out of 6,703 on the rolls. This was sufficient to approve the request for a contract for 200 pupils at $108, or a total of $21,600.

Immaculate Conception School, Crow Creek: A petition, dated February 27, 1906, was signed by 21 members of the tribe, representing 81 shares out of 1,009 on the rolls. This was not sufficient to cover the contract for 65 children at $108 requested, and the Catholic Bureau reduced its request to 37 pupils; a contract was thus drawn for a total of $3,996, instead of $7,020. In addition, two Lower Brule students attended that school, but because the total attendance averaged only 36, settlement was made for $3,887.66.

St. Francis School, Rosebud: The petition, March 26, 1906, was signed by 212 Indians, representing 669 shares out of the 4,986 on the rolls. A contract was duly entered into for 250 pupils at $108 per capita or a total of $27,000. Because of the injunction suit, no payments had been made. Average attendance was 233, so that the total claim finally amounted to only $25,164.

Leupp explained the 1906 contracts at great length in an article in the *Outlook* in June, in order, as he said, "to give a prompt account of my stewardship." He worked out the figures for the Sioux and Cheyenne reservation contracts, indicating exactly the per capita amount due each Indian from the tribal funds, how much was spent for the government schools and how much contracted for the Catholic schools, and how those expenditures affected the remaining funds due to each Indian. The following section about the Rosebud Reservation gives an example of his care:

> On the Rosebud Reservation in South Dakota are 4,986 Indians, each of whom is entitled to $50.15 from the tribal income of the year. Of these, 669 are represented on a petition for a contract with St. Francis' Mission School, involving $27,000. The shares of the petitioners would make a total of $33,550.35, so that they will have a balance to their credit of $6,550.35, or $9.79 apiece. The non-petitioners number 4,317, controlling an aggregate of $216,497.55, and the Government schools cost this year $76,836, which will leave them a balance of $139,661.55, or $32.35 apiece. Had there been no diversion of money to the mission school, there would have been $173,211.90 to be divided between 4,986 Indians, at the rate of $34.73 each; so that the petitioners will be credited with $24.94 less, each, than they would have been but for their petition, while the shares of the non-petitioners suffer a deduction of $2.38.[25]

Leupp's calculations were an interesting bit of arithmetic, but they were academic, as he well knew. "As no money is actually paid out in any of these cases," an Indian Office memorandum noted, "the deductions are all on a purely theoretical basis, to be used in a final adjustment if one should be made hereafter." The point was not lost on the Catholics. The diminution of the funds due the Indians would take place only in the event of the distribution of the funds, Lusk noted in a letter to Ketcham, but as a matter of fact there would never be a distribution of the funds, since the particular funds in question were appropriated annually by Congress and would cease to be appropriated when the necessity for them ended. Lusk wanted Ketcham to be sure to explain this to the missionaries and the Indians.[26] It should be noted, too, that Leupp's calculations assumed that the cost of the government schools would remain the same if no money were diverted to the mission schools, but the cost certainly would have gone up substantially if the Catholics had been forced to close their schools on the reservations.

The problems involved in obtaining the requisite signatures on the petitions for the use of tribal funds harassed the Catholic missionaries, and the prelates who directed the Bureau of Catholic Indian Missions in the fall of 1906 tried once more to eliminate the petitions and have the contracts simply renewed from year to year. The case was especially critical among the Menominee Indians, and on October 8, 1906, the prelates formally appealed to the President that the petition then in circulation among the Menominees for a contract for the fiscal year ending June 30, 1907, be withdrawn and that similar petitions not be sent to the other tribes involved in contract schools. When Leupp answered the appeal negatively, asserting, first, that to renew contracts without new petitions would be "an act of bad faith to the Indians" because the past petitions specified one year as the period for which the Indians were approving use of their money and, second, that any arrangements extending beyond one year would result in administrative difficulties, Cardinal Gibbons sent a long letter to Roosevelt arguing against the Commissioner's position.[27]

Gibbons noted that the use of the trust funds was discretionary with the executive and insisted that the Indians, having once signified their desire to spend the trust funds for the mission schools, would not expect to be asked to sign each year. If the petition then circulating among the Menominees could be withdrawn, he said, the difficulties and hardships that would be encountered in getting signatures would be avoided and it would be better for "these illiterate and suspicious people." Nor did he think the administrative difficulties were so great that they could not be overcome. The financial burdens to the Catholics of operating the schools while awaiting contracts were great, for it had been necessary to borrow at heavy interest in order to keep the schools open. "This is one of the reasons why, with the best disposition possible on our part," Gibbons said, "we are unable to look upon the present policy otherwise than in the light of a policy of obstruction."[28]

Roosevelt was incensed by the Cardinal's letter, which appeared to him as an ungrateful response for all that he and Leupp had done for

JAMES CARDINAL GIBBONS. As Archbishop of Baltimore, Cardinal Gibbons was one of the board of prelates who directed the work of the Bureau of Catholic Indian Missions. He was a highly respected churchman, and his strong voice aided the cause of the Catholic mission schools. (Photograph from the Library of Congress)

THEODORE ROOSEVELT. As President of the United States, Roosevelt
acted favorably toward the demands of Catholics for protection of their
interests in Indian education. (Photograph from the Library of Congress)

the Catholic mission schools, and he fired back a long and strongly worded letter. He stood firmly behind Leupp and his policy and rejected most of Gibbons's arguments.[29]

> You speak of the policy of Commissioner Leupp as one of obstruction [he began]. I must with all emphasis say that Commissioner Leupp's action thruout this entire matter has had my hearty approval. Not only do I feel that he could not with propriety have acted otherwise than he did act, but I must add my great regret that information should have been given you which should cause you to speak of him in this way, inasmuch as he has uncomplainingly accepted attack after attack from members of various Protestant bodies because of the very fact that he has acted with such scrupulous fairness toward the Catholic schools. I hardly think you can be aware of the great pressure brought to bear upon Mr. Leupp —and, indeed, for that matter upon me also—to get us to abandon our position as regards the Catholic Indian schools. This pressure came from the leading representatives of many of the Protestant religious bodies. Mr. Leupp utterly disregarded these protests, as I disregarded them, because we shall pay no heed to any religious body when the question is of refusing to do injustice to, or I may add, of refusing to show favoritism to, any particular religious body. I accordingly wish it understood that I assume full responsibility for what Mr. Leupp has done in this matter.

Roosevelt took issue with Gibbons's assertion that the President had full discretionary authority for the use of the trust funds and could thus use them without petitions from the Indians. "I have announced not once but repeatedly," he wrote, "not only to Father Ketcham and to those interested in behalf of the Catholic schools, but also to the Protestant bodies interested in our attitude, that my whole course was based upon the theory of using these trust funds where I had power in accordance with the wishes of the Indians as expresst to me. I have never for one moment contemplated acting, and never shall act, without regard to the wishes of the Indians." To withdraw the petitions as Gibbons asked would be to abandon the only principle upon which he was justified in granting aid to the Catholic schools at all—the express will of the Indians. That had been the justification of his course in reply to the Episcopalian bishops who had visited him to protest. To dispense with the petitions would be fatal.

The President, however, was willing to concede one point. He directed the Indian Bureau to have the petition of the Menominees drawn up for five years rather than for one. "I trust that Father Ketcham's Bureau will turn in and help to make that petition a success, just as the petition a year ago was a success, and I am certain that if the Bureau turns in with this purpose, no difficulty whatever will be found really to exist." Roosevelt noted. As a final remark, the President said that Leupp was willing to do for the Menominee school what had been done elsewhere earlier—"to purchase the Catholic Indian school, and to cover the present teaching force, regardless of garb, into the classified service, so that they shall continue their work unchanged." [30]

Roosevelt's letter was a stern one, but Father Ketcham was not disturbed by it. "We have gained a great deal," he told Gibbons, "and this letter is written in such a way that if Protestants raise an outcry against what has been granted, it can be used very effectively to silence the outcry." Ketcham reported that he had talked with Leupp for several hours and that, aside from resentment at being called an obstructionist, the Commissioner was affable and ready to please the Catholics in any way possible, even to the point of advocating a revival of the old contract system if an opportunity ever arose. "I think we will have smooth sailing now for six months or a year," Ketcham said, "and I venture to say that the President will be disposed to accede with alacrity to the very next request your Eminence may make of him—provided, of course, there is no question of forcing Mr. Leupp to take back water in something that he has already done; and I have a hope that Mr. Leupp will not act precipitately hereafter." [31]

Father Ketcham went out to the Menominee reservation to promote the signing of the petition and found the Indians "completely filled with false ideas and fears" and apprehensive that by signing they might lose their rights to annuity payments. He charged that this state of mind had been induced by hostile agitation against the petition, and he urged the Commissioner to instruct the agent at Keshena to explain the situation clearly to the Indians who came to sign. But in the end it all turned out well for the Catholic school. Because the government school on the reservation could not accommodate all the Indian children, the Indian Bureau treated the mission school as supplemental to the government school and used Indian moneys on an equal basis between the two. In January 1907 a sufficient number of signatures were obtained to provide for the full amount required by the Menominee contract. [32]

There were continuing irritations about the petitions, for they were divisive on some of the reservations and there was always the possibility, feared by the Catholics, that insufficient signatures would be obtained to keep up the number of students in the schools from year to year. The injunction suit caused additional uncertainty about the petitions and the contracts. The delay in the decision postponed the signing of the petitions, and in 1907 the Catholic Bureau tried once again to get the President to waive the petitions for the year.[33] But in general the procedure became routine, as petitions were sent out by the Indian Office and contracts were issued for the Catholic mission schools.[34]

The final success in getting the contracts considerably softened Father Ketcham's views about Commissioner Leupp. Gone were the irritations that arose from delays and uncertainty—which the priest was inclined to attribute to Leupp—and the Commissioner's affability in dealing with the Catholic Bureau and his concern to see Catholic students treated fairly in the government schools created conditions of friendliness that must have been welcome to both sides. Ketcham used the occasion of his annual report of 1906 to express his opinion. "Commissioner Leupp," he wrote, "is undoubtedly the best and most efficient Indian Commissioner that the United States has ever had. He is, without question, the Indians' friend, and has practical and correct ideas as to what should be done for them. In the main, his views coincide with those of the Catholic missionaries, at least in so far as the education and temporal welfare of the Indians are concerned, and, far from being antagonistic, he is sympathetic towards the efforts of any religious body which conducts itself becomingly to Christianize, civilize and educate the Indians." While admitting that Leupp and the Bureau had not always agreed, he refused to charge this to prejudice on Leupp's part and declared that the Catholic schools were greatly indebted to him for his sense of justice and his fearlessness in carrying out his policy. Earlier, in the *Indian Sentinel*, Ketcham had urged Catholics to read Leupp's annual report—"the most remarkable as well as the best report ever issued from the Indian Office"—for in it the Commissioner advocated the gradual development of the Indians into civilization and the preservation of Indian music and art, with the object of making good Indians, not turning the Indians into white men. "In this contention," Ketcham noted, "he has espoused the traditional policy of Catholic missionaries in contradistinction to that of Protestant missionaries."[35]

Father Ketcham's new admiration for Commissioner Leupp, it should be noted, stood in dramatic contrast to the growing dissatisfaction that the Protestant Indian reform groups came to feel toward the man. The Indian Rights Association especially disagreed with some of Leupp's policies and came to feel that he was deliberately disregarding its advice and undermining its influence. When the Association's officers attempted to investigate an alleged violation of Indian rights at the Crow Agency in Montana, they were turned away, and the organization fought unsuccessfully to defeat the Senate confirmation of a special inspector sent to look into the charges. "Heretofore our endeavors to correct wrongs in the Indian Service," Herbert Welsh lamented, "have on the whole been sympathetically received by the Indian Department and our cooperation accepted. Mr. Leupp, in my opinion, clearly intends to drive the Indian Rights Association from the field." [36] Leupp was criticized severely, too, for his handling of a case involving Navajo Indian outlaws, who were arrested and confined without specific charges and without trial.[37] The Indian Rights Association was delighted when Leupp resigned in 1909. "It is a cause of congratulations," the president of the Association wrote, "that a commissioner whose egotism had made it impossible for him to catch other people's point of view, should give place to one of more open mind and a less assured infallibility." [38]

The Stephens Bill and the Lacey Act

Running parallel to the struggle on the reservations to procure the necessary petitions which would permit new contracts for the Catholic schools was a renewal of the drive in Congress for explicit prohibition of the use of tribal funds for mission schools. When the Fifty-ninth Congress opened on December 4, 1905, the Indian Rights Association was all set to start its agitation in what was practically a replay of the activity of a year earlier.

Having learned that attempts to gain their end by amendments to the annual Indian appropriation bills were destroyed by points of order (on the ground that the amendments proposed new legislation), the opponents of the Catholic schools now sought direct legislation. To that end, Congressman Stephens on December 13, 1905, introduced a bill (H.R. 7067) "to prohibit the use of Indian trust funds for the purpose of educating Indian children in sectarian schools." The bill would have extended the 1897 prohibition against appropriations for education in sectarian schools to cover trust funds or interest thereon held by the government for the benefit of any tribe, and the prohibition was to continue "so long as such trust fund belongs to any Indian tribe." [1]

The bill was referred to the Committee on Indian Affairs, of which Congressman Sherman was chairman and Stephens a member, and when it was due for consideration, the Indian Rights Association opened its campaign. "Stephens needs all the ammunition he can collect now to support his bill," Brosius wrote to Sniffen on January 13, 1906. Sniffen went through his regular routine. He wrote to the secretaries of the mission boards in New York, sending them a pertinent clipping from the *New York Evening Post* of January 18 and the names of the committee members to whom they were urged to write. Then he made a trip to New York to promote the campaign with the secretaries, and he took care as well to see Lyman Abbott of the *Outlook* and DeWitt Morrell. He received help, too, from Charles Saunders, who got four friends to join him in writing to nineteen members of Congress—seventy-six letters in all. Saunders reported that he had persuaded his friends to join the Indian Rights Association. But he warned: "We are interested particularly in the phase of the Indian question dealing with sectarian schools and join simply on that account. So you may expect us to drop out, if the Association lets up in this fight." Sniffen thanked Saunders for his help and assured him, "We are in this fight to the finish, and have no idea of relinquishing our efforts until a positive result has been accomplished." DeWitt Morrell kept up his fight against Sherman in New York state. "Sherman never can live down his dirty record, last year, in the Indian trust fund matters," he wrote; "not even if he grows wings." [2] Nor did Abbott let Sniffen down. In an article entitled "Indian Church Schools: The Way Out," he urged support of the Stephens bill, which he asserted was "simply an extension of the principle that Congress has already adopted, and may almost be said to have been suggested by the President's phrase that the practice of giving such appropriations 'will be continued unless the Congress should decree to the contrary.'" [3]

Sniffen was optimistic. "We have been pushing the trust fund matter pretty vigorously . . . ," he wrote to the missionary at Crow Creek Agency, "I have been interviewing people, as well as writing to others, urging that letters be sent to the members of the House Committee in favor of the bill. The responses to our requests were very satisfactory, and it now remains to be seen what effect it will have in Washington." Meanwhile Brosius kept a sharp lookout for possible slips in the capital. He noted that "Lusk of the Catholic Bureau here has been importuning the members of the Ind. Committee of the House of Rep., urging that they do not support Stephens' Bill on trust funds." Somehow, to Brosius and Sniffen, such action on the part of Catholics to influence legislators seemed inherently evil and the sign of a political conspiracy on the part of the Catholic Church, while their own identical efforts were never viewed in anything but a positive, wholesome light. Brosius wrote to Sniffen: "It now seems very important that every effort be made *at once* to secure the co-operation of persons over the country, notably the workers in the Church denominations in N. Y., so as to impress upon the different members of the Indian Committee (especially at this juncture) the importance of its passage." [4]

The Indian Committee of the House in its deliberations sought the views of Commissioner Leupp and sent him (through the Secretary of the Interior) a copy of the bill. Brosius watched its transit carefully.

"Stephens bill was promised to be forwarded to Commr. a week ago," he reported, "Today I inquired at Indian Office, and it was not there. I called upon Stephens who inquired at Sherman's Committee room— the clerk in charge stated to him that the bill was sent to Secretary on yesterday (Jan 31)—so we have to keep an eye all along the line—or it will be *knifed* by some Papist, I fear." [5]

Brosius need not have feared, for Leupp got the bill in good time and sent a detailed report to the Secretary of the Interior, who forwarded it to the committee, with his concurrence. Leupp noted the "acrimonious popular controversy" and the "excitement among some of the Indian tribes concerned"—all of which greatly increased the correspondence of the Indian Office—and he asserted that "a conclusive statement by the lawmaking body, one way or the other, would be most welcome." Not only would such action dissipate the dispute, but it would open the way for the passage of a law allotting the trust funds to individual Indians, who could then contribute to the support of the schools of their choice. Leupp could not resist, however, submitting a revised version of the bill, which he thought would make it simpler and clearer. [6]

While the Protestants repeated their old tactics to induce a public outcry in favor of Stephens's bill, the Catholics sat quietly on the sidelines. Since the bill was a separate piece of legislation, not an amendment to an essential appropriation bill, Ketcham hoped that it could be disposed of without any agitation at all, simply by "a sufficient number of friends on the Committee." At one point he discarded his optimistic stand and drew up a plan of action by which the Marquette League and other Catholic societies as well as individuals and bodies of citizens would flood the Indian Committee with resolutions, but before he started the campaign Sherman convinced him that it would do more harm than good and that the Stephens bill would be defeated without it. So nothing was done on a public scale—except for some agitation by Professor Scharf, who on his own initiative stirred up petitions in Milwaukee and other parts of the Midwest. [7]

The Committee voted down the Stephens bill on February 8. "Stephens told me the vote was strictly along party lines,—the Democrats voting *for* his bill," Brosius reported. "This shows that the Republicans have caucussed upon the measure and decided not to interfere with the President's order as published, in his letter last winter." Sniffen knew where to place the blame. "When an administration is concerned more about the question of votes than matters of right and wrong," he wrote to one partisan, "it is not surprising that such a political machine as the Roman Catholic Church has so often proved is treated with marked consideration." To another he wrote, "It seems to me that the Romanists can get pretty nearly anything they want from the Administration."[8]

Stephens's response to his defeat was to prepare another collection of documents to enter into the *Congressional Record*, an enterprise that Brosius and Sniffen endorsed and assisted by supplying materials. Ketcham, meanwhile, hoped that the issue would quietly stay killed. Unless it were revived in the Senate, he thought it would be very unfortunate if any further notice were taken of the bill. And even if some measure were introduced in the upper house, he felt confident that it would "be immediately laid to rest" through the efforts of Senator Aldrich.[9]

The Stephens bill to outlaw the use of trust funds for sectarian schools was but one part of a two-pronged attack. The other was the drive to segregate the funds, to individualize them, that is, so that each Indian would have control of his own share of the moneys and there would be no general tribal funds upon which contracts could be based. The two objectives ran a parallel course as the Protestants sought to cut out the Catholic use of money held in the United States Treasury in the Indians' name.

The prohibition embodied in the Stephens bill was a simple attempt to protect the principle of the separation of church and state as the Protestants understood it, a continuation in a direct line of the campaign against the Catholic contract schools that began about 1890. The allotment of the trust funds, on the other hand, had a more complex history. Fundamentally, the notion was an outgrowth of the movement to detribalize the Indians that had reached a peak in the General Allotment Act (Dawes Act) of 1887. The allotment of tribal reservation lands in severalty to individual Indians provided by that legislation was itself a capstone to a long period of agitation for individualizing landholdings. And the motivation—although land greed was satisfied by the results— was primarily philosophical. The idea was almost universally held by the white humanitarians and government officials who formulated American Indian policy that communal ownership and civilization could not coexist.[10]

It was soon realized that the Dawes Act had touched only one element of communal property—the land. Still in tribal control were the sizable sums of money held in trust for the tribes by the federal government. If individualization of landownership was essential for bringing

the Indians into the mainstream of American society, then individualization of the trust funds was logically necessary as well. Theodore
Roosevelt in his first state of the union message, on December 3, 1901,
announced: "The General Allotment Act is a mighty pulverizing engine
to break up the tribal mass. It acts directly upon the family and the
individual." Then he moved to the next step. "We should now break
up the tribal funds, doing for them what allotment does for the tribal
lands." [11] Roosevelt was merely echoing what had already become a
staple in the program of the Board of Indian Commissioners, the Indian
Rights Association, and the Lake Mohonk Conference. He in fact had
adopted the very phrases from an address of Merrill E. Gates, secretary
of the Board of Indian Commissioners and president of the Lake
Mohonk Conference, at Lake Mohonk in October 1900. Gates had pictured two actions to correct remaining evils about the Indians. The first
was to end polygamy and to regulate marriage relations among the
Indians. The second was to break up the tribal funds, which perpetuated
tribalism and thus the Indian problem. [12]

Gates continued to hammer at the same theme, spending a lot of his
opening remarks at the 1901 conference on the same topic, with stress
on the "intensely conservative force of vested funds in maintaining an
established order of things"; he provided the outline of a law that would
break up the tribal funds and place the individual shares to the credit
of the Indians in the Treasury. The following year he delivered a special
address entitled "The Next Great Step to Break up Tribal Funds into
Individual Holdings," in which he repeated his arguments, and the
Lake Mohonk Conference included in its platform a recommendation to
segregate the tribal funds into individual holdings "for the good of the
Indian and for his protection from the machinations of designing white
men." [13]

The Board of Indian Commissioners did not let the matter rest. It
argued in 1901 that "the expectation of annuities and of a share of undivided tribal funds keeps Indians out of civilized life and prevents them
from engaging in self-supporting labor. In general, it tends to pauperize
and degrade them." It was all part of "the new method" of Indian
policy, the breaking up of tribal reservation life and the training of the
Indians in the duties of American citizenship. "The conviction that
Indians can be educated to the right use of property as individuals,
and by *learning as individuals responsibility in the use of money*," the
Board of Indian Commissioners report said in 1902, "and the further
conviction that *relying upon annuity payments to the tribe as a mass*,

prevents the formation of any proper sense of responsibility for earning money, have led this board to advocate earnestly measures for breaking up these tribal funds." [14]

The Indian Rights Association, too, had been concerned about the communal tribal funds. Brosius in his report of 1902 spoke for the Association:

> Public opinion is gradually being aroused to the anomalous condition of the Indian tribes regarding the perpetual tribal relation— the transmitting from parent to child an interest in the communal property that of itself might continue forever. Such a system renders futile the best efforts to create a sense of individuality, and to arouse a feeling of responsibility among the members of the tribe, which is absolutely essential to advancement. The Indians themselves frequently appeal for a division of their trust funds. This shows an awakening of that proper sense of self-interest which controls civilized man. [15]

Such concern of the humanitarian reformers for the breaking up of the tribal funds, it should be noted, was reflected in the Indian Office. Commissioner Jones called the trust funds "a constant menace to the welfare of the Indian." He proposed in 1900 to set aside part of the funds to maintain the reservation schools and then to divide the rest among the individual Indians. Their interests in common thus broken up, the Indians would come to realize "their own responsibility and prepare to find their proper place in the body politic." [16]

This developing agitation for treating the trust funds as the communal lands had been treated in the Dawes Act did not end when the contract school issue arose at the end of 1904. Added then to these traditional reformers' views of the relation between the tribal funds and the progress of Indian civilization was a new and important element: segregation of the funds came to be looked upon, not only as good in itself for Indian welfare, but as an effective means of solving the problem caused by dipping into the tribal funds to support Catholic Indian schools. The Indian Rights Association and its supporters wanted to divide up the trust funds to prevent the Catholics from getting any money that came from the general tribal resources in which non-Catholic Indians had an interest. Government officials like Roosevelt and Leupp favored the division of the funds as a solution to an irritating problem, in which they were caught between Catholic pressures and anti-Catholic pressures. If all Indians controlled their own shares of the funds, they could spend them or not for missions schools as they chose.

As the controversy developed, the Indian Rights Association and its supporters adopted their double legislative program, first to immediately forestall Catholic use of the trust funds by an explicit Congressional prohibition (either through an amendment to the Indian appropriation bill or by a special piece of legislation), and second—or coordinately —to individualize the trust funds (again by an amendment to the appropriation bill or by a separate measure). Lyman Abbott saw the two measures as supplementary to each other and as taking "this troublesome question out of politics." Sniffen was more candid; in February 1905, when both types of amendment were under consideration in the Senate, he said: "If one or both remain in the bill when it passes, we are in a position to prevent any further diversion of the trust funds." [17] The anti-contract agitation was, in fact, the impetus that brought the segregation of the trust funds before Congress. Strongly recommended by Roosevelt in his letter of February 3, 1905, outlining the procedures for the use of the funds for contract schools, and urged repeatedly by Commissioner Leupp as *the* solution to the vexing problem of the contract schools, the breaking up of the tribal funds had a considerable legislative history.

In the midst of the uproar over the Stephens amendment and the Bard amendment in the third session of the Fifty-eighth Congress, a bill to segregate the trust funds (H.R. 18516) was introduced on January 30, 1905, by Congressman John F. Lacey, a standpat Republican member of the Indian Affairs Committee. The measure provided that the President at his discretion could designate tribes "sufficiently advanced in civilization to be prepared to receive and manage their individual shares of the tribal funds." Their funds were to be allotted in severalty to the members, each of whom would have his own account credited to him in the United States Treasury. When the President thought it would be in the best interests of the individual Indians, he could order the distribution and payment of such funds, or the interest thereon, to them. The bill was reported favorably with some minor amendments by the Committee on Indian Affairs on February 9. The Committee noted that some individual tribes had already had their funds allotted and argued that it would be better to pass general legislation that would allow the executive to act as occasions arose. "Your committee was of the opinion," the report concluded, "that the best interests of the Indian in the future required that the individuals should ultimately become members of the common citizenship of the country and that individualism among them should be encouraged." Attached to the report was a letter from Commissioner Leupp giving the bill his unqualified approval and one from the Secretary of the Interior, Ethan Allen Hitchcock, who concurred. For good measure the Committee added Roosevelt's letter of February 3, 1905, in which he had strongly supported Lacey's bill and hoped that Congress would immediately enact it.[18]

There was no hint in the Committee's report itself that the contract school issue had any part in the deliberations, but the question was raised by Congressman Stephens when the bill was finally considered by the House on March 3. He asked if the law would prevent the payment of trust funds to sectarian schools, and Lacey replied that it would so far as the money was allotted to individual Indians. "The bill," he said, "as far as it goes, is in that direction." When Stephens insisted and said he wanted the bill to go further and actually prohibit the use of trust funds for mission schools, Lacey retorted that that issue was not involved in his bill and that such an amendment would not be germane to it. The House passed the bill without further debate.[19] But there was no time left in the session to work the measure through the Senate, and it died with the end of the Congress. The Senate in the meantime, however, had made its own attempt to provide for the allotment of the tribal funds by means of an amendment to the Indian appropriation bill. The amendment, proposed by the Committee on Indian Affairs, was similar to Lacey's bill in the House, but it was struck down on a point of order offered by Senator John C. Spooner, of Wisconsin, on the basis that it was general legislation.[20]

Both sides thought it only a matter of time. Father Ketcham wrote to Father Digmann at St. Francis Mission early in April: "The Lacey Bill is a question of the future. I think that it will lead to the loss of the compensation we are receiving from tribal funds; but, in one sense of the word, it is a logical outcome of the contentions we made about the Indian's use of his own money, and taking into consideration the pressure that is behind it, I have an idea that it will become a law at the next session of Congress. Mr. Bonaparte is very much opposed to it, but I look upon it as one of the inevitables—it is like the fate of the Indians." Herbert Welsh, in a statement appealing for funds for the Indian Rights Association, reported his confidence that the efforts that were being made would result in the prompt passage of the Lacey bill.[21]

When the Fifty-ninth Congress convened in December 1905, even before Congressman Stephens could get his trust fund bill introduced, Lacey on December 7 reintroduced a bill to segregate the Indian funds (H.R. 5290). The wording of the bill was exactly that of the bill passed by the House in the previous Congress.[22]

While the new bill was still in committee and before any action had been taken on the measure, the waters were considerably muddied by an alternative bill (H.R. 17113) introduced on March 21, 1906, by Congressman Charles H. Burke, of South Dakota.[23] Instead of authorizing the President to designate tribes deemed fit for allotment of the funds and then to order the distribution of the funds—a wholesale action following the pattern of the Dawes Act—Burke's bill dealt only with *individuals* considered ready to manage their own affairs, and it included the following proviso:

> That no apportionment or allotment shall be made to any Indian until such Indian has first made an application therefor, and before any portion thereof is paid, such Indian shall file a release of any further interest in the tribal or trust funds of such tribe or tribes of which he may be a member, such release to cover any funds that may thereafter be deposited to the credit of such tribe or tribes.

Burke told Leupp that there was not much difference between his bill and Lacey's and believed that it would meet much less opposition. What he wanted with his bill was merely to get his ideas into the discussion; he did not want to eliminate Lacey's bill but hoped to amend it.[24]

Although Burke may have honestly felt that there was little difference between the two bills, the proponents of the Lacey bill were seriously upset by Burke's measure, for it practically eliminated the general segregation of the funds they desired by requiring that the individual Indian make application for the allotment. Brosius quickly addressed letters to Congressmen Sherman, Lacey, and Stephens, in which he spoke forcefully against Burke's bill. He argued that the principal contention of the friends of the Indian was that the tribal relation "defeats the effort for individual advancement and responsibility, a weakness so apparent in all systems of communal ownership of property." Burke's bill would not remedy that evil, for it would affect only those Indians who applied for the allotment of their pro rata share of money. And precisely those who needed the law would be least likely to take advantage of it. "The members of a tribe that might have an incentive to seek for a separation from the tribal yoke," he said, "will quite naturally be of the brighter element, and not so much in need of legislation of this character to stir them to action, while on the other hand those Indians who ought to be spurred to action and greater individual effort will make no application for a pro-rata share under the operation of the proposed legislation." Moreover, Brosius was afraid that the provision calling for the Indians to give up their right to any future tribal funds would deter individuals who might otherwise be interested. "In brief," he concluded, "the bill seems to fail in meeting the present needs of tribal Indians, as viewed from the standpoint of seeking to make independent and self-supporting Red Men." In a postscript he urged the Congressmen to support instead Lacey's bill, H.R. 5290. The president of the Indian Rights Association, Charles C. Binney, sent a letter to all members of Congress urging support of the Lacey bill, arguing as Brosius had done on the basis of civilizing the Indians.[25]

Although the arguments against Burke's bill and in favor of Lacey's were all couched in the old reformist terms, looking to the civilizing influence of private property and condemning the debilitating effects of communal ownership of the trust funds, the different effect of the two bills on the contract school issue was much in the minds of the Indian Rights Association officers. Sniffen thought that, while the Burke bill would provide for individual cases, "yet by keeping the fund intact it could be more readily reached by such schemes as the diversion for support of sectarian schools, than if the segregation were made."[26]

Burke sent Binney a copy of his bill and asked for his comments, and Binney replied with a long letter almost identical with the one Brosius had written to Sherman, Lacey, and Stephens. Binney's letter elicited in turn a comprehensive defense of his position from Burke, who argued that "it is very much easier to legislate by degrees, than it is to undo what may be done by going too far in enacting new legislation." He told Binney that he thought it was precisely the brighter element that the bill should be aimed at, for only they had reached the stage of advancement and civilization that made them capable of managing their own affairs. He did not believe, he said, that an Indian should be forced to separate himself from his tribe. Moreover, and this was an important point, his provision had some chance of being passed in Congress, whereas the Lacey one did not. Burke ended by urging the advocates of the Lacey proposition to support the bill as it was reported in its revised form.[27]

The action of the Committee on Indian Affairs was a victory for Burke, a defeat for Lacey. The Committee, while keeping the same number of the bill that Lacey had introduced, voted to strike out everything after the enacting clause of the original bill and substitute Burke's measure.[28] When the bill was reported on April 6, 1906, Lacey somewhat lamely explained what had been done. Although he himself held firm to his belief that the distribution of the trust funds ought not to be wholly dependent upon the application of the individual Indian but that the President should be authorized on his own initiative to designate Indians to receive the allotments, the Committee had decided otherwise. And by limiting the allotments to Indians who applied for them, the Treasury would be spared the expense and labor of opening a large number of individual accounts. There was only desultory debate on the floor of the House. Questions were raised about the relation of the allotment of land to the allotment of trust funds, but there was no mention of the sectarian schools. Lacey ended by saying that the bill certainly was "good as far as it goes." The bill passed on May 7, 1906, and was sent to the Senate for concurrence.[29]

Brosius was unhappy. "The primary object sought by the Lacey Bill—that of breaking up the communal interests in the tribal funds, as the allotment of lands has done for the tribal holdings of realty—," he wrote, "is altogether defeated by the measure adopted by the House of Representatives. It is inconceiveable from a disinterested standpoint, why the Committee should not urge the principle involved in the Lacey measure."[30]

It is difficult to determine exactly why the switch occurred and how much the sectarian Indian school issue had to do with it. The same forces that lay behind the Burke Act of 1906, which modified the Dawes Act by postponing citizenship for allotted Indians, seem to have been at work here (as Burke's sponsorship of the new measure and his arguments in support of it make clear). The absolute faith of the Indian Rights Association and similar humanitarian reformers in the immediate civilizing power of a division of tribal property—be it land or money—was not held by Congress, for the experience of allotment of land under the Dawes Act indicated that not all Indians were ready for the sudden immersion into the white man's economic world. Congressman Sherman, powerful as chairman of the Indian Committee, was reported to disapprove of the Lacey bill, and Commissioner Leupp, who the Indian Rights Association promoters hoped would stand firm for Lacey's proposal, was apparently willing to settle for Burke's. Lacey himself was said to have agreed to the revision rather than have his bill laid aside altogether.[31]

Brosius, as might be expected, drew his own conclusions. "I feel quite sure," he wrote to Sniffen, "that the influence of the R. C. [Roman Catholics] has wrought the change in the minds of the Committee." There is no record, however, of public agitation on the part of the Catholics against the original Lacey bill or for the Burke revision, for they were caught on the principle of individual choice for the Indians on which they based their argument for use of the trust funds. While the revised Lacey bill was pending in the Senate, Lusk wrote to Ketcham about it: "I don't see how it can hurt us much, nor can I see how it would be possible for us to make any headway in opposition to its passage, for it seems a reasonable and proper thing when an Indian is capable of managing his own affairs that he should be permitted to do so, and in doing so, to be allowed the use of his own money."[32]

The Senate delayed action on the bill until the second session of the Fifty-ninth Congress. Then on December 17, 1906, Senator Moses E. Clapp, of Minnesota, for the Committee on Indian Affairs, reported the bill with amendments. The Committee had replaced the President with the Secretary of the Interior, who was "authorized and directed" to designate Indians to receive the allotments. And the allottee was permitted to retain his right to subsequent additions to the trust funds instead of signing away those rights when receiving his allotment of funds. When the Senate came to consider the bill on February 14, however, it recommitted it to the Committee. When the Committee returned it the following day, it had inserted a new section, which authorized the Secretary of the Interior to pay shares of the trust funds to "any Indian who is blind, crippled, decrepit, or helpless from old age, disease, or accident."[33] This still did not quite satisfy the Senate. During the consideration of the Committee's report on February 15, Senator Spooner observed that the language of the bill was mainly permissive but that the first section of the bill contained the mandatory phrase "authorized and directed," and he moved to strike out the words "and directed," an amendment Senator Clapp accepted. Once more the bill was recommitted to the Committee, which returned it with Spooner's amendment included, and in that form it passed the Senate on February 18.[34]

The House, however, refused to accede to the Senate amendments, and the bill was sent to a conference committee, which in general accepted the Senate amendments. The House members of the committee, in reporting the results to the House, noted two major differences between the House and Senate versions of the bill—the change from the President to the Secretary of the Interior in making the allotments and the retention by the Indian allottees of rights to future additions to the trust funds. Both of these changes were supported by the conferees. The House and Senate both agreed to the conference report on February 25, and the bill became law on March 2.[35]

The Indian Rights Association was displeased with the outcome. Although it asked its supporters to push for the passage of the bill (no doubt thinking that something was better than nothing), it let its dissatisfaction be known and urged a return to the principles of the original Lacey bill. After the measure became law, the Indian Rights Association did not relent in its advocacy of a more radical law. The Lacey Act did "not meet the present need," for it did not correct the enervating effects of communal property.[36]

The reformers kept urging. The Board of Indian Commissioners in 1907, 1908, and 1909 repeated its recommendations and its arguments.[37] These moves disturbed the Catholic Bureau, for it had become accustomed to the support of the schools from the trust fund contracts and did not want to close its schools for lack of that financial aid. Ketcham's biggest fright came in 1909. He noticed a newspaper dispatch in the *Washington Post* for February 20, 1909, about the report and recommendations of a special committee of the Board of Indian Commissioners, of which Archbishop Ryan was a member. The report indicated that the Board planned to do everything in its power to have the tribal funds broken up and distributed to the Indians, and Ryan's agreement was implied. Ketcham was shocked, and he relayed his dismay to Ryan. "I have a hope that, notwithstanding the recommendation of the Commissioners, we may be able to prevent such a disastrous thing being done by Congress," he wrote. And he continued:

Your Grace is aware that if this is done we will lose our eight large schools that are supported out of these Tribal Funds. In addition to these eight, I hoped we might have others. The Indian Rights Association and the Commissioners for a number of years have been agitating this question. They use specious reasoning to make their position plausible, but there is no doubt that the chief object the manipulators have in view is the depriving us of any help in our educational work from these funds. This is clear to me by things that have been said to me by Commissioner Leupp, by Mr.

Brosius and by Dr. Merrill E. Gates. I trust your Grace will not forbid me to do all that I can in Congress toward preventing this being done. If the Funds are broken up, the first thing in order will be for the Bureau to determine upon a policy of discontinuing its schools, for experience has proved that they cannot be kept up by the voluntary offerings of the faithful, and even with Mother Katharine's help, all of them would not have been kept up this long had we not secured the valuable assistance from the Tribal Funds.[38]

But, as so often happened, Ketcham's fears evaporated. It is true that in 1911 Brosius, noting the "partial success" and the "makeshift substitute" of the Lacey Act of 1907, declared that the time had arrived for a new attempt to divide up the tribal funds, and he reported that the Indian Office had a change of opinion regarding the advisability of such legislation. In January of that year Secretary of the Interior Richard A. Ballinger sent to the House Committee on Indian Affairs the draft of a bill to amend the Lacey Act by broadening the classes of Indians to whom the Secretary could pay pro rata shares of the trust funds. Although the committee reported the bill favorably, the House did not act.[39] And, in fact, no further legislation came from Congress to divide the communal trust funds of the tribes. The Catholic Bureau continued unabated to draw upon them for its mission schools. It had won another victory.

Quick Bear v. Leupp

FROM the first intimation of renewal of federal support for Catholic mission schools, the idea kept popping up in the minds of the schools' opponents that the way to end the practice was by a court injunction. Such a legal stoppage was part of Bishop Hare's original suggestions, and the Indian Rights Association initially gave the idea strong support, looking at legal action as a means of arousing public sentiment against the Catholic schools even if the suit was lost. Roosevelt and Leupp both contributed to the movement by their willingness—and in Leupp's case one might almost say eagerness—to have the issue settled once and for all by the courts. It was start and stop on the matter, however, as other measures were given priority.

Because the results were not very satisfying when Sniffen sounded out the secretaries of the mission boards in December 1904 about the possibility of their assuming the costs of legal proceedings, the Executive Committee of the Indian Rights Association at its meeting of January 4, 1905, referred the question of instituting a suit to its Law Committee, with power to act. The Law Committee on February 1 unanimously reported against doing anything for the present. The law, the Committee thought, gave the President and the Secretary of the Interior discretion in the use of the Indian funds in their hands. Unless something could be found on which to build a strong case, the Committee saw no use in litigation. "The only advantage would be a greater ventilation of the question," it said, "and it did not seem desirable that the Association should attempt to advertise itself by what would necessarily be a rebuff in the courts." [1] So the matter rested in an uneasy limbo, while the Indian Rights Association and its supporters tried other roads to reach their goal—hoping for adverse rulings from the Attorney General, a change of heart on the part of Roosevelt and the Commissioner of Indian Affairs, Congressional action to prohibit the use of the trust funds for sectarian schools, obstruction of the petitions upon which the contracts were based, or, finally, the segregation of the funds into the hands of individuals, so that there would no longer be any tribal funds upon which the Catholics could draw. As each of these avenues was blocked, it was inevitable that a new look would be given to the possibility of an injunction.

The idea seems to have been raised in an effective way by the Reverend Aaron B. Clark at Rosebud, who wrote to Sniffen in early March 1906 urging a suit. When Sniffen broached the subject with Brosius, the Washington agent sent a negative reply, however. He thought there was no more likelihood of successful proceedings than there had been a year before when the Law Committee had voted the idea down, but he suggested approaching the Law Committee again. Soon Clark arrived in the East to promote his views. He stopped first in Philadelphia to see Sniffen, who remarked: "I will be very much surprised if Mr. Clark's visit to the East, Washington in particular, does not result in a pretty vigorous stirring up of the Trust Fund matter. He is loaded to the muzzle, and when he gets properly started something is likely to happen." [2] Sniffen, meanwhile, began to sound out the president of the Indian Rights Association, Charles C. Binney, who was himself a lawyer, and the Law Committee. The Committee began to go over the matter again to see if there was "any good ground" for instituting a suit. [3]

Each rebuff to the Indian Rights Association's campaign against the Catholic use of the tribal funds moved the Association forward another step toward legal action. The substitution of Burke's measure for allotting the trust funds in place of the Lacey measure supported by the Indian Rights Association was one such block, and Brosius on April 13 decided that "it appears all the more advisable to bring that injunction suit to prevent the use of trust and treaty funds." And on the seventeenth he reported confidentially to Sniffen that he had been told, "quite reliably," that the Attorney General believed that the law would not sustain use of the *treaty* funds, but since the President had promised them to the Catholics for the current year, the Attorney General thought it wise not to render a decision lest he embarrass the administration. "The President," Brosius concluded, "is about as likely to use the treaty funds for next fiscal year, as otherwise—change his mind *again*, unless he is prohibited *now* from doing so. They have invited a trial and decision of the case in Court, and ought not to complain if injunction is resorted to." Sniffen's reasoning was the same. He wrote to Charles Saunders after the suit had been decided upon: "All efforts to accomplish anything through legislation at the present session seems to be useless; the powers that be evidently feel that the influence of certain ecclesiastics is too strong to be resisted." [4]

On April 21 the decision was made. The Law Committee voted: "That Mr. Binney, as a member of this committee, be authorized and requested to institute such proceedings as may be necessary to determine the legality of the use of treaty funds for sectarian schools, and that all necessary disbursements and expenses required for this purpose will be paid by the Association." [5]

To be sure, there was risk involved. If the courts decided that even the treaty funds could be used, the Catholics would benefit, for the President had outlawed their use after one year. Brosius thought there was no possibility of such a decision, and anyway, the President's prohibition after a year could not be depended upon. Moreover, Leupp was favorable to the suit and promised to supply the necessary information. Nor could the advantages of a public court case be forgotten. "It seems to me that the proposed suit ought to do more than anything yet attempted in the way of bringing this matter before the public," Sniffen asserted, "and should it be decided against us, then the sentiment ought to be sufficiently strong to bring about some definite action on the part of Congress. It seems to me," he added, "it is better to have the matter settled than to let it remain in the present uncertain state." [6]

Binney, who was to handle the case, went to Washington to confer with Brosius and with Leupp. Out of the conferences came a couple of essential decisions about the suit. After talking with Leupp, Binney concluded that trust funds as well as treaty funds should be included in the injunction, on the ground that there was "some chance that the courts may hold the trust funds are annually appropriated, although not mentioned in the 'budget.'" And it was determined to bring the action against the Rosebud contract only, assuming that what was decided by the courts in the one case would be applicable to all. [7]

One thing remained to be done: to find some Rosebud Indians in whose name the Indian Rights Association could enter the suit. At first it was thought that the business council of the tribe should appeal for action, but since some of the members might possibly be Catholics, that plan was deemed infeasible. What was needed was the names of some Indians, as representative members of the tribe, who could give Brosius power of attorney to bring the action on their behalf and on behalf of other members of the tribe. Brosius appealed to Clark to pick out the proper Indians. If Clark did not intend to return immediately to the West, Brosius wanted the name of "the proper white person to write, so that a proper power of attorney can be filled out and executed by the Indian members of the tribe." Clark went in person to Washington to give Brosius the data he needed.[8]

The Indian Rights Association liked to act in public as though it were no more than the helpful agent of the Indians in the case, and it would begin its announcements about having undertaken the suit with the phrase "at the earnest request of representative Rosebud Indians."[9] But it was clear to all, as Leupp wrote in the *Outlook*, that the suit was brought "by three Indians as nominal complainants, but actually by the Indian Rights Association." The Indian Rights Association, however, wanted to keep its actions secret until the suit was actually entered, and Sniffen wrote in strictest confidence to his friends not to mention the suit. "It will be all the more of a surprise to our friends, the enemy," he wrote to one, "when it is made known through the regular channels."[10]

At last all was ready. Just after noon on May 11, 1906, Brosius as solicitor for the plaintiffs, filed a bill in equity in the Supreme Court of the District of Columbia.[11] The bill read:

> REUBEN QUICK BEAR, RALPH EAGLE FEATHER and CHARLES TACKETT, on behalf of themselves and all other members of the Sioux Tribe of Indians of the Rosebud Agency, S. D., *Plaintiffs*
>
> *vs.*
>
> FRANCIS E. LEUPP, Commissioner of Indian Affairs, ETHAN ALLEN HITCHCOCK, Secretary of the Interior, LESLIE M. SHAW, Secretary of the Treasury, CHARLES H. TREAT, Treasurer of the United States, and ROBERT J. TRACEWELL, Comptroller of the Treasury, *Defendants*.[12]

After a statement of the treaties and laws which set up the trust fund and the treaty fund of the Sioux and citation of the act of June 7, 1897, which set the Congressional policy of no appropriations for any sectarian schools, the case was stated. It was charged that Leupp had made or intended to make a contract with the Bureau of Catholic Indian Missions for the St. Francis Mission Boarding School on the Rosebud Reservation for the fiscal year ending June 30, 1906, with compensation to be paid out of the trust or treaty funds, or from both. Such payments were unlawful diversions of the funds and contrary to the Congressional policy of 1897 and would be of great injury to the plaintiffs and other Indians of the Rosebud Agency by seriously depleting the funds, in which they had a common interest. They had never requested nor authorized any payment to the Catholic Bureau.

The plaintiffs then asked, as relief, a permanent injunction against Leupp to restrain him from executing any contract with the Catholic Bureau for St. Francis School, against Leupp and Hitchcock to restrain them from paying out any money from the Sioux funds to the Catholics, and against Shaw, Treat, and Tracewell to enjoin them from drawing any money from the Treasury or paying warrants in favor of the Catholic Bureau for the mission school at Rosebud. In an affidavit attached, the three Indians stated that the petitions in support of the contracts had been signed by a minority of tribe and that three-fourths of the tribe were opposed to such use of the funds.

Brosius, as soon as the bill was filed, passed out prepared statements to the press, and he ordered one hundred extra copies of the bill to circulate to supporters. Sniffen, for his part, corresponded with newspaper editors and other friends, informing them of the suit and sending to many a copy of the bill of injunction.[13]

It was not immediately clear what the response of the defendants would be or just how they would handle the case. The Catholic Bureau, of course, hoped that the Department of Justice would be asked to defend the government officials, and Lusk conferred with Senator Aldrich (who suggested that Cardinal Gibbons write to the President urging a vigorous defense) and with Charles W. Russell of the Attorney General's office. If the Department of Justice were indeed called upon, Russell thought the work would fall to him. "He does not believe it will be necessary for us to employ a lawyer," Lusk wrote to Ketcham, who was absent from Washington, "as, in his opinion, our interests will be fully looked after by whoever represented the Government."[14]

On May 16, Secretary of the Interior Hitchcock formally requested the Attorney General to defend him and the Commissioner of Indian Affairs in the suit. The Attorney General's office directed Daniel W. Baker, United States Attorney for the District of Columbia, to take charge of the case, with Stuart McNamara as an assistant.[15] The Catholic Bureau for a short while kept to its original opinion that it would not need to employ counsel since the Department of Justice would look after its interests. Bonaparte, however, while praising Baker, strongly advised Ketcham that it would be useful to have associated with him in the case "someone more directly identified with our interests and perhaps of wider professional experience." He recommended a lawyer from Baltimore, Edgar H. Gans, as remarkably well suited for the task and reported that the Attorney General had indicated he would be happy to associate as special counsel with Mr. Baker anyone the Catholic Bureau wished to employ, provided the Bureau paid the fees. The actual defense of the case thus came to rest on Gans as special counsel. The Marquette League agreed to bear the costs, and Cardinal Gibbons gave his approval.[16] There was some question about whether the government lawyers would agree to accept all the information that Gans and the Catholics wanted to put into the answer to the bill and whether, if they did not, the Bureau should file a separate answer on its own behalf, but in the end Gans went forward with the case simply in his position as special counsel. The attorneys for the government appeared to be willing to let him handle the arguments as he saw fit. Brosius reported that McNamara had said that since there was "a sectarian phase to the case," he was glad not to have to argue it himself and was quite willing for Gans to take charge.[17]

There was long delay. The Indian Rights Association suspected that it was intentional and meant to aid the defendants, but Leupp assured Brosius that the postponement was the result only of the heavy schedule of business in the Department of Justice. The Indian Rights Association, however, took the precaution of amending its bill, so that it would apply to any future contract and not only to the one for 1906.[18]

The delay also disturbed the Catholics, for it added further confusion to the problem of the 1906 contracts. These contracts had been requested in June 1905, the petitions had been returned to the Indian Office early in 1906, yet no approval of the contracts was immediately forthcoming. Only when the injunction was entered did the Indian Office act, asking the President on May 26 to approve the contracts. Being assured that the justices would not consider the execution of the contracts a discourtesy to the court, pending the hearing of the case, he approved the contracts for 1906. But the 1907 contracts were up in the air. Even if the suit were won, would there be time to gather the petitions and get the contracts issued in time? Not until the middle of December did Leupp sign and file the answer drawn up by Gans.[19]

The defendants' answer explicitly denied that the contracts violated any law of Congress and that the payments under the contracts would deplete the funds or diminish the payments that might be made to the plaintiffs. It then supplied a long exposition of the history of the contracts, an analysis of the treaties and laws involved in the trust funds and the treaty funds for the Sioux, and citations of the laws of the 1890s by which the appropriations for contract schools had gradually been eliminated. It argued that there was no fundamental difference between the trust funds and the treaty funds, insofar as they were not public money of the United States but belonged instead to the Indians, and that all the prohibitions and limitations placed by Congress on the executive in making payments to sectarian schools did not apply at all to these funds.[20]

In a decision dated April 15, 1907, Justice Ashley M. Gould of the Supreme Court of the District of Columbia rendered his opinion. He held that the trust funds could be used but that the treaty funds could not.[21]

Gans was terribly disappointed, and he wrote to Bonaparte, who on December 12, 1906, had been appointed Attorney General: "The decision comes as somewhat of a surprise to us, because Father Ketcham, Mr. McNamara and myself all received the very decided impression at the time of the argument that Mr. Justice Gould was entirely impressed with the correctness of our views, and we fully expected a decision in our favor." He wrote immediately to McNamara telling him to appeal the case insofar as it concerned the treaty funds. "Although the case is an uphill one, as I told you weeks ago," he wrote to Ketcham, "there is no reason for giving up the fight until the last effort has been made."[22] Meanwhile the Indian Rights Association, too, was displeased with the outcome and decided to appeal the part of the decision that pertained to the use of the trust funds.[23]

The cross appeals of the government and the Indian Rights Association were filed in the United States Court of Appeals of the District of Columbia on May 9, 1907. Both sides presented briefs on the double case, reasserting the timeworn arguments for and against the use of the trust funds and the treaty funds for sectarian schools. Brosius and Binney presented the argument before the court for the Indian Rights Association, and Gans, Baker, and McNamara again represented the government and the Catholic Bureau. The brief on behalf of Quick Bear tried to extend the case by tying it to the constitutional prohibition against an "establishment of religion." While admitting that there was no explicit constitutional issue at stake, the brief argued that Congress had been influenced in cutting off the appropriations for the contract schools by "other reasons, more fundamental" than the source of funds and that the foremost of these reasons was clearly connected with the First Amendment. If there was to be a "wall of separation" built between the United States and every religious denomination, it said, it followed that the government was bound to follow "an undenominational rule of conduct" and could never act in a sectarian capacity either in the use of its own funds or as trustee for the funds of others. While it may have been desirable for the government to aid the contract schools as a temporary expedient, this was action in a sectarian capacity and too clearly inconsistent with a thoroughly undenominational rule of conduct and with the spirit of the Constitution to be maintained any longer than necessary.[24]

The Court of Appeals adjourned for the summer months before it handed down its decision, and it was not until November 29, 1907, that Justice Daniel Thew Wright, of the Supreme Court of the District of Columbia, who sat in the hearing in place of Justice Charles H. Robb, delivered the opinion.[25] The court analyzed in considerable detail the nature and character of the two funds involved, recalling the provisions of the Sioux treaty of 1868, which provided for educational facilities for a set period of years (a provision extended in 1889), and the act of 1889, which provided the three-million-dollar Sioux trust fund in return for the cession of parts of the Great Sioux Reserve. In creating these funds, the court argued, Congress had "made public money Indian money." In the one instance it paid a treaty debt, in the other a debt for lands. "The money," it said, "has changed owners; what had been money of the public in the Treasury of the United States is now money of the Indians in the Treasury." These moneys were quite distinct from the gratuitous appropriations made by Congress for Indian education, and the court spoke at length about the distinction between the two classes of money. It cited the acts of Congress year by year, showing that the Indian appropriation acts listed separately and distinctly the funds intended for fulfilling treaty stipulations and those for "support of schools." And it noted that the provisos through the 1890s reducing the amount that could be used for contract schools and the final prohibition against using any of them for sectarian education were all attached to the second class of appropriations, that is, to the gratuitous grant of public funds for Indian education. In regard to the first group of funds, the government acted as a "trustee," in the second as a "voluntary donor." Congress could attach restrictions to the latter without applying the limitations to the former. And, the court said, that is what Congress had done.

The court then considered the statement "It is hereby declared to be the settled policy of the government to hereafter make no appropriation whatever for education in any sectarian school," found in the acts of 1896 and 1897. Did it, as the complainants contended, limit Congress as thoroughly as a direct legislative prohibition? The court said no, for it noted that the statements were in fact followed in succeeding years by a continued (although reduced) appropriation for the contract schools. Thus, though the policy was enunciated in 1896, in 1897 Congress made such appropriations; the policy was repeated in 1897, but new appropriations were made in 1898. So the court concluded: "If the declaration of 1896 was then intended as announcing a permanent policy to control the future, Congress in 1897, in its wisdom, saw the necessity of departing from it and wiped it out by appropriating in that year; and if the declaration of 1897 was currently intended as announcing a permanent policy for the future, it in turn was wiped out by appropriating in 1898; so that, as the matter appears, these declarations both stand nullified; and there remains nothing declarative of policy save in the act of 1898 the expression, 'this being the final appropriation for sectarian schools.'" And all of this, anyway, applied only to the gratuity, not to the trust or treaty funds.

For the sake of argument, the court was willing to assume that the provisos in the laws did announce "a definite, fixed, and permanent policy." But what precisely was that policy? "Is it," the court asked, "the policy of depriving a religious Indian of the liberty of educating his children in a school of his own sect, at the cost of his own money? Or is it the policy of declining to educate an Indian in religious schools gratuitously, at the cost of public donations, which are not his and to which he had no claim as matter of right?" The questions, of course, were rhetorical.

The First Amendment to the Constitution, the court concluded, rather than prohibiting the Indians' use of trust or treaty funds for education of their children in sectarian schools, in fact supported it. "It seems inconceivable," the decision read, "that Congress shall have intended to prohibit them from receiving religious education at their own cost, if they desire it; such an intent would be one to 'prohibit the free exercise of religion' amongst the Indians; and such would be the effect of the construction for which the complainants contend." The court had set the argument of the Indian Rights Association on its head.

The court then concluded: "We are therefore of the opinion that the so-called declaration of policy, the limitations and restrictions found in the various appropriation acts under the title 'Support of Schools,' concern only moneys appropriated under that particular title,—that is to say, the gratuitous appropriations of public money to the cause of Indian education,—and have nothing to do with the expenditure of the Indian 'treaty fund,' nor with the proceeds of the Indian 'trust fund.'" There was no difference between the two funds in this regard, so the decision affected both alike. The Court of Appeals affirmed the decree of the lower court insofar as it denied the injunction respecting the trust funds and reversed it insofar as it enjoined payment from the treaty funds. The lower court was directed to dismiss the bill, at the cost of the complainants.

Gans was much relieved by the decision. "We were fighting against such heavy odds, considering the adverse opinions of the Attorney-General's office, and the traditions of the Indian Bureau," he confided to Ketcham, "that I felt at times we would not succeed, although I always felt confident the position we took was not only just, but legally right." To Gans, Ketcham sent the "most earnest congratulations on the signal victory for right and justice." [26]

The effect of the decision upon the payment of funds to the Bureau of Catholic Indian Missions for the contract schools was not immediately clear. The payment had been withheld on the St. Francis contract for 1906 after the injunction was requested, and the contracts for 1907 were held up pending the outcome of the suit. Gans took the issue much to heart because he believed that the government owed the schools the money, for they had gone ahead with their services as though the contracts had been made. If, as was likely, the case were appealed to the Supreme Court, the decision might not be reached for another year or more and the result would be "extremely disastrous" to the missions. He wanted Attorney General Bonaparte to prevail upon the President to withdraw his prohibition against paying out treaty funds beyond the 1906 fiscal year until the courts had decided the issue. The loss from the contracts for 1907 and 1908 would amount to about two hundred thousand dollars, "simply on account of the filing of a bill which the Court of Appeals and the Supreme Court of the United States would dismiss." [27] Bonaparte sent a copy of Gans's letter to the Secretary of the Interior and informed him that he could find no objection whatever to making the contracts for the current year. The original injunction applied only to the single school of St. Francis, and when the mandate from the Court of Appeals went down, even that injunction would be dissolved. Further appeal to the Supreme Court would delay the decision, but he felt sure that the appeal would not be sustained. Bonaparte was less sure about the 1907 contracts, thinking that perhaps recourse might have to be made to Congress for those payments. [28]

The Indian Rights Association hesitated about appealing the case to the Supreme Court. Dubois Miller of the Law Committee did not think that it was worthwhile to appeal; Binney was of a different mind, but after the two men consulted about the matter, they decided to go ahead, and Binney started to prepare a brief.[29] The brief, bearing the names of Binney as solicitor for appellants, with Miller and Hampton L. Carson as counsel, was largely a repetition of the brief submitted to the Court of Appeals. The chief argument was that there was no difference between the trust and treaty funds held by the government for the Indians and the public moneys appropriated by Congress and that the Congressional prohibition against spending money for education in sectarian schools applied to all equally.[30]

The defendants' brief was submitted again by Gans as special counsel. He was assisted this time by Henry M. Hoyt, Solicitor General of the United States, although Gans himself did most of the work. As he explained to Hoyt, "You have probably already seen from the record that this is a case in which the Government of the United States is somewhat a neutral party, the real defendant being the Catholic Indian Bureau. It was this condition of affairs that led President Roosevelt to appoint me a special counsel, so as to represent as vigorously as possible the standpoint of the Catholic Bureau." He drew up the brief, following in substance the brief submitted to the Court of Appeals, although Hoyt requested a chance to look at the typewritten draft or the proofs of the brief before it was printed. In the presentation before the Supreme Court Gans was to develop the case fully and take about an hour and a half, while Hoyt would close the case, using twenty to thirty minutes. Attorney General Bonaparte took no part in arguing the case, but his name was entered ahead of Hoyt's on the brief.[31] Bonaparte, however, signed the motion to advance the hearing of the case, which Gans had drawn up at his suggestion and which was submitted for the defendants late in January. The motion noted the embarrassment faced by the fiscal officers of the government because of the uncertain status of the contracts and the heavy loss that would be incurred by the Catholic Indian schools by continued delay in perfecting the contracts, and it urged a hearing of the case in time for the contracts for 1908 to be issued. The case was argued before the Supreme Court on February 26 and 27. The Indian Rights Association lawyers entered a short *Appellants' Brief in Reply*, which Hoyt and Gans decided not to answer with an additional brief of their own.[32]

Chief Justice Melville Weston Fuller delivered the opinion of the court on May 18, 1908. It was a full concurrence with the opinion of

Justice Wright in the Court of Appeals and affirmed that court's decree. Fuller, in explaining the court's decision, emphasized as the lower court had done the essential difference between gratuitous appropriations of public moneys and moneys "belonging really to the Indians" in payment of debts. And he quoted the statement of the Court of Appeals about the prohibition of the free exercise of religion if the Indians were denied the right to use their own money to educate their children in religious schools of their choice.[33]

Bonaparte, who had been on hand when the court handed down its decision, wrote to congratulate Gans on the victory. "It is hardly accurate to say that I *heard* this," he wrote, "for the Chief Justice, who delivered the opinion, spoke so low that it was very difficult to make out what he said. However, I heard enough to learn that we had gained the case."[34]

The Indian Rights Association was, of course, disappointed with the final outcome, for the Supreme Court had overturned its arguments of long standing. It wondered whether the Protestant churches should now seek the use of trust and treaty funds for their own mission schools or attempt once more to secure legislation forbidding such use of Indian funds. In the end it consoled itself with the thought that the money currently spent for contracts did not exceed the proportionate shares of the Indians requesting the contracts.[35]

Quick Bear v. *Leupp* was a major triumph for the Catholic Indian missions, for it settled favorably the legality (and the constitutionality) of the use of the tribal funds, for which the Catholics had been contending for a decade.[36]

Religious Instruction in Government Indian Schools

I⊤ was a principle agreed to by both Protestants and Catholics that instruction in Christianity was fundamental in the education of Indian youth. To fit Indians for citizenship in a Christian nation (which all considered the United States to be), it was imperative that religious training precede or parallel the industrial and literary learning that was intended to prepare the pupils of the tribes for full participation in white American society. The government's long reliance on missionary societies to maintain schools for the Indians was predicated upon this basic premise. The contract schools, whether Protestant or Catholic, saw it as their sacred duty to demolish the paganism of their charges and replace it with a "pure" religion, that is, Christianity.

The rapid and extensive development of a government Indian school system after 1890 created a troublesome problem. If these national schools, supported by increasing appropriations by Congress, were to become the major if not sole educational force among the Indians, how was the religious training, considered so essential, to be provided? Lyman Abbott, a thorough secularist when it came to direct support of religion in government schools, believed that the influence of religious-minded teachers in the schools would be enough to place the little Indians in a proper atmosphere, while formal religious instruction could be a missionary activity quite apart from the schools. But a more general conclusion was that the government schools themselves should make provision for religious instruction, taking care only that it be "undenominational" or "non-sectarian" to avoid violating the principle of the separation of church and state.

The series of *Rules for Indian Schools*, which the Office of Indian Affairs began to issue in 1890, without apologies directed that the Indian pupils be required to attend church services. The *Rules* for 1890 in section 39 said:

The Sabbath must be properly observed. There shall be a Sabbath school or some other suitable service every Sunday, which pupils shall be required to attend. The superintendent may require employés to attend and participate in all the above exercises; but any employé declining as a matter of conscience shall be excused from attending and participating in any or all religious exercises.[1]

While this was unexceptionable to Protestants, since it was understood that the "suitable service" would be Protestant in nature, the Catholics were far from pleased. At first they charged that nonsectarian schools would be "godless" and that "the Government must either enlist in the cause the services of Christianity, or be doomed to utter failure in its attempt to civilize the Indian."[2] The Protestants, however, did not intend to hand the Indians over to a completely godless, secular education. They intended that Protestant values should continue to be inculcated by god-fearing men and women in the government schools; they argued that the government schools would in fact retain a Christian character. An example of the Protestant position was an editorial in the *Independent* on May 5, 1892. The editor pointed to the government boarding school at Carlisle, Pennsylvania.

> This school is presided over by Captain Pratt, an earnest Christian man, and most of the teachers and other employes connected with the institution are active members in Christian churches. There is a preaching service at school every Sabbath afternoon; there is a Sunday-school exercise for all who desire to attend in the morning; Catholic pupils are expected to attend their own services in the neighboring city of Carlisle; there is a weekly prayer meeting, conducted by the students, and largely participated in by others, there is an active, vigorous Young Men's Christian Association, having close relationship with the Christian associations of the country and doing a valuable work, and in addition to all this there are many influences, directly and indirectly, brought to bear upon the pupils, seeking to develop their Christian characters and to inculcate in their minds the highest ideals of Christian living.

Similar work, the editor pointed out, was being done in other "Government non-sectarian schools."[3]

Father Stephan attacked this position vigorously. In December 1893 he accepted an invitation to present to the Board of Indian Commissioners at their meeting with the missionary boards a report on the work of the Catholic Bureau. Although not appearing in person, he sent a statement, which was read by the secretary to the assembled conference. It was a typically intemperate outpouring and created something of a disorder at the staid meeting.[4]

The priest asserted that "some sort of religious education becomes necessary to the Indians, as a basis upon which to rear a fabric of general knowledge sufficient to qualify him as a member of civilized society." And he pointed out that, inevitably, whatever religious education the Indians got would in some sense be sectarian because whoever taught it would of necessity teach it according to his own denominational views. Then he delivered a pointed accusation: "What I do object to is that the effort now being made to secularize, to 'non-sectarize' the Indian schools, is a dishonest, hypocritical one, whose sole aim and purpose it is to drive the Catholic Church out of the Indian educational and missionary field, in which it has gained glorious laurels, and to substitute for its influence and teachings the influence and teachings of other religious bodies." At this, Thomas J. Morgan, the ex-Commissioner, rose to a point of order. "I do not feel," he declared, "that we are called upon to be called liars and hypocrites. If this man wants to make these charges personally let him come here and make them." Morgan was overruled by the chair, and the reading continued, the presiding officer trying to maintain an air of decorum in the proceedings.

Assuredly, Stephan's tone was offensive, but the point he made was not without merit. "Non-sectarian" was quite a relative term. "If any Christian teaching at all be allowed," he asked, "is not that 'sectarian' as between Christians and Jews, Buddhists and Atheists? Equally, much might be taught that would be 'non-sectarian' as between the views of the leading Protestant denominations, but which would be 'sectarian' as to Catholics." That the "non-sectarian" schools advocated by Morgan and his supporters were in fact Protestant schools, if not indeed specifically Baptist or Methodist or Presbyterian, can hardly be questioned. Stephan charged: "The most extreme claimants for secularization now would be found incorporating all the elements of their peculiar religious systems in the Indian schools when once they had control, and the sectarian phenomena of 'revivals,' Young Men's Christian associations, Christian Endeavor societies, King's Daughters, and so on, would be introduced in the 'non-sectarian' schools, as they have been hitherto."

While the Catholic insistence upon continuation of the Catholic contract schools, in which the faith of the Catholic Indian children could be preserved and strengthened, met repeated defeat during the 1890s until government appropriations were cut off entirely by 1900, some

consideration for Catholic Indians in the government schools was forthcoming. Instead of general Sunday services that all pupils were required
to attend, provisions were made for students to attend their own churches wherever possible. The *Rules for the Indian School Service* for 1894,
1898, and 1900 declared: "Pupils of Government schools shall be encouraged to attend the churches and Sunday schools of their respective
denominations, and shall be accompanied by employes detailed by the
superintendent for that purpose. Pupils who can not thus be accom-
modated shall be assembled during some suitable hour for religious and
ethical exercises of a strictly undenominational character." [5]

These general directives, however, were not explicit enough to provide the encouragement of religious activities that all wanted, nor did
they afford the specific protection that Catholic missionaries wanted for
their charges.

A paradigm of the problem of religious instruction in government
Indian schools was the Carlisle school, praised by the editor of the
Independent. Its relations with Catholics underwent sharp change, as
did the government's policy in regard to the rights and privileges of
Catholic students in the federal boarding schools.

The anti-Catholic posture of Captain Pratt, head of Carlisle, was
clear throughout the 1890s. As early as 1891 the Catholic Bureau attacked him for intemperate statements in the *Red Man*, a Carlisle publication. And when Stephan in 1895 wrote to Father Henry Ganss, then
pastor of St. Patrick's Church at Carlisle, about conditions at the Indian
school, the priest reported critically. Although he admitted that Pratt
and the other school authorities had been courteous to him, Ganss found
that his limited contact with the Catholic pupils was "unable to counter-
balance the overt and insidious influences that are sapping the faith of
our children." Some of the brightest pupils in the school were the children of Catholic parents and raised under Catholic influences, he noted,
but as soon as they entered the atmosphere of Carlisle, "the deathknell
of their faith was sounded." Of Captain Pratt, Ganss reported, "a more
rabid bigot could not be found," whose "mania assumes the type of
demoniac phrenzy." As late as the spring of 1899, Ganss continued his
attack on Pratt in private letters to Stephan. "The mission schools do
the work," he wrote, "and Carlisle School reaps the reward. The Faith
is implanted by the missionary fathers,—only for Carlisle to uproot
it." [6]

A good part of Pratt's hostility toward the Catholics came from his
belief (for which there was certainly some foundation) that Catholic

missionaries in the West refused to send students to Carlisle, and, of course, his anti-Catholic reaction to that situation merely increased Catholic antagonism. Pratt, too, believed so strongly in the government schools for Indians (especially off-reservation schools like Carlisle) that he could not abide the success of the contract schools on the reservations. It is understandable that he flirted with the APA and the League for the Protection of American Institutions, which opposed those schools. When Ganss asked for special privileges to instruct and minister to the Catholic pupils at Carlisle, Pratt stood firm, and in this he was backed by Commissioner Jones, who told him, "You have been eminently fair with them, probably more so than they deserve, and it has now reached that point where you must take a decided stand." [7]

Then, suddenly, at the beginning of the new century there was a change in the relations of the Catholics and Carlisle. A modus vivendi worked out between Ganss and Pratt for the religious welfare of the Catholic pupils became a model which was offered to all the government schools. What brought about the revolution can only be surmised. The ending of the contract school system by Congress in 1899 perhaps removed one of Pratt's irritants. It may have been the irresistible pressure of Ganss's fundamentally ecumenical temperament and his willingness—far ahead of his times—to cooperate with Protestants. No doubt both Ganss and Pratt realized that benefits would accrue to both sides if peace could be declared; the Catholic students would get protection if not special privileges at Carlisle, and the Catholic missionaries in the field, finding that Carlisle would not inevitably mean the ruin of the Catholic faith for the students, would be more helpful in finding students to fill Pratt's school. Nor could political considerations be entirely discounted. Jones and Pratt in September 1900 exchanged critical views about the "catering" of the Republican Campaign Committee to "religious fanatics," but Jones added: "However, I am very glad that you made the concessions you did to the Priest at Carlisle as I think, laying aside all politics, that it will be for the best interests of the school to be as much at peace with them as possible. While you understand my position in regard to these people, I still realize that they have some claims upon us, and unless they materially interfere with the workings of the school, I am very glad to comply with their reasonable requests and will do as much for them as for any other denomination and no more." [8]

By 1901 the Bureau of Catholic Indian Missions was pointing to the "Carlisle Plan" as an arrangement to be imitated. Jones wrote to Pratt in November 1901 to find out just what this plan was, noting that the Catholic Bureau had requested for its priests at several of the larger schools privileges similar to those granted at Carlisle. He wanted, he said, to provide some sort of uniformity of action in the matter throughout the Indian service.[9] Pratt replied at once with a brief statement of what the Catholics were allowed:

> The Catholic sisters meet the Catholic students in the school rooms from six to seven Tuesdays and Thursdays of each week. They have also a meeting at the church between nine and ten on Sundays, the same hour we have for Sunday school for the remainder of the children here. In all these services the Catholics have all the boys and girls belonging to their denomination. . . . We have a Sunday afternoon preaching service and a Sunday evening meeting at which all students without reference to creed are required to be present unless there should be some special service in town at which the minister requests the presence of his members, but such occurrences are very rare. There has been no objection on the part of the Catholic church to the presence of the Catholic students at the morning prayers of the school in the dining room, nor at the Sunday afternoon and evening services.[10]

The Catholics, however, remained ambivalent about the Carlisle practice. On the one hand, they used the "Carlisle Plan" as a lever to get comparable privileges at other government schools. At Haskell Institute, for example, Superintendent H. B. Peairs refused the request of the Catholics to instruct Catholic pupils at the school on the ground that "under the regulations of the Indian Office religious instruction of a sectarian character is prohibited in Indian schools." And he added: "We have careful religious instruction in this school, but it is always non-sectarian." That reasoning infuriated Ketcham, who sent Jones a sharp rejoinder. "We contend," he insisted, "that it is absolutely impossible to give religious instruction which is purely non-sectarian, since the instruction imparted must necessarily be colored by the views and prejudices of the teacher to a greater or less extent, and hence in its very nature must be sectarian. The instruction given to Catholic children will be either Catholic, anti-Catholic, or at best non-Catholic; and non-Catholic training, in its relation to Catholic children, is just as sectarian in its essence as Catholic training would be to Protestant children." Ketcham pointed to the experience at Carlisle, where there was "the greatest harmony and peace," and Jones in fact directed Peairs to accord the Catholics the same privileges at Haskell that they had at

Carlisle.[11] Jones sent similar instructions, after receiving complaints from Father Ketcham, to the schools at Santa Fe, Fort Defiance, and Phoenix.[12]

On the other hand, Catholics complained continually about the status of Catholic students at government schools, because so much depended upon the good will of each school superintendent and his staff. The superintendents would make some concessions and then throw obstacles in the way of the priests and sisters. Ketcham on the whole found the situation "far from satisfactory."[13] Even at Carlisle there were difficulties in the "outing system," by which students were sent out to live with farm families in the area for summer work. There were few Catholic families to take the students, so most of the Catholics found themselves in Protestant homes, and Ketcham considered the outing system "more dangerous to the faith of Catholic children than the Government schools themselves." But Ganss managed to work out with the superintendent at Carlisle a system of "Outing Rules" and "Supplementary Rules Governing Catholic Patrons," which eased the situation.[14]

Commissioner Jones was sincere in his attempt to satisfy all parties, Catholics included. On December 20, 1902, he issued Education Circular No. 87 to all Indian agents and school superintendents.[15] It was a detailed directive and became the fundamental document in providing uniformity of religious instruction throughout the government Indian schools.

The pupils were expected to attend the churches to which they or their parents or guardians belonged, and the agents and superintendents were to urge the children to attend. The officials, however, were directed to use no force to compel attendance unless they had written instructions to do so from the parents. Proselytizing among the pupils by pastors, priests, employees, or pupils was strictly forbidden, and no pupil under eighteen was allowed to change his church membership without the knowledge of the school superintendent and the consent of his parents or guardians. But pupils who did not belong to any church were urged to affiliate with some denomination. Two hours of instruction time on weekdays were to be allowed missionaries for religious classes at times agreed upon with the superintendent which would not interfere with regular school duties. It was planned that this would be a joint meeting of all pupils taught by various missionaries in turn, but those denominations whose membership was sufficiently large and who desired their own religious instruction were to have their "religious sensibilities" respected by being allowed to withdraw from the common instruction for lessons at the same hour conducted by their own minister or priest. Church and mass attendance on Sundays at times agreed upon were to be "strictly insisted upon" by the school superintendent. All who wished were to be allowed to attend confession and communion, and permission was to be granted for special services if arranged for at least a day in advance.

Jones hoped that these detailed instructions would put an end to complaints and conflicts, and he urged the agents and superintendents to cooperate loyally with religious authorities in furnishing Indian pupils in the government schools with religious instruction of the faith to which either the pupils or their parents adhered. But he demanded cooperation, too, from the missionaries. They were to avoid "unseemly discussion of sectarian matters, proselyting, or other conduct which would tend to create strife among religious denominations," and if any caused trouble, they were to be debarred from the privileges outlined in the circular.

These instructions of the Indian Office in 1902 seem to have satisfied the Protestants, for they were well entrenched in the government schools, and Circular No. 87 did not interfere with their interests in any appreciable degree. For the Catholics it was quite a different matter, for they feared that the faith of the Catholic pupils was still endangered. Year by year they reported that bigotry and proselytizing were rampant in the government schools. Ketcham's report submitted to his superiors in November 1902 had appended to it a series of letters from missionaries telling about the unsatisfactory conditions, and in subsequent years his reports hammered on the same theme. In January 1904 he sent out a letter of inquiry to priests in the areas in which Catholic Indians attended government schools, asking how Circular No. 87 was working and whether "we could in conscience advocate this system as a substitute for our Catholic Indian Mission schools?" The replies fitted into Ketcham's own position—that the instruction permitted might retard loss of faith but that it could not be compared to what the children would get in Catholic schools.[16]

What the Catholics objected to, in essence, was the atmosphere of the government schools. The majority of the teachers and the tone they imparted to the schools were Protestant (if not in some cases actually anti-Catholic). Ketcham saw no sure way out of the difficulty except the Catholic mission schools. "So long as Protestantism is Protestantism and Catholicity is Catholicity," he concluded, "a child in the hands of Protestant teachers will ordinarily develop either into a Protestant or a misbelieving Catholic." [17]

The problem, of course, as Ketcham recognized, was twofold. First, although the Indian Office in Washington had exhibited a liberal spirit, superintendents and other employees on the spot rendered it somewhat ineffective. Haskell Institute under superintendent Peairs was an especially sore point because of the large number of Catholic students in attendance, and the Catholic Bureau kept up a barrage of attacks upon the school.[18] But, second, the success at any given school depended very largely on the priests and sisters who could be furnished to minister to the students. Ketcham admitted: "It is rare that a priest can be found who will undertake such a mission, or who will devote the requisite amount of time to it. This work demands undoubted zeal and patience. It calls for a priest who can attract the children and command the esteem and good will of those in Authority." He lamented that the Indian Office was as helpless to control its superintendents and teachers as the Catholic Bureau was to provide adequate opportunities for worship and religious instruction.[19] A good case in point was the government boarding school at Fort Spokane, at which, Ketcham complained, the superintendent was frustrating the instruction of Catholic pupils, but where the old Jesuit missionary Aloysius Folchi was clearly an obstacle to harmonious relations.[20]

Where there were good priests and sisters available, the Catholic pupils were well served. Father Ganss and the Sisters of the Blessed Sacrament (Mother Katharine's congregation) at Carlisle made the rules work there. Even Haskell came to be looked upon as a model school, as Ketcham reported in 1906:

> For years these children were deprived of the Sacraments, and opportunities to learn and to practice their religion. Thanks to Bishop [Thomas F.] Lillis, conditions have entirely changed, and all this has been accomplished by the right man in the right place—the Rev. George J. Eckart—who, about a year ago, was given charge of the children of this school. The same Superintendent remains, but, instead of the trouble that existed in former years, perfect peace and harmony reign, and not one complaint has been brought to the attention of the Bureau by Father Eckart. . . . The children hear Mass regularly, approach the Sacraments frequently, and receive ample religious instruction. It is a pity that for twenty years the Catholic pupils of this school should have been systematically perverted, and that the progress of so great an evil was not arrested

sooner. With the exception of Carlisle, Haskell presented the best results of any of the schools, and if we consider what has been done and the short time in which it has been accomplished, it may be said to be surpassed by none.[21]

Jones's Circular No. 87 was aimed at one of the needs of the Catholic students in the government Indian schools, that is, a protected opportunity for Catholic worship and instruction. It sought to provide equality of rights and privileges for all denominations, including Catholic, in regard to specialized religious services pertaining to each group. But there was another serious problem—the common assembly programs of a religious nature that all students, Catholic as well as Protestant, were expected to attend. Repeated remonstrances by superintendents that the religious services were nonsectarian made little sense to Catholics. The services and activities may indeed not have been denominational in the sense of being strictly Methodist or Baptist or Presbyterian, but they were decidedly Protestant, with Protestant Bible, Protestant hymns, and Protestant Sunday school lessons. This troublesome situation was not corrected by Circular No. 87.[22]

De-Protestantizing the Common Religious Services

I⟋ was left to Jones's successor, Francis E. Leupp, to work upon the irritating problem of the common exercises. He seriously tried to accommodate the Catholics, and to that end he asked Ketcham to send him a memorandum listing the "class of troubles against which your people have to contend." It was his goal, he said, "to systematize our school work and to reduce to a minimum, at least, the friction which cannot always be avoided in dealing with the religious aspects of a school question." He wanted to look into any trouble spots identified by Ketcham and to see whether regulations could be devised that would satisfy the Catholics without interfering with the proper discipline of the schools. Leupp also asked Ketcham to point out hymns, prayers, or scripture translations used in the schools that offended Catholics and indicated his willingness to make use of Catholic hymns, prayers, and translations that might not be too strongly objected to by Protestant missionaries. The priest enumerated the obligations that the Church imposed upon Catholic parents and children, the concessions Catholics would like to have in the government schools, and the rights they could not under any circumstances voluntarily consent to give up. He asked that no priest or minister be permitted to lead the undenominational common programs so that children of one religious denomination would not be forced against their will to receive instruction from a minister of a different church. Priests or ministers might be invited to address the assemblies on good morals and conduct, but all strictly religious teaching would be given only to the children segregated into denominational groups.[1]

Leupp moved ahead on two fronts. He began by seeking ways to more fully accommodate the Catholics in schools where there were large numbers of them and where local school authorities and Catholic officials were willing to cooperate. In a letter of remarkably irenic tone, he wrote on September 21, 1906, to Burton B. Custer, who had recently been appointed superintendent of the United States Indian School at Albuquerque, New Mexico.[2] He wrote, Leupp said, about the religious aspect of the school service and "to suggest that you have now an opportunity to take the first step in an important departure which I contemplate in this domain."

Leupp expressed his personal conviction that the government of the United States was of and for *all* religious faiths and that the separation of church and state—"the chief tenet of our patriotic creed"—required that any school system conducted at public expense eliminate all religions or adopt one that would be as nearly universal as possible. His own choice, he said, would be the former. Not that he would abolish religion from the schools but that he would confine the schools' own teaching to good morals and leave everything of a dogmatic nature to missionary bodies, whose work with the Indian children he would encourage. "The children should have impressed upon them by their teachers in the Government employ," he said, "such simple virtues as kindness to each other and to all living things; the control of their passions; charitableness of judgment and gentleness of speech and action; cleanliness of body and mind; honesty and unselfishness; and, in short, all those elements of human conduct which make for better relations between fellow men and react with a wholesome influence upon individual character. Whatever went beyond this and dealt with the duty of mankind toward a higher power, I should commit to the keeping of the missionary organizations."

But such an ideal situation, Leupp admitted, was beyond his control. He had inherited a situation in which a religious system was already planted in the Indian schools. It was his duty, then, to administer the system as fairly as possible with regard to the equal rights and privileges of all the missionary groups who were involved with the Indians. He found in the schools, "already established and in full operation," religious exercises "of what is called an undenominational character." The several churches had endeavored to unite upon a common basis of worship with as few distinctly sectarian features as possible. "In arranging the religious features of the assembly exercises of the schools," he noted, "the Presbyterian has avoided any emphasis on his doctrine of foreordination, and the Methodist has done the same with his doctrine of free-will, and the Baptist with his preference for immersion, the general spirit manifested being one of concession."

Then he came to the point of his letter. "The only Christian church," he wrote, "which still seems not to have been drawn into the brotherhood is the Catholic, which numbers among its communicants a very large Indian contingent." Although the Catholics considered vital certain beliefs and observances with which other Christian churches did not agree, Leupp insisted that they should stand on an equal footing with the others. He hoped that the Catholic Church could be brought into the same harmonious relation with the non-Catholic churches as those churches had among themselves, and to that end he urged "a little further extension of the same spirit of liberality and tolerance of differences of opinion which, among the several non-Catholic bodies, develops so kindly a state of feeling." He, in fact, wanted the non-Catholics, in a distinctly Christian spirit, to go "somewhat further than half way to reach a common meeting ground." To make sure that he was understood, he offered Custer some concrete examples.

In the choice of hymns for the general assembly meetings, why not choose those "in which the Catholics could join with as much fervor as the non-Catholics, and the non-Catholics as the Catholics?" In the matter of scripture readings, there were passages of great beauty and religious spirit that are the same in the Catholic and non-Catholic versions of the Bible: "Why could not the readings be confined to these?" Of the two variant forms of the Lord's Prayer that appear in Matthew and Luke, that in Matthew contained a concluding passage of which the Catholics doubted the authenticity. Why, then, not use the one that avoids offense? Such changes in practice, Leupp remarked, would result in a service that was "a broadly undenominational one instead of its being merely common to a *part* of the Christian organization."

But Leupp went beyond this ecumenical proposal for the common assembly exercises and recommended other actions to satisfy the Catholics. They should be allowed and encouraged to provide religious teachers for the Catholic students so long as the proper discipline of the schools was not interfered with. The superintendent should provide the means for Catholic children to go to Catholic churches near at hand for Sunday services. A separate room should be set aside during Sunday school hours so that Catholic pupils could have their own instruction. And special time should be allowed for Catholic pupils to prepare for confession and to participate in Holy Communion. In these ways, Leupp argued, "without in the least transgressing the general authority of the school, it would be quite practicable to exercise the utmost liberality in the field of religious observance."

Leupp chose Albuquerque as the place to give his plan a trial because he believed the idea would appeal to Custer and because the geographical location of Albuquerque with the nearby Catholic missions would give the idea a chance to develop in a congenial atmosphere. He urged Custer to confer with Father A. M. Mandalari, the local priest, and to prepare with him a report of arrangements made. If the experiment succeeded, he told Custer, "it will do more to dissipate the petty frictions over religious matters which have hampered the growth of our Government school system than any other one step which has been taken since that system was founded." He was optimistic enough to believe, he said, that if the plan were given a chance, "we shall see our Catholic friends, who have hitherto held aloof on grounds of conscience from the general support of our schools, lending cordial aid and encouragement to them." At least he thought it was worth the attempt. If the scheme worked at Albuquerque, Leupp planned to adopt it at other schools, "using the success of Albuquerque as an argument to prove that what some of our fainter-hearted friends of our educational establishment have regarded as impossible is not impossible at all, but needs only the right method of approach with the right spirit behind it to be thoroughly effective." [3]

Custer and Mandalari accepted Leupp's proposal and drew up a set of "Rules Regarding the Religious Instruction of Catholic Indian Pupils in the Government School at Albuquerque, New Mexico," dated March 1, 1907. Passing over without any mention at all the suggestions for ecumenical common services that would be agreeable to both Catholics and Protestants, the rules concentrated instead on guarantees to the Catholics that their children would be properly provided with Catholic services and instruction. The agreement specified that the children were to be sent to the Church of the Immaculate Conception each Sunday for mass and that they would be taught Sunday school each week by the sisters (both exercises were to be compulsory), that additional time would be granted for special religious exercises, that confessions would be heard once a month, and that time would be allowed for a three-day annual retreat. The rules appointed the pastor as "chaplain for the Catholic pupils at the school," and the priest and the sisters pledged themselves "to work in harmony with the rules of the school, to inculcate respect for authority, order and discipline, and to assist the school officials to elevate the school to a high degree of educational efficiency." [4]

It was pretty much the sort of concordat that Leupp had had in mind. Signed by both the superintendent and the pastor, the rules were a great step toward guaranteeing that the religious rights of the Catholic pupils would be respected. Leupp was rightly pleased with his efforts and the initial response they had received at Albuquerque, and he reported that his letter to Custer had "commended itself to leading religious teachers among the Protestant faiths."

While these negotiations were in progress, the Indian Office also sought to get precise information from the field about the religious practices carried on at the schools. On April 22, 1907, Acting Commissioner Charles F. Larrabee sent Education Circular No. 150 to the agents and superintendents.[5] Because there was very little uniformity throughout the Indian service in the religious exercises given to the pupils, the agents and superintendents were directed to report in full on the religious exercises provided in both boarding and day schools under their care. Larrabee was insistent: "I do not mean for you to make a mere perfunctory report saying 'We have an exercise once a week consisting of bible reading, a prayer and two hymns, and we ask a blessing before meals and return thanks after it,' or anything of that sort. What I want is an *explicit* and *particularized* statement, even to such apparently little matter as saying grace before meals in use in each of the schools." And he asked for the number of pupils who were recognized members of a church, broken down by denomination, as well as the number of those not affiliated with any church.

He instructed that the report include descriptions of how the pupils were sent to churches of their choice and how the choice was made; how often they attended and what penalties were imposed for failure to attend; when and how often religious exercises were conducted by ministers and priests at the school and what the nature of those exercises was; how pupils were permitted to change from one denomination to another and whether the parents requested that their children be compelled to attend any particular church. "In short," Larrabee concluded, "let your entire report give everything essential for a thorough understanding of what you are doing on this important subject."

The superintendents took the charge seriously. More than one hundred replies to the circular presented in the explicit and particularized manner the Indian Office wanted a full picture of religious instruction.[6] Most reported a Sunday school taught by employees in the regular classrooms for a set period each week, frequently using the International Sunday School Lessons, a uniform set of lessons specifically designated for each Sunday of the year. The lessons were selected by a special committee under the sponsorship of the American Sunday School Union, a committee composed largely of Methodists, Presbyterians,

Baptists, Episcopalians, and Congregationalists. The lessons were basically selections from the Bible—so that much of the Bible was covered in a cycle of years—with quarterly review sessions and some lessons devoted to missionary work and to temperance. A "Golden Text" was given for each Sunday, and other verses were designated for memorization.[7]

There was also a common religious meeting for all students in the assembly room of the school on Sunday evening, at which Gospel hymns were sung, selections of Scripture were read, some prayers were recited, and a talk given by the superintendent or one of the employees or by a minister or priest of the vicinity. The Gospel hymns were taken from popular revivalist hymnals, prepared originally by Dwight Moody and Ira Sankey for revival meetings and reprinted in many forms.[8] Many of the superintendents went out of their way to note that these evening exercises were "undenominational and nonsectarian."

At most schools grace was offered before meals, sometimes a short silent prayer with heads bowed, more often a recited or sung verse. Popular was this brief song:

> God is great and God is good,
>   And we thank Him for this food:
> By His hand must all be fed,
>   Give us, Lord, our daily bread.[9]

Usually, too, there was a night prayer recited in common under the supervision of the matrons. Commonly, the Lord's Prayer was used.

Wherever possible, the pupils were allowed to go away from the schools for Sunday services to the churches of their choice. They were accompanied by employees, and strict measures were taken to prevent truancy. In other cases, denominational services were given at the school itself by the various pastors of the area. Sometimes, where large enough groups existed to warrant it, denominational Sunday school or weekday evening instruction or services were held at the school.

Many schools reported active YMCA and YWCA programs under the direction of the superintendent or some employee or run by the students themselves. Haskell Institute was a case in point. The school reported 337 Catholic pupils out of a total of 759 (which included 106 of no particular church). The Episcopalians counted 95, Methodists 82, Baptists 68, and Presbyterians 51, together with a few of other Protestant churches. Services for the Catholic students were provided each

Sunday morning by the priest from Lawrence, and during the afternoon Sunday school period there were special classes for Catholic children, who were taught the catechism by some of the older students, while the Protestant children were organized into classes and taught the International Sunday School Lessons by the regular teachers. There were junior and senior YMCA and YWCA organizations, associated with the state associations. Although the meetings of these groups were voluntary, they were well attended—but there was no provision for Catholic groups of a comparable nature. The superintendent noted the general religious atmosphere of the school. "It would not be fair to the many faithful Christian employes not to speak of the many, many heart to heart talks with pupils which are given, and which we sometimes believe are more effective and more lasting in good results than any set program can possibly be." And he concluded that "the religious life of the students is conscientiously looked after by employes, Y.M.C.A. and Y.W.C.A. secretaries, and the pastors of the various churches of Lawrence." [10] It is not hard to see why there was dissatisfaction among Catholics with such an arrangement, in which the school and its employees furnished a rich set of religious activities for the Protestants, while the Catholics had to rely on the Lawrence pastor, already overworked with his own parish duties, and on their own older students.

The problems that the Indian Office was trying to meet occurred, of course, chiefly at schools of mixed population, like Haskell. Where the total population of a given government school was of one denomination, in many respects the school could be considered of that group. Thus the Fort Totten Indian School was made up entirely of Catholic pupils, whose parents directed that they be sent to Catholic services at a chapel a mile away. There were song services, too, on Sunday evening. The superintendent reported: "There is certainly not in the [Indian] service a school where it could more properly be said, that the pupils are all of one religious faith and that, Catholic." [11] Similarly, among the Pueblos, who were almost entirely Catholic, the religious activities of the pupils at the day schools were provided by the Catholic church of each pueblo. At the Santa Fe Boarding School, where the great majority of pupils were Catholic, the boys and girls were taken to Catholic services in the city, and on Sunday afternoons the sisters from the St. Catherine mission school came to hold religious exercises and to instruct the Catholic children in their faith. There was also a nonsectarian Sunday school and daily prayers. "I am pleased to say," the superintendent reported, "that there is a good feeling existing between the churches of the different denominations in Santa Fe regarding our Indian children; most of them are Catholic, and there is no denominational contention." [12]

On the other hand, schools that belonged entirely or predominantly to one Protestant denomination fell into its camp. The superintendent of the Fort Mojave School, for example, reported that the Presbyterian missionary held a regular church service each Thursday evening, which advanced pupils were required to attend. Employees of various denominations assisted in the service, which consisted of songs, Scripture reading, prayer, and a sermon addressed especially to the children. "While it is a Presbyterian service," the superintendent said, "it would be regarded as non-sectarian by any Protestant." On Sunday evening a song service was held in the school chapel, with a talk by an employee on some Bible topic. And each Sunday morning there was a Sunday school, divided into the regular grades of the school. The lessons, Sunday school papers, and other Sunday school helps were donated by the Presbyterian Mission Board in Philadelphia. With a Monday evening chapel talk by the superintendent, grace before meals, and a prayer at bedtime, there was a distinctly religious atmosphere to the school. It was for all practical purposes a Presbyterian school. [13]

Two points were clear in the answers to the survey. First, the government through its Indian schools assumed the obligation of providing Christian religious instruction for the Indian pupils, although it tried not to give anyone a handle for the charge that it was promoting any one sect or denomination. The schools were clearly agents of Christianization; no concern of any kind was paid to the Indians' native religions. Second, despite repeated assurance that the government-sponsored activities were undenominational or nonsectarian, it is obvious that most of the exercises provided in common for the pupils at schools of mixed religious affiliation were, in some vague way at least, Protestant. One can understand, given the Catholic view of these things, why there were objections to the Scripture readings, the Gospel hymns, the Sunday school lessons, and the pervasive YMCA groups.

Early in January 1908 Leupp took his second step. He sent a copy of his letter to Custer and of the "Rules" drawn up at Albuquerque to the superintendents of government Indian schools where there were a sizable number of Catholics and some concern for them by the local Catholic authorities. He urged the superintendents to take the Albuquerque arrangement as a model and to use the Custer letter as a statement of the broad policy of the Indian Office. [14]

The replies Leupp received in response to his request for criticisms and questions were gratifying. The superintendents replied at length, describing their reactions and their own relations with the Catholic pupils. Nearly all were in favor of Leupp's proposals and reported cooperation and good will on both sides in the relations of the various denominations at their agencies.[15]

One of the best letters came from Major W. A. Mercer, superintendent of the Carlisle school, who had replaced Pratt in 1904. He reported that he was already following Leupp's policy. He enclosed a printed copy of his own "Rules Governing Catholic Pupils at the U.S. Indian Industrial School, Carlisle, Pa.," which antedated Custer's "Rules" by exactly three months. The two sets of rules were so similar in content and even in phraseology that Mercer strongly intimated that the Carlisle rules must have been the pattern for those drawn up at Albuquerque.[16] The Carlisle experience, like that at Albuquerque, showed what was possible when reasonable men on both sides cooperated. Father Ganss, in fact, was so well pleased with the arrangement at Carlisle that in January 1907 he sent out a circular letter to Catholic pastors in the Indian country, for whom he described the "tolerant and helpful character" of Carlisle. "The anxiety hitherto manifested in allowing Catholic pupils to come to Carlisle," he wrote, "need no longer exist. Catholic endeavor and work is permitted with the most praiseworthy readiness through the generosity of the School authorities. The faith and morals of our children are safeguarded as well as they possibly can be in any Government School. The presence of a Catholic chaplain just appointed [Ganss himself] and the activities of six of Mother Katharine Drexel's Sisters, women consecrated to the Indian work; obligatory attendance at mass on part of the pupils; instructions and other privileges always cheerfully accorded, place Carlisle in the forefront of schools that invite the attendance and patronage of our missionaries." Ganss hastened to explain that he was not trying to undercut the Catholic schools on the reservations by taking children away from them, for Carlisle, after all, lacked "those two imperative requisites of Catholic education, *atmosphere and environment*." But for advanced students, he insisted, Carlisle was the government school to which they ought to be sent.[17]

Ganss's position was a delicate one, a tightrope to be walked between unreasonable condemnation of the government schools like Carlisle, which were seriously seeking to be fair to their Catholic students, and such praise of the schools as would lead to a conclusion that Catholic mission schools—and the tremendous financial efforts that had to be made to support them—were in fact unnecessary. A little more than a year earlier, when he had been asked by Father Ketcham to write up for the *Indian Sentinel* an account of affairs at Carlisle, Ganss had refused, for he considered that such a report would be "both injudicious and hurtful to our Indian work." He added: "It would reveal a feature and phase of the Indian question, which had better be kept as quiet as possible. If the unintelligent reader would see that Uncle Sam makes princely provision for the Indians at the Government Schools, and the church can apply her machinery without let or hindrance, like at Carlisle, both under Gen. Pratt and Maj. Mercer, why it would seal the channels of beneficence that support our work. True, I championed this work in public print several times,—but the motive inspiring my action was always the contradiction of error and falsehood about the local school,—not really exalting it as an ideal institution for a Catholic child." [18]

Ganss, however, backtracked a bit from this policy of secrecy when he wrote an article on Catholic Indian work for the *Messenger*, a widely circulated journal published by the Jesuits in New York. In one segment of the three-part article he noted "the gradual disappearance of the old-time distrust and bitterness existing between the Catholic and Government schools," and he spoke favorably of the government's recent actions to rout out from the Indian service anti-Catholic superintendents. Although he noted the importance of Catholic schools, with the possibility they offered of deepening the faith of their students, he urged attention to the Catholic students who perforce would have to attend the government schools. "The religious opportunities offered to Catholic pupils," he wrote, "are of a character that can no longer be overlooked or neglected, nor dismissed with a contemptuous shrug of the shoulder or a scornful smile of incredulity." He urged that "unusually bright, alert and promising pupils after finishing their courses in the mission school" be transferred to government schools, where their studies might be continued to good advantage with "fostering religious safeguards." "If the pupil will not preserve his faith under such indirect church supervision," he said, "he will certainly not preserve it in the world, when he must fight the battle of faith single-handed." His desire for Catholics to cooperate with the government schools was clear throughout the article. "The pacific and liberal overtures of the Indian School Department," he concluded, "should be met both without suspicion or distrust, and with frankness and confidence. The opportunities it offers

HENRY G. GANSS. A learned and energetic priest, Father Ganss, as pastor at Carlisle, Pennsylvania, worked out a successful program for Catholic pupils at the Carlisle Indian School which became a model for other government schools. (Photograph from the Marquette University Library)

FRANCIS E. LEUPP. Leupp, during his term as Commissioner of Indian Affairs (1904–1909), came to support much of the Catholic program for their Indian schools. At first considered an obstacle by the Catholic leaders, he came to be a friend and supporter. (Portrait from the *Indian Craftsman*, April 1909)

for methodic devotions and instructions should be repaid with grateful recognition and energetic correspondence. . . . The Government Indian school should no longer cause the spine-creeping sensations of a charnel house for slaughtered Catholic aboriginal innocents." [19]

To Father Ketcham, in the midst of his struggles to find support, both private and federal, for Catholic mission schools, this was "insidious, covert treason in the ranks." And he was incensed that the Jesuit journal, "which more than any other diffuses Catholic information throughout the country," could have published the article. "There can be no question that Father Ganss' ideas must be to have Carlisle supersede the Catholic Indian Missions," he wrote to a Jesuit confidant. "For the life of me I cannot understand how a publication of the Society of Jesus can be made his tool in carrying out his nefarious policy." [20] But Ketcham cooled down after this initial response, and there was no public break between the two priests, each devoted strongly in his own way to the Catholic Indian cause.

The Carlisle rules, like those from Albuquerque, dealt with rights and privileges accorded Catholic students to have their own services and instructions. They did not address themselves to Leupp's concern about an arrangement of the *common* assembly services that would not be objectionable to Catholics. The Commissioner did not let this matter drop. After consultation "with leading authorities of the Catholic Church and three or four Protestant churches which maintain missions in the Indian field," he issued a set of additional instructions to govern "all assembly religious exercises—that is, those in which the entire pupil body takes part, as distinguished from the several Sunday school exercises under separate denominational or undenominational control." Leupp was very explicit:

1. Substitute the Revised Version for the King James Version of the Bible, for the scriptural readings, confining them to the four Gospels and the Acts of the Apostles.
2. Use either form of the Lord's Prayer given in the Revised Version.
3. For the singing, use the "Carmina for Social Worship," omitting the following hymns: Nos. 106, 108, 110, 111, 119, 161, and 165.
4. Until further notice, these will be the only strictly religious exercises used at the assembly meetings. [21]

The problems encountered in arriving at these new regulations can be seen in Archbishop Ryan's reaction to a set of scriptural readings proposed by Leupp: "I have looked over the Scripture Readings. I find them all taken from the Protestant Bible. The single word '*which*' applied to God the Father, would stamp the 'Lords Prayer' as sectarian. The new version has 'who' (as we have it) but the old one is retained in the book you left me. There are many other reasons why I can have nothing to do with it." [22]

Finding an appropriate hymnbook was also a problem. Leupp picked out hymns from non-Catholic sources for a new songbook he was planning to compile. These he submitted to a panel of Catholic priests, including Father Ketcham, who culled out those they considered objectionable. Then, since the Commissioner was willing to add some specifically Catholic hymns, Ketcham marked out for him a number in a Catholic hymnal published in New York. He explained to the publisher the importance of the project, but he was unable to get permission to use the hymns. Ketcham appealed to the members of the Marquette League to force the publisher's hand, but without avail. [23]

The *Carmina for Social Worship*, which Leupp ultimately adopted, was intended to be a replacement for the widely used *Gospel Hymns*. It was geared more particularly for the use of children than the common adult hymnals and had, as the preface noted, "a larger number of didactic hymns of high character admitted than would be appropriate in a book for adults." [24] The hymns proscribed by Leupp were "Onward, Christian Soldiers" and another martial-spirited hymn, which he may have considered inappropriate for students being educated for peaceful citizenship, and some that were considered objectionable by the Catholic censors for too heavy a stress upon the Bible as the rule of faith or for some other doctrinal reason.

Leupp may have left office thinking that he had solved the problems of religious instruction in the government Indian schools, and there can be no doubt that the Catholic position had been considerably improved. Father Ketcham praised Leupp for what he had done, but he still had criticism about what went on in individual schools and concluded that "no Commissioner will ever be able to secure uniformly fair treatment of Catholic pupils in all Government schools, as his efforts must in many instances be thwarted by the bigotry and duplicity of inferior employees." This all confirmed his opinion that government schools could never adequately supply the religious needs of the Catholic Indian pupils. [25]

Leupp left to his successor, Robert G. Valentine, the task of dealing with critical Protestant reaction to the new arrangements and of finally refining and promulgating a uniform set of rules to replace the old Circular No. 87 and the amendatory regulations and suggestions of Leupp. Valentine drew up a draft of a new set of regulations, incorporating the principles and prescriptions that Leupp had originated, and called upon the religious groups to comment upon them before they were officially issued.

The chief objections came from the Indian Committee of the Home Missions Council. The Council, organized in 1908, represented a federation of denominations carrying on mission work in the United States, and its Indian Committee comprised five members from the denominations doing extensive work among the Indians, namely, Baptist, Congregational, Methodist, Protestant Episcopal, and Presbyterian. Its spokesmen on the question of religious instruction were Thomas C. Moffett of the Indian Committee and Charles L. Thompson, president of the Home Missions Council. Both men were connected with the Board of Home Missions of the Presbyterian Church.[26]

In November 1909 representatives of the Indian Committee met with F. H. Abbott, Acting Commissioner of Indian Affairs, and at his suggestion the Committee sent to the Indian Office a detailed statement about the proposed regulations. These Protestant spokesmen made a number of strong points. First, they objected to compulsory attendance at denominational services as "not in harmony with the purpose of our government," and they asked that the school superintendents not be required to compel children to attend any sectarian or denominational services. Second, they objected to the watered-down religious instruction that was permitted for common assembly exercises. Third, they criticized the restrictions which limited the choice of Bible selections and forced the schools to leave out "the Old Testament stories, including the tales of patriarchal days, of pastoral life and country life, with the heroic and prophetic descriptions which particularly appeal to the Indian mind and heart." And they did not like "the expurgated hymn book," *Carmina for Social Worship*, which they described as "unfamiliar." They asked specifically for the removal of the restriction on "Onward, Christian Soldiers" and other hymns. Finally, they objected to having the superintendents count and list students by denominations, "compelling them to recognize denominational distinctions among their pupils, and to distinguish and place in groups the pupils who ought to be molded into one body by common school interests and by recognition of a common standard of Christian civilization." What they wanted, in short, was a return to the old ways that Leupp had tried to correct.[27]

Commissioner Valentine did not pay the attention to their wishes that the Protestant mission leaders expected, although he seems to have gone about getting recommendations and comments on his proposed regulations in a methodical way. In December 1909, during an extended conference with Indian school superintendents, chiefly from the non-reservation boarding schools, he spent one session on the question of religious instruction, to which representatives of the Bureau of Catholic Indian Missions and of Protestant churches were invited. Although the invitation was issued too late for Moffett and his colleagues to attend, Merrill E. Gates, secretary of the Board of Indian Commissioners, who was much in sympathy with Moffett's group, and some local Protestant clergymen spoke for their side of the issue. The meeting, Gates reported in a confidential letter to Moffett, was "friendly in spirit and in words." Father Ketcham presented the Catholic position and commended the regulations from Carlisle (although he said that he was not entirely pleased with them). Gates spoke for the Protestants and read to the gathering the November statement of the Home Missions Council. Then the superintendents were asked to tell about the practices at their schools and to indicate how the Carlisle regulations would affect them. Gates remarked: "The superintendents seemed to me to be afraid of offending that very strong church organization which Father Ketcham represents; but this impression of mine may have been my fancy." Valentine asserted that "this matter of religious instruction is in many respects the most difficult that the Bureau has to handle," and that he was determined to make the final decision himself and to accept responsibility for it.[28]

Moffett's Indian Committee held itself in readiness to act and to come to Washington to confer with Valentine, but it was not called upon. Gates had a conference with Valentine at the beginning of February about the matter of religious instruction and was assured by the Commissioner that no final promulgation of regulations would be made without consultation with the Protestant group. But the Home Missions Council heard no more until Secretary of the Interior Richard A. Ballinger on February 19 sent them (as he at the same time sent to Father Ketcham) a draft of the regulations he proposed to issue on March 1. He had "carefully considered" the protests made by the Council in its letter of November 11, Ballinger said, and he had "modified the former draft in so far as the points you raised appealed to me." [29]

Thompson was not pleased. He shot back a note to Ballinger, asserting that Valentine had assured them that they would be consulted again, yet now the regulations were ready to be issued and they had not had a chance to criticize them. "The changes which on our suggestion you have made in the proposed rules," he told the Secretary, "are so few and unimportant, that our committee deems it necessary to lay the matter before you in another interview." He was invited to send his statement in writing instead. [30]

The "General Regulations for Religious Worship and Instruction of Pupils in Government Indian Schools" came out on March 12, 1910, over Valentine's signature. They represented a compromise, but since they followed Leupp's provisions for protecting the rights of Catholic students as well as Protestant, weakening, if not obviating, the Protestant character of the common assembly exercises, they must be considered a victory for the Catholics. [31]

Catholics, in fact, so considered them. Cardinal Gibbons told Valentine that the regulations appeared to cover the ground adequately. "No doubt all lovers of justice and liberty will applaud your course," he wrote, "and I take it for granted the various non-Catholic religious organizations will be as pleased as we are." Father Ketcham received two hundred copies of the "General Regulations," which he quickly dispatched to Indian missionaries, asking them to write a note of thanks to the Commissioner. The priests were prompt to write to Valentine; they praised the regulations and complimented the Commissioner for promulgating them. "Truly, they give all possible chances to Catholic pupils to follow their religious convictions, and to their pastors ample opportunities to look after their spiritual welfare," wrote a Jesuit missionary from Oregon; "the justice and fairmindedness of those regulations make their author worthy of the highest encomiums." Another, from St. Francis Mission, declared: "There is not a word, nor yet an implied principle in them, to which a fair and unbiased mind can take exception. In the now famous slogan, it is a 'square deal' for all." Ketcham himself praised the new regulations as "vastly an improvement on all preceding ones," and he rejoiced that the "'non-sectarian' Sunday School is at last abolished." He noted that the Protestant bodies were displeased, although they were given equal rights in the document. "Why this displeasure?" Ketcham asked. "Is it because under the new regulations they cannot by means of the machinery of the State force all children, Catholics included, to attend Protestant services and listen to Protestant discourses?" [32]

The Protestants publicly accepted the outcome with good grace, if without enthusiasm. Thompson wrote to Valentine to acknowledge receipt of the regulations. He especially liked, he said, the section that allowed ministers and priests to come to the schools to address the pupils. Though he would have preferred fewer restrictions upon the superintendent in what was allowed for the common services, Thompson said that his group was "sure that the regulations as a whole can have the cordial acceptance of all denominations." [33]

It had been something of an ordeal for Valentine, for he had given much time and thought to framing the regulations, yet he realized that it was impossible to please everyone. His goal had been, he said, to issue them in a form that "would be, on the one hand, least objectionable to anyone, and on the other, carry the most possible of the spirit that goes to make all that is best in life." If given a fair trial, the regulations, he hoped, would "solve automatically many of the perplexing questions before the Office." [34]

Valentine checked carefully on the operation of the regulations. In January 1911 he sent a telegram to many of the superintendents asking for a report on the total number of children of each denomination and exact details on how the regulations were carried out "paragraph by paragraph," and in March he sent out letters of similar tone to others. The replies of the superintendents—some quite perfunctory, others full of particulars—reported few difficulties. The biggest block to full compliance seemed to be the *Carmina for Social Worship*, which was not easily accepted as a substitute for the well-liked *Gospel Hymns*, even when it was available, which it often was not. [35]

When Valentine addressed the Indian Rights Association meeting on December 14, 1911, he spoke candidly about the difficulties in getting full compliance with the regulations. He found superintendents who were not carrying them out to the letter, in some places the *Carmina for Social Worship* was not being used, and he noted cases of proselytizing. But overall he enthusiastically backed the regulations. They clearly showed, he said, that

while the government must assume only an attitude of widest hospitality to each and every religious belief, and must hold the schools exactly even between all religious beliefs at any common exercises, that fact should not be allowed to stand in any one's mind as an excuse for discouraging or putting the slightest obstacle in the way of, or retarding by a merely passive attitude, the religious work in our schools and reservations. It is my own firm belief that religion in some form is absolutely necessary to the right development of the Indians throughout the Indian country; and I feel this so strongly that were the government boarding school to be a bar to the proper carrying out of its fullest functions by any denomination in that boarding school, I think it would be a less evil to abandon the boarding school than to lose that religious spirit.[36]

The "General Regulations for Religious Worship and Instruction" were aimed at boarding schools. The day schools, in which the students spent only the classroom hours and then returned to their homes, presented a different and less serious problem. Yet Valentine received requests from various missionary boards for regulations governing these schools, too. On March 15, 1911, the Commissioner thereupon sent a draft of a circular to eleven individuals representing churches concerned with the Indian schools (including leaders of Catholic, Baptist, Presbyterian, and Methodist groups, as well as Merrill E. Gates, secretary of the Board of Indian Commissioners, and S. M. Brosius, agent of the Indian Rights Association). In it he noted the sharp differences between the boarding schools and the day schools. In the former, he said, the Indian Office, "being in a semi-parental relation, feels that the theory of the separation of the church and state does not justify it in excluding all religious endeavor from the schools," lest the students be deprived of religious training altogether. In the latter, the churches in the vicinity had the same access to the Indian pupils as they did to students in white public schools, and the Indian Office had no responsibility for religious instruction. But since often there were not suitable facilities for religious classes available in the community, Valentine suggested that the Indian schools provide classrooms for such religious exercises as the various ministers wanted to provide. He stipulated only that the religious work not interfere with regular classes and that the students be made to understand "that attendance at these meetings is in no sense a part of the Government's school work for them, and that they are there simply by courtesy of the Government, at the invitation of the missionary."[37]

This circular raised no storm. Eight of the eleven to whom it was sent replied, and they uniformly voiced no objections. Only Father

Ketcham offered an alternative suggestion—that in schools where all the pupils were of the same denomination some religious instruction could be made a part of regular class exercises.[38]

The Catholic Bureau's agitation for consideration of its interests in the government Indian schools and the willingness of the Indian Office to react favorably can be seen in these regulations concerning religious instruction.[39] A happy solution seemed to have been reached, yet the new rules, unfortunately, did not ease all the tensions between Protestants and Catholics, for the Protestants soon found a new issue on which to take a stand.

Religious Garb and Insignia

A final battle between the Catholic and Protestant forces occurred in 1911 and 1912 over the question of religious garb and insignia in government Indian schools. It was an extensive and virulent controversy. Archbishop Ireland noted in 1912 "a recrudescence of anti-Catholic feeling in the country" after long years of peace and saw "violent bigotry stalking through the land." The religious garb issue reflected to a large degree the new animosity.[1]

The question arose because of the practice of the government from time to time of taking over Indian mission schools and supporting them as regular government schools—but with the old teaching staffs intact. The government found this a ready solution for expanding its school system when mission schools, especially with the withdrawal of contract money, would have been forced to close, leaving certain groups of Indians who had depended upon them without any educational facilities. For the Catholics, desperately attempting to maintain their Indian schools in the face of financial troubles, the practice was most welcome, for it meant that the entire support for the schools then fell to the federal government while, for all practical purposes, the schools continued to be run just as they had been before, with the priests and nuns teaching the children and the atmosphere and activities of the schools still thoroughly Catholic. It was common for Catholics to speak of the converted institutions as "our schools."

Although there were instances of Catholic nuns being paid by the government for teaching in Indian schools going back to 1874, when the peace policy of President Grant was in effect, a serious problem arose only in the 1890s, after government Indian school teachers and other personnel had been placed under civil service rules.[2] On June 3, 1895, the Secretary of the Interior asked the Civil Service Commission to include the teachers and matrons at four schools (none of which were run by Catholics) in the classified service without examination. John R.

Proctor, president of the Civil Service Commission, replied favorably, comparing the case to that of upgraded post offices, in which the old personnel were brought into the classified service when the change was made. Vacancies occurring thereafter, however, were to be filled from the registers of the Civil Service Commission.[3] The persons involved were said to be "covered in" or "blanketed in" to the civil service.

On the basis of this authorization the government continued to take over mission schools. Commissioner of Indian Affairs Valentine reported in 1910 that, including the four schools in the original approval of 1895, twenty-three mission schools had been taken over and the employees covered in to the classified service. Those originally under Protestant auspices apparently disappeared into the federal system, leaving little trace. The Catholic schools, because of the distinctive garb worn by the teachers, remained visible. At the beginning of 1912, ten such schools were identified (some boarding schools and some day schools), with an estimated forty-six religious employees.[4]

Protestant agitation against the continuance of Catholic teachers with distinctive garb in these schools began in the summer of 1910 through the Home Missions Council. In June, Valentine received a memorandum with questions from Charles L. White, secretary of the Home Missions Council, and he was visited by a committee representing that organization and the newly organized Federal Council of American Churches. These men asked if the practice of covering in the mission schools was consistent with the spirit and rules of the Indian Office, whether it was permissible to display emblems of a denominational character in such schools, whether any garb of a sectarian or denominational character should be worn by teachers in the schools, what legal warrant there was for blanketing in the schools, and whether the practice amounted to "sectarian discrimination."[5]

The Commissioner replied with straightforward answers to the queries, noting the Civil Service Commission's authorization of 1895, which required only that vacancies be filled through regular procedures. He said that if special religious emblems were displayed, he would insist upon their removal, but he knew of no law prohibiting a person in the Indian service from wearing "any distinctive garb, either sectarian or otherwise, which is unobjectionable from a moral standpoint"; there were no rules regarding what kind of clothing could or could not be worn in Indian schools. Valentine denied that the exception to civil service rules was equivalent to sectarian discrimination.[6]

In June 1911 the Indian Rights Association began its own drive to prohibit the wearing of religious garb in government schools. Brosius drew up a resolution calling upon the Secretary of the Interior for full information on the matter, which he handed to Congressman Stephens for introduction in the House. Stephens dutifully complied and introduced a resolution of inquiry (H.Res. 216). It called upon the Secretary of the Interior to furnish information showing in detail the number of schools covered in—including details of purchase or lease, the religious denomination originally controlling each school, and the names of the personnel involved. The Secretary was asked also to report whether any religious garb, emblems, or symbols of particular religious denominations were permitted in the schools.[7]

The resolution was referred to the Committee on Indian Affairs, which did not take any action on it. Stephens, as chairman of the Committee, then wrote directly to the Secretary of the Interior for the information called for by the resolution. A reply came from Samuel Adams, Acting Secretary of the Interior, ten days later.[8]

Stephens's action set off a violent reaction from the Catholics. He was looked upon as their bête noire in Congress, and this latest move was considered only one more indication of his hostility. "He has been, ever since he has been in public life," Charles Lusk noted, "our pronounced opponent, never failing to show his hand when the occasion offered." Lusk considered the resolution "on its face a direct attack upon us."[9] Father Ketcham took the occasion of an address to the Knights of Columbus in Washington on Columbus Day to excoriate Stephens and to urge the Democratic party not to tie itself to the Congressman's coattails. Stephens's bigotry, he said, was a peril to the Democratic Party and he asked if the party was willing to shoulder that burden. He was especially concerned that the Democrats, gaining control of the House in the Sixty-second Congress, had made Stephens chairman of the Committee on Indian Affairs. The speech was only the beginning of a publicity campaign against Stephens. A statement entitled "Mr. Stephens of Texas a Peril" was sent to the editors of Catholic papers, who reported fully on Ketcham's speech under such headlines as "Catholic Indian Work Threatened" and "An Old-Style Texas Bigot." Ketcham thought that the agitation in the Catholic press had some effect and that perhaps Speaker of the House Champ Clark would see the necessity of "putting Mr. Stephens right."[10]

But as usual there was criticism that this was unwarranted political interference. The action of the Knights of Columbus in response to Ketcham's plea was picked up by the *Independent*, which asserted:

"We are by no means in a hurry to object to the wearing of crosses, Christian Endeavor pins or the dress of the sisters, but we do object to requiring the Knights of Columbus to enter into a political conflict to defeat Mr. Stephens for re-election, or to defeat his party if it should follow his lead." And it quoted a Catholic paper from Chicago which stated, "It is quite certain that Representative Stephens, of Texas, is a bigot and bigots must not be allowed to run at large without at least being branded, especially if they dwell under the open skies of illimitable Texas." [11]

Meanwhile, the Home Missions Council renewed its interests in the religious garb question. It appointed a Washington lawyer, Henry B. F. Macfarland, as a special counsel, and Macfarland began to collect information from the Indian Office. [12] The first action taken by the lawyer was a statement, dated November 27, 1911, addressed to the United States Civil Service Commission. Macfarland asked what warrant in law the practice of covering in the private school teachers had —for neither the Attorney General nor any other law officer had ruled on it. Then he presented a long argument to show that the practice was in fact contrary to the Civil Service Act and to rules and regulations of the Civil Service Commission. The point of the argument was that the analogy made with the post offices was unsound, since in that case two types of government institutions were involved, not the transfer of persons from a private institution to a government one. There was no mention of the Catholic Church or of the principle of separation of church and state, and the concern expressed was to assure that teachers in the government schools met the requisite standards, a goal that could not be achieved if teachers were accepted into the classified service without competitive examinations. [13]

Ketcham was aware, he said, "that a storm was brewing, that some one was 'making medicine,' as the Indian expresses it." In talking with Secretary of the Interior Walter L. Fisher about Congressman Stephens's attitude on the matter, he had been told that Fisher had been receiving protests and that considerable opposition was developing. But the Secretary had assured him that if the protests were to be acted upon, he would give Ketcham a hearing to present his side of the question. Ketcham had no inkling from Valentine that any action by his office was contemplated. [14]

It came, then, as a sharp blow when, without any warning or the promised hearing, Valentine on January 27, 1912, issued a circular on the subject to all superintendents of Indian schools (Circular No.

Robert G. Valentine. Successor to Leupp as Commissioner of Indian Affairs, Valentine received much attention for his circular prohibiting the wearing of religious garb in government Indian schools. (Portrait from *Indian Rights Association Report*, 1909)

WILLIAM HOWARD TAFT. President Taft was considered a friend of the Catholic Indian Schools. His revocation of Valentine's garb order won him much abuse from anti-Catholic forces. (Photograph from the Library of Congress)

601). This order became the point of such active controversy that it is well to give it here in full:

> In accordance with that essential principle in our national life —the separation of church and state—as applied by me to the Indian Service, which as to ceremonies and exercises is now being enforced under the existing religious regulations, I find it necessary to issue this order supplementary to those regulations, to cover the use at those exercises and at other times, of insignia and garb as used by various denominations. At exercises of any particular denomination there is, of course, no restriction in this respect, but at the general assembly exercises and in the public school rooms, or on the grounds when on duty, insignia or garb has no justification.
>
> In Government schools all insignia of any denomination must be removed from all public rooms, and members of any denomination wearing distinctive garb should leave such garb off while engaged in lay duties as Government employees. If any case exists where such an employee cannot conscientiously do this, he will be given a reasonable time, not to extend, however, beyond the opening of the next school year after the date of this order, to make arrangements for employment elsewhere than in Federal Indian Schools.[15]

The Home Missions Council immediately sent a telegram to President Taft, saying that the order was "so manifestly American in spirit, so judicial and righteous" that the Council heartily approved and commended it. It asked that nothing be permitted to weaken its force and requested a conference with the Secretary of the Interior on the matter.[16]

Ketcham went directly to President Taft and convinced him that the order had been given by Valentine without consultation with either the President or the Secretary of the Interior. Because of the importance of the question, Taft informed Secretary Fisher that the order should be revoked, restoring the status quo, after which both sides could be heard and a proper decision arrived at before the beginning of the new school year in September, when Circular No. 601 was to take effect. "I may say to you confidentially that in the interview I have had with Father Ketcham," Taft told Fisher, "I told him that I didn't think there was any case at all for his insignia, and church and religious pictures, that they properly ought not to remain in a public school house; but that the question of garb presented different considerations that we would give thought to in the interval." He sent to Fisher the substance of a statement to be issued and suggested that it be discussed with Valentine in case the Commissioner had some modification that would be more agreeable to him.[17]

Fisher then drew up two alternative statements for the President to consider. They were identical insofar as they set forth the background of the case, but they differed in the form the President's action was to take. "Suggestion No. 1" noted that Circular No. 601 would not take effect until the fall and that in the meantime a hearing would be held, but it allowed Valentine's order to stand. Fisher reported that this was the form he preferred. He had been visited, he said, by representatives of the Protestant denominations, and he thought that the first alternative would meet with the least objection from them.[18]

Taft, passing over the Secretary's preference and the wishes of the Protestants, chose "Suggestion No. 2," which he embodied in a formal letter to Fisher on February 3. While asserting his belief in "the principle of the separation of the Church and State on which our Government is based," he saw a special difficulty in the fact that the teachers in the transferred schools had been officially included in the classified service and were protected by the civil service law. "The Commissioner's order," he said, "almost necessarily amounts to a discharge from the Federal Service of those who have thus entered it. This should not be done without a careful consideration of all phases of the matter, nor without giving the persons directly affected an opportunity to be heard." He concluded: "I direct that it [the order] be revoked and that action by the Commissioner of Indian Affairs in respect thereto be suspended until such time as will permit a full hearing to be given to all parties in interest and a conclusion to be reached in respect to the matter after full deliberation."[19] Fisher immediately sent the President's directive to Valentine, and the Commissioner, having no choice but to comply, on February 6 issued a new order (Circular No. 605) revoking Circular No. 601.[20]

Both sides geared up for the hearing that Taft had promised. Each stirred up a furor of public agitation in favor of its own position and prepared a legal brief for presentation of its arguments at the hearing.

The Catholics worked through a number of organizations. The Central Verein, a German Catholic federation, through the director of its Central Bureau in St. Louis, F. P. Kenkel, kept in close contact with Ketcham, who sent sample letters that could be used to write to Taft, to Speaker of the House Clark, and to various Congressmen. Kenkel reported considerable letter writing, to the President, to Clark (especially from the German societies in Missouri, the Speaker's home state), and to appropriate members of Congress. He intended, he said, to write to all the thirteen hundred societies affiliated with the Central Verein, asking them to write to their Congressmen.[21] The American Federation of Catholic Societies, through its national secretary, Anthony Matre, also eagerly pitched in. Matre on February 9 sent a telegram to Taft with a subtle political touch: "The American Federation of Catholic Societies, representing three million members, is informing its affiliated societies of your action in revoking the Valentine anti-garb order. We deeply appreciate your fearless action in promptly rescinding this measure and know that your conduct in this matter will meet with the hearty approval not only of the fifteen million Catholics in the U.S. but by all fair-minded citizens."[22]

Matre sent to each of the affiliated societies a printed notification, dated February 10, 1912, marked "Very Important and Urgent—Action Should be Taken at Once." He said that Cardinal Gibbons requested all the Catholic societies to send a letter of congratulations to Taft for revoking Valentine's order and to Champ Clark, protesting the attitude of Congressman Stephens against Catholic interests, especially in the garb issue. Sample messages were provided, but the societies were instructed to vary the form of the letters, and they were told that the Cardinal urged no publicity about the sending of the letters lest it stir up counter moves on the part of Protestant societies. Matre reported that the results were excellent—all the national organizations and various state and county federations responded, as well as a number of bishops. He had received assurances, too, from Clark that Stephens would let up on the matter. "On the request of the Cardinal," he added, "I have also informed our Oklahoma Societies to urge Hon. Congressman Ferris to 'break away' from Mr. Stephens. The Oklahoma societies and K. of C. Councils have promptly attended to the request."[23]

Ketcham appreciated the good work done by the letters, for they had made many Congressmen "sit up and take notice." But he was not convinced that anyone had readily persuaded Stephens to change his views. The Texas Congressman had assured Speaker Clark that he would treat all churches alike, and Ketcham found that position quite unsatisfactory. The Protestants, he noted, had few Indian schools compared with the Catholics, and any restrictions applied across the board would affect them but little, while the Catholics would suffer serious losses. "There is the additional fact to consider," he noted, "that the ordinary school is Protestant in its tone and teaching, and serves to all intents and purposes the ends of a Protestant Mission school."[24]

The Marquette League, too, through its president, Eugene Philbin, addressed the President to express the appreciation of "every member of the Marquette League and indeed of all Catholics throughout the country," for the "broad justice" he displayed in rescinding the anti-garb order. And the second vice-president of the League, Andrew J. Shipman, wrote an article on the Valentine order for the *Columbiad*, a journal of the Knights of Columbus. The League was ready, too, to take action to counteract an article hostile to the Catholics that appeared in the *New York Herald* on March 12, but Ketcham cautioned against a head-on attack, preferring to wait until the hearing had taken place lest there seem to be an attempt by public agitation to influence the Secretary's decision.[25]

Meanwhile Ketcham was in touch with both Bonaparte and Edgar Gans for legal counsel on the anti-garb issue. Bonaparte was asked to draw up a formal brief for use at the hearing, and as the date of the hearing approached, Ketcham pushed him to hurry with the work. On March 27 the lawyer sent his finished work to Ketcham, a brief entitled "In the Matter of Religious Garb and Insignia in Indian Schools: Brief Submitted in Behalf of the Bureau of Catholic Indian Missions by Charles J. Bonaparte."[26]

Bonaparte discussed the law relative to garb and could find no uniform or prescribed dress for teachers in the Indian service. Without such a law or regulation, he argued, an employee of the government had the same right as any other citizen to dress as his taste dictated, provided the dress was decent and did not interfere with the discharge of his duties. He cited a Pennsylvania case which supported the wearing of sectarian garb. Unless Congress prescribed by statute the dress of *all* teachers in government Indian schools, to single out one group was "a disingenuous and oppressive usurpation of authority" and "unjust discrimination." He noted that the wishes of the Indians concerned had not been considered and that the great majority of the children affected were Catholic and had never found anything offensive in their teachers' dress. "As a matter of fact," he wrote, "the wishes of the Indians have always been disregarded when hostile action was taken against the Catholic schools." After quoting from *Quick Bear* v. *Leupp*, Bonaparte declared that Valentine's anti-garb order was another attempt to prohibit the free exercise of religion and a violation of the very principle on which he professed to base it. Nor could he find any support for the order in civil service rules.

While holding firm on the garb issue, Bonaparte conceded the point on insignia. He granted that nothing offensive to anyone should be exhibited on the walls of the classrooms. Although it was Protestant clergymen who objected to the Catholic insignia, not the children or their parents, he was willing to give in, for he considered the point a minor one. "If sectarian prejudice can be allayed," he concluded, "and those engaged in the great work of civilizing and christianizing the Indians can be spared the impediments to their work arising from denominational jealousy and intolerance by having bare walls for their school rooms, by all means let the walls be bare." Bonaparte's decision in the matter was a pragmatic one. He wrote to Ketcham when he submitted the brief: "I have acted on the theory that the President would probably direct the crucifixes and other insignia or religious emblems to be removed from the walls of the school rooms and decide that the Sisters could dress as they pleased. This seems to me very much the most probable outcome, and as it would give us, for practical purposes, all that we wanted, I thought it advisable to ask for what we are likely to get, especially since this is pretty near all that we want." [27]

The issue on insignia, in fact, had already been decided, for Ketcham had paid attention to Taft's suggestion and had directed (after consultation with Cardinal Gibbons) that the crucifixes, statues, and Catholic pictures should be removed from all the public rooms of the schools. The teachers were advised to do this quietly and gradually so as not to attract the attention of the children. By the time of the hearing, Ketcham hoped to be able to state that there were no Catholic insignia to be found in the government schools. [28]

When it came time for the hearing, Bonaparte was unable to attend, but the Catholic Bureau, in addition to Ketcham and Lusk, was represented again by Edgar Gans, in whom Bonaparte and the Bureau continued to have high confidence. [29]

Active Protestant support of Valentine's order continued to come from the Indian Rights Association and the Home Missions Council, and the argument was based on the principle of separation of church and state (with its corollary of anti-Catholicism). Sniffen saw the President's revocation of Circular No. 601 as "at the instance of the Roman Church authorities" and spoke of it as "this surrender to Rome." He and the president of the Indian Rights Association, the Reverend Carl E. Grammer, set a campaign of protest rolling. "This is a time," Sniffen said, "calling for aggressiveness and vigor." Grammer at once drew up a letter to the President, which was presented to the Executive Committee of the Indian Rights Association for approval. The letter, signed by both Grammer and Herbert Welsh, protested the suspension of Valentine's order, which "makes plain a fundamental principle of our Government and is for the best interest of the civil service." The whole arrangement of covering in mission schools was deprecated as an "introduction of ecclesiastical questions into politics." In the schools in question the children would certainly draw the conclusion that "the Government schools are Roman Catholic or that this is a Roman Catholic Government." And the letter noted—once again—the action of Congress in the 1890s cutting off appropriations to sectarian schools.[30]

The letter was intended also as a propaganda piece and was sent to interested individuals, to editors of newspapers, and to the associated press representative in Philadelphia. The result in the newspapers, however, was disappointing. Only the Philadelphia *North American* printed it substantially complete. The poor showing Sniffen attributed to the fact that "the press of the country is largely Romanized, and consequently the interests of that church are carefully looked after by these moulders of public opinion." It was to him just a part of "the main scheme to completely dominate this country."[31] Grammer kept active in the matter. He wrote to Brosius asking him to collect specific information about religious dress and insignia placed before the eyes of students in the covered-in schools, and he wrote to Valentine to commend him on his stand. As the days passed he pressed both the President and the Secretary of the Interior to hold the hearing soon and informed them that the Indian Rights Association could be ready on short notice to present its views. He got carried away in his enthusiasm for the anti-Catholic cause, however, and occasionally uttered nonsense. "The situation which makes it necessary for the Roman Catholics to have an agency in Washington," he wrote to one supporter, "shows by the existence of such an agency, its opposition to the principles of our government."[32]

The Indian Rights Association was materially aided by the Home Missions Council, which independently pursued a campaign against the revocation of the Valentine order. The Council drew up a statement on "Separation of Church and State in Indian Schools," which it sent out to the secretaries of the home mission boards of all the Protestant churches, asking them to publish it in their denominational papers. The emphasis again was on the violation of the principle of separation of church and state. The use of teachers in religious garb, the statement said, was "un-American in view of the fact that children educated under the care of instructors robed in religious insignia cannot receive their education in that complete liberty of mind and freedom from church restraint, the lack of which has wrought untold harm in foreign countries."[33] The Council sought to collect express statements (and where practicable sworn affidavits) about sectarian influence in the covered-in schools and prepared material for presentation at the hearing. It invited the Indian Rights Association, the National Indian Association, the YMCA, and the YWCA to join with it "in opposing actions in the administration of Indian schools which we deem to be un-American."[34] The material was printed up in pamphlet form, with a plea to the recipients to write immediately to President Taft asking that Valentine's order be affirmed. The Council itself distributed the pamphlet widely and sent copies to the Indian Rights Association as well.[35] Letters by the hundreds flowed into Washington, a flood in support of Valentine's order that made the Catholic letters look like a trickle.[36]

The Council leaders looked forward eagerly to the Secretary's hearing and aimed to have a large delegation there. Dr. Thompson, the president of the Council, arranged for a preliminary get-together at the Shoreham Hotel on the day scheduled for the hearing.[37]

All this agitation was highly newsworthy. Religious papers and the secular press covered the matter thoroughly, being supplied by the partisans with appropriate material. Valentine's original order as well as the revocation of the order were widely reported, and the partisan positions of pro-Protestant and pro-Catholic papers polarized the issue. The *Catholic Union and Times* of February 8, 1912, proclaimed "The Perfidy of Robert Valentine" in its headline, while the *Truth Seeker* of February 17 trumpeted, "Another Concession to Rome at the Expense of American Principles." And the journals of opinion kept their readers informed as the conflict developed.[38]

The hearing took place as scheduled on April 8, running from 10:30 in the morning to 5:15 in the afternoon, with about sixty persons in attendance. A large number of persons spoke. Samuel Scoville, Jr., made a statement on behalf of the Indian Rights Association, and Macfarland spoke as counsel for the Home Missions Council; Father Ketcham, Lusk, and Gans represented the Catholic position (no doubt relying on Bonaparte's brief); and there were remarks by Secretary Fisher and a number of others present, including John D. Bradley, secretary of the Washington Secular League. Commissioner Valentine read a long apologia for his action, which Sniffen reported was "a full and most comprehensive review of his action" and "practically unanswerable." [39]

Valentine, having been severely rebuffed by the President and the Secretary of the Interior for his precipitant action in issuing Circular No. 601, had prepared himself thoroughly to vindicate his action. He had drawn up four long memoranda containing information about the order, which he sent to Fisher on March 20 for his use in connection with the hearing and which he used in preparing the brief he read at the hearing.[40] The memoranda had a strong coloring of anti-Catholic sentiment, for Valentine was obviously annoyed by Catholic agitation. The Commissioner was particularly outspoken in the section called "Attitude of Bureau of Catholic Indian Missions," for which he had dredged up a variety of Catholic statements in order to show that the Catholics had been hostile to Grant's peace policy (despite Father Ketcham's statement about Catholic cooperation), that they aimed to draw the Protestant Indian children into their fold, and that they had a long history of opposing all nonsectarian schools. The Catholic motives and purposes, he concluded, "are such that no officer of the United States can take cognizance of them, or in any degree permit them to influence his official action." He had issued Circular No. 601, he indicated to Fisher, only after careful consideration extending over several months. His trip to the West in November 1911 had especially impressed upon him the need for the order.[41]

The formal brief used by Valentine at the hearing, while less anti-Catholic in tone, was forthright justification of Circular No. 601. The issue was "simple, clear-cut, and susceptible of exact statement," he said, and he proceeded to set it forth in logical steps: (1) The separation of church and state was an "essential principle of American policy"; (2) the education of youth was a government function, and public schools were the instruments of the state for the exercise of that function; (3) religious garb and insignia in the government schools conflicted with the essential principle. Valentine developed the third point at great length, insisting that it was "a matter of plain psychology" that the ecclesiastical robes and insignia exerted a sectarian influence. He argued:

> . . . the unspoken declarations and intimations of the garb are so striking and pronounced, are so constantly and necessarily asserting their cause, that the mere presence of the dress in a school room lends the school a denominational character. The teachers appear not in their capacities as public officers and teachers, but

as ecclesiastical persons. The effect is inevitable: No child can be expected, as no adult should be asked, to keep in mind the distinction. The result is all the respect inspired by the teacher's office, all the tendency so natural among all children and intensified among Indians—toward emulation of the teacher,—is drafted to serve the mission of the ecclesiastic.[42]

Valentine added a history of the contract school question to show that the government had long insisted on nonsectarian Indian schools and admitted the contract schools only as a temporary expedient. He spoke of the dependence of the Indians as wards of government and the duty of the government to educate them in a proper appreciation of American principles. "How can it be," he said, "that we are doing our whole duty by the Indians when in that governmental agency with which they come into the most direct and intimate relation—in the one concrete expression of the Government which avowedly represents at once the fulfillment of our pledge and the hope of the Indian in America— they see a standing denial consistently asserting itself in graphic and unmistakable manner of one of the very principles which professedly we are seeking to secure to them, the principle that the church has no part as such in the state?" He had issued Circular No. 601, he concluded, "to please no one and to offend no one, but only in the performance of official duty."[43]

The Protestants, despite their protestations that the arguments in favor of Valentine's order carried the day at the hearing, did not let matters rest. Henry Macfarland immediately drew up a long new brief on behalf of the Home Missions Council, which was accepted also by the Indians Rights Association and the Federal Council of the Churches of Christ in America. The brief repeated the standard Protestant arguments against the garb and cited numerous cases which were asserted to bear on the subject.[44] The Indian Rights Association ordered three hundred copies of the brief for distribution among its interested friends.[45] The Catholics were not greatly worried by this new effort. Bonaparte and Gans conferred about it and decided that it would not materially affect the Secretary's decision. Bonaparte also examined Valentine's statement at the hearing and came to the same conclusion.[46]

The fires were kept burning by an explosive campaign carried on by the Reverend Randolph H. McKim, rector of the Episcopal Church of the Epiphany in Washington. McKim insisted that Catholics placed on the walls of government schools pictures showing that all but Catholics were damned. He had reference to the so-called "Two Roads" chart, a pictorial catechism used by the Catholic missionaries in their mission schools. The Protestant view of the device was well expressed by the Reverend Aaron B. Clark, who described it as "extremely and most offensively sectarian."

> It is, indeed, a most graphic portrayal of the chief events of Bible History, up to the founding of the Christian Church. But then, having made out that the Church was founded upon Peter as chief of the Apostles, the Chart goes on to show in the centuries after Christ that "the principal heresies lead the souls from the good to the bad road" giving as exemplars of these heresies Luther, Mahomet and Arius. Farther on, "the infallible Pope directs and blesses the efforts of the children of the Church" (i.e., Roman Catholics). "The devil, the father of lies, drives his own children toward the abyss." By this teaching of the chart all who remain Protestants are sent straight to hell, depicted as a place of flames and tortures. All the virtues are depicted along the way which leads up by Peter's chair and on through "purgatory" to where Mary presents souls to Christ in Heaven.
>
> All vices are shown on the side of the Protestants along the way that leads only to Hell in the end.
>
> It is difficult to conceive a more graphic way of teaching children and ignorant adults to curse all Protestants and oppose them.[47]

McKim's exposé was quickly defused, for the Catholic missionaries denied that any such picture was used in the government schools or that they taught that all Protestants were damned, and neither McKim nor his supporters were able to bring forth any evidence to support their charges.[48]

While Secretary of the Interior Fisher was making up his mind on the garb issue, whether to support the Commissioner of Indian Affairs or to continue the revocation of Circular No. 601, Valentine was much in the news. He had become the key figure in the dispute, and both Protestants and Catholics speculated about how long he would stay in office, for he was under attack on a number of fronts. Ketcham was increasingly hostile to Valentine, although he did not publicly attack him. He complained that the Commissioner "constantly is slyly and plausibly and continually embarrassing us in every way possible," and he urged the Federation of Catholic Societies to bring pressure to bear on President Taft to have Valentine removed.[49]

Rumors were thick in July and August about Valentine's resigning, which he denied firmly. The Indian Rights Association, taking no chances, began an active campaign to be sure that a suitable replacement was appointed if Valentine could not be retained. It liked J. George Wright, Commissioner to the Five Civilized Tribes, but discarded him because he was "*very* friendly with the Catholics," and this would be unsuitable at a time when "the question of Catholic aggression" was so important. The Association settled on Edgar B. Meritt, who headed the law section of the Indian Office, as their candidate and pushed steadily for his appointment.[50]

Valentine resigned on September 10, 1912, asserting that he did so in order to work for Roosevelt's Bull Moose Party, but the newspapers alluded to the troubles over the anti-garb order. And his Protestant supporters saw the garb question as the cause.[51]

Valentine's letter of resignation came before any announcement of a resolution of the issue. Fisher had reached his decision in a letter addressed to Valentine on August 24, 1912, but the document was not made public, awaiting the President's approval. Fisher hoped to satisfy both sides. He noted that the question was one of administrative policy, not of statutory or constitutional law, and he declared that "as a matter of wise and far-seeing administrative policy the wearing of a distinctive religious garb by teachers in Government schools for the Indians should not be permitted." But, because of the circumstances by which those religious now in the service had been covered in, he decided that they should be allowed to continue without having to discard their special garb. No more religious teachers would be accepted, and gradually the "mistake" would be corrected as the vacancies were filled from the regular civil service lists. He insisted, in addition, that all teachers, whether Protestant or Catholic, refrain from sectarian instruction or the use of their positions for sectarian ends. To this simple, straightforward decision, the Secretary added a long discussion of the policy, much of which was an attempt to answer various points raised on both sides at the hearing of April 8, especially the Protestant contention that the practice was unlawful and unconstitutional. The immediate and complete exclusion of all religious garb and the dismissal of those who continued to wear it, as representatives of some Protestant denominations and of the Washington Secular League urged, he considered unnecessary, unreasonable, and unwise.[52]

Taft waited until September 23 to issue his approval of Fisher's decision. It was a brief summary of the Secretary's opinion and a statement of full concurrence.[53] Like any real compromise, the President's statement did not fully satisfy either side. The president of the Marquette League told the members that it "shows the good will of President Taft and is greatly valued," but that it "is not all that was hoped for by those interested in Catholic Indian mission work." Charles Thompson, president of the Home Missions Council, commended the President for the statement of principle in his letter, but he expressed strong regret that the wearing of religious garb was allowed to continue. Sniffen wrote that it was "just about what we expected, and . . . certainly NOT UNFAVORABLE to the Roman Catholics." He expected the Catholics to show their gratitude by voting the Republican ticket in November.[54]

The garb controversy brought the tension between the Catholic Bureau and the Indian Rights Association to the breaking point. When Sniffen wrote to Ketcham in November 1912 to ask if the Bureau would like to send a representative to a conference on Indian matters to be held in connection with the annual meeting of the Indian Rights Association, Ketcham bitterly rejected the invitation. He wrote:

> I have always been desirous of working hand in hand with all organizations which have the benefit of the Indian as their aim. I have tried to get along with all in amity and peace. I have not succeeded. Notwithstanding the help I have always willingly and cheerfully extended to others I generally speaking find other organizations ready to band together at any time in an effort to discredit and hamper the work in which I am engaged. I am speaking from an experience of about twelve years. I believe in reciprocity. If the Indian Rights Association is willing to help me in my efforts for the Indians I am willing to help them. If they are not disposed to do this, it is better for each organization to pursue its own course without any attempt to give out the impression that there is mutual understanding and concord where none such exists.[55]

Ketcham's disgust with the Indian Rights Association did not adequately reflect the situation of the Catholic Indian schools at the end of 1912, for the Catholics had come a long way since the low point of 1900 when the contract school funds were cut off. The Catholic Bureau's campaigns, in fact, had largely succeeded. The principle that Catholic Indian parents had some say in where their children went to school and how their share of tribal money was spent for education had been pretty well established. The revocation of the Browning Ruling, the restoration of rations to children in mission schools, the Supreme

Court decision that trust and treaty funds could be designated by the Indians for support of mission schools, and the rights accorded Catholic pupils in government Indian schools had all been Catholic victories. The weakened version of the Lacey bill that became law in 1907 benefited the Catholics by preserving the tribal funds on which they drew. Even the compromise on the religious garb issue meant that the Catholic nuns teaching in the government schools were not to be thrown out because they wore their religious habits (although no new ones were to be admitted).

The Protestant opposition to Catholic growth in Indian education, after initial success in the 1890s, thus in the long run was ineffective, and the bitter anti-Catholicism that accompanied much of the struggle, while irritating, did not win wide national support and was rejected by the responsible officials of the government who made the crucial decisions regarding the Catholic cause. The political weight of the Catholics in the nation and their successful lobbying for their interests in the Indian school question gave them a more widely accepted role in national affairs, and it was no longer possible to think of management of Indian affairs without some consideration of Catholic views. Symbolic of this new status was Catholic representation on the Board of Indian Commissioners, an established principle after 1902. Father Ketcham's appointment to the Board in December 1912 was a fitting capstone to his arduous career on behalf of Catholic Indian interests; he was an active, able, and respected member of that body.[56] Protestant carping, to be sure, did not completely die out, and anti-Catholicism reappeared from time to time, but Catholics, as the old evangelical Protestant Indian reformers declined in influence, had clearly come of age in Indian affairs.

Petition of Sioux Indians, Rosebud Reservation

To the Commissioner of Indian Affairs:

We, the undersigned duly enrolled members of the Sioux tribe of Indians, located on the Rosebud, South Dakota reservation under the jurisdiction of the United States Indian Agent, Rosebud Agency, South Dakota, hereby respectfully request and petition you to enter into a contract with the Bureau of Catholic Indian Missions of Washington, D.C., for the care, maintenance and education of Two Hundred and Fifty (250) children of the said tribe in St. Francis Mission school located at Rosebud Agency, South Dakota for the fiscal year 1906, to be paid for out of our trust and treaty funds known as "Interest on Sioux $3,000,000 fund" and "Education Sioux Nation" and "Subsistence and Civilization of the Sioux."

We further request that whatever ratable share or interest may be due each of us, or each of our children, in the aforesaid fund, shall be used for said contract for the fiscal year 1906, and

We further unqualifiedly agree and understand that in event said contract is made and entered into as heretofore requested, that such share or shares so used shall be deducted from whatever payments of money, like annuities, etc., or issues of clothing, subsistence, etc., or other benefits which may hereafter arise in the distribution of the same to the Indians of such nation.

We further state that it is the clear understanding of each of us, that each petitioner and each of petitioner's children, will thus receive less by such amount than otherwise.

We further agree that eligible pupils of said tribe may be enrolled and paid for in said school under said contract, provided children of petitioners have the preference, and there are total shares of all petitioners sufficient for the entire number.

WITNESS our signatures at _____ agency _____
_____ on _____, 19_____.
[Signatures]

SOURCE: Records of the Bureau of Indian Affairs, Letters Sent, Education, vol. 562, pp. 259–60, National Archives, Record Group 75.

Contract for St. Francis Mission School, Rosebud Reservation, South Dakota

Whereas, on June 6, 1905, application was made by the Bureau of Catholic Indian Missions of Washington, D.C., to the Commissioner of Indian Affairs, requesting that a contract be made with the said Bureau for the care, education and maintenance, during the fiscal year 1906, of Two Hundred and Fifty (250) Indian pupils at $108 per capita in the St. Francis Mission School situated on the Rosebud Reservation, South Dakota, payable from the funds of said Indians;

Whereas, under date of March 26, 1906, a petition duly signed by Two Hundred and Twelve (212) members of the Sioux tribe of Indians of the Rosebud Agency, South Dakota, was filed, asking that a contract be entered into with said Bureau in accordance with its request.

Now, therefore, this agreement, made and entered into this First day of July, 1905, by and between F. E. Leupp, Commissioner of Indian Affairs, for and on behalf of the United States of America, party of the first part, and the Bureau of Catholic Indian Missions of Washington, D.C., party of the second part,

Witnesseth; That said parties have covenanted and agreed, and by these presents do covenant and agree to and with each other as follows:

Article 1. The party of the second part, for and in consideration of the compensation hereinafter named, agrees—

1. To support, maintain, and educate under this contract, at the Industrial boarding school on the Rosebud Reservation, South Dakota, known as St. Francis Mission Boarding School, with a capacity and the necessary appliances for the healthful accommodation of at least Two Hundred and Fifty (250) pupils, during twelve months commencing July 1, 1905, in a manner satisfactory to the party of the first part, an average, if practicable, of Two Hundred and Fifty (250) eligible Sioux Indian Pupils of the said Rosebud Reservation, South Dakota, the total number of all pupils attending the school at any one time not to exceed its capacity.

2. That no pupil is to be enrolled under this contract who is under six or over twenty years of age, provided, however, that any Sioux pupil of the said Rosebud Reservation, South Dakota, over twenty and under twenty-three years of age, who was attending said school during the fiscal year 1905 and is otherwise eligible, may be continued in said school during the current fiscal year.

3. That all children, before being accepted as pupils by the party of the second part, shall be certified to the Commissioner of Indian Affairs by the agency physician, or other authorized physician, as in good health and sound physical condition.

4. That the pupils be procured under this contract by the party of the second part are to be obtained only from children of duly enrolled members of said Sioux tribe on the said Rosebud Reservation, South Dakota, and entitled to share in the funds hereinafter designated.

5. That children otherwise eligible who were in attendance at other schools during the twelve months preceding the date of this contract shall not be received for this school without special authority therefor from the Commissioner of Indian Affairs.

6. To provide for said school a sufficient number of employees to conduct it to the satisfaction of the party of the first part, presenting satisfactory evidences of the qualifications of each instructor, all employes to converse with pupils under their charge in English, and to be able to speak and write in the English language fluently and correctly; to instruct the male pupils of said school in gardening and farming and care of stock, or such other industries as are suitable to their reservation; to instruct certain of the male pupils in mechanical trades; to instruct the female pupils in cookery, laundering, needlework, dairy work, and general housewifery; to teach all the pupils in the ordinary branches of an English education; to teach the effects of alcoholic drinks and narcotics upon the human system, as required by act approved May 20, 1886; to observe with appropriate public exercises all national holidays; to instruct pupils as to the duties and privileges of American citizenship, explaining to them the fundamental principles of the Government, and to train them in such a knowledge and appreciation of our common country as will inspire them with a wholesome love of it.

7. To supply the pupils of said school with suitable and sufficient clothing, subsistence, lodging accommodations, medical attendance, medicines, school books, stationery, school appliances, and all other articles necessary to their personal comfort; and also to supply the

school with mechanical tools, seeds, and all other articles necessary in a properly conducted industrial school.

8. To have school-room exercises on five and industrial exercises on six days in each week, legal holidays excepted; and excepting also vacation not to exceed two months within the first quarter of the fiscal year, unless expressly agreed, provided that period is covered by this contract, during which vacation there need be no school-room exercises, and the pupils may, in the discretion of the party of the second part, be relieved from industrial work, and permitted to visit their homes at no expense to the party of the first part for transportation either going or returning.

9. To report concerning said school as required, and upon blank forms to be furnished by the party of the first part.

10. To not transfer this contract or any interest therein, as provided by section 3737 of the United States Revised Statutes, to any other party or parties, it being understood that if this contract or any interest therein shall be transferred by the party of the second part, by that act the party of the first part will be relieved from all obligations under the contract; but all rights of action for breach of the contract by the party of the second part will be reserved to the party of the first part.

Article 2. The party of the first part, in consideration of the faithful performance of the aforesaid agreements and stipulations by the party of the second part, agrees—

1. To pay said party of the second part at the rate of Twenty-seven Dollars ($27.00) per quarter as compensation for every pupil in attendance under the provisions and restrictions of this contract and authorized to be received under section 4, Article 1, hereof. It is agreed, however, that any fractional quarter created by section 8, Article 1, shall, as far as relates to compensation, be considered a full quarter, and that the average attendance during the remaining portion of said quarter shall be considered as the average attendance for the full quarter, provided there shall not be paid to the party of the second part, under this contract, as compensation for the fiscal year a sum aggregating more than Twenty-seven Thousand Dollars ($27,000.00).

2. To make payments under this contract from either or all of the funds of the Sioux tribe of Indians designated technically as "Interest on Sioux Fund," "Education Sioux Nation" and "Support of Sioux of different Tribes, Subsistence and Civilization," as may be decided by the party of the first part.

3. To make these payments to the party of the second part at the

end of every quarter, upon vouchers in duplicate duly certified to by the United States Indian Agent, Rosebud Agency, South Dakota, that the said Industrial Boarding School has been maintained and managed according to the true intent and meaning of this contract.

Article 3. The party of the first part reserves the right—

1. To abrogate this contract in the following manner and for the following reasons: (a) On a notice of fifteen days, given in writing to the party of the second part, provided that the party of the second part has failed to comply with the agreements and stipulations of this contract, the fifteen days' notice to be counted from and to include the day on which the notice is served personally by a duly authorized officer of the United States Government on the party of the second part, or is left by such officer at the school-house of the Mission Boarding School above mentioned; (b) on a notice of sixty days, given in writing to the party of the second part, and for any reasons satisfactory to the party of the first part, the sixty days' notice to be counted from and to include the day on which the notice is served personally upon or is left at the school-house of the party of the second part, in the manner provided above for serving notice of the abrogation of this contract for failure of the party of the second part to comply with the agreements and stipulations thereof.

2. To make inspections of the said school, and to require the party of the second part at any time immediately to dismiss from the service of the school all school employees who may be considered by the party of the first part not qualified for the respective positions occupied by them in the school.

Article 4. It is expressly agreed and stipulated by and between the parties to this contract—

1. That this contract may by mutual consent be changed, altered, modified, amended, or abrogated in whole or in part, provided such change, alteration, or modification does not affect the rate, or amount of compensation, or fund out of which payment is to be made, or eligibility of pupils.

2. That no member of or delegate to Congress, officer, agent, or other employee of the Government shall be admitted to any share or part in this contract, or derive any pecuniary benefit therefrom.

3. That where the word "eligible"—in relation to children or pupils—occurs in this contract it is mutually understood that said children or pupils are those provided for under section 4, Article 1, hereof.

Article 5. This agreement is made subject to the approval of the Secretary of the Interior.

IN WITNESS WHEREOF, the undersigned have hereunto subscribed their names and affixed their seals the day and year of this agreement as hereinbefore written.

Witnesses:

_____

_____ }   _____

For party of first part.   Commissioner of
                                  Indian Affairs

_____

_____ }   _____

For party of second part.

SOURCE: Records of the Bureau of Indian Affairs, Education Division, Memoranda, vol. 1905–1907, pp. 199–203, National Archives, Record Group 75.

General Regulations for Religious Worship and Instruction of Pupils in Government Indian Schools

1. Pupils shall be directed to attend the respective churches to which they belong or for which their parents or guardians express a preference.

2. Should a question arise as to which church pupils belong, they shall be classed as belonging to a certain denomination as follows:

(a) Those whose names are to be found on the baptismal record of said denomination, or who have been formally received as members of such denomination, or who belong to families under its instructions, except where the children are under 18 years of age and parents or lawful guardians make written request that the child be instructed in some other religion.

(b) Those who, regardless of previous affiliations, Christian or pagan, having attained the age of 18 years, desire to become members of any denomination.

(c) Those of any religion whatever, under 18 years of age (or over that age, unless they make voluntary protest), whose parents or lawful guardians, by written request, signify their desire that their children shall be reared in a certain denomination.

3. Ample provision shall be made for the conveyance of those who are too young or unable to walk in cases where the church services are held at a distance from the school. Hours of services are to be agreed upon betweeen the attending pastor and the superintendent. Where these services can not be held in or near the school on Sunday, the pupils must be sent to church on week days, provided arrangements can be made between the attending pastor and the superintendent so as not to conflict with regular school duties.

4. Pupils shall not change church membership without the knowledge of the superintendent and consent of parents or guardians.

5. Pupils who belong to no church are encouraged to affiliate with

some denomination—preference being left to the pupil if he be 18 years of age or to the parent or guardian if the child be under 18 years of age.

6. Proselyting among pupils by pastors, employees, or pupils is strictly forbidden.

7. Method and promptness and a pervasive desire to cooperate with the discipline and aims of the schools must characterize the work of those to whom the spiritual interests of the pupils are intrusted.

8. Two hours on week days are allowed each church authority for religious instruction, the hours to be decided upon by superintendent and pastor.

9. Each Sunday all pupils belonging to a certain denomination shall attend the Sunday school taught, either at the school or in a near-by church, when by mutual consent of the attending pastor and the superintendent such a place has been selected.

10. Pupils will have every facility in attending confession, preparatory classes, and communion by handing their names to their religious instructors, and these in turn shall hand the names to the matron or disciplinarian—this as a precaution to account for the presence of the pupil.

11. Truancy, tardiness, or misconduct on the part of pupils attending church or Sunday school, either away from or at the school, must be promptly reported to the superintendent.

12. For special services in church or at the school, special permission, granted at least a day in advance, must always be procured from the superintendent.

13. In the general school assembly exercises, as distinguished from the several Sunday school exercises under separate denominational control, the following *only* must be observed for the strictly religious part:

(a) Substitute the revised version for the King James version of the Bible for scriptural readings, and confine these to the four Gospels and the Acts of the Apostles.

(b) Either form of the Lord's Prayer as given in the revised version.

(c) For song exercises use the "Carmina for Social Worship," omitting the following hymns: Nos. 106, 108, 110, 111, 119, 161, and 165.

(d) These assembly exercises are to be conducted by the superintendent of the school, or some employee or pupil designated by him; but not a minister or priest unless the superintendent should be one, in which case he acts ex officio.

(e) The privilege of addressing the school at these exercises will be cordially offered to all ministers and priests; but doctrinal instructions or denominational teachings must not be permitted.

14. Regular and compulsory attendance is demanded on the part of all pupils at the regular assembly exercises conducted by the superintendent of the school.

15. Superintendents shall be required to carry out these regulations. They are required not only to cooperate loyally with this office in holding the balances equally between all churches, granting them equal privileges and excluding special privilege, but must not under any circumstances allow their personal prejudices or church affiliations to bias them in any way.

R. G. VALENTINE, *Commissioner*.

March 12, 1910.

SOURCE: Printed Copy in Records of the Board of Indian Commissioners, Reference Material, Schools (Sectarian), National Archives, Record Group 75.

Abbreviations Used in the Notes

AAB	Archives of the Archdiocese of Baltimore
BCIM	Bureau of Catholic Indian Missions Records
BCIM *Report*	*Report of the Bureau of Catholic Indian Missions*
BIA	Records of the Bureau of Indian Affairs, National Archives, Record Group 75
BIC	Records of the Board of Indian Commissioners, National Archives, Record Group 75
BIC *Report*	*Report of the Board of Indian Commissioners*
CCF	Central Classified File
CIA *Report*	*Report of the Commissioner of Indian Affairs*
CJB	Charles J. Bonaparte Papers
DC	District of Columbia
DJ	General Records of the Department of Justice, National Archives, Record Group 60
ID	Indian Division
IRA	Indian Rights Association Papers
IRA *Report*	*Report of the Executive Committee of the Indian Rights Association*
LM	*Proceedings of the Lake Mohonk Conference of Friends of the Indian*
LR	Letters Received
LS	Letters Sent
NA	National Archives
OSI	Records of the Office of the Secretary of the Interior, National Archives, Record Group 48
RG	Record Group

Notes

Chapter 1

1. Grant's peace policy has been studied extensively; see Francis Paul Prucha, *American Indian Policy in Crisis: Christian Reformers and the Indian, 1865–1900* (Norman: University of Oklahoma Press, 1976), pp. 30–63, and the references cited there.

2. Some weak attempts to involve Catholics centered on the Reverend George Deshon, a Paulist priest who had been a classmate of Grant's at West Point. When asked in 1896 about the matter, Deshon replied: "Prest Grant never offered to put a Catholic in the Board of Indian Comrs. . . . F. D. Dent, Grant's brother in law, and who was a long time in the White House, asked me if I would be willing to be one of the Commissioners, and I declined. He said Grant would appoint me if I would consent. I did not see that I could do the least good in that crowd of bigots who would ignore me and bolster themselves by serving with a Catholic man on the board and therefore I declined." Joseph A. Stephan to George Deshon, January 15, 1896, and Deshon to Stephan, January 18, 1896, BCIM, 1896, DC. See also references to Father Deshon and the peace policy in Peter J. Rahill, *The Catholic Indian Missions and Grant's Peace Policy, 1870–1884* (Washington: Catholic University of America Press, 1953).

3. An annual report was published by the Board of Indian Commissioners. These reports include the proceedings of the meetings with the missionary societies and present an excellent picture of the mood of the reformers as well as of the activities undertaken.

4. The distribution of agencies with a tabulation of the number of Indians involved is given in CIA *Report*, 1872, pp. 461–62. The work of the Catholics under the program is discussed in Rahill, *Catholic Indian Missions*; that of the Methodists in Robert Lee Whitner, "The Methodist Episcopal Church and Grant's Peace Policy: A Study of the Methodist Agencies, 1870–1882" (Ph.D. diss., University of Minnesota, 1959). See also Robert H. Keller, Jr., "The Protestant Churches and Grant's Peace Policy: A Study in Church-State Relations, 1869–1882" (Ph.D. diss., University of Chicago, 1967).

5. Strong Catholic attacks on Grant's policy appeared in *Address of the Catholic Clergy of the Province of Oregon, to the Catholics of the United States, on President Grant's Indian Policy, in Its Bearings upon Catholic Interests at Large* (Portland, Oreg.: Catholic Sentinel Publication Co., 1874) and in *Catholic Grievances in Relation to the Administration of Indian Affairs: Being a Report Presented to the Catholic Young Men's National Union, at Its Annual Convention, Held in Boston, Massachusetts, May 10th and 11th, 1882* (Richmond, Va., 1882). The question of religious freedom on the reservations is treated in Rahill, *Catholic Indian Missions*, pp. 273–331.

6. The full story of the organization of the Bureau and its activities up to 1884 is given in Rahill, *Catholic Indian Missions.* See also *The Bureau of Catholic Indian Missions: The Work of the Decade Ending December 31, 1883* (Washington, 1884); *The Bureau of Catholic Indian Missions, 1874 to 1895* (Washington: Church News Publishing Co., 1895); *The Catholic Encyclopedia*, s.v. "Indian Missions, Bureau of Catholic," by William H. Ketcham.

7. See Consuela Marie Duffy, *Katharine Drexel: A Biography* (Philadelphia: Peter Reilly Co., 1966), which is based upon the extensive archives of the Sisters of the Blessed Sacrament. A similar but undocumented work is Katherine Burton, *The Golden Door: The Life of Katharine Drexel* (New York: P. J. Kenedy and Sons, 1957).

8. J. A. Stephan to Katharine Drexel, June 11, 1885, Archives of the Sisters of the Blessed Sacrament.

9. Marty to James Cardinal Gibbons, May 31, 1889, printed flyer, AAB, 86-K-10. See also *Statistics of Catholic Indian Education, July 1, 1886, to June 30, 1887, Issued by the Bureau of Catholic Indian Missions, Washington, D.C., March, 1887*, ibid., 82-P-4.

10. By 1889, out of $530,905 in contract school funds, $347,672 was distributed to Catholic schools. The Presbyterians, with $41,825, ran a poor second. CIA *Report*, 1890, p. xvii.

11. For the establishment of these organizations, the make-up of their membership, and their reform ideas, see Prucha, *American Indian Policy in Crisis*, pp. 132–68. The quotation is from LM, 1885, p. 1.

12. Painter to Welsh, October 12, 1887, IRA (reel 2).

13. Welsh to Armstrong, October 14, 1887, ibid. (reel 68). McLaughlin was frequently cited by Welsh as a Catholic friend who was on his side in the controversy.

14. Welsh to Ward, October 14, 1887, and Welsh to Rhoads, October 14, 1887, IRA (reel 68); Painter to Welsh, October 17, 1887, ibid. (reel 2). The *Independent* supported the Protestant position by occasional editorials. See vol. 40 (February 9, 1888): 170; (October 25, 1888): 1371.

15. Welsh to Anna L. Dawes, October 19, 1887, IRA (reel 68); Dawes to Welsh, October 21, 1887, ibid. (reel 2). William H. Hare, Episcopal Bishop in Dakota, was well aware of the Catholic encroachments and sought support from other Protestant bodies. See letter to Hare from St. Mary's School, Rosebud Reservation, January 9, 1888, and J. M. Reid, corresponding secretary of the Mission Board, Methodist Episcopal Church, to Hare, February 27, 1888, Historical Archives Collection, The Episcopal Church in South Dakota, Sioux Falls.

16. Welsh to W. H. Ward, October 29, 1887; Welsh to Anna L. Dawes, December 1, 1887; Welsh to F. F. Ellinwood, February 2, 1888, IRA (reels 68 and 69).

17. *Church at Home and Abroad* 4 (July 1888): 55.

18. Welsh to Vilas, July 9, 1888, IRA (reel 69).

19. Vilas to Welsh, July 20, 1888, ibid. (reel 3). Welsh's letter to Vilas and the Secretary's reply were published in *Church at Home and Abroad* 4 (September 1888): 209.

20. CIA *Report*, 1888, p. xv.

21. LM, 1888, p. 94.

22. For Abbott's work in Indian affairs, see Ira V. Brown, *Lyman Abbott, Christian Evolutionist: A Study in Religious Liberalism* (Cambridge: Harvard University Press, 1953), chap. 8.

23. LM, 1888, pp. 11–16.
24. Ibid., pp. 33, 102. The story of the Boston public school controversy is told in Robert H. Lord, John E. Sexton, and Edward T. Harrington, *History of the Archdiocese of Boston*, 3 vols. (New York: Sheed and Ward, 1944), 3:75–85, 110–18, 126–33.
25. See, for example, the remarks of the Reverend Charles S. Shelton, of the American Missionary Association, LM, 1888, p. 20.
26. Ibid., pp. 32, 36.
27. Ibid., pp. 94–95.

Chapter 2

1. Some of the material in this chapter is taken from my *American Indian Policy in Crisis: Christian Reformers and the Indian, 1865–1900* (Norman: University of Oklahoma Press, 1976), chap. 10.
2. For the facts of Morgan's career, see *Dictionary of American Biography*, s.v. "Morgan, Thomas Jefferson," by Conrad Henry Moehlmann, and a biographical sketch written by Morgan himself, attached to a letter of Morgan to E. W. Halford, January 14, 1889, OSI, Appointments Division, Commissioner of Indian Affairs, 1889.
3. Morgan to Harrison, November 26, 1888; Morgan to E. W. Halford, January 14, 1889; Morgan to Harrison, May 22, 1889; Morgan to John W. Noble, June 13, 1889, ibid.
4. Thomas J. Morgan, *Studies in Pedagogy* (Boston: Silver, Burdett and Co., 1889), pp. 327–28, 348–50.
5. LM, 1889, p. 16.
6. Ibid., pp. 107–8; BIC *Report*, 1889, p. 4. Memorials in support of Morgan were sent to Congress by the Baptist Conference and by the Women's National Indian Association. *Senate Journal*, 51st Cong., 1st sess., ser. 2677, pp. 13, 56.
7. There is a sketch of Stephan in *Indian Sentinel*, 1902–1903, pp. 2–5. His early career is described in Anthony J. Posen, "Joseph Andrew Stephan: Indiana's Fighting Priest," *Social Justice Review* 69 (September 1976): 150–58; (October 1976): 188–91. See also Peter J. Rahill, *The Catholic Indian Missions and Grant's Peace Policy, 1870–1884* (Washington: Catholic University of America Press, 1953), pp. 252–53, 261–62, 266, 339–40.
8. Daniel Dorchester, *Romanism versus the Public School System* (New York: Phillips and Hunt, 1888), p. 185. In an address before a conference of the Evangelical Alliance in 1887, Dorchester spoke strongly against the "peril from Romanism." *National Perils and Opportunities: The Discussions of the General Christian Conference, Held in Washington, D.C., December 7th, 8th and 9th, 1887* (New York: Baker and Taylor Co., 1887), pp. 29–37. For a sketch of Dorchester, see *Dictionary of American Biography*, s.v. "Dorchester, Daniel," by Frederick T. Persons.
9. National Educational Association, *Journal of Proceedings and Addresses*, 1888, p. 158.
10. An extensive account of Catholic opposition to Morgan is found in Harry J. Sievers, "The Catholic Indian School Issue and the Presidential Election of 1892," *Catholic Historical Review* 38 (July 1952): 129–55. See also the detailed study by Mary Edward Lijek, "Relations between the Office of Indian Affairs and the Bureau of Catholic Indian Missions, 1885–1900" (M.A. thesis, Catholic University of America, 1965). A pamphlet devoted to the charge that Catholics were being removed from jobs is

Memoranda Relative to Removals and Appointments in the Indian School Service; it reprints an article from the *National Democrat*, October 5, 1889, called "To Make Rome Howl." Archbishop John Ireland, of St. Paul, wrote to President Harrison in mid-August with specific charges of dismissal of Catholics, and Cardinal Gibbons endorsed the complaints. Harrison dismissed the charges by saying his investigation had indicated that the dismissals were made because of insubordination or incompetence. Ireland to Harrison, August 19, 1889; Gibbons to Harrison, August 27, 1889; Harrison to Ireland, September, 1889 (transcript), Benjamin Harrison Papers, Library of Congress, series 1 (reels 22 and 23). See also Bishop James O'Connor to Gibbons, August 11, 1889, AAB, 86-H-5, and George L. Willard, vice-director of the Bureau of Catholic Indian Missions, to Gibbons, August 23, 1889, ibid., 86-J-10.

11. Welsh to Williams, October 19, 1889; Welsh to Briggs, October 21, 1889; Welsh to Armstrong, November 7, 1889; and Welsh to Morgan, November 18, 1889, IRA (reel 70).

12. Morgan to Gibbons, October 22, 1889, AAB, 86-R-9; Gibbons to Morgan, October 24, 1889, ibid., 86-S-1; Morgan to Gibbons, November 2, 1889, ibid., 86-T-2.

13. Welsh to Gibbons, undated, AAB, 97-Y-5; Welsh to Bonaparte, November 12, 1889, IRA (reel 70). Bonaparte's early public career is well described in Eric F. Goldman, *Charles J. Bonaparte, Patrician Reformer: His Earlier Career* (Baltimore: Johns Hopkins Press, 1943).

14. Welsh to Morgan, November 15, 1889, IRA (reel 70).

15. Ireland to Gibbons, November 20, 1889, AAB, 86-U-5.

16. Numerous examples of the protest forms are in BCIM, 1890, DC (undated items). See also John A. Kuster to Stephan, January 14, 1890, ibid. The scrapbooks of newspaper clippings kept by the Catholic Bureau give ample evidence of Catholic press opposition to Morgan.

17. Morgan to E. W. Halford, December 21, 1889, with copy of Stephan's statement attached, Benjamin Harrison Papers, series 1 (reel 24); Morgan to Dawes, January 6, 1890, Records of the Office of the Commissioner of Indian Affairs, LS, vol. 1889–1890, pp. 296–319, NA, RG 75. See also Morgan to the Secretary of the Interior, November 26, 1889, ibid., pp. 254–66.

18. Stephan to Katharine Drexel, December 15, 1889, and January 14, 1890, Archives of the Sisters of the Blessed Sacrament. Stephan mentioned Senators Daniel W. Voorhees, of Indiana, James K. Jones, of Arkansas, George G. Vest, of Missouri, and John J. Ingalls, of Kansas, as some who would support him.

19. Welsh to Frank Wood, December 24, 1889, IRA (reel 70). The extensive correspondence carried on by Welsh is in the same file. He wrote, for example, to Mrs. Amelia Quinton, secretary of the Women's National Indian Association, urging her to bring pressure to bear in the new western states. Welsh to Quinton, November 29, 1889, ibid.

20. Welsh to Henry W. Farnam, November 25, 1889; Welsh to J. W. Harding, December 21, 1889; Welsh to Morgan, December 24, 1889; and Welsh to D. L. Kiehle, February 3, 1890, ibid.

21. Welsh to Armstrong, January 4, 1890, ibid.

22. *Journal of the Executive Proceedings of the Senate*, 27:65, 66, 353–54, 449–50, 461–63. The executive proceedings on the confirmation were leaked to the press and appeared in the *Washington Post*, January 12, 1890, reprinted ibid., pp. 461–62.

23. George W. Norris to Dawes, February 13, 1890, and Morgan to Dawes, Febru-

ary 14, 1890, Henry L. Dawes Papers, Library of Congress; Welsh to Morgan, February 14, 1890, IRA (reel 70).

24. LM, 1890, pp. 51–58; BIC *Report*, 1890, p. 4. The National League for the Protection of American Institutions was organized in 1889 "to secure constitutional and legislative safeguards for the protection of the common school system and other American institutions, to promote public instruction in harmony with such institutions, and to prevent all sectarian or denominational appropriations of public funds." It proposed a sixteenth amendment to the Constitution to carry out these objectives. Its list of adherents included many prominent men, among them active Indian reformers. Donald L. Kinzer, *An Episode in Anti-Catholicism: The American Protective Association* (Seattle: University of Washington Press, 1964), pp. 56–57; National League for the Protection of American Institutions, *A Petition concerning Sectarian Appropriations for Indian Education* (New York, 1892). The anti-Catholic activities of the National League are thoroughly recounted in James M. King, *Facing the Twentieth Century: Our Country, Its Power and Peril* (New York: American Union League Society, 1899).

25. BIC *Report*, 1890, pp. 168–69.

26. Morgan to E. W. Halford, January 13, 1891, Records of the Office of the Commissioner of Indian Affairs, LS, vol. 1890–1892, pp. 118–20, NA, RG 75.

27. *Congressional Record*, 22:2709. This was part of a long debate in the House over funds for contract schools. Ibid., pp. 2698–2709.

28. Morgan to Bureau of Catholic Indian Missions, February 27, 1891, BIA, LS, Education.

29. Stephan to Morgan, April 29, 1891, BIA, LR, 1891–15961. The debate Stephan referred to is in *Congressional Record*, 22:2698–2709. Persons mentioned by him were Congressman Myron H. McCord, Republican of Wisconsin, and a Professor G. E. Bailey of Washington, D.C.

30. Transcript of conference with Chapelle and Lusk, June 10, 1891, BIA, Summaries of Work Completed and Records Relating to Mission Schools, pp. 392–99; Morgan to E. W. Halford, June 17, 1891, Records of the Office of the Commissioner of Indian Affairs, LS, vol. 1890–1892, p. 247. Chapelle's report of the conference is in Chapelle to Stephan, July 19, 1891, BCIM, 1891, DC; it is very hostile toward Morgan. Morgan sent a copy of the transcript of the conference to Gibbons with a conciliatory statement. Morgan to Gibbons, June 18, 1891, AAB, 88-R-2. See copy of the transcript, AAB, 86-Q-6/1.

31. Morgan to Chapelle, June 30, 1891, Records of the Office of the Commissioner of Indian Affairs, LS, vol. 1890–1892, p. 266; Morgan to the Secretary of the Interior, July 3, 1891, ibid., p. 264; Morgan to Chapelle, July 2, 1891, BCIM, 1891, DC. The last of these letters, together with other correspondence concerning Morgan's decision to stop dealing with the Catholic Bureau, is printed in CIA *Report*, 1891, pp. 161–70. In order to be consistent, Morgan also began to deal with individual Protestant schools directly instead of through the mission boards. See letters of Morgan to secretaries of various missionary societies, July 29, 1891, BIA, LS, Education.

32. Morgan to Gibbons, July 16, 1891, AAB, 88-T-3.

33. Welsh to Morgan, July 18, 1891, copy in Benjamin Harrison Papers, series 2 (reel 77). This was one of a series of letters received by Morgan in support of his action of which he forwarded copies to Harrison's secretary. See also Morehouse to E. W. Halford, July 22, 1891, and King to Harrison, July 24, 1891, ibid.

34. Gibbons to Morgan, July 12, 1891, copy in Benjamin Harrison Papers, series 1

(reel 32); Chapelle to the Commissioner of Indian Affairs, July 8, 1891, CIA *Report*, 1891, pp. 164–67. Chapelle and Lusk sought aid in their struggle against Morgan from important churchmen, who they thought might have influence with the President. See Lusk to Archbishop John Ireland, July 15 and 19, 1891, and Chapelle to Cardinal Gibbons, July 17, 1891, BCIM, 1891, DC. Morgan countered such activity by presenting his side directly to the same prelates. See Morgan to Gibbons, July 14, 16, and 18, 1891, and Morgan to Ireland, July 18, 1891, Records of the Office of the Commissioner of Indian Affairs, LS, vol. 1890–1892, pp. 280, 291–95, 298, 299–300. On July 30, 1891, Morgan had an interview with Ireland, in which the Archbishop seemed to acquiesce in Morgan's move against the Catholic Bureau. Transcript of interview in BIA, LR, 1891–27825½. See also Morgan to the Secretary of the Interior, July 30, 1891, BIA, LS, Education. There is a discussion of Gibbons's part in the controversy between Morgan and the Catholic Bureau in John Tracy Ellis, *The Life of James Cardinal Gibbons, Archbishop of Baltimore, 1834–1921*, 2 vols. (Milwaukee: Bruce Publishing Co., 1952), 2:389–94.

35. Lusk to Stephan, July 24, 1891, BCIM, 1891, DC.

36. Morgan to Halford, July 20, 1891, and Morgan to Harrison, July 21 and 22, 1891, Benjamin Harrison Papers, series 1 (reel 32). Morgan reported that Francis E. Leupp, then correspondent for the *New York Evening Post*, had congratulated him on his courage and wisdom and said that those he had talked to were practically unanimous in approval. "He said," Morgan wrote, "they looked upon it as having no partisan nor sectarian influence whatever, but, as an important action in the interest of good government. He said it seemed to them anomalous and dangerous that a sectarian body of *any* kind could be maintained here at the Capital to dictate to the Government." Morgan to Harrison, July 23, 1891, ibid.

37. Morgan's letter has not been found, but its contents are clear from the reply he received.

38. Salpointe to Stephan, April 16, 1891, enclosed in Chapelle to Morgan, May 9, 1891, BIA, LR, 1891–17054.

39. Morgan to Salpointe, July 29, 1891, BIA, LS, Education.

40. Ibid.

41. Salpointe to Morgan, September 11, 1891, BIA, LR, 1891–33650; Morgan to Salpointe, October 6, 1891, and October 22, 1892, BIA, LS, Education. Information on the operation of St. Catherine's School can be found in J. B. Salpointe, *Soldiers of the Cross: Notes on the Ecclesiastical History of New-Mexico, Arizona and Colorado* (Banning, Calif., 1898), pp. 273–74. For biographical data on Salpointe, see Sister Edward Mary Zerwekh, "John Baptist Salpointe, 1825–1894," *New Mexico Historical Review* 37 (January 1962): 1–19; (April 1962): 132–54; (July 1962): 214–29. Morgan's criticism of St. Catherine's seems to be corroborated by Stephan, who wrote to Katharine Drexel on February 27, 1889: "The Archbishop Salpointe is no manager. . . . Father Jouvenceau is careless. . . . The Sisters don't care and have not more interest in the Indians than an old Jew in a hog." Quoted ibid., p. 152. There is an account of the habeas corpus episode in Lijek, "Office of Indian Affairs and the Bureau of Catholic Indian Missions," pp. 33–43.

42. LM, 1892, pp. 60–64.

43. A history of that partnership is R. Pierce Beaver, *Church, State, and the American Indians: Two and a Half Centuries of Partnership in Missions between Protestant Churches and Government* (St. Louis: Concordia Publishing House, 1966). Beaver's

account of "The Dissolution of the Partnership" is on pp. 161–68. Documents on the official withdrawal of the Presbyterians, Baptists, Episcopalians, Congregationalists, and Methodists are appended to Morgan's annual report. CIA *Report*, 1892, pp. 177–82.

44. The election is thoroughly treated in Sievers, "Catholic Indian School Issue."

45. *Report of Rev. J. A. Stephan, Director, to Rt. Rev. Bishop M. Marty, President of the Bureau of Catholic Indian Missions, for the Year 1891–'92* (Washington, 1892), p. 1. Stephan certainly disliked Harrison; to a Jesuit missionary he wrote of the President: "He is a hater of Catholics and believes firmly what he learned in his Presbyterian catechism that the Pope is anti-Christ, and the Catholics are Idolators." Stephan to L. Van Gorp, June 20, 1892, BCIM, 1892, DC.

46. John A. Kuster to Stephan, January 14, 1890, BCIM, 1890, DC.

47. This and numerous other clippings from Catholic newspapers exhibiting the virulent attacks upon Morgan are in the scrapbooks of the Bureau of Catholic Indian Missions. There is no doubt that these attacks were intemperate and in many cases petty. Archbishop Patrick J. Ryan, of Philadelphia, said that the Catholic papers had come to "the lowest ebb of gross personal abuse," and he wanted the bishops to issue a manifesto against it. Ryan to Gibbons, August 17, 1892, AAB, 90-C-4.

48. December 3, 1892, quoted in Sievers, "Catholic Indian School Issue," p. 131. Father Stephan had worked hard in the campaign. He was then seventy years old and in poor health, and he offered his resignation from the Bureau. Bishop Martin Marty, president of the Bureau, and Cardinal Gibbons were willing to accept the resignation and agreed upon the Reverend P. F. Hylebos, vicar general of the Tacoma diocese, as a successor, but in fact no change was made and Stephan continued in office. Stephan to Marty, September 20, 1892, AAB, 90-G-3; Marty to Gibbons, November 30, 1892, ibid., 90-S-6; Gibbons to Marty, December 5, 1892, ibid., 90-T-5.

Chapter 3

1. The phrase is quoted in Harry J. Sievers, "The Catholic Indian School Issue and the Presidential Election of 1892," *Catholic Historical Review* 38 (July 1952): 155.

2. Ryan to Gibbons, January 26, 1893, AAB, 91-D-9; Gibbons to Cleveland, January 30, 1893, ibid., 91-D-10; W. S. Cantrell and others to the President, February 17, 1893, OSI, Appointments Division, Appointment Files, March 4, 1893–March 3, 1897, Commissioner of Indian Affairs. Herbert Welsh, who had strongly urged Oberly's retention in office in 1889, now criticized him because of alleged violations of civil service regulations and strongly urged C. C. Painter, Washington agent of the Indian Rights Association, as the new Commissioner. As an alternate, however, Welsh suggested James McLaughlin, a highly respected Indian agent. "McLaughlin," Welsh wrote, "is a Roman Catholic but would I believe be perfectly fair in his treatment of other denominations." Welsh to Cleveland, January 13 and March 15, 1893, Grover Cleveland Papers, Library of Congress, series 2 (reels 72 and 73).

3. For accounts of this anti-Catholicism, see Donald L. Kinzer, *An Episode in Anti-Catholicism: The American Protective Association* (Seattle: University of Washington Press, 1964); Humphrey J. Desmond, *The A.P.A. Movement: A Sketch* (Washington: New Century Press, 1912); Charles Louis Sewrey, "The Alleged 'Un-Americanism' of the Church as a Factor in Anti-Catholicism in the United States, 1860–1914" (Ph.D. diss., University of Minnesota, 1955); Gustavus Myers, *History of Bigotry in the United States* (New York: Random House, 1943), pp. 219–47; and John Higham, *Strangers in*

the Land: Patterns of American Nativism, 1860–1925 (New Brunswick: Rutgers University Press, 1955). A contemporary account and strong condemnation of the APA is Washington Gladden, "The Anti-Catholic Crusade," *Century Magazine* 47 (March 1894): 789–95. Herbert Welsh condemned the persecution of Catholics by the APA as "un-American and un-Christian." *City and State*, June 18, 1896, p. 3.

4. See Francis P. Cassidy, "Catholic Education in the Third Plenary Council of Baltimore," *Catholic Historical Review* 34 (October 1948): 257–305; (January 1949): 414–36.

5. Thomas J. Morgan, *Roman Catholics and Indian Education* (Boston: American Citizen Company, 1893), p. 2.

6. Clippings from *Chicago Herald*, October 14, 1893, and *San Francisco Chronicle*, November 4, 1895, in BCIM scrapbooks.

7. *Congressional Record*, 26:5928–29.

8. Ibid., pp. 5929–32.

9. Ibid., 26:5999–6055; 27:6238–39.

10. Ibid., 27:6309. See also the debate on June 16, ibid., pp. 6423–24, 6434–35. The Senate received numerous petitions against the use of funds for sectarian schools. Ibid., 26:7816, 7877.

11. Act of August 15, 1894, *United States Statutes at Large*, 28:311.

12. Report of the Secretary of the Interior, 1894, in *House Executive Document* no. 1, pt. 5, 53d Cong., 3d sess., ser. 3305, p. vi. Smith restated his position in his report for 1895, in *House Document* no. 5, 54th Cong., 1st sess., ser. 3381, pp. vii–viii. Hoke Smith's biographer says that Smith "suggested a compromise that proved acceptable," but he makes no mention of the strong opposition to Smith that came from the Catholic Bureau. The "compromise" was acceptable to the Protestant-dominated Congress and to the Indian Rights Association but hardly to Father Stephan and his supporters. Dewey W. Grantham, Jr., *Hoke Smith and the Politics of the New South* (Baton Rouge: Louisiana State University Press, 1958), pp. 76–80.

13. Fred L. Israel, ed., *The State of the Union Messages of the Presidents, 1790–1966*, 3 vols. (New York: Chelsea House, 1966), 2:1783; CIA *Report*, 1894, p. 17.

14. IRA *Report*, 1893, pp. 20–23. This position was reiterated in the *Report* for 1894, pp. 8–9, and these statements were referred to in subsequent years as the firm position of the Association.

15. Welsh to C. C. Painter, October 14, 1893, IRA (reel 72); Welsh to Gibbons, November 7, 1893, AAB, 92A-G-1. Welsh's letter was sparked by an article of Gibbons's in the *Review of Reviews*, in which Welsh detected an adherence to the principle of complete separation of church and state. Welsh asked whether Gibbons's "maturer judgment on it [the question of the contract schools] coincides with mine." Gibbons replied that the contract schools were doing good work and were still necessary and that he saw no reason to discontinue them. Gibbons to Welsh, November 14, 1893, AAB, 92A-H-1. Welsh sent copies of his correspondence with Gibbons to a number of friends, including Lyman Abbott, who on his own published it in the *Outlook*. Welsh was incensed by this action and apologized to Gibbons, but he ultimately concluded that no harm had been done. Welsh to Gibbons, December 4, 1893, AAB, 92A-L-10; Welsh to Abbott, December 2, 4, and 5, 1893, IRA (reel 72).

16. Welsh to Carl Schurz, March 24, 1894, IRA (reel 73) and other correspondence of April and May in the same file. Welsh also carried on the campaign through the pamphlets of the Indian Rights Association: *The Secretary of the Interior and the Indian*

Education Problem—A Rift in the Cloud (Philadelphia: Indian Rights Association, 1894); *The Position of Superintendent of Indian Schools Threatened—A Serious Danger to Be Averted* (Philadelphia: Indian Rights Association, 1894); *Indian School Welfare* (Philadelphia: Indian Rights Association, 1894).

17. Welsh to Hailmann, November 16, 1894, IRA (reel 73); Welsh to Evans Woolen, October 20, 1896, ibid. (reel 74).

18. Stephan to Gibbons, Ryan, and Corrigan, December 21, 1894, BCIM, 1894, DC.

19. Act of March 2, 1895, *United States Statutes at Large*, 28:904. See also *Congressional Record*, 27:993–96, 1112–14. A table showing the schools with contracts for fiscal year 1896, indicating location, number of pupils, religious community in charge, and government allotment, appears in *The Bureau of Catholic Indian Missions, 1874 to 1895* (Washington: Church News Publishing Co., 1895), pp. 22–25.

20. Stephan to William F. Harrity, December 19, 1895, BCIM, 1895, DC.

21. Stephan to Sherman, February 3, 1896, BCIM, 1896, DC. A similar letter was written on February 13 to Senator William B. Allison, chairman of the Committee on Appropriations. Ibid.

22. Stephan to Ryan, March 3, 1896, ibid.

23. *Congressional Record*, 28:2080–88; Leupp's "Washington Letter" of March 4, 1896, in *City and State*, March 5, 1896, p. 6.

24. *Congressional Record*, 28:3813–14. The whole debate of April 10, 1896, is on pp. 3812–22. Carter was supported by Senator Pettigrew and others and opposed chiefly by Senators Henry Cabot Lodge, of Massachusetts, and Jacob H. Gallinger, of New Hampshire.

25. *Congressional Record*, 28:4208–14, 6357.

26. Circular of Stephan to Superintendents of Catholic Indian Boarding and Day Schools, June 15, 1896, BCIM, 1896, DC. One school that fell victim to the Congressional cutting of funds was St. Joseph's Indian Normal School at Rensselaer, Indiana, which Father Stephan had founded in 1888 with Mother Katharine's funds as a sort of Catholic counterpart to the Carlisle Indian Industrial School. The history of the school is a valuable example of what the Bureau of Catholic Indian Missions was attempting, the opposition of Morgan and Dorchester, and the ultimate collapse because of lack of funds. The school was an off-reservation boarding school meant for advanced students and thus was not typical of the reservation schools, which the Catholics fought harder to retain. An excellent account of the school is given in Dominic B. Gerlach, "St. Joseph's Indian Normal School, 1888–1896," *Indiana Magazine of History* 69 (March 1973): 1–42.

27. *Congressional Record*, 29:2043. The full debate on the topic is on pp. 2039–47.

28. Herbert Welsh, *A Response to Senator Pettigrew* (Philadelphia: Indian Rights Association, 1897); Welsh to J. H. Gallinger, February 24, 1897; Welsh to Francis E. Leupp, February 24, 1897; Welsh to Mrs. L. H. Daggett, March 19, 1897, IRA (reel 74).

29. *Congressional Record*, 29:2080–83, 2964; Act of June 7, 1897, *United States Statutes at Large*, 30:79. The act passed by the second session of the Fifty-fourth Congress was not signed by the President, but it was reintroduced immediately when the Fifty-fifth Congress met and passed during the first session of that Congress.

30. Stephan to Gibbons, Ryan, and Corrigan, March 10, 1897, BCIM, 1897, DC.

31. Arthur Wallace Dunn, *From Harrison to Harding: A Personal Narrative Cover-*

ing a Third of a Century, 1888–1921, 2 vols. (New York: G. P. Putnam's Sons, 1922), 1:197. See also Kinzer, *An Episode in Anti-Catholicism*, p. 224.

32. Stephan to E. Vattman, January 11, 1897, and Stephan to William McKinley, January 19, 1897, BCIM, 1897, DC.

33. Stephan to Archbishop Frederick X. Katzer, April 22, 1897, and James O'Keefe to Stephan, April 28, 1897, BCIM, 1897, DC.

34. "Memorandum Relative to Catholic Indian Schools from Bureau of Catholic Indian Missions," September 24, 1897, AAB, 95-S-9/1. There is some indication that the Catholics in 1897 began an attempt to get petitions from the Sioux Indians for the use of tribal funds to continue the schools. Bishop Hare in April 1897 sent an inquiry to Episcopalian missionaries to find out about such petitions, and he received some positive answers, but apparently no petitions were sent to Washington. Joseph W. Cook to Hare, April 8, 1897; C. E. Snavely to Hare, April 10, 1897, and P. J. Deloria to Hare, April 28, 1897, Historical Archives Collection, The Episcopal Church in South Dakota, Sioux Falls. A petition from the Menominee Indians, April 19, 1897, sent to the Commissioner of Indian Affairs, is printed in *Senate Document* no. 179, 58th Cong., 3d sess., ser. 4766, pp. 3–5. For agitation on the Menominee matter, see Stephan to Mother Katharine, June 8, July 4, and August 1, 1898, BCIM, 1898, DC; Senator Thomas H. Carter to Lusk, July 19, 1898, ibid.; Lusk to Carter, January 11, 1899, ibid., 1899, DC.

35. "Memorandum in the matter of appropriation for the support of Indian contract schools during the fiscal year ending June 30, 1899," January 3, 1898; Lusk to Archbishop Ireland, January 4, 1898; Lusk to J. Haven Richards, January 14, 1898; Lusk to Stephan, January 16, 1898, BCIM, 1898, DC. The same file contains letters of Lusk to senators and others urging a 40 percent figure for the contract schools. Ryan's address is printed in *Indian Schools: Statement of Archbishop Ryan before Senate Committee, 4th Feb., 1898*, copy in BIC, Reference Material, Schools (Sectarian).

36. Act of July 1, 1898, *United States Statutes at Large*, 30:587; Lusk to Gibbons, February 10, 1898; Lusk to Stephan, April 15, 1898; Lusk to Ryan, June 1, 1898, BCIM, 1898, DC. The Senate amended the House's 20 percent to read 30 percent without debate on February 10, 1898. *Congressional Record*, 31:1612.

37. Stephan to Gibbons, Ryan, and Corrigan, July 28, 1898, BCIM, 1898, DC.

38. Printed copy of minutes of the annual meeting of the archbishops, October 12, 1898, AAB, 96-Q-2; *Petition of James Cardinal Gibbons . . . Praying Congress for a Reopening of the Indian Contract School Question . . .* , December 5, 1898, printed copy in BCIM. The archbishops at their meeting voiced some criticism of Father Stephan's accounting for the salary money he received from Mother Katharine. The criticism drew a sharp rejoinder from the petulant old man in a letter to Cardinal Gibbons: "I have had a hard and constantly worrying life during 14 years while I am in the Bureau. My assistants generally went after 4 o'clock to baseballs, to theatres, playing cards and enjoying themselves, while I was sitting in my office untill late at nights, alone, studying how to overcome the obstacles laid in my ways by congress, the A.P.A.s, their satellites, their sympathizers, & religious fanatics. Financially I would have done better to be the Assistant Director than Director. I go out of the Bureau—as God is my witness —a poor malignant [*sic*] priest." He again offered to resign, but he probably did not mean to be taken seriously, for at the end of the letter he noted, "I am working on the promised 'memorial' for Congress and shall send it to Your Eminence, as soon as it is finished." Stephan to Gibbons, October 21, 1898, AAB, 96-Q-6.

39. Gibbons to bishops, December 5, 1898, pp. 1–2, printed copy in BCIM.

40. Stephan to Secretary of War D. S. Lamont, February 29, 1897, printed copy in BCIM. See also Stephan to Secretary of the Interior C. N. Bliss, June 26, 1897, and Bliss to Stephan, July 1, 1897, BCIM, 1897, DC. Bliss said that Pratt had been cautioned and that no further complaints about him had been heard.

41. BCIM *Report*, 1899, pp. 5–6; Jones to Pratt, September 30 and December 26, 1899, William A. Jones Papers, State Historical Society of Wisconsin. Pratt's anti-Catholicism in regard to Indian education is thoroughly examined in Everett Arthur Gilcreast, "Richard Henry Pratt and American Indian Policy, 1877–1906: A Study of the Assimilation Movement" (Ph.D. diss., Yale University, 1967), pp. 262–75.

42. Gibbons to bishops, December 5, 1898.

43. Act of March 1, 1899, *United States Statutes at Large*, 30:942. The Senate had inserted into the bill a provision to continue payments at a 20 percent level; when the House refused to concur, the conference committee cut the figure to 15 percent and added the clause about the final appropriation. *Congressional Record*, 32:1556–57, 2527. See also R. F. Pettigrew to Lusk, January 10, 1899, and Stephan to Gibbons, February 8, 1899, BCIM, 1899, DC.

44. Memorandum dated August 1, 1898, BCIM, 1898, DC.

Chapter 4

1. Circular of Stephan to Superintendents of Catholic Indian Contract Schools, April 11, 1900; Jones to Bureau of Catholic Indian Missions, June 22, 1900; Stephan to Jones, June 29, 1900, BCIM, 1900, DC.

2. William H. Ketcham to Senator Henry Teller, March 11, 1904, BCIM, 1904, DC.

3. Stephan to Horstmann. January 17, 1900, and Lusk to Horstmann, January 20, 1900, BCIM, 1900, DC.

4. Draft, ibid.

5. *Congressional Record* 33:1463, 1741–74, Appendix, pp. 50–53. On May 24, 1900, Congressman Little entered into the *Record* a memorandum from Commissioner William A. Jones, which was a rebuttal of Fitzgerald's remarks on the contract schools. Fitzgerald replied in a long speech entered into the *Record*, in which he declared that Jones's statement was "a covert, contemptible, and despicable attack upon and slur upon the missionary work so long done by the people of a particular faith. It is a scandalous, although indirect, reflection on the Catholic missions of this country, unjustifiable, unworthy, and constituting a disgraceful abuse of official power." Jones's memorandum is printed in *Congressional Record* 33:5989–90. Fitzgerald's reply is printed ibid., Appendix, pp. 550–55.

6. Lusk circular to Superintendent of Catholic Indian Contract Schools, February 6, 1900, and Lusk to Senator Thomas H. Carter, February 23, 1900, BCIM, 1900, DC.

7. Lusk to E. R. Dyer, February 13, 1900; Lusk to Bishop Horstmann, March 2, 1900; Lusk to Bishop George Montgomery, March 6, 1900; Stephan to Ryan, March 7, 1900; Stephan to Bishop Henry Elder, May 15, 1900, BCIM, 1900, DC. The action in the Senate can be traced in *Congressional Record*, 33:3877–90, 3916–19.

8. Stephan to Ryan, March 7, 1900, BCIM, 1900, DC.

9. Stephan to Elder, May 15, 1900, ibid.

10. Stephan to Lusk, June 1, 1900, ibid.

11. BCIM *Report*, 1899–1900, pp. 3–4. See also Lusk to Horstmann, March 2, 1900, and Stephan to Elder, May 15, 1900, BCIM, 1900, DC.

12. Stephan to Ryan, June 30, 1900, and Stephan to Horstmann, July 14, 1900, ibid. Stephan's role in initiating a federation is seen in a series of letters, June to October, 1900, from Stephan and Lusk to Theodore Thiele, a Chicago layman who was influential in the organization of the American Federation of Catholic Societies. Ibid.

13. BCIM *Report*, 1899–1900, p. 10; Stephan to Mother Katharine, July 23, 1900, BCIM, 1900, DC.

14. Stephan to Superintendents of Catholic Indian Schools, July 14, 1900, ibid.

15. Information on Ketcham's life is taken from M. Imelda Logsdon, "Monsignor William Henry Ketcham and the Bureau of Catholic Indian Missions" (M.A. thesis, Catholic University of America, 1949).

16. Ryan to Ketcham, August 2 and 26, November 6, 1900, BCIM, 1900, DC; Ryan to Gibbons, November 2, 1900, AAB, 98-L-1; Ryan to Lusk, November 22, 1900, BCIM, 1900, DC.

17. Ketcham to Ryan, December 20, 1900, ibid.

18. Copy of memorandum in BCIM, 1901, DC. See also Ketcham to Gibbons, April 20, 1901, ibid.

19. Ketcham to Ryan, January 18, 1901, ibid.

20. Jones to the Secretary of the Interior, February 12, 1901, BIA, LS, Education. The trust fund part of this letter is printed in *Senate Document* no. 179, 58th Cong., 3d sess., ser. 4766, pp. 32–35. See also Jones's "Memorandum Relating to Contract or Sectarian Schools," November 12, 1902, ibid., pp. 36–41. The question of the use of Indian trust funds was referred to the Board of Indian Commissioners for an opinion. The Board, in a formal resolution, unanimously decided against the use of the funds for denominational schools. Minutes of January 25, 1901, BIC, typed copies, p. 270.

21. Jones to the Secretary of the Interior, September 28, 1900, Records of the Office of the Commissioner of Indian Affairs, LS, volume 1900–1901, pp. 111–22, NA, RG 75. Jones was not opposed to religious influences in the education of Indian children. When the Jesuit John J. Wynne sent Jones a copy of *A Vanished Arcadia*, by R. B. Cunninghame Graham, a history of the missionary work of the Jesuits among the Indians of Paraguay, Jones replied: "I fully agree with you that there was no mistake there and that the same good could and can be accomplished by others as well as by Jesuits if religious influences were employed. While I have been in favor of Government Schools, my early training was of such a character that I can never get over the idea that all true education must be based upon religion, and the more of it we have in the training and instruction of children, the more permanent and lasting will be its effect." Jones to Wynne, January 4, 1901, William A. Jones Papers, State Historical Society of Wisconsin.

22. BCIM *Report*, 1900–1901 and 1901–1902, p. 28; Ketcham to Gibbons, April 20, 1901, BCIM, 1901, DC.

23. Ketcham to archbishops, October 10, 1901, copy in Archives of the Sisters of the Blessed Sacrament; extracts from the letter are printed in *Appeal on Behalf of the Negro and Indian Missions in the United States* (N.p., 1902), pp. 2–3.

24. BCIM *Report*, 1899, pp. 3–4. Stephan repeated his plea in his last report as director of the Bureau. BCIM *Report*, 1899–1900, pp. 6–7. In a letter to Mother Katharine, March 27, 1900, Stephan said, "My idea would be to supplement the Bishop's

work by sending through the country eight of ten priests to preach and lecture to the people on the Indian schools question, and take up collections." BCIM, 1900, DC.

25. Ryan to Ketcham, January 17, 1901, BCIM, 1901, DC; BCIM *Report*, 1901–1902, pp. 1–2, 5.

26. John J. Wynne to Ketcham, March 8, 1905, BCIM, 1905, DC.

27. For information on the establishment of the Society, see BCIM *Report*, 1900–1901 and 1901–1902, pp. 5–7, and BCIM *Report*, 1903–1904, pp. 1–3, 38–40. The BCIM records for 1902 and 1903 are full of information about the varied activities.

28. Ketcham to Gibbons, October 5, 1901, BCIM, 1901, DC.

29. *Indian Sentinel*, 1902–1903, pp. 24, 28–33. The periodical was issued as an annual from 1902 to 1916. It became a quarterly in July 1916, a monthly in January 1936, a bimonthly in January 1957, and a quarterly again in 1962, the last year of publication. It was primarily a vehicle for keeping alive interest in Catholic Indian missions and promoting support for the schools. It contained accounts and pictures from the various missions and schools, as well as reports of the activities of the Catholic Bureau.

30. *Dictionary of American Biography*, s.v. "Ganss, Henry George," by George I. Chadwick; "The Reverend Henry G. Ganss, Mus. D.," *Records of the American Catholic Historical Society* 24 (June 1914): 179–82.

31. Mother Katharine to Gibbons, September 26, 1901, AAB, 99-B-6; *Indian Sentinel*, 1902–1903, p. 26; BCIM *Report*, 1900–1901 and 1901–1902, p. 7. The considerable correspondence between Ganss and Ketcham in BCIM, 1902 and 1903, DC, indicates tension between the two men.

32. Statement in BCIM, 1903, DC.

33. BCIM *Report*, 1903–1904, pp. 15, 38–39; *Indian Sentinel*, 1904–1905, p. 29.

34. BCIM *Report*, 1906, p. 29. The annual reports of the Catholic Bureau give statistics on the receipts for each year from various sources.

35. Ketcham to E. Eyre, first president of the Marquette League, January 20, 1904, BCIM, 1904, DC.

36. Eyre to Ketcham, May 27, 1904, ibid. The files of BCIM, 1904 and 1905, are full of materials dealing with the organization and early activities of the League. The circular is reprinted in BCIM *Report*, 1904–1905, pp. 19–21. See also Charles Warren Currier, "The Marquette League," *Indian Sentinel*, 1906, pp. 4–6.

37. BCIM *Report*, 1904–1905, pp. 20–21.

38. The annual reports of the Catholic Bureau show the contributions of the Marquette League.

39. Ketcham to Gibbons, November 16, 1901, BCIM, 1901, DC; Gibbons to Roosevelt, March 29, 1902, AAB, 99-N-7; Welsh to the President, March 20, 1902, and Welsh to Philip C. Garrett, March 27, 1902, IRA (reel 75); Garrett to Welsh, March 29, 1902, ibid. (reel 16).

40. Bonaparte's Indian activities are well described in Eric F. Goldman, *Charles J. Bonaparte, Patrician Reformer: His Earlier Career* (Baltimore: Johns Hopkins Press, 1943).

41. BCIM *Report*, 1903–1904, p. 35.

42. Ganss to Welsh, February 28, 1902, IRA (reel 16); Welsh to Ganss, March 1, 1902; J. LeRoy to A. K. Smiley, March 5, 1902; and Welsh to Philip C. Garrett, March 18, 1902, ibid. (reel 75).

43. LM, 1902, pp. 43–47, 55–56, 130–32, 180; Ganss to Smiley, September 25, 1903, Smiley Family Papers, Quaker Collection, Haverford College. The Smiley Family Papers contain a good many indications of the Protestant-Catholic accord.

44. Ganss to Sniffen, November 10, 1902, IRA (reel 16).
45. Ganss to Ryan, November 24, 1902, AAB, 100-D-7.

Chapter 5

1. Morgan to Charles S. Kelsey, October 12, 1891, and Browning to J. George Wright, October 26, 1894, BIA, LS, Education.
2. W. H. Clapp to the Commissioner of Indian Affairs, September 21, 1896, BIA, LR, 1896-36613E; Browning to Clapp, September 30, 1896, BIA, LS, Education.
3. BCIM *Report*, 1898, pp. 4–5; Lusk to Ryan, January 26, 1898, BCIM, 1898, DC. For action in the House of Representatives, see *Congressional Record*, 31:1056.
4. BCIM *Report*, 1899, pp. 6–7. Cardinal Gibbons had condemned the Browning Ruling in his petition to Congress in 1898. *Petition of James Cardinal Gibbons . . . Praying Congress for a Reopening of the Indian Contract School Question . . .*, December 5, 1898, p. 10. Printed copy in BCIM.
5. Stephan to Horstmann, October 24, 1899, with attached memorandum, and Horstmann to Stephan, November 17, 1899, BCIM, 1899, DC. See also Stephan to Mother Katharine, September 28, 1899, ibid. Senator Hanna sent a memorandum to Commissioner Jones, with pointed questions about the Browning Ruling, about the alleged bigotry of Richard H. Pratt at Carlisle Indian Industrial School, and about the continued appropriations for Hampton Institute, which the Catholics contended was a sectarian school. Jones refuted the charges in a letter to Hanna, March 14, 1900, William A. Jones Papers, State Historical Society of Wisconsin.
6. Memorandum of Ketcham, BCIM, 1901, DC (undated items). See also Bishop George Montgomery to W. A. Jones, March 15, 1901, enclosed in F. A. Hitchcock to Jones, October 12, 1901, BIA, LR, 1901-56942E.
7. Jones to the Secretary of the Interior, February 12, 1901, BIA, LS, Education. The quotations in the paragraphs following are from this letter.
8. A brief account of these actions appears in BCIM *Report*, 1900–1901 and 1901–1902, pp. 2–3. A much more detailed story is given in Ketcham to Bonaparte, August 14, 1903, CJB, LR. The facts are also reported in Jones to the Secretary of the Interior, August 29, 1901, BIA, LS, Education. Copies of the telegrams exchanged between Secretary of the Interior E. A. Hitchcock and the Acting Secretary, Thomas Ryan, May 6, 1901, are in Private Papers of Ethan Allen Hitchcock, 1880–1909, Subject File, Miscellaneous Indian Affairs, in a folder marked "Browning Ruling," NA, RG 200. This file contains copies of most of the essential documents dealing with the matter. In reply to Thomas Ryan's inquiry (instigated by Archbishop Ryan), Hitchcock said: "You can assure His Grace Archbishop Ryan that the Browning order will be revoked."
9. Jones to the Secretary of the Interior, August 29, 1901, BIA, LS, Education. Jones sent on to Hitchcock correspondence he had received about a conflict between the government schools and the mission school at the Tule River Agency in California, which he said fed his doubts about the wisdom of abrogating the ruling.
10. Jones to the Secretary of the Interior, September 26, 1901, copy in Private Papers of Ethan Allen Hitchcock, Subject File, Miscellaneous Indian Affairs, "Browning Ruling."
11. Hitchcock to the Commissioner of Indian Affairs, October 12, 1901, BIA, LR, 1901-56942E. News of the suspension was sent to the Bureau of Catholic Indian Missions by Jones on October 22, 1901, BIA, LS, Education.

12. Jones to the Bureau of Catholic Indian Missions, October 30, 1901, and Jones to the Secretary of the Interior, November 4, 1901, ibid. The abrogation of the ruling was reported in the *New York Times*, October 31, 1901.

13. Records of the Education Division, Circulars Issued by the Education Division, 1897–1909, NA, RG 75. The circular was approved by the Secretary of the Interior on January 18, 1902. It is printed in full in BCIM *Report*, 1900–1901 and 1901–1902, p. 9.

14. Education Circular no. 84, November 1, 1902, Circulars Issued by the Education Division, 1897–1909; Jones to the Secretary of the Interior, February 12, 1901, BIA, LS, Education.

15. BCIM *Report*, 1900–1901 and 1901–1902, pp. 9–10.

16. Hare to Jones, November 7, 1902, and Jones to Hare, November 14, 1902, Historical Archives Collection, The Episcopal Church in South Dakota, Sioux Falls.

17. Gates to Abbott, November 29, 1901, BIC, Reference Material, Schools (Sectarian). The dossier of letters on the Browning Ruling is in this same file.

Chapter 6

1. Agreement ratified February 28, 1877, *United States Statutes at Large*, 19:256.

2. A. C. Tonner to Indian Agent, Shoshone Agency, July 28, 1900, BIA, LS, Education; *Rules for the Indian School Service, 1900* (Washington: Government Printing Office, 1900), p. 40.

3. Jones to agents, August 27, 1901, BIA, LS, Finance.

4. Jones's long letter to the Secretary of the Interior, September 28, 1900, lamenting the pressures put on the Indian Office by the Catholics made no mention of the rations question. Records of the Office of the Commissioner of Indian Affairs, LS, vol. 1900–1901, pp. 111–22. In reply to a complaint from St. Patrick's Mission Boarding School at Anadarko, Oklahoma, about the cessation of essential rations, Jones justified his action on the basis of the Congressional policy. Jones to the Secretary of the Interior, November 22, 1901, OSI, ID, LR, 1901-9832.

5. Hare to the Secretary of the Interior, November 15, 1901, ibid., LR, 1902-111.

6. Jones to the Secretary of the Interior, January 6, 1902, BIA, LS, Finance. The quotations in the paragraphs following are from this letter.

7. See William Langford to D. M. Browning, December 17, 1895, BIA, LR, 1905-50897E.

8. George B. Cortelyou, secretary to the President, to Knox, January 30, 1902, DJ, Year File no. 2290-02. A copy of Jones's letter of January 6 was sent to Knox with the notation that the President thought "the position of the Interior Department in this matter is correct, and that, under the law it cannot do as Bishop Hare desires," but that the judgment of the Department of Justice was wanted.

9. Attorney General to the President, February 10, 1902, DJ, Year File no. 2290-02. There is some question whether the decision was officially sent to Roosevelt. The jacket says "Opinion not sent," and in 1905, the Attorney General wrote: "Responding to your request over the telephone this morning, I beg to transmit herewith correspondence in this Department in regard to the distribution of rations by the Interior Department to Indian children in Episcopal schools. Your attention is called to the fact that the opinion prepared by this department on February 10, 1902, to the President, was never sent. I am informed, however, that in some manner this opinion got into the Congressional Record, but was subsequently withdrawn. Assistant Attorney General Purdy, who had

immediate charge of this matter, advises me that ex-Attorney General Knox talked with the President personally about it at the time and reached the conclusion that nothing should be done about it." Attorney General to William Loeb, Jr., secretary to the President, January 26, 1905, ibid. In discussing the history of the case in a letter of January 5, 1905, however, Bishop Hare quotes the opinion of Knox and says, "This opinion was sent to me by the President, as his answer to my appeal." Printed copy in BIC, Reference Material, Schools (Sectarian). The opinion is also printed in *Senate Document* no. 179, 58th Cong., 3d sess., ser. 4766, pp. 35–36.

10. Letter of Hare, January 5, 1905, printed copy in BIC, Reference Material, Schools (Sectarian). The Indian Rights Association supported the use of rations for mission schools. IRA *Report*, 1902, pp. 22–24.

11. BCIM *Report*, 1903–1904, pp. 25–26.

12. Special aid came from Theodore B. Thiele, a Catholic layman in Chicago, who put pressure on the Illinois Senators, William E. Mason and Shelby M. Cullom, and who promised help from the German Catholic societies in Chicago. The Catholic Bureau eagerly accepted the help. Thiele to Lusk, November 27 and December 16, 1901, and Lusk to Thiele, December 11, 1901, BCIM, 1901, DC.

13. Ketcham to the President, January 25, 1902, OSI, ID, LR, 1902-1343.

14. Bonaparte to Ryan, October 1, 1902, CJB, LS.

15. Bonaparte to Ryan, October 6, 1902, ibid.; Roosevelt to the Attorney General, July 25, 1903, DJ, Year File no. 2290-02.

16. Gates to Bonaparte, December 26, 1902, CJB, LR; Minutes, October 23, 1902, BIC, typed copies, p. 279.

17. Bonaparte to Ryan, December 24, 1902, CJB, LS; Ryan to Bonaparte, December 26, 1902, ibid., LR.

18. James's report has not been found, but its contents can be reconstructed from Bonaparte's minority report, cited below.

19. Bonaparte's minority report is printed in a pamphlet by Congressman Edward Morrell, of Pennsylvania, *Rations to Indian School Children*, dated February 4, 1903, pp. 11–13. Copy in DJ, Year File no. 2290-02.

20. Bonaparte to Ryan, December 24, 1902, and Bonaparte to Herbert Welsh, December 24, 1902, CJB, LS.

21. Minutes, January 21–23, 1903, BIC, typed copies, pp. 280–82.

22. Minutes, January 23, 1902, ibid., pp. 283–84. Bonaparte reported the action in detail to Herbert Welsh when he sent him a copy of the resolution. Bonaparte to Welsh, January 26, CJB, LS.

23. Bonaparte to Ketcham, January 27, 1903, ibid.; Ketcham to Bonaparte, January 31, 1903, ibid., LR.

24. *Congressional Record*, 36:2182. Ketcham was very hostile toward Lodge. He wrote: "This is not the first time that Senator Lodge has killed this measure, nor is it the only occasion upon which he has shown his antipathy to the Catholic Indian schools. From the beginning of the agitation of the question of discontinuing 'contract schools' down to the present, he has ever been on guard, ready to defeat every measure that might tend to ameliorate the condition of these schools. Senator Lodge is not only a bigot, but he appears to delight in being as conspicuous as possible in his anti-Catholic work. It is well that all Catholics should know their foes, and of these we are of the opinion that few, if any, will be found the equal of Senator Lodge." *Indian Sentinel*, 1903–1904, p. 28.

25. Ketcham to Philbin, March 10, 1903, and John J. Wynne to Ketcham, July 14 and September 17, 1903, BCIM, 1903, DC.

26. Bonaparte to Ryan, October 1 and 6, 1902, CJB, LS.

27. Philbin to Bonaparte, July 16, 1903, ibid., LR; Bonaparte to Ryan, August 1, 1903, ibid., LS.

28. Roosevelt to the Attorney General, July 25, 1903, DJ, Year File no. 2290-02; Ryan to H. M. Hoyt, Assistant Attorney General, July 31, 1903, ibid.; Bonaparte to the Attorney General, August 1, 1903, ibid.; Bonaparte to Ryan, August 1, 1903, CJB, LS.

29. *Rations to Indian School Children: Argument of Hon. Edward Morrell, Representative of the Fifth Pennsylvania District*, February 4, 1903; letters of Bonaparte to Ryan, Ketcham, and Philbin, August 13, 1903, CJB, LS.

30. Ketcham to Bonaparte, August 14, 1903, ibid., LR; Bonaparte to Ryan, August 22, 1903, ibid., LS.

31. Philbin to Bonaparte, August 14, 1903, ibid., LR; Bonaparte to Philbin, August 19, 1903, ibid., LS.

32. Bonaparte to Philbin, August 27 and December 1, 1903, and Bonaparte to Ryan, October 21, 1903, ibid.; Philbin to Bonaparte, December 8, 1903, ibid., LR.

33. Bonaparte to Hitchcock, February 27, 1904; Bonaparte to Philbin, December 14, 1903; Bonaparte to Ryan, February 11, 1904; Bonaparte to Ketcham, February 20 and 23, 1904, CJB, LS; Bonaparte to Roosevelt, February 24, 1904, Theodore Roosevelt Papers, Library of Congress, series 1 (reel 42); Roosevelt to Bonaparte, February 25, 1904, *The Letters of Theodore Roosevelt*, ed. Elting E. Morison, 8 vols. (Cambridge: Harvard University Press, 1951–54), 4:739–40; Bonaparte to the Attorney General, February 27, 1904, DJ, Year File no. 2290-02.

34. The brief is in DJ, Year File no. 2290-02.

35. Ketcham to Bonaparte, February 22, 1904, CJB, LR. Bonaparte wrote: "I learn from Father Ketcham that a spirit decidedly more friendly than formerly towards Catholics and Catholic interests seems to prevail at the Indian Bureau and in the Department of the Interior, and I must say that Secretary Hitchcock professes entire good will towards us. He gave as one reason for wishing me to undertake the investigation of alleged abuses in the Indian Territory the fact that I was a more or less prominent Catholic." Bonaparte to Ryan, October 21, 1903, CJB, LS.

36. Philbin to Bonaparte, July 13, 1903, ibid., LR; Bonaparte to Ryan, August 1, 1903, and Bonaparte to Philbin, August 1, 1903, ibid., LS.

37. *Proceedings of the American Federation of Catholic Societies*, 1902, pp. 51–56.

38. Ibid., 1903, p. 114.

39. Ibid., p. 96; ibid., 1904, p. 29. Ketcham sent thanks to the national secretary of the Federation. Ketcham to Anthony Matre, April 4, 1904, BCIM, 1904, DC.

40. Ketcham to Wynne, November 10, 1903, BCIM, 1903, DC; Ketcham to Ryan, January 6, 1904, ibid., 1904, DC.

41. *Congressional Record*, 37:151; BCIM *Report*, 1903–1904, p. 28; Ketcham to Gibbons, January 16, 1904, BCIM, 1904, DC.

42. Ketcham to Bonaparte, February 22, 1904, CJB, LR. To Mother Katharine ne wrote, "It is certainly time for thanksgiving to our dear Lord—the clouds have parted and a ray of sunshine has burst through." In a postscript he added, "You must help us to reelect President 'Teddy' & Senator Aldrich—they both deserve it." Ketcham to Mother Katharine, March 7, 1904, Archives of the Sisters of the Blessed Sacrament.

43. *United States Statutes at Large*, 33:217. Commissioner Jones reported: "Whether the language of the item will produce the desired result is, in my opinion, very questionable. In any event it seems to throw the responsibility upon the [Indian] Bureau and the [Interior] Department, which I think is unfair." Jones to O. H. Platt, March 8, 1904, William A. Jones Papers, State Historical Society of Wisconsin.

44. Copy of flyer attached to Ketcham to Bonaparte, March 25, 1904, CJB, LR; Bonaparte to Ketcham, April 5, 1904, ibid., LS; Ketcham to Bonaparte, April 6, 1904, ibid., LR. The rations due were not always promptly provided, and Ketcham complained about the delay to the Commissioner of Indian Affairs. Ketcham to F. E. Leupp, October 19, 1906, BIA, LR, 1906-92408E; Ketcham to Leupp, November 21, 1906, ibid., 1906-102307E.

45. Ketcham to Bonaparte, February 23 and March 7, 1905, CJB, LR.

46. Act of June 21, 1906, *United States Statutes at Large*, vol. 34, pt. 1, p. 326; BCIM *Report*, 1905–1906, pp. 9–10. A memorandum of September 1906 provided a set of regulations for carrying out this provision. Records of the Education Division, Memoranda, vol. 1905–1907, p. 369, NA, RG 75.

47. BCIM *Report*, 1906, pp. 32–33; ibid., 1908, p. 35; ibid., 1909, p. 17; ibid., 1910, p. 19.

48. Ibid., 1908, p. 35.

49. S. M. Brosius to M. K. Sniffen, April 16, 1906, IRA (reel 18); Sniffen to Brosius, April 18, 1906, ibid. (reel 77).

50. BCIM *Report*, 1903–1904, p. 36; ibid., 1904–1905, pp. 45–46. The latter repeated an editorial from the *Indian Sentinel*, 1905–1906, pp. 30–39.

51. BCIM *Report*, 1903–1904, p. 37; *Indian Sentinel*, 1905–1906, p. 39. See also BCIM *Report*, 1904–1905, pp. 67–68.

52. Ketcham to Harkins, March 23, 1904, BCIM, 1904, DC.

53. Ketcham to priests in Rhode Island, October 18, 1904, ibid. See also Ketcham to Archbishop John M. Farley, of New York, August 25, 1904, ibid.

54. Ketcham to Gibbons, November 28, 1904, ibid. There are no studies of the 1904 election that investigate Catholic votes and their effect on the election; a recent scholarly study of the election has little to say about Catholics. William H. Harbaugh, "Election of 1904," in *History of American Presidential Elections, 1789–1968*, ed. Arthur M. Schlesinger, Jr., and Fred L. Israel, 4 vols. (New York: Chelsea House, 1971), 3:1965–94. There are indications that some Democrats felt aggrieved by Catholics voting for Republicans and that Democratic support for the Catholic Indian missions was consequently weakened. See John J. Wynne to Ketcham, February 21, 1905, BCIM, 1905, DC.

Chapter 7

1. "Memorandum in the Matter of the Use of 'Tribal Funds' for the Education of Indian Children in Mission Schools," undated, in *Senate Document* no. 179, 58th Cong., 3d sess., ser. 4766, pp. 42–43.

2. Ketcham to the President, January 5, 1904, ibid., pp. 43–45.

3. Ibid.

4. Ketcham to Mother Katharine, January 21, 1904, Archives of the Sisters of the Blessed Sacrament.

5. Memorandum, January 22, 1904, DJ, Year File no. 2290-02. An account of the

meeting based on the records in the Justice Department is given in a letter of Attorney General W. H. Moody to the President, February 2, 1905, in *Senate Document* no. 179, pp. 59–61.

6. Petition, April 19, 1897, ibid., pp. 3–5. The Indian agent, in forwarding the petition, added his strong support for the continuation of the school. Thomas H. Savage to the Commissioner of Indian Affairs, May 10, 1897, ibid., p. 3.

7. Osage petition, June 1902, ibid., pp. 5–6.

8. Jones to the Secretary of the Interior, February 20, 1904, and Francis E. Leupp to the Secretary of the Interior, January 17, 1905, ibid., pp. 52–54. See also the table included in Leupp to the Secretary of the Interior, February 21, 1905, ibid., p. 2. These contracts had been specifically requested in a letter of Ketcham to Jones, January 27, 1904, ibid., p. 10.

9. Charles S. Lusk to Jones, August 3, 1904, ibid., p. 15.

10. Rosebud petition, June 30, 1904; Crow Creek petition, June 1904; and Pine Ridge petition, June 21, 1904, ibid., pp. 15–18.

11. Ketcham to Jones, August 15, 1904, and Tongue River petition, June 15, 1904, ibid., pp. 19–20. Jones sent the prepared contracts for execution by the Catholic Bureau on August 16. Jones to Ketcham, August 16, 1904, ibid., p. 20.

12. Ketcham to Jones, October 1, 1904, and Quapaw council resolution, September 3, 1904, ibid., p. 21. The Indian Office sent the contracts to Ketcham on October 25. A. C. Tonner, Acting Commissioner, to Ketcham, October 25, 1904, ibid., p. 23. There is historical background on St. Mary's of the Quapaws School in Ralph E. Curtis, Jr., "Relations between the Quapaw National Council and the Roman Catholic Church, 1876–1927," *Chronicles of Oklahoma 55* (Summer 1977): 211–21. See also Velma Nieberding, "St. Mary's of the Quapaws," ibid. 31 (Spring 1953): 2–14.

13. This information is supplied in Leupp to the Secretary of the Interior, January 17, 1905, and February 21, 1905, in *Senate Document* no. 179, pp. 2, 53. Although running for the fiscal year from July 1, 1904, to June 30, 1905, the contracts were signed at various times. See Jones's letters to the Secretary of the Interior, August 17 and October 29, 1904, ibid., pp. 54–55.

14. Ibid., pp. 12–14.

15. Sniffen said at the beginning of 1905: "In Mr. Welsh's temporary retirement, the responsibility for carrying on our work has devolved largely on me. By way of personal explanation, it might be said that I have literally grown up in the office under Mr. Welsh's personal guidance for twenty-one years, and, naturally, I am well grounded in his methods and thoroughly familiar with the work in all its phases." Sniffen to Miss E. F. Mason, March 21, 1905, IRA (reel 76). The correspondence between Sniffen and Brosius in the Indian Rights Association Papers is one of the richest sources for the history of the controversy. The stand of the Indian Rights Association, together with a number of pertinent documents, is given in IRA *Report*, 1904, pp. 6–21, under the heading "Perverting Tribal Trust Funds."

16. *Word Carrier* 33 (September–October 1904): 1, copy in BIC, Reference Material, Schools (Sectarian). Riggs sent marked copies of the *Word Carrier* to the Indian Rights Association. Sniffen to Riggs, November 16, 1904, IRA (reel 76).

17. Hare to the Commissioner of Indian Affairs, October 10, 1904, BIA, LR, 1904-75292; Commissioner to Hare, October 12, 1904, printed in Hare to Brosius, November 7, 1904, in *Senate Document* no. 179, pp. 48–49.

18. Hare's reaction is reported in a circular letter dated January 5, 1905, copy in

BIC, Reference Material, Schools (Sectarian); an abbreviated form of the letter is printed in *Senate Document* no. 179, pp. 25–27.

19. Hare to Brosius, November 7, 1904, in *Senate Document* no. 179, pp. 48–49. Agitation over news of the petition at Rosebud is described in Aaron B. Clark to Hare, November 12 and 25, 1904, Historical Archives Collection, The Episcopal Church in South Dakota, Sioux Falls.

20. Sniffen to Brosius, November 11 and 14, 1904, IRA (reel 76); Brosius to Sniffen, November 16, 1904, ibid. (reel 17).

21. Sniffen to A. L. Riggs, November 16, 1904, and Sniffen to Brosius, November 16, 19, and 21, 1904, ibid. (reel 76); Brosius to Sniffen, November 18, 20, 21, and 22, 1904, ibid. (reel 17). Brosius requested copies of the petitions of Rosebud and Crow Creek from the Commissioner of Indian Affairs on November 17, 1904, and Jones sent the petitions on November 19. *Senate Document* no. 179, p. 23.

22. Sniffen to S. B. Griffin of the *Republican*, November 25, 1904, and Sniffen to W. H. Ward of the *Independent*, November 26, 1904, IRA (reel 76).

23. Sniffen to Brosius, November 28 and 29, 1904, ibid.

24. Sniffen to Hare, December 1, 1904, and Sniffen to Brosius, December 1, 1904, ibid.

25. Reuben Quick Bear and others to President of the Indian Rights Association, December 5, 1904, ibid. (reel 17).

26. Petition of Rosebud Sioux Indians to Commissioner of Indian Affairs, December 12, 1904, in *Senate Document* no. 179, p. 24. There are other Indian protests in *Senate Document* no. 170, 58th Cong., 3d sess., ser. 4766.

27. S. M. Brosius, for the Indian Rights Association, to the Secretary of the Interior, December 12, 1904, OSI, ID, LR, 1904-12045; and printed in *Senate Document* no. 179, p. 50.

28. Clark and Cross to the President of the Indian Rights Association, December 6, 1904, IRA (reel 17).

29. Hare to Sniffen, December 3, 1904, ibid.

30. Separate letters of Sniffen to Morehouse, Thompson, Woodbury, Leonard, Janney, and Lloyd, December 3, 1904, ibid. (reel 76).

31. Morehouse to Roosevelt, December 12, 1904; Lloyd to Sniffen, December 1904; J. W. Cooper to Sniffen, December 6, 1904; Thompson to Sniffen, December 23, 1904, ibid., (reel 17).

32. Sniffen to Hare, December 24, 1904, ibid. (reel 76); A. B. Leonard and others to Roosevelt, December 31, 1904, OSI, ID, LR, 1905-300.

33. Morehouse to Sniffen, December 8 and 13, 1904, and Janney to Sniffen, December 15, 1904, IRA (reel 17).

34. See, for example, Cortland Whitehead, Bishop of Pittsburgh, to the President, December 7, 1904, and J. S. Johnston, Bishop of West Texas, to the President, December 9, 1904, OSI, ID, LR, 1904-11991 and 1904-12215. The letter sent by Sniffen to Johnston, December 5, 1904, is in *Senate Document* no. 179, p. 49.

35. Scarborough to Sniffen, December 7, 1904, IRA (reel 17).

36. Roosevelt to Bishop George Worthington, December 10, 1904, sent to Sniffen by John M. Wood, of the Episcopal Missionary Society, December 17, 1904; acting secretary of the President to Morehouse, December 14, 1904, sent to Sniffen by Morehouse, December 15, 1904, ibid.

37. Brosius to Sniffen, December 9 and 11, 1904, ibid. Brosius later told Sniffen,

"It is the publicity that will be given the matter that will do the good in my opinion— not the probability of winning, as I do not believe we could win the suit, although some are inclined to think we might." Brosius to Sniffen, December 29, 1904, ibid.

38. Sniffen to Brosius, December 1, 13, and 14, 1904; Sniffen to Scarborough, December 13, 1904, ibid. (reel 76).

39. Brosius to Sniffen, December 17, 1904, and Hare to Sniffen, December 28, 1904, ibid. (reel 17).

40. Sniffen to Brosius, December 19, 1904; Sniffen to John W. Wood, December 19, 1904; Sniffen to Charles L. Thompson, December 24, 1904; Sniffen to J. W. Cooper, December 24, 1904, ibid. (reel 76).

41. Sniffen to Brosius, December 27 and 31, 1904, ibid.; Brosius to Sniffen, December 28, 1904, ibid. (reel 17).

Chapter 8

1. *Congressional Record*, 39:249. For concern in finding an appropriate Congressman to introduce the resolution, see Sniffen to Brosius, December 10, 1904, and Sniffen to H. L. Morehouse, December 16, 1904, IRA (reel 76).

2. *Congressional Record*, 39:649; Report of Leupp, January 17, 1905, in *House Document* no. 249, 58th Cong., 3d sess., ser. 4832.

3. Ketcham to Bonaparte, January 21, 1905, BCIM, 1905, DC.

4. Minutes of the Executive Committee, January 4, 1905, IRA (reel 18).

5. Letters of Sniffen to H. L. Morehouse, A. S. Lloyd, C. L. Thompson, J. W. Cooper, and A. B. Leonard, January 4, 1905; Executive Committee to Sherman, January 5, 1905, and to Leupp, January 5, 1905; Sniffen to Abbott, January 5, 1905, ibid. (reel 76).

6. Sniffen to Leonard, Thompson, Cooper, and Morehouse, January 6, 1905; Sniffen to James, January 6, 1905, ibid.

7. Sniffen to King, January 7, 1905, ibid. There is a copy of the form letter, January 7, 1905, which urges letters and telegrams to members of the committee in support of the Stephens clause, in the same file.

8. King to Sniffen, January 10, 1905, IRA (reel 18); Sniffen to Strong, January 19, 1905, ibid. (reel 76); Strong to Sniffen, January 26, 1905, ibid. (reel 18).

9. *Indian Trust Funds for Sectarian Schools* (Philadelphia: Indian Rights Association, 1905); Sniffen to Brosius, January 10, 1905, IRA (reel 76).

10. Ganss to Sniffen, January 28, 1905, ibid. (reel 18); Sniffen to Ganss, February 1, 1905, and Sniffen to Brosius, January 30, 1905, ibid. (reel 76).

11. Brosius to Sniffen, January 16, 1905, ibid. (reel 18).

12. Sherman letter quoted in Sniffen to Brosius, January 11, 1905, ibid (reel 76). Sniffen received a copy of Sherman's reply to Morehouse enclosed in Morehouse to Sniffen, January 10, 1905, ibid. (reel 18).

13. Morehouse to Sniffen, January 10, 1905, ibid.; *Indian Trust Funds for Sectarian Schools*, p. 8.

14. Sniffen to Abbott, January 5 and 20, 1905, IRA (reel 76); "A Mischievous Appropriation," *Outlook* 79 (January 21, 1905): 149–50; "Indian Appropriations for Sectarian Schools," *Outlook* 79 (January 28, 1905): 221–22.

15. "Unfair Indian Fighting," *Outlook* 79 (February 4, 1905): 263–65; "The State, the Church, and the Indian," *Outlook* 79 (February 11, 1905): 370–72.

16. Ketcham to Joseph J. Murphy, editor of the (Boston) *Republic*, January 30, 1905, BCIM, 1905, DC; Lusk to Bonaparte, January 31, 1905, CJB, LR. See other correspondence between Ketcham and Catholic editors in BCIM, 1905, DC. A draft of Ketcham's reply, entitled "Facts regarding the question treated in The Outlook of January 21, 1905, under the caption, 'A Mischievous Appropriation,'" is in BCIM, 1905, DC.

17. *Congressional Record*, 39:3941.

18. *Indian Tribal Funds: The Case for the Catholic Indians Stated, with the Record Made in Congress of the Debate by the Senate on the Issue of the Mission Schools* (New York: Marquette League, 1905), pp. 25–26.

19. *Congressional Record*, 39:1196. At this point in the proceedings, Stephens read into the *Congressional Record* a large number of documents concerning the use of tribal funds for sectarian schools, including reports of Commissioner Leupp on the 1904 contracts, Bishop Hare's letter of January 5, 1905, the letter of the Reverend Aaron B. Clark and James F. Cross, December 6, 1904, and numerous protests from Indians and others. Ibid., pp. 1196–1201. See also Sniffen to Brosius, January 23, 1905, IRA (reel 76).

20. Memorandum of Leupp, enclosed in Hitchcock to Bishop Alexander Mackay-Smith, January 9, 1905, ibid. (reel 18). Leupp's document is printed in IRA *Report*, 1904, pp. 14–15.

21. This is the form in which the amendment was proposed to the Senate by the Committee on Indian Affairs on February 28, 1905. *Congressional Record*, 39:3613. There is a long discussion of "The Diversion of Trust Funds," with reprinting of pertinent documents, in IRA *Report*, 1905, pp. 4–23; see also ibid., 1906, pp. 4–10.

22. Brosius to Sniffen, January 25, 1905, IRA (reel 18); Sniffen to Brosius, January 26, 1905, and letters of Sniffen to C. L. Thompson, A. S. Lloyd, and A. B. Leonard, January 27, 1905, ibid. (reel 76); form letter, Brosius to Merrill Gates, BIC, Reference Material, Schools (Sectarian).

23. *Indian Appropriation Bill, 1905: Hearing before the Subcommittee of the Committee on Indian Affairs of the Senate of the United States* (Washington: Government Printing Office, 1905), pp. 13–17.

24. Ibid., pp. 17–23. There is a typed copy of "Statement by S. M. Brosius before the Sub-Committee of the Senate Committee on Indian Affairs" in IRA (reel 18). There are copies of Scharf's weekly "Washington Letter" in BCIM, 1903, DC. No. 13, February 23, 1903, is full of abuse of Senator Lodge and Congressman Stephens.

25. Brosius to Sniffen, January 31, 1905, IRA (reel 18). The extensive coverage of the whole tribal funds question stimulated by the Bard amendment can be followed in the BCIM scrapbooks. The clippings, chiefly from February and March 1905, were gathered by a clipping service and came from a wide variety of papers, Catholic, Protestant, and secular, from all sections of the country. The *New York Times*, February 1, 1905, gave first-page coverage to the Bard accusations; it printed Cardinal Gibbons's denial of any formal connection of Scharf with the Catholic Church on February 2. See also "The Indian School Blunder," *Independent* 58 (February 9, 1905): 333–34.

26. Ketcham to Archbishop Ryan, February 4, 1905; Ketcham to John Connolly, March 17, 1905; Ketcham to William M. McGinnis, March 17, 1905, BCIM, 1905, DC. See also BCIM *Report*, 1904–1905, pp. 51–52.

27. Sniffen to Brosius, February 2, 1905, IRA (reel 76).

28. *Indian Appropriation Bill, 1905*, pp. 63–66.

29. Ibid., p. 75.

30. Ibid., pp. 63–65.

31. Ibid., p. 74.

32. Ibid., p. 77. At this point Leupp entered the first Lacey bill into the record, as well as other documents from the Commissioner's office giving data on the contracts with the Catholic schools.

33. Roosevelt to the Secretary of the Interior, February 3, 1905, in *Senate Document* no. 179, 58th Cong., 3d sess., ser. 4766, pp. 61–62. The President's letter was widely reported in the press; see *New York Times*, February 5, 1905, and BCIM scrapbooks. The letter cut short an attempt on the part of the Catholic Bureau to get approval from ᵗhe Attorney General, an attempt that centered on the drawing up of a brief by Bonaparte to be submitted to the Attorney General. See correspondence between Ketcham and Bonaparte, January–February 1905, CJB; Bonaparte to the President, January 28 and 30, 1905, ibid., LS; Bonaparte to Attorney General William H. Moody, February 7, 1905, DJ, Year File no. 2290-02.

34. Ketcham to Edward L. Hearn, February 16, 1905, BCIM, 1905, DC.

35. Abbott to Roosevelt, February 11, 1905, Theodore Roosevelt Papers, series 1 (reel 52); Roosevelt to Abbott, February 12, 1905, *The Letters of Theodore Roosevelt*, ed. Elting E. Morison, 8 vols. (Cambridge: Harvard University Press, 1951–54), 4: 1120–21; "The President and the Indian: A Step Backward," *Outlook* 79 (February 18, 1905): 417–19.

36. Brosius to Sniffen, February 2, 1905; form letter, February 4, 1905, IRA (reel 18). A long list of names of people to whom the form letter was sent is at the end of the February entries (reel 18).

37. Sniffen to Villard, February 7 and 9, 1905, IRA (reel 76). The *Baptist Home Mission Monthly* 27 (March 1905): 91, 112–14, printed Brosius's statement before the Senate subcommittee and Morehouse's protest to Congressman Stephens and editorialized strongly against the Catholic contracts.

38. Brosius to the President, February 10, 1905, IRA (reel 18); letters of Sniffen to *Evening Post*, *Republican*, *Public Ledger*, *Transcript*, *Herald*, *Times*, and *Record*, February 14, 1905, ibid. (reel 76).

39. *Congressional Record*, 39:2513, 2627; Brosius to Sniffen, February 14, 1905, IRA (reel 18). The documents are printed in *Senate Document* no. 179, 58th Cong., 3d sess., ser. 4766.

40. *Congressional Record*, 39:2705, 3190; Brosius to Sniffen, February 15, 1905, IRA (reel 18). The reply of the Secretary of the Interior, February 28, 1905, is printed in *House Document* no. 374, 58th Cong., 3d sess., ser. 4832.

41. Brosius to Senators, February 16, 1905, and Brosius to Sniffen, February 16, 1905, IRA (reel 18); Sniffen to Brosius, February 17, 1905, ibid. (reel 76).

42. These are printed in *Senate Document* no. 170, 58th Cong., 3d sess., ser. 4766.

43. The Records of the United States Senate, NA, RG 46, have close to two hundred of these petitions from New Jersey alone; see Senate 58A-K6. See also Records of the United States House of Representatives, HR 58A-H8.1, Committee on Indian Affairs, Indian Schools #5058, NA, RG 233. Sniffen declared that the *Congressional Record* showed that every lodge of the Junior Order had sent in a protest. Sniffen to DeWitt C. Morrell, March 11, 1905, IRA (reel 76).

44. Thomas B. Minahan to Ketcham, February 23, 1905, BCIM, 1905, DC; George W. Heer to Roosevelt, February 23, 1905, BIA, LR, 1905-16674E.

45. Sniffen to William H. Gladden, February 21, 1905, IRA (reel 76). See also Snif-

fen to Brosius, February 21, 1905; Sniffen to Erving Winslow, February 22, 1905, and Sniffen to a number of others on the same date, ibid.

46. Ketcham to Bonaparte, February 18, 1905, CJB, LR; Bonaparte to Ketcham, February 22, 1905, ibid., LS.

47. Ketcham to Bonaparte, February 19, 1905, ibid., LR.

48. The Senate debate on this matter, February 28, 1905, is in *Congressional Record*, 39:3613–23. See also Ketcham to John Connolly, March 17, 1905, BCIM, 1905, DC.

49. *Congressional Record*, 39:3866–69, 3920, 3929, 3979.

50. Bonaparte to Ketcham, March 8, 1905, CJB, LS; John Ireland to Ketcham, March 9, 1905; E. Eyre to Ketcham, March 13, 1905; Ketcham to John Connolly, March 17, 1905, BCIM, 1905, DC.

51. Sniffen to Brosius, March 4, 1905, IRA (reel 76). Sniffen and Brosius sought to find out from Stephens who did the "dirty work" in the confidential sessions of the conference committee. Brosius to Sniffen, March 10, 1905, IRA (reel 18). Congressman Stephens explained his position at considerable length in a speech in the House on March 3, 1905. *Congressional Record*, 39: Appendix, pp. 53–64.

52. Sniffen to Oliver H. Bales, March 6, 1905; Sniffen to Charles R. Saunders, March 16, 1905, IRA (reel 76). Sniffen wrote to Brosius: "If the fight has to be renewed at the next session, we are in a position now to organize a more formidable opposition. We had very little this session to thoroughly arouse the country as it can be aroused. Still, I think we did everything that was possible." Sniffen to Brosius, March 4, 1905, ibid. See also Sniffen to Mary P. Lord, March 17, 1905, ibid.

53. Sniffen to Brosius, March 4, 1905, ibid. See also Sniffen to Oliver H. Bales, March 6, 1905, and Sniffen to DeWitt C. Morrell, March 7, 1905, ibid.

54. Sniffen to Morrell, March 11, 1905, ibid.; Brosius to Sniffen, March 10, 1905, ibid. (reel 18).

55. *Indian Appropriation Bill: Use of Indian Trust Funds* (Washington, 1905), copy in BIC, Reference Material, Schools (Sectarian). The original material is in *Congressional Record*, 39:3613, 3616–19, 3622, 3623, Appendix, pp. 61–63.

56. Letter of Sniffen to editors, April 10, 1905, IRA (reel 76). There is extended correspondence between Brosius and Sniffen about the production of the pamphlet, March 9–June 1, 1905, IRA.

57. Sniffen to DeWitt C. Morrell, May 12, 1905, IRA (reel 76); Brosius to Sniffen, May 16, 1905, ibid. (reel 18).

58. Brosius to Sniffen, April 17, 1905, ibid.; Sniffen to Brosius, April 21, 1905, ibid. (reel 76). For some of Morrell's diatribes against the Catholic Church, see his letters to Sniffen of June 12, October 20 and 24, 1905, ibid. (reel 18).

59. Morrell to Sniffen, February 20 and May 18 (two letters), 1905, ibid.

60. Morrell to Sniffen, May 18 and June 26, 1905, and Morrell to Brosius, August 24, 1905, ibid.; Sniffen to Morrell, June 9, 1905, ibid. (reel 76).

61. Sniffen to Morrell, March 18 and October 9, 1905, ibid. The extensive correspondence between Sniffen and Saunders is in IRA (reels 18 and 76).

62. *Indian Tribal Funds: The Case for the Catholic Indians Stated, with the Record Made in Congress of the Debate by the Senate on the Issue of the Mission Schools* (New York: Marquette League, 1905), p. 4; John J. Wynne to Ketcham, March 8, 1905, BCIM, 1905, DC; BCIM *Report*, 1904–1905, pp. 22–23.

63. Ketcham to Joseph H. Fargis, president of the Marquette League, May 24, 1905,

BCIM, 1905, DC. Sniffen was not worried by the Marquette League publication. He wrote to Brosius after receiving a copy: "It seems to me that what you have prepared is about all we need to put out." Sniffen to Brosius, May 15, 1905, IRA (reel 76). The fall meeting of the Lake Mohonk Conference in 1905 came out strongly on the side of the Indian Rights Association in opposition to the contract schools, although the Catholic position was also presented. LM, 1905, pp. 187–91.

Chapter 9

1. Lusk to the Commissioner of Indian Affairs, June 6, 1905, copy in DJ, Year File no. 2290-02; C. F. Larrabee to the Secretary of the Interior, June 16, 1905, OSI, ID, LR, 1905-6373.

2. Lusk to Digmann, June 21, 1905, BCIM, 1905, South Dakota, St. Francis; CIA *Report*, 1905, pp. 34–40. The report gives a list of the funds available and a detailed statement of the procedures to be followed in getting petitions and pro rating the funds. The procedures followed a memorandum of Leupp to J. H. Dortch, May 15, 1905, copy in BCIM, 1905, DC.

3. Lusk to Aldrich, August 13, 1905, ibid. See also other letters of July and August in the same file. There is an unsigned copy of an opinion addressed by the Attorney General to the Secretary of the Interior, August 11, 1905, but apparently it was not sent. DJ, Year File no. 2290-02. President Roosevelt informed Cardinal Gibbons that he had written to the Secretary of the Interior to push the matter forward. Roosevelt to Gibbons, August 12, 1905, AAB, 102-M-3.

4. Ketcham to John F. McQuade, November 15, 1905, BCIM, 1905, DC.

5. Ketcham to John F. McQuade, November 24, 1905, ibid.; Ketcham to Bonaparte, December 1, 1905, CJB, LR.

6. Memorandum, December 8, 1905, BCIM, 1905, DC.

7. Bonaparte to Ketcham, December 22, 1905, ibid.

8. Roosevelt to the Commissioner of Indian Affairs, December 23, 1905, copy in BIA, Education Division, Memoranda, vol. 1905–1907, pp. 256–58. This letter became the basis for Leupp's actions.

9. Moody to the President, January 4, 1906, DJ, Year File no. 2290-02. There is a copy in BCIM, 1906, DC.

10. Leupp to Ketcham, January 2, 1906, BIA, LS, Education.

11. Ketcham to Aldrich, January 4, 1906, BCIM, 1906, DC; Ketcham to Bonaparte, January 5, 1906, CJB, LR; Bonaparte to Ketcham, January 6, 1906, ibid., LS.

12. Leupp to the Indian Agent, Rosebud Agency, January 11, 1906, BIA, LS, Education. Similar letters were sent to the other agents.

13. Leupp to Superintendent, Seneca Training School, January 15, 1906, ibid.

14. Ketcham to Aldrich, January 18, 1906, with memorandum enclosed, BCIM, 1906, DC.

15. Roosevelt to Aldrich, January 21, 1906, Theodore Roosevelt Papers, Library of Congress, series 2, vol. 60, pp. 466–67 (reel 340); Roosevelt to Leupp, January 25, 1906, ibid., vol. 61, pp. 19–20 (reel 340); Leupp to Roosevelt, January 26, 1906, ibid., series 1 (reel 62).

16. Sniffen to Brosius, May 10, 1905, IRA (reel 76).

17. Clark to Hare, February 6, 1906, Historical Archives Collection, The Episcopal

Church in South Dakota, Sioux Falls; telegram, Leupp to Agent, Pine Ridge, February 7, 1906, BIA, LS, Education.

18. *Indian Sentinel*, 1907, pp. 26–28. Ketcham called the Protestant methods "low & tantalizing." He wrote: "The preacher has stirred up the Sioux who are not Catholics by miserable cartoons and doggerel rhymes—he has made a college yell out of Fr. Digman's [*sic*] name & mine." Ketcham to Mother Katharine, March 29, 1906, Archives of the Sisters of the Blessed Sacrament.

19. Florentine Digmann, "History of St. Francis Mission, 1886–1922," pp. 155–61, typescript copy in Holy Rosary Mission Records, series 11, box 1, Marquette University Library; Clark to Hare, February 13, 1906, Historical Archives Collection, The Episcopal Church in South Dakota.

20. Agent's letter, quoted in Leupp to Ketcham, February 26, 1906, BIA, LS, Education.

21. BCIM *Report*, 1905, p. 7.

22. C. F. Larrabee to E. A. Hitchcock, May 26, 1906, BIA, Letters Sent by Acting Commissioner Charles F. Larrabee, 1905–1908; Jesse E. Wilson, Acting Secretary of the Interior, to the Attorney General, June 26, 1906, DJ, Year File no. 2290-02.

23. CIA *Report*, 1906, pp. 51–58.

24. Lusk to Ketcham, May 4, 1906, BCIM, 1906, DC.

25. Francis E. Leupp, "Indian Funds and Mission Schools," *Outlook* 83 (June 9, 1906): 318.

26. Memorandum on determination of trust and treaty funds for schools, undated but filed in August 1906, BIA, Education Division, Memoranda, vol. 1905–1907, pp. 307–8; Lusk to Ketcham, June 27, 1906, BCIM, 1906, DC.

27. The prelates' letter of October 8, 1906, and Leupp's reply could not be found. Information here is taken from Gibbons to the President, November 1, 1906, BCIM, 1906, DC.

28. Gibbons to Roosevelt, November 1, 1906, BCIM, 1906, DC.

29. Roosevelt to Gibbons, November 8, 1906, ibid. Quotations in the paragraphs following are from this letter.

30. The question of extending the petitions to cover more than one year of contracts had been considered by Roosevelt earlier, and he thought it unwise to have the petitions signed every year. Roosevelt to Leupp, October 20, 1906, Theodore Roosevelt Papers, series 2, vol. 67, p. 464 (reel 343). He had told Gibbons on October 27, "I will make this new petition [with the Menominees] for one year or five years as your Board may desire." Roosevelt to Gibbons, October 27, 1906, ibid., vol. 68, p. 108 (reel 343).

31. Ketcham to Gibbons, November 10, 1906, AAB, 104-H-2.

32. Lusk to Ketcham, December 15, 1906, BCIM, 1906, DC; Lusk to Ketcham, January 6, 1907, ibid., 1907, DC; Ketcham to Leupp, January 21, 1907, BIA, LR, 1907-6658E. The contract is in BIA, Education Division, Memoranda, vol. 1907–1910, pp. 49–53.

33. Lusk to Ketcham, May 15, 1907, BCIM, 1907, DC. For hints of later problems, see Ketcham to Ryan, December 10, 1907, ibid.; Lusk to Ketcham, January 13, 1908, ibid., 1908, DC.

34. See, for example, Lusk to Ketcham, August 19, 1910, ibid., 1910, DC; F. Abbott, Acting Commissioner, to Ketcham, June 5, 1913, ibid., 1913, DC. For the contracts themselves, see OSI, CCF, 5-6, Box 1445; BIA, Education Division, Memoranda,

vol. 1907–1910. See also renewed agitation by the Indian Rights Association against the use of the funds in 1912. IRA *Report*, 1912, pp. 14–19. Carl E. Grammer, president of the Indian Rights Association, sent a long argument against the use of tribal funds to the Secretary of the Interior, but the Interior Department refuted his arguments one by one. Grammer to the Secretary of the Interior, November 26, 1912, and Assistant Secretary of the Interior Lewis C. Laylin to Grammer, March 19, 1913, OSI, CCF, 5–6, Schools, Contract, Box 1445.

35. BCIM *Report*, 1906, pp. 44–45; *Indian Sentinel*, 1906, p. 27. Leupp responded to Ketcham's moderate reporting of the tribal funds issue in the Bureau's report of 1905–1906 with a friendly word of appreciation. Leupp to Ketcham, May 12, 1906, BCIM, 1906, DC.

36. IRA *Report*, 1908, pp. 4–20; Welsh to Richard H. Dana, January 25, 1909, IRA (reel 78).

37. IRA *Report*, 1908, pp. 32–35.

38. Statement of Carl E. Grammer, published in the *North American* (Philadelphia), June 16, 1909. For a sympathetic appraisal of Leupp's term as Commissioner of Indian Affairs, see Necah Furman, "Seedtime for Indian Reform: An Evaluation of the Administration of Commissioner Francis Ellington Leupp," *Red River Valley Historical Review* 2 (Winter 1975): 495–518.

Chapter 10

1. *House Journal*, 59th Cong., 1 sess., ser. 4903, p. 142. An identical bill (H.R. 18859) had been introduced by Stephens in the third session of the Fifty-eighth Congress, on February 9, 1905, but it died immediately. *House Journal*, 58th Cong., 3d sess., ser. 4754, p. 288. The bills, like others cited, can be seen in the collection of bills and resolutions in the Library of Congress, which is also available on microfilm.

2. Brosius to Sniffen, January 13, 1906; Saunders to Sniffen, January 30, 1906; Morrell to Sniffen, February 10, 1906, IRA (reel 18); letters of Sniffen to H. L. Morehouse, A. S. Lloyd, A. B. Leonard, C. L. Thompson, and J. W. Cooper, January 25 and 26, 1906; Sniffen to Brosius, January 26, 27, and 30, 1906; Sniffen to Saunders, February 2, 1906, ibid. (reel 77). There are numerous other letters on the matter in the files.

3. *Outlook* 82 (February 3, 1906): 247–48. The same article urged support of the Lacey bill.

4. Sniffen to H. Burt, February 6, 1906, IRA (reel 77); Brosius to Sniffen, January 15 (filed under February 15) and January 25, 1906, ibid. (reel 18).

5. Brosius to Sniffen, January 31, 1906, ibid.

6. Leupp to the Secretary of the Interior, February 8, 1906, BIA, LS; Education.

7. Ketcham to Joseph Fargis, president of the Marquette League, January 2 and 12, 1906, BCIM, 1906, DC. See the petitions protesting against the Stephens bill in Records of the United States House of Representatives, HR 59A-H9.1, Committee on Indian Affairs, NA, RG 233. A number of petitions refer the Congressmen to Scharf for more information.

8. Brosius to Sniffen, February 8, 1906, IRA (reel 18); Sniffen to Mary C. Collins, February 23, 1906, and Sniffen to A. B. Clark, March 2, 1906, ibid. (reel 77).

9. Sniffen to Brosius, February 23, 1906, ibid.; Brosius to Sniffen, February 27, 1906, ibid. (reel 18); Ketcham to John J. Wynne, March 3, 1906, BCIM, 1906, DC.

10. The Dawes Act and its antecedents are discussed in Francis Paul Prucha, *American Indian Policy in Crisis: Christian Reformers and the Indian, 1865–1900* (Norman: University of Oklahoma Press, 1976), pp. 227–57.

11. Fred L. Israel, ed., *The State of the Union Messages of the Presidents, 1790–1966*, 3 vols. (New York: Chelsea House, 1966), 2:2047.

12. LM, 1900, pp. 18–20. Gates repeated much of the same material in BIC *Report*, 1900, pp. 9–10. The topic had concerned the Board also in the previous year. Ibid., 1899, pp. 17–18.

13. LM, 1901, pp. 5–8; ibid., 1902, pp. 9, 118–29.

14. BIC *Report*, 1901, p. 7; ibid., 1902, p. 22. Italics are in the original. The Board continued its advocacy. See ibid., 1903, pp. 11–12; ibid., 1904, pp. 5–10.

15. IRA *Report*, 1902, p. 25.

16. CIA *Report*, 1900, pp. 11–12.

17. *Outlook* 82 (February 3, 1906): 248; Sniffen to William J. Cleveland, February 27, 1905, IRA (reel 76).

18. *House Journal*, 58th Cong., 3d sess., ser. 4754, p. 234; *House Report* no. 4547, 58th Cong., 3d sess., ser. 4762. My attention was first directed toward the relationship between the allotment of tribal funds and the contract school controversy by a graduate seminar paper on the Lacey Act by Robert Schrader.

19. *Congressional Record*, 39:3978; *House Journal*, 58th Cong., 3d sess., ser. 4754, p. 435.

20. *Congressional Record*, 39:3525, 3619, 3643–44.

21. Ketcham to Digmann, April 5, 1905, BCIM, 1905, South Dakota, St. Francis; form letter of Welsh, June 21, 1905, IRA (reel 18).

22. *House Journal*, 59th Cong., 1st sess., ser. 4903, p 107.

23. Ibid., p. 702.

24. Burke to Leupp, March 23, 1906, BIA, LR, 1906-26055. Burke sent a copy of the bill to Leupp for his comments.

25. Letters of Brosius to Sherman, Lacey, and Stephens, March 27, 1906; Binney to members of Congress, March 28, 1906, IRA (reel 18).

26. Sniffen to Brosius, March 30, 1906, ibid. (reel 77).

27. Binney to Burke, April 4, 1906, ibid.; Burke to Binney, April 7, 1906, ibid. (reel 18).

28. Burke to Binney, April 17, 1906, ibid. For another account of what went on in the committee, see Brosius to Sniffen, April 1, 1906, ibid.

29. *House Report* no. 2950, 59th Cong., 1st sess., ser. 4907; *Congressional Record*, 40:6470–71; *House Journal*, 59th Cong., 1st sess., ser. 4903, p. 970.

30. IRA *Report*, 1906, p. 49.

31. Brosius to Sniffen, April 1 and 13, 1906, IRA (reel 18); Sniffen to Brosius, April 6, 1906, ibid. (reel 77).

32. Brosius to Sniffen, April 13, 1906, ibid. (reel 18); Lusk to Ketcham, December 18, 1906, BCIM, 1906, DC.

33. *Senate Journal*, 59th Cong., 2d sess., ser. 5058, pp. 51, 278, 283; *Senate Report* no. 4634, 59th Cong., 2d sess., ser. 5060; *Senate Report* no. 6687, 59th Cong., 2d sess., ser. 5060.

34. *Congressional Record*, 41:3012–13; *Senate Report* no. 6698, 59th Cong., 2d sess., ser. 5061; *Senate Journal*, 59th Cong., 2d sess., ser. 5058, p. 300.

35. *House Report* no. 8068, 59th Cong., 2d sess., ser. 5065; *Senate Journal*, 59th Cong., 2d sess., ser. 5058, p. 344; *House Journal*, 59th Cong., 2d sess., ser. 5059, p. 523; *United States Statutes at Large*, 34:1221–22.

36. Brosius to Sniffen, January 7 and 8, 1907, IRA (reel 19); form letter of Herbert Welsh, January 14, 1907, ibid.; IRA *Report*, 1907, pp. 40–41.

37. BIC *Report*, 1907, p. 17; ibid., 1908, pp. 8 ff, 21; ibid., 1909, p. 19.

38. Ketcham to Ryan, February 20, 1909, BCIM, 1909, DC. See also Ketcham to Mother Katharine, February 20, 1909, and Ketcham to Mother M. James, February 26, 1909, ibid.

39. IRA *Report*, 1911, pp. 28–29; *House Report* no. 925, 62d Cong., 2d sess., ser. 6132; *House Report* no. 422, 63d Cong., 2d sess., ser. 6559.

Chapter 11

1. Minutes of Executive Committee, January 4 and February 1, 1905, IRA (reel 18).

2. Sniffen to Brosius, March 9 and 20, 1906, ibid. (reel 77); Brosius to Sniffen, March 13, 1906, ibid. (reel 18).

3. Sniffen to Brosius, March 21, April 10 and 20, 1906, ibid. (reel 77); Brosius to Sniffen, March 23 and April 6, 1906, ibid. (reel 18); Sniffen to DeWitt C. Morrell, April 10, 1906, ibid. (reel 77).

4. Brosius to Sniffen, April 13 and 17, 1906, ibid. (reel 18); Sniffen to Saunders, May 8, 1906, ibid. (reel 77).

5. Minutes of the Law Committee, April 21, 1906, ibid. (reel 18).

6. Brosius to Sniffen, April 23, 1906, ibid.; Sniffen to Brosius, April 24, 1906, ibid. (reel 77).

7. Brosius to Sniffen, April 26, 1906, and Brosius to A. B. Clark, April 26, 1906, ibid. (reel 18).

8. Brosius to Clark, April 26, 1906, ibid.; Sniffen to Brosius, April 27, 1906, ibid. (reel 77).

9. See, for example, Sniffen's letters to the editors of the *Boston Herald*, *Boston Transcript*, *Springfield Republican*, and *Evening Post*, May 11, 1906, ibid. The Indian Rights Association maintained that "the plaintiffs are Indians, persons directly interested, who have consistently opposed this use of the treaty and trust funds, and who wish to test its legality. The Association has aided them to assert what they believe to be their legal rights, but is in no sense a party to the suit." IRA *Report*, 1907, p. 22.

10. Francis E. Leupp, "Indian Funds and Mission Schools," *Outlook* 83 (June 9, 1906): 319; Sniffen to Mrs. H. Burt, April 28, 1906 (filed after May 9), IRA (reel 77).

11. Brosius to Sniffen, May 11, 1906, IRA (reel 18). Bonaparte was surprised to learn that the bill had been signed by Brosius as solicitor, for he had not known that Brosius was a member of the bar. Bonaparte to Ketcham, June 4, 1906, CJB, LS. But Brosius had been admitted to the bar in September 1904, as he joyfully wrote to Sniffen. Brosius to Sniffen, September 19, 1904, IRA (reel 17).

12. *Bill in Equity, in the Supreme Court of the District of Columbia*, May 11, 1906, no. 26271. Since the case was appealed twice, the bill also appears in the transcript of record of the higher courts. The printed briefs and records of the case are listed in the Bibliography, with an indication of depositories in which they can be found.

13. Brosius to Sniffen, May 11, 1906, IRA (reel 18); Sniffen letters to various per-

sons, May 11, 15, and 16, 1906, ibid. (reel 77). Sniffen kept up such correspondence through the summer.

14. Lusk to Ketcham, May 14, 1906, BCIM, 1906, DC.

15. Hitchcock to the Attorney General, May 16, 1906, and the Acting Attorney General to Daniel M. Baker, May 16, 1906, DJ, Year File no. 2290-02.

16. Lusk to Philbin, May 18, 1906, and Lusk to Ketcham, June 26, 1906, BCIM, 1906, DC; Bonaparte to Ketcham, June 4, 1906, CJB, LS.

17. Brosius to Binney, November 23, 1906, IRA (reel 19).

18. Sniffen to William H. Gladden, July 23, 1906, ibid. (reel 77); Brosius to Binney, September 10, 1906, ibid. (reel 19).

19. Daniel W. Baker to the Attorney General, May 29, 1906, March 22 and 26, 1907, DJ, Year File no. 2290-02; Lusk to Ketcham, December 15, 1906, and Ketcham to Gans, January 21, 1907, BCIM, 1907, DC.

20. *Brief on Behalf of Defendants, in the Supreme Court, District of Columbia, in Equity*, no. 26271. It appears also in the transcript of record of the higher courts and is printed "substantially in full" as a footnote in *United States Reports*, 210:56–71.

21. The decree is printed in *Transcript of Record* for *Quick Bear* v. *Leupp* (Supreme Court), p. 47. April 15 is the official date of the decree, but the decision was announced earlier. Brosius sent Sniffen on April 5 a clipping from the *Washington Post* giving the substance of Gould's decision. Sniffen to Brosius, April 6, 1907, IRA (reel 77).

22. Gans to Bonaparte, April 8, 1907, DJ, Year File no. 2290-02; Gans to Ketcham, April 8, 1907, BCIM, 1907, DC.

23. Sniffen to H. Burt, April 11, 1907, and Sniffen to Charles Saunders, April 11, 1907, IRA (reel 77). See also Sniffen letters to Bishop Hare and other supporters, April 17, 1907, ibid.

24. *Brief for Reuben Quick Bear, et al., in the Court of Appeals of the District of Columbia, April Term, 1907*, nos. 1786 and 1787; *Brief for Appellees in No. 1786, and Appellants in No. 1787*, in the Court of Appeals for the District of Columbia, April Term, 1907 [Brief for the government]. By this time there had been changes in the government officers named in the suit, and the Court of Appeals, on McNamara's motion, substituted James R. Garfield for Hitchcock and George B. Cortelyou for Shaw. Record of May 21, 1907, Court of Appeals of the District of Columbia, in Records of the United States Supreme Court, Appellate Case Files, no. 20972, NA, RG 267. This is repeated in *Transcript of Record* for *Quick Bear* v. *Leupp* (Supreme Court), p. 52.

25. *Reports of Cases Adjudged in the Court of Appeals of the District of Columbia* (New York: Lawyers Co-operative Publishing Co., 1908), 30:151–64. This is also printed in *Transcript of Record* for *Quick Bear* v. *Leupp* (Supreme Court), pp. 54–62.

26. Gans to Ketcham, December 3, 1907, and Ketcham to Gans, November 30, 1907, BCIM, 1907, DC.

27. Gans to Bonaparte, December 2, 1907, DJ, Year File no. 2290-02. See also the memorandum of Gans to Bonaparte, December 5, 1907, ibid.; Gans to Ketcham, December 8, 1907, BCIM, 1907, DC.

28. Bonaparte to James R. Garfield, December 7, 1907, OSI, CCF, 5–6, Indian Office—Bureau of Catholic Indian Missions—Contracts, Box 1445.

29. Sniffen to Brosius, December 10 and 12, 1907, and Sniffen to A. B. Clark, December 17, 1907, IRA (reel 77).

30. *Appellants' Brief, in the Supreme Court of the United States, October Term, 1907*, no. 569.

31. *Brief for Appellees, in the Supreme Court of the United States, October Term, 1907*, no. 569; Gans to Hoyt, February 7 and 15, 1908, DJ, Year File no. 2290-02; Hoyt to Gans, February 6, 8, and 18, 1908, ibid.

32. Gans to Gibbons, January 25, 1908, AAB, 106-A-8; *Motion to Advance Argument and Hearing of Case, in the Supreme Court of the United States, October Term, 1907*, no. 569; *Appellants' Brief in Reply, in the Supreme Court of the United States, October Term, 1907*, no. 569; Hoyt to Gans, March 5, 1908, DJ, Year File no. 2290-02.

33. *United States Reports*, 210:77–82.

34. Bonaparte to Gans, May 20, 1908, CJB, LS. Gans was paid six thousand dollars for his work, a sum that, at the suggestion of Cardinal Gibbons and with the approval of Father Ketcham, was charged to the schools that benefited from the favorable decisions of the courts. Lusk to Gans, May 22, 1908; Gans to Lusk, May 25, 1908; Lusk to Ketcham, June 13, 1908; Ketcham to Lusk, July 25, 1908, BCIM, 1908, DC. There is no indication that any approach for funds was made to the Marquette League, which originally had offered to contribute to the cost of the legal proceedings. The Indian Rights Association during the litigation wrote to various individuals asking for funds to support the case, but it appears that Binney and the other Association lawyers connected with the case did not receive a fee.

35. IRA *Report*, 1908, pp. 24–25.

36. Small crises arose in 1915, when there was danger that Congress might not extend the appropriation of Sioux treaty funds, and when the Comptroller of the Treasury prohibited the use of tribal funds for Catholic schools among the Choctaws and Chickasaws, but in the end Congressional action removed the difficulties. See Rev. Wilbur F. Crafts, of the International Reform Bureau, to Gibbons, February 26, 1915, AAB, 115-H-11; Gibbons to Crafts, March 3, 1915, ibid., 115-J-8; Ketcham to Gibbons, May 24, 1916, ibid., 115-R-12; Bonaparte to Lusk, May 17, 1915, ibid., 115-R-4. In May 1916, Ketcham wrote: "This session of Congress has been the most trying ordeal through which I have passed. The opposing forces have been more determined and insidious in their work than ever before and have been unscrupulous in their methods. They not only have deliberately falsified issues and published erroneous statements, but they have likewise misstated the attitude of the Prelates of the Church." But in the same letter he noted that he had been "victorious in every issue." Ketcham to Gibbons, May 24, 1916, AAB, 117-E-5.

Chapter 12

1. *Rules for Indian Schools, with Course of Study* (Washington: Government Printing Office, 1890), sec. 39, p. 10. This section, with a provision that employees who absented themselves needed to file a written statement to be forwarded to the Indian Office, was repeated in *Rules for Indian Schools, with Course of Study, List of Text-Books, and Civil Service Rules* (Washington: Government Printing Office, 1892), sec. 90, p. 18.

2. L. B. Palladino, *Education for the Indian: Fancy and Reason on the Subject: Contract Schools and Non-Sectarianism in Indian Education* (New York: Benziger Brothers, 1892). Father Palladino included the information from this pamphlet as well as other attacks on Thomas J. Morgan's Indian school plans in his book *Indian and White in the Northwest: A History of Catholicism in Montana, 1831–1891*, 2d ed. rev. (Lancaster, Pa.: Wickersham Publishing Co., 1922), pp. 108–37.

3. *Independent* 44 (May 5, 1892): 624–25.

4. Stephan's statement and the reaction to it are in BIC *Report*, 1893, pp. 112–15.

5. *Rules for the Indian School Service* (Washington: Government Printing Office, 1898), sec. 195, p. 25. The identical text was used in the *Rules* for 1900; the *Rules* for 1894, section 69, had omitted the reference to employees accompanying the pupils.

6. J. A. Stephan to John W. Noble, Secretary of the Interior, April 7, 1891, printed in BCIM *Report*, 1891–92, pp. 20–24; Ganss to Stephan, April 7 and 15, 1899, and Stephan to Ganss, April 14, 1899, BCIM, 1899, DC.

7. Jones to Pratt, April 2, 1898, Records of the Office of Commissioner of Indian Affairs, LS, vol. 1895–1899, p. 192. Ganss warned Stephan about Jones, noting that he was "a *persona gratissima* to Pratt, which is ample evidence that he is not a friend of our cause." Ganss to Stephan, April 15, 1899, BCIM, 1899, DC. Pratt's anti-Catholicism is discussed in Everett Arthur Gilcreast, "Richard Henry Pratt and American Indian Policy, 1877–1906: A Study of the Assimilation Movement" (Ph.D. diss., Yale University, 1967), pp. 261–75.

8. Jones to Pratt, September 20, 1900, Records of the Office of the Commissioner of Indian Affairs, LS, vol. 1900–1901, p. 89. See also Jones to Pratt, September 25, 1900, ibid., p. 103.

9. Jones to Pratt, November 5, 1901, BIA, LS, Education.

10. Pratt to the Commissioner of Indian Affairs, November 7, 1901, BIA, LR, 1901-63098E. A formal statement (undated) of the rules relative to religious instruction at Carlisle is printed in BCIM *Report*, 1900–1901 and 1901–1902, pp. 10–11.

11. Peairs to Lusk, October 12, 1901, enclosed in Ketcham to Jones, October 30, 1901, BIA, LR, 1901-61063E; Jones to Superintendent, Haskell Institute, November 30, 1901, and Jones to Bureau of Catholic Indian Missions, November 30, 1901, ibid., LS, Education.

12. Jones to Superintendent, Indian School, Santa Fe, January 18, 1902, and Jones to Ketcham, January 18, 1902, BIA, LS, Education; Ketcham to Jones, March 5, 1902, ibid., LR, 1902-13761E; Jones to U.S. Indian Agent, Navaho Agency, Fort Defiance, Arizona, March 18, 1902, and Jones to Ketcham, March 18, 1902, ibid., LS, Education; Ketcham to Jones, May 19, 1902, ibid., LR, 1902-29724E; A. C. Tonner to Superintendent, Indian School, Phoenix, June 12, 1902, and Tonner to Bureau of Catholic Indian Missions, June 12, 1902, ibid., LS, Education.

13. BCIM *Report*, 1900–1901 and 1901–1902, pp. 11–12, 21.

14. Ibid., 1903–1904, pp. 68–69; Ketcham to Mother Katharine, January 26, 1903, BCIM, 1903, DC. The rules are printed in BCIM *Report*, 1906, pp. 50–52.

15. BIA, Circulars Issued by the Education Division, 1897–1909. The circular is reprinted in BCIM *Report*, 1903–1904, pp. 44–46. The *New York Times*, December 21, 1902, said the circular had for its object "the settlement of the long-standing religious controversy concerning the education of Indian children" and noted that the new rules made general the rules of the Carlisle Indian School.

16. BCIM *Report*, 1900–1901 and 1901–1902, pp. 21–32; ibid., 1903–1904, pp. 47–69.

17., Ibid., 1900–1901 and 1901–1902, p. 28.

18. Rev. J. C. McCourt to Ketcham, November 2, 1904, enclosed in Ketcham to Jones, November 11, 1904, BIA, LR, 1904-83988E; Jones to Ketcham, November 18, 1904, and Jones to Superintendent, Haskell Institute, November 18, 1904, ibid., LS, Education; H. B. Peairs to the Commissioner of Indian Affairs, November 30, 1904, ibid., LR, 1904-83988E; and A. C. Tonner to Bureau of Catholic Indian Missions, De-

cember 6, 1904, ibid., LS, Education. In 1909, when Peairs was put forward as a candidate for the post of Commissioner of Indian Affairs, Ketcham strongly fought against the appointment. He wrote to the president of the Marquette League: "This man must not under any circumstances be appointed. For years he kept the priest out of his school which had several hundred Catholic children in it, and even at the present time, although he has been forced to allow the priest entrance, he thwarts his work in every way possible. Haskell Institute has been simply a proselytizing institution and hundreds of Catholic children have gone there to lose their faith." Ketcham to Philbin, January 30, 1909, BCIM, 1909, DC.

19. BCIM *Report*, 1904–1905, pp. 55–56.

20. Ketcham to Jones, October 10, 1903, BIA, LR, 1903-65460E; Jones to Indian Agent at Colville, October 22, 1903, ibid., LS, Education; Frank F. Avery, Superintendent, Fort Spokane Boarding School, to Albert M. Anderson, Agent, Colville Agency, October 27, 1903, enclosed in Anderson to Jones, November 12, 1903, ibid., LR, 1903-75232E; Jones to Indian Agent, Colville Agency, November 27, 1903, and Jones to Ketcham, November 27, 1903, ibid., LS, Education.

21. BCIM *Report*, 1906, p. 52. See reports on other schools, ibid., pp. 52–56.

22. Some Protestants saw the problem, too. Commissioner Jones reported to the Secretary of the Interior that Bishop Hare asserted "that the phase of religion taught in the great majority of the Government schools among the Sioux, except in cases where the Roman Catholics dominate the situation as on the Standing Rock Reserve, is distinctly Protestant; that the Gospel Hymns are supplied to the Government schools in large quantities by the Government and are in frequent use. These books present religion in a form which is approved by Methodists and Congregationalists, and others, but not in the form in which some other denominations think religion should be presented to the young, for example the Episcopal and Roman Catholic bodies. He individually, does not object, for the adoption of this form is, he believes, a well-meant effort of the Government to deal with a very difficult and, he fears, troublesome problem; but the Roman Catholics do object and protest and put their protestations before the public in forms which appeal not only to prejudice but to equity." Jones to the Secretary of the Interior, January 14, 1902, OSI, ID, LR, 1902-569.

Chapter 13

1. Leupp to Ketcham, April 10, 1906, BCIM, 1906, DC; BCIM *Report*, 1906, pp. 47–49.

2. Leupp to Custer, September 21, 1906, BIA, CCF, 3115-08, 816 General Service. The quotations in the paragraphs following are from this letter.

3. Before dispatching the letter to Custer, Leupp sent a draft of it to Roosevelt for his approval. The President cautiously endorsed the idea. "I think the experiment well worth trying," he wrote, "It could not succeed if it were introduced everywhere at once, but having in view what you say about Mr. Custer and Father Marinelli [*sic*], there is a good chance that it may succeed at Albuquerque. Upon the measure of success, and the reception given to the plan, will of course depend how far we can adopt it elsewhere." Roosevelt to Leupp, September 17, 1906, Theodore Roosevelt Papers, Library of Congress, series 2, vol. 66, p. 449 (reel 343).

4. Copy in BIA, CCF, 3115-08, 816 General Service.

5. BIA, Circulars Issued by the Education Division, 1897–1909.

6. These replies can be located in BIA, Index to Letters Received, 1907, under "Religious Instruction."

7. There is a good description of the lessons in Edwin Wilbur Rice, *The Sunday-School Movement, 1780–1917, and the American Sunday-School Union, 1817–1917* (Philadelphia: American Sunday-School Union, 1917), section 9, "International Lessons —1872–1925," pp. 294–317. See also the more detailed book by John Richard Sampey, *The International Lesson System: The History of Its Origin and Development* (New York: Fleming H. Revell Co., 1911).

8. See, for example, *Gospel Hymns Nos. 1 to 6*, by Ira D. Sankey, James McGranahan, and George C. Stebbins (New York: Biglow and Main Co., and Cincinnati: John Church Co., 1895), which contains 739 hymns. The preface to this edition notes: "In addition to the large number of Gospel Hymns and Sacred Songs in this collection there will also be found over 125 of the most useful and popular Standard Hymns and Tunes of the Church."

9. This appears as hymn no. 260 in *Gospel Hymns Nos. 1 to 6*.

10. H. B. Peairs to the Commissioner of Indian Affairs, May 7, 1907, BIA, LR, 1907-45087E.

11. C. M. Ziebach to the Commissioner of Indian Affairs, May 17, ibid., 1907-48214E.

12. G. Crandall to the Commissioner of Indian Affairs, May 4, 1907, ibid., 1907-44404E.

13. Charles S. McNichols to the Commissioner of Indian Affairs, May 13, 1907, ibid., 1907-47283E.

14. BIA, CCF, 3115-08, 816 General Service. Leupp had asked Ketcham to supply him with a list of government Indian schools in which there were a considerable number of Catholic children. Leupp to Ketcham, November 19, 1907, BCIM, 1907, DC. The BCIM *Report*, from 1907 on, included tables showing "Catholic Instruction in Non-Reservation Government Boarding Schools" and "Catholic Instruction in Government Indian Day Schools."

15. Answers to Leupp's letter, dated January and February 1908, are filed in BIA, CCF, 3115-08, 816 General Service.

16. Mercer to Leupp, January 14, 1908, with Carlisle "Rules" enclosed, ibid.

17. A copy of this printed letter is enclosed in Mercer to Leupp, January 14, 1908.

18. Ganss to Ketcham, September 17, 1906, BCIM, 1906, DC.

19. H. G. Ganss, "The Present Status of the Catholic Indian Problem," *Messenger* 48 (November 1907): 430–41. Earlier sections of the article, dealing with the history of Catholic Indian schools, appeared ibid., (July 1907): 48–59; (October 1907): 337–45. The series of articles was reprinted by the Marquette League as a pamphlet, *The Present Status of the Catholic Indian Problem* (New York, 1907), copy in Holy Rosary Mission Records, series 12, box 1, Marquette University Library.

20. Ketcham to George de la Motte, October 15, 1907, BCIM, 1907, DC. Ketcham also thought that Ganss's article made too little of the work of the Catholic Bureau. See Ketcham to Ganss, October 15 and 19, 1907, and Ganss to Ketcham, October 17, 1907, BCIM, 1907, DC.

21. Education Circular no. 249, October 31, 1908, BIA, Circulars Issued by the Education Division, 1897–1909. It is printed in BCIM *Report*, 1908, p. 50.

22. Ryan to Ketcham, January 6, 1908, BCIM, 1908, DC.

23. Ketcham to Philbin, April 19, 1907, ibid., 1907, DC. See other letters between Ketcham and Philbin, April and May, 1907, ibid.

24. *Carmina for Social Worship*, comp. and ed. Rev. Lewis A. Mudge and Rev. Herbert B. Turner (New York: A. S. Barnes and Co., 1894 and 1898). There is a copy in the Music Division of the Library of Congress.

25. BCIM *Report*, 1908, pp. 48–50, 60–69. The letters from missionaries quoted in the *Report*, however, generally have a more optimistic tone than Ketcham's own statements.

26. The history and organization of the Home Missions Council is set forth in a pamphlet by William R. King, *History of Home Missions Council with Introductory Outline History of Home Missions* (New York: Home Missions Council, 1930).

27. Moffett and Charles L. White to Valentine, November 11, 1909, BIA, CCF, 71330-09, 816 General Service. There is also a copy enclosed in Moffett to Merrill E. Gates, November 15, 1909, BIC, General Correspondence, 1899–1918, Societies 1901–1913.

28. Gates to Moffett, December 10, 1909, ibid.

29. Moffett to Gates, December 14, 1909, and Gates to Moffett, February 2, 1910, ibid.; Ballinger to Thompson, February 19, 1910, BIA, CCF, 15191-10, 816 General Service; Ballinger to Ketcham, February 19, 1910, ibid., 15192-10, 816 General Service.

30. Thompson to Ballinger, February 24, 1910, ibid., 14338-10, 816 General Service; telegram, Valentine to Thompson, February 25, 1910, ibid.

31. Copy in BIC, Reference Material, Schools (Sectarian); printed also in BCIM *Report*, 1910, pp. 36–39.

32. Gibbons to Valentine, March 24, 1910, BIA, CCF, 28146-10, 816.1 General Service; Ketcham to priests, March 26, 1910, BCIM, 1910, DC; M. A. Dimier to Valentine, April 13, 1910, and Florentine Digmann to Valentine, April 10, 1910, BIA, CCF, 21913-10, 816 General Service; BCIM *Report*, 1910, p. 39.

33. Thompson to Valentine, March 16, 1910, BIA, CCF, 21913-10, 816 General Service.

34. Valentine to Thompson, March 18, 1910, and Valentine to Anna L. Dawes, March 18, 1910, ibid.

35. See letters of Valentine to the superintendents and their replies in BIA, CCF, 6503-11, 816 General Service. There are other replies ibid., 7563-11, 816 General Service.

36. Draft of address, IRA (reel 24).

37. Valentine to missionary boards, March 15, 1911, BIA, CCF, 92015-10, 816 General Service.

38. Ketcham to the Commissioner of Indian Affairs, March 17, 1911, ibid.; letters from others are in the same file. In a memorandum of August 21, 1911, J. H. Dortch, in charge of the Education Division, summarized the replies. Ibid.

39. In an ironic turnabout, the YMCA director at Carlisle in 1912 complained about Catholic pressures, which forced him to dismiss Catholic pupils from the YMCA and suspend social affairs lest they create jealousy among the Catholics, who could not attend. "Of course this is a government affair and cannot well be changed during the present administration," he wrote, "especially during the administration of the present Superintendent of this school. Mr. Friedman is doing everything in his power to block any work of the Y.M.C.A., simply because he is dominated by the Catholic element, and is really held in office through their influence, so you see we are in a pretty bad situation. I am residing on the school grounds, and they are quite anxious to have me removed,

but so far nothing has been done effectively. I am here in the interests of the Protestant denominations as the Protestants are taken care of in the Y.M.C.A. and proselyting is prevented thereby." James W. W. Walker to F. W. Farr, December 11, 1912, copy in IRA (reel 26).

Chapter 14

1. The broader question of religious garb in public schools is discussed in Alvin W. Johnson and Frank H. Yost, *Separation of Church and State in the United States* (Minneapolis: University of Minnesota Press, 1948), pp. 115–24. For the revival of anti-Catholic sentiment in these years, which was reflected in the garb issue, see John Higham, *Strangers in the Land: Patterns of American Nativism, 1860–1925* (New Brunswick: Rutgers University Press, 1955), pp. 175–82. Archbishop Ireland's statement is in Ireland to Gibbons, June 8, 1912, AAB, 110-L-5.

2. An account of civil service reform in Indian administration is given in Francis Paul Prucha, *American Indian Policy in Crisis: Christian Reformers and the Indian, 1865–1900* (Norman: University of Oklahoma Press, 1976), pp. 353–72.

3. John R. Proctor to the Secretary of the Interior, June 10, 1895, BIA, CCF, 47724-10, 816.2 General Service.

4. Valentine to Bishop Earl Cranston, June 18, 1910, ibid. A list of the schools and information on the employees covered in at particular schools is contained in a file labeled "Schools taken over from religious denominations and private parties and changed to Government schools under letter of 1895, Civil Service Commission," ibid., 13128-12, 816.1 General Service. A brief account of Catholic schools transferred to government control is given in William H. Ketcham, *Religious "Garb" and "Insignia" in Government Indian Schools* (Washington: Bureau of Catholic Indian Missions, 1912).

5. Letter and memorandum of White to Valentine, June 10, 1910, BIA, CCF, 47724-10, 816.2 General Service.

6. Valentine to Bishop Earl Cranston, chairman of the Joint Committee of Home Missions Council and the Federal Council, June 18, 1910, ibid.

7. Brosius to Sniffen, June 21, 1911, IRA (reel 24); *Congressional Record*, 47:2438. The resolution is printed in Ketcham, *Religious "Garb"*, p. 12.

8. Samuel Adams, Acting Secretary of the Interior, July 22, 1911, copies in IRA (reel 24) and BCIM, 1911, DC. For information on the inaction of the Committee on Indian Affairs, see Charles S. Lusk to Ketcham, September 13, 1911, BCIM, 1911, DC. Stephens's letter to the Secretary of the Interior, July 13, 1911, cited in Ketcham, *Religious "Garb"*, could not be found.

9. Lusk to Ketcham, October 5, 1911, BCIM, 1911, DC.

10. A copy of the statement is in BCIM, 1911, DC. The BCIM scrapbooks include numerous clippings from Catholic newspapers, November–December 1911, which printed the statement and discussed Stephens's threat to the Catholic schools. See also Ketcham to F. W. Hoppman, December 16, 1911, BCIM, 1911, DC.

11. *Independent* 71 (December 14, 1911): 1348.

12. Correspondence between Macfarland and the Indian Office, beginning September 14, 1911, BIA, CCF, 81081-11, 816 General Service.

13. Macfarland to the United States Civil Service Commission, November 27, 1911, copy in OSI, CCF, 5-114, Religious Garb in Indian Schools.

14. Ketcham, *Religious "Garb"*, p. 5. For a very candid expression of Ketcham's

views, see his letter to John J. Wynne, February 8, 1912, BCIM, 1912, DC. In it he speaks of his conversation with Champ Clark, his disappointment in the lack of support from Catholic Congressmen, and his hope of keeping both parties favorable to the Catholics in the garb issue. He concludes with this evaluation of Valentine: "Confidentially, I will say that Mr. Valentine is not a bigot in any sense of the word. He has been extremely kind to us on many occasions but at all times very 'slippery.' He would not object to wear the religious garb himself if he thought it would do him any good. He apparently is a man utterly devoid of principle and religion. I think there is no doubt that his famous order was not influenced by prejudice or bigotry but that it was an act of treason pure and simple to many of his best friends perpetrated for personal ends."

15. BIA, Circulars, Box 514-640. The circular is printed in Ketcham, *Religious "Garb"*, p. 13, and copied often in other literature on the subject.

16. Charles L. Thompson, president of the Home Missions Council, to the President, February 1, 1912, printed in Ketcham, *Religious "Garb"*, p. 13.

17. Taft to Fisher, February 2, 1912, Walter F. Fisher Papers, Library of Congress, Secretary's Private Files, Official, Indian, box 12.

18. Fisher to Taft, February 3, 1912, William Howard Taft Papers, Library of Congress, series 6, case file no. 515C (reel 397). The two draft "suggestions" are attached.

19. Taft to the Secretary of the Interior, February 3, 1912, Fisher Papers, Secretary's Private Files, Official, Indians, box 12; printed also in Ketcham, *Religious "Garb"*, p. 14.

20. Fisher to Valentine, February 3, 1912, BIA, CCF, 13128-12, 816.1 General Service. For Circular no. 605, see BIA, Circulars; it is also printed in Ketcham, *Religious "Garb"*, p. 15.

21. Ketcham to Kenkel, February 6, 1912, and Kenkel to Ketcham, February 8, 1912, ibid. Some of the Congressmen who received letters from the Catholic societies entered them into the records of the House, much to the dismay of the senders, who had not foreseen that their resolutions would thus be made public. Ketcham attributed the publication to "the intense bitterness and activity of Protestant societies and clergymen, especially here in Washington." Ketcham to Anthony Matre, March 14, 1912, ibid. For examples of presentation of the petitions in the House, see *Congressional Record*, 48:3126, 3240, 3293. All the petitions were referred to the Committee on Indian Affairs.

22. Telegram, Matre to the President, February 9, 1912, Fisher Papers, Secretary's Private Files, Official, Indian, box 12.

23. Form letter of Matre, February 10, 1912, and Matre to Ketcham, March 1, 1912, BCIM, 1912, DC. There is a massive file of letters from Catholic groups and individuals in OSI, CCF, 5-114, General, Indian Office, Religious Insignia in Indian Schools.

24. Ketcham to Matre, March 8, 1912, BCIM, 1912, DC.

25. Philbin to the President, February 14, 1912; Byrne to Ketcham, March 13 and 15, 1912; Ketcham to Byrne, March 14 and 16, 1912; Philbin to members of the Marquette League, March 23, 1912, BCIM, 1912, DC. See also Andrew J. Shipman, "Stretching the Constitution," *Columbiad*, undated clipping in BCIM scrapbooks.

26. Ketcham to Gans, February 29 and March 14, 1912, BCIM, 1912, DC; Ketcham to Bonaparte, March 26, 1912, CJB, LR; Bonaparte to Ketcham, March 27, 1912 (two letters), BCIM, 1912, DC. A printed copy of the brief is in OSI, CCF, 5-114, Religious Garb in Indian Schools. It might be noted that in April 1909 Bonaparte had been formally appointed legal adviser to the Bureau of Catholic Indian Missions, a post with no salary.

BCIM *Report*, 1909, p. 3; Ketcham to Bonaparte, April 27 and 30, 1909, CJB, LR; Bonaparte to Ketcham, April 29, 1909, ibid., LS.

27. Bonaparte to Ketcham, March 27, 1912, BCIM, 1912, DC.

28. Form letter of Ketcham to priests and nuns in government schools, February 7, 1912, and Ketcham to Gans, February 29, 1912, BCIM, 1912, DC. Commissioner Valentine in a letter to Cardinal Gibbons, June 20, 1912, declared that the statements in Bonaparte's brief and the statements of the Catholics at the hearing on April 8 had convinced him that the question of insignia was closed and that he anticipated no further misunderstanding on the score of pictures and insignia. BIA, CCF, 13993-12, 816 General Service.

29. Ketcham to Gans, March 30, 1912, and Bonaparte to Ketcham, April 1, 1912, BCIM, 1912, DC.

30. Sniffen to Annie Fuller, February 5, 1912; Sniffen to Brosius, February 5, 1912; Sniffen to Welsh, February 5, 1912; Grammer to E. J. Moore, February 6, 1912; Sniffen to C. L. Thompson, February 7, 1912, IRA (reel 80); Grammer and Welsh to the President, February 8, 1912, ibid. (reel 25), also printed in IRA *Report*, 1912, pp. 10–11.

31. Sniffen to C. L. Thompson, February 7, 1912; Sniffen to Thomas C. Moffett, February 9, 1912; Sniffen to Herbert Marten, February 10, 1912, IRA (reel 80).

32. Grammer to Brosius, February 13, 1912, ibid.; Grammer to Valentine, February 13, 1912, BIA, CCF, 13993-12, 816 General Service; Grammer to the President, February 24, 1912; Grammer to the Secretary of the Interior, February 24, 1912; Grammer to Mrs. Brinton Coxe, February 13, 1912, IRA (reel 80).

33. C. L. Thompson to Sniffen, February 6, 1912, IRA (reel 25). A copy of the statement is attached. Thomas C. Moffett in *The American Indian on the New Trail: The Red Man of the United States and the Christian Gospel* (New York: Presbyterian Department of Missionary Education, 1914), pp. 235–36, wrote: "This [Circular no. 601] offered a special opportunity for service on the part of the Indian Committee of the Home Missions Council. United Protestantism was enabled in this instance to present a solid front." For use of this material in the denominational press, see, for example, *Missions: A Baptist Monthly Magazine* 3 (April 1912): 254, 297–99. The editor declared that the Catholic Church in the garb issue showed "the perilous and insidious side of a great ecclesiastical system." The journal of the National Indian Association declared: "It becomes essentially a question of separation or non-separation of Church and State. It is idle talk to say it is a mere 'fuss about clothes.' To permanently revoke the order of the Commissioner of Indian Affairs would be to take a long stride backward in the march of our national life." *Indian's Friend*, May 1912, p. 9.

34. Report of the meeting of the Executive Committee of the Home Missions Council, February 8, 1912, in Moffett to Grammer, February 8, 1912, IRA (reel 25). See also minutes of the meeting of the Indian Committee, Home Missions Council, February 14, 1912, enclosed in Charles L. White to Sniffen, February 21, 1912, and Sniffen to Brosius, February 8, 1912, ibid.

35. Charles L. White to Sniffen, March 2, 1912, ibid. There is a copy of the pamphlet in BIA, CCF, 13993-12, 816 General Service.

36. See the large number of letters—to President Taft, to Secretary Fisher, and to Commissioner Valentine—filed in OSI, CCF, 5-114, General, Indian Office, Religious Insignia in Indian Schools. A good many are printed forms. There was some confusion about whom the letters of protest were to be sent to. Apparently many of the letters from Baptists were sent only to the President and not also to the Secretary of the Interior

and to the Commissioner of Indian Affairs, and the Baptists apologized to Valentine for the oversight. C. L. White to Valentine, May 4, 1912, and Bruce Kinney to Valentine, May 8, 1912, BIA, CCF, 13993-12, 816 General Service. There are a great many letters to the President about the revocation of the garb order, from both Catholics and Protestants, in the Taft Papers, series 6, case file no. 515C (reels 397–98). Some of the Protestant letters are very anti-Catholic in tone. There are also letters to Taft accusing him of having sold out to the Catholic Church—with the garb issue as one point of complaint—in the Taft Papers, series 6, case file no. 2139 (reels 426–27). The President's secretary replied to those condemning the revocation of Valentine's order with a simple statement: "The order of the Commissioner of Indian Affairs to which you refer was not intended to go into effect before September 1st, next, and the President's order was merely to preserve the *status quo* in order to give full opportunity to all parties in interest to be heard before the matter is finally determined." Ibid., case file no. 515C (reel 397). There is a brief account of anti-Catholic attacks on Taft in Henry F. Pringle, *The Life and Times of William Howard Taft*, 2 vols. (New York: Farrar and Rinehart, 1939), 2:833–34.

37. Moffett to Sniffen, April 3, 1912, IRA (reel 25). The Council hoped to get representatives at the hearing from the Boston Indian Citizenship Committee, but that organization failed to act in time. J. Weston Allen, vice-chairman of the Boston Indian Citizenship Committee, to Sniffen, April 10, 1912, ibid.

38. See "Religious Garb in Indian Schools," *Independent* 72 (February 15, 1912): 374–75; "Religious Garb in Indian Schools," *Literary Digest* 44 (February 24, 1912): 379–80; "Critics of Religious Garb in Indian Schools," *Literary Digest* 44 (March 2, 1912): 428; "Indian Government Schools," *Outlook* 100 (March 30, 1912): 718–19. There is much information on the controversy in the BCIM scrapbooks.

39. I could find no formal record of the hearing aside from two sets of typed pages —one of five pages and another of three pages, not consecutive—which appear to be transcripts of the hearing, in BIA, CCF, 92015-10, 816 General Service. Sniffen to Miss Mateer, April 8, 1912, IRA (reel 25), reports briefly on the meeting. An undated and unsigned document entitled "The Hearing before the Secretary of the Interior" presents a Catholic view of the affair. It says in part: "The Secretary's room was crowded with advocates of the order—representatives of the Indian Office, of the Indian Rights Association, of the Home Missions Council, Protestant pastors of Washington, Adventists, atheists, Secular league people and wild-eyed fanatics who never in all their lives had done one act of kindness or helpfulness for the Indians." BCIM, 1912, DC.

40. The memoranda, attached to Valentine to Fisher, March 20, 1912, were the following: Memorandum I contained a long history of the contract schools, a bitter statement headed "Attitude of Bureau of Catholic Indian Missions," a review of the contracts made for the use of tribal funds, and a series of recommendations; Memorandum II was a collection of data from the Constitution, acts of Congress, court cases, and civil service regulations against sectarian instruction in schools; Memorandum III contained brief material dealing with the sales and leases by which the government took over sectarian schools; and Memorandum IV was a long historical narrative entitled "Notes on Educational Policies and Activities on Behalf of Indians." OSI, CCF, 5-114, General.

41. Memorandum I, ibid. See also the long letter of Sniffen to Welsh, February 17, 1912, IRA (reel 80), in which Sniffen reports a meeting with Valentine, in which the Commissioner explained his action.

42. Copy of Valentine's statement, OSI, CCF, 5-114, Religious Garb in Indian Schools.

43. Ibid.

44. *Reply Brief of Henry B. F. Macfarland, Counsel . . . in the Matter of the Circular Order No. 601* . . . , a twenty-five-page pamphlet, dated April 13, 1912, ibid., file 5-114, General. A typewritten copy of the brief, dated April 11, 1912, is in IRA (reel 25). For Indian Rights Association support of Macfarland's efforts, see Brosius to Executive Committee of the Indian Rights Association, April 11, 1912, ibid.

45. Brosius to Sniffen, April 14, 1912, and Sniffen to Brosius, April 15, 1912, ibid.

46. Bonaparte to Ketcham, April 16, 1912, CJB, LS; Bonaparte to Ketcham, April 20, 1912, BCIM, 1912, DC.

47. Unsigned copy of Clark to Brosius, March 8, 1912, IRA (reel 25). The chart, a foot wide and more than five and one-half feet long, is labeled "Pictorial Catechism, composed by Rev. Father A. Lacombe, O.M.I., Missionary, used with success for the speedy and easy instruction of Indians, children and uneducated people." It was published in Montreal by C. O. Beauchemin & Fils. There is a copy, mounted on cloth and showing signs of heavy use, in the Holy Rosary Mission Records, Marquette University Library. An account of Lacombe's creation of the chart is given in Katherine Hughes, *Father Lacombe: The Black-Robe Voyageur* (Toronto: McClelland and Stewart, 1920), pp. 201–3.

48. Correspondence between McKim and Lusk, May–June, 1912, BCIM, 1912, DC; Brosius to Sniffen, May 14, 1912, and Sniffen to Brosius, May 15, 1912, IRA (reel 25); Gibbons to Valentine, June 8, 1912, and Valentine to Gibbons, June 20, 1912, BCIM, 1912, DC. An article in the *Washington Post*, June 28, 1912, presents both sides of the controversy. The Catholic Bureau wrote to the schools involved in the garb issue and received letters from them all denying that any religious pictures were displayed in their schools. The letters are in BCIM, 1912, DC.

49. Ketcham to J. K. Kenkel, August 27, 1912, BCIM, 1912, DC. See also Ketcham to J. J. Wynne, August 28, 1912, and other correspondence in the same file.

50. See Brosius to Sniffen, June 26 and July 2, 1912, and subsequent correspondence, IRA (reel 26).

51. Valentine to the President, September 10, 1912, Taft Papers, series 6, case file no. 25A (reel 358). Attached to the letter is the four-page statement Valentine prepared for the press to explain the reasons for his resignation. For a Protestant view, see Brosius to Sniffen, July 2, 1912, IRA (reel 26). For newspaper coverage of Valentine's resignation, see BCIM scrapbooks.

52. *Religious Garb in Indian Schools: Letter of the Secretary of the Interior to the Commissioner of Indian Affairs* (Washington, 1912). As late as January 1933 there were still five employees in the Indian schools wearing religious garb on the basis of this decision. Johnson and Yost, *Separation of Church and State*, p. 122 n.

53. Printed statement of Taft, *Religious Garb in Indian Schools*, September 23, 1912, copy in CJB, Subject File, Indians (printed matter). For comments on the statement, see "Catholics and Indian Schools," *Outlook* 102 (October 5, 1912): 234–35; "The Nuns'-Garb Question," *Literary Digest* 45 (October 12, 1912): 626. The considerable newspaper coverage of the President's action can be followed in the BCIM scrapbooks.

54. Eugene Philbin to members of the Marquette League, October 3, 1912, BCIM,

1912, DC; Charles L. Thompson to the President, October 18, 1912, Taft Papers, series 6, case file no. 515C (reel 398); Sniffen to Annie Fuller, October 4, 1912, IRA (reel 26); IRA *Report*, 1912, pp. 8–14.

55. Ketcham to Sniffen, November 13, 1912, IRA (reel 26). See also Ketcham to Sniffen, November 19, 1912, ibid.; Sniffen to Ketcham, November 15, 1912, ibid. (reel 80).

56. Ketcham replaced Cardinal Gibbons on the Board. The Cardinal, who had been appointed when Archbishop Ryan died in 1910, resigned because he was too busy to take an active part in the Board's work and recommended to Taft that Ketcham be appointed in his stead. Taft to Gibbons, November 30, 1912, AAB, 111-G-6; Ketcham to Gibbons, December 3, 1912, ibid., 111-H-4.

Bibliography

1. Bureau of Catholic Indian Missions Records

These records, maintained at the headquarters of the Bureau in Washington, D.C., from 1874 to 1977, are now deposited in the Marquette University Library. They consist of incoming and outgoing correspondence of the Bureau, arranged by year, and within year by place. Most of the correspondence used in this study is filed under District of Columbia, since it concerns the activities of the director and other officers of the Bureau.

The collection also includes a number of scrapbooks with extensive newspaper clippings dealing with topics of concern to the Bureau and a large collection of snapshots and photographs of missions and mission schools.

The following printed reports of the Bureau or its director are in the collection.

The Bureau of Catholic Indian Missions: The Work of the Decade, Ending December 31, 1883. Washington: Bureau of Catholic Indian Missions, 1884.

The Bureau of Catholic Indian Missions, 1874 to 1895. Washington: Church News Publishing Co., 1895.

Report of Rev. J. A. Stephan, Director, to Rt. Rev. Bishop M. Marty, President of the Bureau of Catholic Indian Missions, for the Year 1891–'92. Washington: Gedney and Roberts Co., 1892.

Report of the Bureau of Catholic Indian Missions. 1898–1910.

There are numerous printed flyers and pamphlets, published by the Bureau to promote its activities, including the following:

Ketcham, William H. *Brief Historical Sketch of Catholic Indian Mission Work in the United States of America.* Published in 1913 or later.

———. *Father Ketcham's Address before the Senate Indian Committee.* N.d.

———. *Father Ketcham's Statement before the Subcommittee of the Committee of Indian Affairs, United States Senate, in the Matter of the Use of Indian Tribal Funds for the Maintenance of Sectarian Schools.* Transcript of the hearing on February 3, 1905.

————. *The Indian Rights Association vs. the Rights of the Indians*. A paper read before the Marquette League of New York City, May 19, 1909.

————. *The Indians and Catholic Indian Missions of the United States*.

————. *Our Catholic Indian Missions*. A paper read before the Catholic Missionary Congress, Chicago, November 16, 1908.

————. *Religious "Garb" and "Insignia" in Government Indian Schools*. Washington, 1912.

————. *The Views of Bishops Having Indians in Their Dioceses and of Catholic Indian Missionaries as to What Should Be the Future of Our Catholic Indian Missions*. A report dated October 10, 1907.

————. *What Shall Be the Future of Our Catholic Indian Missions?* An inquiry issued in response to a resolution of October 10, 1905.

Memoranda Relative to Commissioner Morgan's Indian School Policy, and to the Mission School System for the Education of the Indians. Undated, about 1889.

Memoranda Relative to Removals and Appointments in the Indian School Service. Undated, about 1889.

Senator Aldrich and Catholic Indian Missions. Dated November 2, 1904.

Statement of the Case. Undated, about 1912.

Statistics of Catholic Indian Mission and School Work from the Report of the Director of the Bureau of Catholic Indian Missions for 1903–1904.

Stephan, Joseph A. *The Crusade against the Catholic Indian Schools*. A letter to James Cardinal Gibbons, January 26, 1895.

————. *Letter of Monsignor J. A. Stephan, Director Bureau Catholic Indian Missions, Relative to Capt. R. H. Pratt, Superintendent Carlisle Indian Training School*. Letter to Secretary of War D. S. Lamont, February 29, 1896.

The Bureau from 1902 to 1962 published a promotional magazine, the *Indian Sentinel*. It was issued as an annual from 1902 to 1916. It became a quarterly in July 1916, a monthly in January 1936, a bimonthly in January 1957, and a quarterly again in 1962, the last year of publication.

2. Indian Rights Association Papers

This extensive collection of correspondence and printed items is deposited in the Historical Society of Pennsylvania, Philadelphia. It is available on microfilm (136 reels), for which there is a printed guide: *Indian Rights Association Papers: A Guide to the Microfilm Edition, 1864–1973* (Glen Rock, N.J.: Microfilming Corporation of America, 1975). The microfilm edition contains not only the incoming and outgoing correspondence of the Indian Rights Association and of Herbert Welsh, long-time executive secretary and president of the organization, but also organizational records and a complete set of the *Annual Report* and of the numerous publications (pamphlets and leaflets) of the Association. In addition there are miscellaneous government documents and other publications dealing with Indian affairs, which are found in the Association's files.

Particularly pertinent items from the publications of the Indian Rights Association are the following:

Indian School Welfare: Signs of Returning Reason in the House Committee— Superintendent Hailmann and the Question of Economy. 1894.
Indian Trust Funds for Sectarian Schools. 1905.
The Position of Superintendent of Indian Schools Threatened—A Serious Danger to Be Averted. 1894.
A Response to Senator Pettigrew. 1897.
The Secretary of the Interior and the Indian Education Problem—A Rift in the Cloud. 1894.
Shall Public Funds Be Expended for the Support of Sectarian Indian Schools? 1914.

3. Records of the Federal Government in the National Archives

Material from the following record groups was used in this study:

Record Group 46: Records of the United States Senate
    Committee on Indian Affairs, Petitions and Memorials
Record Group 48: Records of the Office of the Secretary of the Interior
    Appointments Division, Commissioner of Indian Affairs
    Indian Division, Letters Received
    Central Classified File, 5-6 and 5-114
Record Group 60: General Records of the Department of Justice
    Year File no. 2290-02
Record Group 75: Records of the Bureau of Indian Affairs
    Letters Received
    Letters Sent
    Circulars
    Central Classified File, 816, 816.1, and 816.2 General Service
    Records of the Education Division
        Circulars Issued by the Education Division, 1897–1909
        Memoranda, 1905–1910
        Record of School Contracts
    Records of the Office of the Commissioner of Indian Affairs
        Letters Sent
    Records of the Board of Indian Commissioners
        Minutes of Meetings

Reference Material, Schools (Sectarian)
General Correspondence, 1899–1918, Societies, 1901–1913
Letters Sent by Acting Commissioner Charles F. Larrabee, 1905–1908
Summaries of Work Completed and Records Relating to Mission Schools
Record Group 200: National Archives Gift Collection
Private Papers of Ethan Allen Hitchcock, 1880–1909
Subject File, Miscellaneous Indian Affairs
Record Group 233: Records of the United States House of Representatives
Committee on Indian Affairs, Petitions and Memorials
Record Group 267: Records of the United States Supreme Court
Appellate Case Files, no. 20972
Record Group 287: Publications of the U.S. Government
Selected publications on Indian schools

4. Other Archives and Personal Papers

Archdiocese of Baltimore, Baltimore, Maryland
Archives of the Archdiocese of Baltimore (Papers of Cardinal Gibbons)
Episcopal Church in South Dakota, Sioux Falls, South Dakota
Historical Archives Collection (copies of selected documents supplied by
the archivist)
Haverford College Library, Haverford, Pennsylvania
Smiley Family Papers, Quaker Collection
Library of Congress, Washington, D.C.
Charles J. Bonaparte Papers
Henry L. Dawes Papers
Walter L. Fisher Papers
Benjamin Harrison Papers
Theodore Roosevelt Papers
William Howard Taft Papers
Marquette University Library, Milwaukee, Wisconsin
Holy Rosary Mission Records
Sisters of the Blessed Sacrament, Cornwells Heights, Pennsylvania
Archives of the Sisters of the Blessed Sacrament
State Historical Society of Wisconsin, Madison, Wisconsin
William A. Jones Papers

5. Printed Congressional Documents (in serial order)

"Indian Tribal Funds," *House Report* no. 4547, 58th Cong., 3d sess., ser.
4762. Report of the Committee on Indian Affairs on the Lacey bill (H.R.
18516) for allotment and distribution of Indian tribal funds.
"Expenditures for Support of Sectarian Schools," *House Report* no. 4826,

58th Cong., 3d sess., ser. 4762B. Report of the Committee on Indian Affairs amending House Resolution no. 502, requesting information from the Secretary of the Interior about expenditures for sectarian schools.

"Use of Indian Trust Fund for Sectarian School Purposes," *Senate Document* no. 170, 58th Cong., 3d sess., ser. 4766. Contains protests of Sioux Indians and others against the use of trust funds.

"Care and Education of Indians in Sectarian and Denominational Schools," *Senate Document* no. 179, 58th Cong., 3d sess., ser. 4766. Documents supplied by the Secretary of the Interior in response to a Senate resolution; contains many key documents relative to use of tribal funds for sectarian schools.

"Expenditure of Indian Trust Funds," *House Document* no. 249, 58th Cong., 3d sess., ser. 4832. Report of the Secretary of the Interior in response to House request for information on use of trust funds for contract schools.

"Use of Indian Funds for Support of Sectarian Schools," *House Document* no. 374, 58th Cong., 3d sess., ser. 4832. Report of the Secretary of the Interior in response to House request for information on use of appropriated funds for sectarian schools.

"Allotment of Indian Tribal Funds," *House Report* no. 2950, 59th Cong., 1st sess., ser. 4907. Report of the Committee on Indian Affairs on the Lacey bill (H.R. 5290) for allotment and distribution of Indian trust funds.

"Allotment of Indian Tribal Funds," *Senate Report* no. 4634, 59th Cong., 2d sess., ser. 5060. Report of the Committee on Indian Affairs on the Lacey bill (H.R. 5290).

"Allotment of Indian Tribal Funds," *Senate Report* no. 6687, 59th Cong., 2d sess., ser. 5060. Report of the Committee on Indian Affairs on the Lacey bill (H.R. 5290).

"Allotment of Indian Tribal Funds," *Senate Report* no. 6698, 59th Cong., 2d sess., ser. 5061. Report of the Committee on Indian Affairs on the Lacey bill (H.R. 5290).

"Allotment and Distribution of Indian Tribal Funds," *House Report* no. 8068, 59th Cong., 2d sess., ser. 5065. Report of the conference committee on the Lacey bill (H.R. 5290).

"Allotment and Distribution of Indian Tribal Funds," *House Report* no. 925, 62d Cong., 2d sess., ser. 6132. Report of the Committee on Indian Affairs on a bill (H.R. 46) to amend the Lacey Act.

"Allotment and Distribution of Indian Tribal Funds," *House Report* no. 422, 63d Cong., 2d sess., ser. 6559. Report of the Committee on Indian Affairs on a bill (H.R. 10832) to amend the Lacey Act.

6. Printed Materials for the Case of *Quick Bear* v. *Leupp*

The various briefs and records of the case are listed below. Aside from those for the Supreme Court of the United States, the documents are difficult to find, and a location for each is indicated. Some of the earlier material also appears in the *Transcript of Record* of the Supreme Court case.

Bill in Equity, in the Supreme Court of the District of Columbia, May 11, 1906, no. 26271. Indian Rights Association Papers, Historical Society of Pennsylvania (microfilm reel 119, no. 80); General Records of the Department of Justice, Year File no. 2290-02, National Archives, Record Group 60.

Brief in Behalf of Defendants, in the Supreme Court, District of Columbia, in Equity, no. 26271. General Records of the Department of Justice, Year File no. 2290-02, National Archives, Record Group 60.

Transcript of Record, Court of Appeals of the District of Columbia, April Term, 1907, nos. 1786 and 1787. General Records of the Department of Justice, Year File no. 2290-02, National Archives, Record Group 60.

Brief for Reuben Quick Bear, et al., in the Court of Appeals of the District of Columbia, April Term, 1907, nos. 1786 and 1787. Indian Rights Association Papers, Historical Society of Pennsylvania (microfilm reel 119, no. 81).

Brief for Appellees in No. 1786, and Appellants in No. 1787, in the Court of Appeals of the District of Columbia, April Term, 1907 (brief for the government). General Records of the Department of Justice, Year File no. 2290-02, National Archives, Record Group 60.

Opinion of Justice Wright, Court of Appeals of the District of Columbia, November 29, 1907, in *Reports of Cases Adjudged in the Court of Appeals of the District of Columbia*, 30:151–64. New York: Lawyers Co-operative Publishing Co., 1908.

Transcript of Record, Supreme Court of the United States, October Term, 1907, no. 569.

Motion to Advance Argument and Hearing of Case, in the Supreme Court of the United States, October Term, 1907, no. 569.

Appellants' Brief, in the Supreme Court of the United States, October Term, 1907, no. 569.

Brief for Appellees, in the Supreme Court of the United States, October Term, 1907, no. 569.

Appellants' Brief in Reply, in the Supreme Court of the United States, October Term, 1907, no. 569.

Opinion of Chief Justice Fuller, May 18, 1908, in *United States Reports*, 210:50.

7. Other Published Government Sources

Annual Report of the Commissioner of Indian Affairs.
Annual Report of the Secretary of the Interior.
Congressional Record.
Journal of the Executive Proceedings of the Senate.

Journal of the House of Representatives.
Journal of the Senate.
United States Statutes at Large.
Israel, Fred L., ed. *The State of the Union Messages of the Presidents, 1790–1966.* 3 vols. New York: Chelsea House, 1966.
Rules for the Indian School Service. (Title varies.) Washington: Government Printing Office, 1890–1904.
Indian Appropriation Bill, 1905: Hearing before the Subcommittee of the Committee on Indian Affairs of the Senate of the United States. Washington: Government Printing Office, 1905.
Indian Appropriation Bill: Use of Indian Trust Funds. Washington, 1912.
Religious Garb in Indian Schools. Statement of William H. Taft, September 23, 1912.
Religious Garb in Indian Schools: Letter of the Secretary of the Interior to the Commissioner of Indian Affairs. Washington, 1912.

8. Contemporary Publications

Address of the Catholic Clergy of the Province of Oregon, to the Catholics of the United States, on President Grant's Indian Policy, in Its Bearing upon Catholic Interests at Large. Portland, Oreg.: Catholic Sentinel Publication Co., 1874.
American Federation of Catholic Societies. *Proceedings of the Convention . . . Held at Cincinnati, December 10th, 11th and 12th, 1901.*
———. *Proceedings of the Second National Convention . . . Held at Chicago, August 5, 6, and 7, 1902.*
———. *Proceedings of the Third National Convention . . . Held at Atlantic City, August 1st to 5th, 1903.*
———. *Proceedings of the Fourth National Convention . . . Held at Detroit, Michigan, August 2, 3, and 4, 1904.*
Appeal in Behalf of the Negro and Indian Missions in the United States. 1902.
Bonaparte, Charles J. *In the Matter of Religious Garb and Insignia in Indian Schools: Brief Submitted on Behalf of the Bureau of Catholic Indian Missions by Charles J. Bonaparte.* N.p., n.d.
Casey, M. P. "Indian Contract Schools." *Catholic World* 71 (August 1900): 629–37.
Catholic Grievances in Relation to the Administration of Indian Affairs: Being a Report Presented to the Catholic Young Men's National Union, at Its Annual Convention, Held in Boston, Massachusetts, May 10th and 11th, 1882. Richmond, Va., 1882.
"Catholics and Indian Schools." *Outlook* 102 (October 5, 1912): 234–35.
"Critics of Religious Garb in Indian Schools." *Literary Digest* 44 (March 2, 1912): 428.
Currier, Charles Warren. "The Marquette League." *Indian Sentinel*, 1906, pp. 4–6.

Dorchester, Daniel. *Romanism versus the Public School System*. New York: Phillips and Hunt, 1888.

Dunn, Arthur Wallace. *From Harrison to Harding: A Personal Narrative, Covering a Third of a Century, 1888–1921*. 2 vols. New York: G. P. Putnam's Sons, 1922.

Elliott, Richard R. "Government Secularization of the Education of Catholic Indian Youth." *American Catholic Quarterly Review* 25 (January 1900): 148–68.

Evangelical Alliance for the United States. *National Perils and Opportunities: The Discussions of the General Christian Conference, Held in Washington, D.C., December 7th, 8th and 9th, 1887*. New York: Baker and Taylor Co., 1887.

———. *National Needs and Remedies: The Discussions of the General Christian Conference Held in Boston, Mass. December 4th, 5th and 6th, 1889*. New York: Baker and Taylor Co., 1890.

Friedman, Moses. "Religious Work in Indian Schools." *Missionary Review of the World* 31 (July 1908): 535–36.

Ganss, Henry G. "The Present Status of the Catholic Indian Problem." *Messenger* 48 (July 1907): 48–59; (October 1907): 337–45; (November 1907): 430–41.

Gibbons, James Cardinal. *Petition of James Cardinal Gibbons, Archbishop of Baltimore, for Himself and on Behalf of the Other Catholic Archbishops of the United States, Praying the Congress for a Reopening of the Indian Contract School Question*. 1898.

Gladden, Washington. "The Anti-Catholic Crusade." *Century Magazine* 47 (March 1894): 789–95.

"Indian Appropriations for Sectarian Schools." *Outlook* 79 (January 28, 1905): 221–22.

"The Indian Bureau and the Catholic Church." *Independent* 40 (February 9, 1888): 170.

"Indian Church Schools: The Way Out." *Outlook* 82 (February 3, 1906): 247–48.

"Indian Funds for Sectarian Schools." *Independent* 63 (December 19, 1907): 1507–8.

"Indian Government Schools." *Outlook* 100 (March 30, 1912): 718–19.

"The Indian School Blunder." *Independent* 58 (February 9, 1905): 333–34.

"The Indian Schools." *Independent* 60 (April 12, 1906): 883–84.

Indian Tribal Funds: The Case for the Catholic Indians Stated, with the Record Made in Congress of the Debate by the Senate on the Issue of the Mission Schools. New York: Marquette League, 1905.

"A Jesuit's Idea of Indian Education." *Independent* 44 (May 5, 1892): 624–25.

King, James M. *Facing the Twentieth Century: Our Country, Its Power and Peril*. New York: American Union League Society, 1899.

"The Knights of Columbus." *Independent* 71 (December 14, 1911): 1348.

Leupp, Francis E. *The Indian and His Problem.* New York: Charles Scribner's Sons, 1910.

————. "Indian Funds and Mission Schools." *Outlook* 83 (June 9, 1906): 315–19.

Macfarland, Henry B. F. *Reply Brief of Henry B. F. Macfarland, Counsel, in the Matter of the Circular Order, No. 601, of the Commissioner of Indian Affairs, of January 27, 1912, respecting Religious Garb and Insignia in Government Indian Schools.* Washington: Press of Bryon S. Adams, 1912.

Marty, Martin. "The Indian Problem and the Catholic Church." *Catholic World* 48 (February 1889): 577–84.

"A Mischievous Appropriation." *Outlook* 79 (January 21, 1905): 149–50.

Moffett, Thomas C. *The American Indian on the New Trail: The Red Man of the United States and the Christian Gospel.* New York: Presbyterian Department of Missionary Education, 1914.

Morgan, Thomas J. *Indian Education.* U.S. Bureau of Education, Bulletin no. 1, 1889. Washington: Government Printing Office, 1890.

————. *The Present Phase of the Indian Question.* Boston: Boston Indian Citizenship Committee, 1891.

————. *Roman Catholics and Indian Education.* Boston: American Citizen Co., 1893.

————. *Studies in Pedagogy.* Boston: Silver, Burdett and Co., 1889.

Morrell, Edward. *Rations to Indian School Children: Argument of Hon. Edward Morrell, Representative of the Fifth Pennsylvania District.* 1903.

Mudge, Lewis A., and Turner, Herbert B., comps. and eds. *Carmina for Social Worship.* New York: A. S. Barnes and Co., 1894 and 1898.

National League for the Protection of American Institutions. *A Petition concerning Sectarian Appropriations for Indian Education.* New York, 1892.

"The Nuns'-Garb Question." *Literary Digest* 45 (October 12, 1912): 626.

Palladino, L. B. *Education for the Indian: Fancy and Reason on the Subject: Contract Schools and Non-Sectarianism in Indian Education.* New York: Benziger Brothers, 1892.

————. *Indian and White in the Northwest: A History of Catholicism in Montana, 1831–1891.* 2d ed., rev. Lancaster, Pa.: Wickersham Publishing Co., 1922.

"The President and the Indian: A Step Backward." *Outlook* 79 (February 18, 1905): 417–19.

"Religious Garb in Indian Schools." *Independent* 72 (February 15, 1912): 374–75.

"Religious Garb in Indian Schools." *Literary Digest* 44 (February 24, 1912): 379–80.

Roosevelt, Theodore. *The Letters of Theodore Roosevelt.* Edited by Elting E. Morison. 8 vols. Cambridge: Harvard University Press, 1951–54.

Ryan, Patrick J. *Indian Schools: Statement of Archbishop Ryan before Senate Committee, 4th Feb., 1898.*

Sankey, Ira D.; McGranahan, James; and Stebbins, George C. *Gospel Hymns Nos. 1 to 6.* New York: Biglow and Main Co., and Cincinnati: John Church Co., 1895.

"The State, the Church, and the Indian." *Outlook* 79 (February 11, 1905): 370–72.

"Trust Funds for Catholic Schools." *Nation* 80 (February 9, 1905): 106.

"Unfair Indian Fighting." *Outlook* 79 (February 4, 1905): 263–65.

In addition to the items listed above, there is some coverage of the contract school issue in such periodicals as *Baptist Home Mission Monthly, Church at Home and Abroad, City and State, Indian's Friend,* and *Missions: A Baptist Monthly Magazine.*

9. Books and Articles

Agatha, Mother M. "Catholic Education and the Indian." In *Essays on Catholic Education in the United States*, edited by Roy J. Deferrari, pp. 523–53. Washington: Catholic University of America Press, 1942.

Beaver, R. Pierce. *Church, State, and the American Indians: Two and a Half Centuries of Partnership in Missions between Protestant Churches and Government.* St. Louis: Concordia Publishing House, 1966.

Berens, John F. "Old Campaigners, New Realities: Indian Policy Reform in the Progressive Era, 1900–1912." *Mid-America* 59 (January 1977): 51–64.

Brown, Ira V. *Lyman Abbott, Christian Evolutionist: A Study in Religious Liberalism.* Cambridge: Harvard University Press, 1953.

Burton, Katherine. *The Golden Door: The Life of Katharine Drexel.* New York: P. J. Kenedy and Sons, 1957.

Cassidy, Francis P. "Catholic Education in the Third Plenary Council of Baltimore." *Catholic Historical Review* 34 (October 1948): 257–305; (January 1949): 414–36.

Curtis, Ralph E., Jr. "Relations between the Quapaw National Council and the Roman Catholic Church, 1876–1927." *Chronicles of Oklahoma* 55 (Summer 1977): 211–21.

Desmond, Humphrey J. *The A.P.A. Movement: A Sketch.* Washington: New Century Press, 1912.

Duffy, Consuela Marie. *Katharine Drexel: A Biography.* Philadelphia: Peter Reilly Co., 1966.

Duratschek, Mary Claudia. *Crusading along Sioux Trails: A History of the Catholic Indian Missions of South Dakota.* St. Meinrad, Ind.: Grail Publications, 1947.

Edwards, Martha L. "A Problem of Church and State in the 1870's." *Mississippi Valley Historical Review* 11 (June 1924): 37–53.

Ellis, John Tracy. *The Life of James Cardinal Gibbons, Archbishop of Baltimore, 1834–1921*. 2 vols. Milwaukee: Bruce Publishing Co., 1952.

Furman, Necah. "Seedtime for Indian Reform: An Evaluation of the Administration of Commissioner Francis Ellington Leupp." *Red River Valley Historical Review* 2 (Winter 1975): 495–518.

Gerlach, Dominic B. "St. Joseph's Indian Normal School, 1888–1896." *Indiana Magazine of History* 69 (March 1973): 1–42.

Goldman, Eric F. *Charles J. Bonaparte, Patrician Reformer: His Earlier Career*. Baltimore: Johns Hopkins Press, 1943.

Grantham, Dewey W., Jr. *Hoke Smith and the Politics of the New South*. Baton Rouge: Louisiana State University Press, 1958.

Harbaugh, William H. "Election of 1904." In *History of American Presidential Elections, 1789–1968*, edited by Arthur M. Schlesinger, Jr., and Fred L. Israel, 3:1965–94. 4 vols. New York: Chelsea House, 1971.

Higham, John. *Strangers in the Land: Patterns of American Nativism, 1860–1925*. New Brunswick: Rutgers University Press, 1955.

Johnson, Alvin W., and Yost, Frank H. *Separation of Church and State in the United States*. Minneapolis: University of Minnesota Press, 1948.

King, William R. *History of Home Missions Council with Introductory Outline History of Home Missions*. New York: Home Missions Council, 1930.

Kinzer, Donald L. *An Episode in Anti-Catholicism: The American Protective Association*. Seattle: University of Washington Press, 1964.

Lord, Robert H.; Sexton, John E.; and Harrington, Edward T. *History of the Archdiocese of Boston*. 3 vols. New York: Sheed and Ward, 1944.

Myers, Gustavus. *History of Bigotry in the United States*. New York: Random House, 1943.

Mitchell, Fredric. "Church-State Conflict: A Little-Known Part of the Continuing Church-State Conflict Found in Early Indian Education." *Journal of American Indian Education* 2 (May 1963): 7–14.

Mitchell, Fredric, and Skelton, James W. "The Church-State Conflict in Early Indian Education." *History of Education Quarterly* 6 (Spring 1966): 41–51.

Nieberding, Velma. "St. Mary's of the Quapaws." *Chronicles of Oklahoma* 31 (Spring 1953): 2–14.

Posen, Anthony J. "Joseph Andrew Stephan: Indiana's Fighting Priest." *Social Justice Review* 69 (September 1976): 150–58; (October 1976): 188–91.

Pringle, Henry F. *The Life and Times of William Howard Taft*. 2 vols. New York: Farrar and Rinehart, 1939.

Prucha, Francis Paul. *American Indian Policy in Crisis: Christian Reformers and the Indian, 1865–1900*. Norman: University of Oklahoma Press, 1976.

Rahill, Peter J. *The Catholic Indian Missions and Grant's Peace Policy, 1870–1884*. Washington: Catholic University of America Press, 1953.
"The Reverend Henry G. Ganss, Mus D." *Records of the American Catholic Historical Society* 24 (June 1914): 179–82.
Rice, Edwin Wilbur. *The Sunday-School Movement, 1780–1917, and the American Sunday-School Union, 1817–1917*. Philadelphia: American Sunday-School Union, 1917.
Sampey, John Richard. *The International Lesson System: The History of Its Origin and Development*. New York: Fleming H. Revell Co., 1911.
Sievers, Harry J. "The Catholic Indian School Issue and the Presidential Election of 1892." *Catholic Historical Review* 38 (July 1952): 129–55.
Stokes, Anson Phelps. *Church and State in the United States*. 3 vols. New York: Harper and Brothers, 1950.
Zerwekh, Sister Edward Mary. "John Baptist Salpointe, 1825–1894." *New Mexico Historical Review* 37 (January 1962): 1–19; (April 1962): 132–54; (July 1962): 214–29.

10. Unpublished Theses and Dissertations

Gilcreast, Everett Arthur. "Richard Henry Pratt and American Indian Policy, 1877–1906: A Study of the Assimilation Movement." Ph.D. dissertation, Yale University, 1967.
Keller, Robert H., Jr. "The Protestant Churches and Grant's Peace Policy: A Study in Church-State Relations, 1869–1882." Ph.D. dissertation, University of Chicago, 1967.
Lijek, Mary Edward. "Relations between the Office of Indian Affairs and the Bureau of Catholic Indian Missions, 1885–1900." M.A. thesis, Catholic University of America, 1965.
Logsdon, M. Imelda. "Monsignor William Henry Ketcham and the Bureau of Catholic Indian Missions." M.A. thesis, Catholic University of America, 1949.
Sewrey, Charles Louis. "The Alleged 'Un-Americanism' of the Church as a Factor in Anti-Catholicism in the United States, 1860–1914." Ph.D. dissertation, University of Minnesota, 1955.
Whitner, Robert Lee. "The Methodist Episcopal Church and Grant's Peace Policy: A Study of the Methodist Agencies, 1870–1882." Ph.D. dissertation, University of Minnesota, 1959.

Index